His Word Became *Flesh*

DAILY DEVOTIONS FOR
PHYSICAL HEALING

MICHELE SNYDER

This book and parts thereof may not be reproduced in any form, stored in a retrieval system or transmitted in a form by any means—electronic, mechanical, photocopy, recording, or otherwise—without prior written permission of the author, except as provided by United States of America copyright law.

EDITOR: Colleen Coffey-Snyder
PROOF-READER: Rich Snyder

Copyright © 2023

Scripture taken from the New King James Version®. Copyright © 1982 by Thomas Nelson. Used by permission. All rights reserved.

Scripture quotations marked "KJV" are taken from the Holy Bible, King James Version (Public Domain).

Scripture quotations marked "AMP" (AMPC) are taken from the Amplified® Bible, Copyright © 1954, 1958, 1962, 1964, 1965, 1987 by The Lockman Foundation. Used by permission. www.Lockman.org

Scripture quotations marked (NIV) are taken from the Holy Bible, New International Version®, NIV®. Copyright © 1973, 1978, 1984 by Biblica, Inc.™ Used by permission of Zondervan. All rights reserved worldwide. http://www.zondervan.com

Scripture quotations marked (NLT) are taken from the Holy Bible, New Living Translation, copyright © 1996, 2004, 2007 by Tyndale House Foundation. Used by permission of Tyndale House Publishers, Inc., Carol Stream, Illinois 60188. All rights reserved. http://www.newlivingtranslation.com/http://www.tyndale.com

Scripture quotations marked "TPT" are from The Passion Translation®. Copyright © 2017, 2018 by Passion & Fire Ministries, Inc. Used by permission. All rights reserved. ThePassionTranslation.com.

Scripture quotations marked "NASB" are taken from the New American Standard Bible®, Copyright © 1960, 1962, 1963, 1968, 1971, 1972, 1973, 1975, 1977, 1995 by The Lockman Foundation. Used by permission. www.Lockman.org

Scripture quotations marked "MSG" or "The Message" are taken from The Message. Copyright 1993, 1994, 1995, 1996, 2000, 2001, 2002. Used by permission of NavPress Publishing Group. http://www.navpress.com/

Strong's Exhaustive Concordance of the Bible is public domain.

Scripture taken from THE MIRROR Copyright © 2012. Used by permission of The Author

Scripture quotations marked "Wuest" are taken from the Kenneth S. Wuest New Testament. Copyright © 1961 Used by permission of Wm. B. Eerdmans Publishing Co. https://www.eerdmans.com

(ESV) - The Holy Bible: English Standard Version Scripture quotations marked "ESV" are from the ESV Bible® (The Holy Bible, English Standard Version®), copyright © 2001 by Crossway Bibles, a publishing ministry of Good News Publishers. Used by permission. All rights reserved. http://www.crossway.org

Scripture quotations marked "Peshitta" are taken from the Holy Bible from the Ancient Eastern Text, George Lamsa's Translation From The Aramaic of the Peshitta Copyright © 1933, 1936, 1940, 1957, 1961, 1967, 1968, used under "fair use guidelines" Originally published by A.J. Holman Company; HarperCollins Publishers http://www.harpercollins.com/

Quotations from the "Thayer's" are taken from Thayer's Greek-English Lexicon of the New Testament, by Joseph H. Thayer Copyright © 2015 by PMA Publishing, used under "fair use guidelines" pmapublishing@yahoo.com

DISCLAIMER

This book is not intended to give medical advice of any kind. I am not a doctor. My personal experiences and opinions regarding the medical field are solely mine; they are not intended to bring condemnation or influence the type of treatments you decide for yourself. No one has the right to tell you the type of protocol you need to follow—that is between you and God.

DEDICATION and ACKNOWLDGEMENTS

This Devotional is dedicated to those who are suffering from disease and pain in their body—*you are not alone!*

To my husband & family, my biggest cheerleaders: thank you for not giving up! You helped me to rise again even stronger than I was before!

To my dear friend and Big Brother in Christ, Tony Myers: I wouldn't have experienced my own healing without your daily (I think I would have gone insane!) help, patience, your quirky way of praying, and the swift kick in the pants when I needed it. You taught me a lot about *Christ*. Churchy people only call Him "Lord" but knowing Him as **Christ**, *my* Healer and *my* Righteousness living on the inside of *me* made all the difference! You put the final blow on my religious beliefs single-handed, magnifying the Holy Spirit's resurrection power giving life to my physical body. You were my "support group" when no one else could listen. I am eternally grateful for your friendship and mentoring! This book would *never* be a possibility without you!

To Don Allen and Dione Guinn of the Midwest Healing Center: You prayed with me, counseled and encouraged me and now we are joined together advancing the Kingdom! I'm on the other side of that prayer line because of people like you! Thank you!

To John G. Lake Ministries and Curry Blake: You were a big part of helping me renew my mind to truth. I absorbed everything you taught about physical healing. At night when I couldn't sleep, I listened to Curry's gentle, calming voice put me to sleep, chase away fears and damaging emotions, while setting my mind on things above. You gave me courage to get out there again and minister to everyone, everywhere I go! Thank you!

FORWARD

I was healed from Lou Gehrig's disease, a journey of which my wife and I essentially travelled alone. I had no clue there were healing ministries and teachings on healing. Indeed, I was not seeking healing, I was seeking to die and get this life over with. Then suddenly and dramatically, Jesus presented himself to me! This is the reason why, after my healing, my heart burned to help others acknowledge their healing. I've gone onward to write five books on healing and I have a healing ministry to help others have their own healing. I have ministered to thousands of people both in person and over the phone. I have met many wonderful people through ministering to them.

Michele Snyder is one of those wonderful people. Roughly five years ago she called me up after hearing my story. Her healing journey was much different than mine because she knew Jesus was her healer and she was all in to have what Jesus had paid for at the Cross. Not only was she determined to have her own healing, she was determined to help others have theirs as well. This was on her heart even while going through her personal hell because of her health.

I remember our first conversation as if it happened yesterday. Her way of speaking was very churchy; by that I mean very much influenced by the Pentecostal culture which has its own language. I thought to myself, *"I need a Christian dictionary to understand this woman!"* She was, in turn, very much shocked at my language and the way I ministered. At one point in our conversation I blurted out *"Gummy worms, where is the improvement?"* Her response was *"mmmm, huh? What do you mean?"* The shock and confusion by my statement was clearly evident even over the phone. She did have improvement that day and I encouraged her to call me every day, if she needed to. She took me up on that offer, and for the next two years she would call me almost every day! Throughout that time we became friends and I consider her my "big" sister. There is no one more qualified to write a daily healing devotional than my dear sister, Michele. In fact, when she told me that she was going to write a healing devotional, I informed her that I had just started to write one myself! I decided not to write that devotional because she's got it fully covered with the Holy Spirit's guidance!

His Word Became Flesh is amazing! If you commit yourself to spending a few minutes every day with this book, there is no doubt in my mind that you will have what is already available... your healing. Having been through it herself, Michele knows about renewing the mind and the concentrated effort that some people need to see their healing. She starts out by giving only the scriptural address of the daily scripture. That is correct! You will have to dust off your Bible (or actually buy one) and turn to that particular scripture for yourself. That is exactly what many of you need.

Not only is the layout purposely thought out, the content of Michele's daily thoughts is equally mined out with precision. The goal is for you to renew your mind with the mind of Christ. That is exactly what this devotional will help you to achieve. Every day when you wake up, reach for this devotional that will be on your night stand and let Michele's words direct your thoughts towards the mind of Christ—then behold your healing is "nigh" and upon you now!

Be Blessed

Be Healed

Be a Blessing!

Tony Myers

P.S. Hey dear friend, do you like how I ended this by being churchy? Just having a little fun at my Big sister's expense, lol!

MY STORY

It was March of 2017. My husband and I had stopped at a local convenience store on our way back from visiting our oldest son who lived in Philadelphia. When I got out of our truck, my left knee felt strangely tight. I chalked it all up to stiffness from the hour drive. From that moment on, my knee became more difficult to bend. I had no other symptoms to make me think it was anything serious, so I just kept going about life as usual.

As the days and weeks passed, I lost mobility of my leg, while symptoms of a sinus infection with a fever set in. I had no idea the pain and stiffness in my knee and the sinus infection were related. I had been under the care of a natural health practitioner for the previous five years and she had no idea what was causing these new symptoms. I followed her protocol and hoped it would all go away—until my knee became infected, hot, swollen, and I couldn't walk any more. The pain was through the roof! My husband had to carry me into her office until we purchased a set of crutches.

One blessing was that my husband began working a very good job for the duration of my illness. The drawback was that he worked in New York four hours away. He drove to New York for the week and came home on the weekends, which meant I spent a lot of time alone in misery and confusion. I had to lie flat on my back with a pillow under my knee to sleep at night. My entire leg and foot became swollen. Even covering my leg with a sheet was excruciating, trapping in the heat. I used ice packs day and night just for a small bit of relief. On a scale from 1 to 10, the pain level was beyond labeling with a number! My sons had to cook and take care of me when they weren't working. Friends and family had to drive me to doctor appointments. Riding in a car was unbearable—even the slightest bump in the road brought agony throughout every bone in my body.

After about six weeks of suffering my husband insisted, *"Get dressed. You're going to a doctor. We've got to find out what this is!"* Against everything within me, we went to the nearest urgent care facility. I had to wait three days for the results of a blood test, but the doctor was pretty sure it was Lyme disease. At first they called and told me that the results of the blood test were negative, and that I needed to pursue treatment with an orthopedic doctor for my knee. About an hour later, they called back and apologized for their mistake. They and had given me the wrong results—I was positive for Lyme. The confusion sent me into a tailspin. This is one reason I personally have a strong aversion to doctors...

"Take this antibiotic and in three weeks go see an Infectious Disease Specialist," the urgent care nurse directed. We did not have medical insurance and no family doctor. When I hobbled into the specialist's office, still on crutches three weeks later, after 21 days of antibiotics, my knee on fire and larger than a grapefruit, he exclaimed, *"In all my twenty years of practicing infectious disease I've never seen anyone with Lyme Disease come into my office on crutches!"* He further stated, *"You've had twenty-one days of antibiotics. You don't have Lyme disease anymore. You must have injured your knee. Go get an MRI."* I couldn't recall any incidence of injury, but I went for the MRI anyway hoping it would reveal the cause of my hot, swollen knee.

The Infectious Disease doctor said that the MRI showed no damage to my knee from injury, but informed me that I could no longer be his patient. He referred me to an orthopedic doctor to have a needle shoved into the joint and fluid drawn to be tested. It hurt like hell! The orthopedic doctor could not draw any fluid out, even after several jabs. By that time, the fluid had absorbed into the tissues surrounding the knee. I had to wear a brace and continue to walk on crutches. She refused to see me for further treatment. *Did I mention that I have a strong aversion to doctors?*

After three months into this mess, a friend suggested a Lyme Disease Specialist that she had gone to herself. This "specialist" would not accept insurance. All blood tests, doctor visits (which were $500 per visit), and medications were out of pocket! He diagnosed me with chronic late stage Lyme disease; which according to him, once it reaches the "chronic" stage, a person has it for life—*a statement I refused to accept!* The pain and swelling started to spread to my other knee. *"Hmm, that shouldn't be happening, you're on two different antibiotics."* He stated, scratching his head. *"No kidding!"* I shot back at him, *"You tell me, you're the doctor!"* I had to find somewhere else to get treated. His protocol was making me so sick that I couldn't eat and I wasn't improving. Severe stomach pain and shortness of breath kept me awake all night in tears!

For the first time in my life, I understood what it was like to be an addict! I was in so much pain that I schemed how to manipulate the specialist and the orthopedic doctor to keep the supply of pain medicine from running out. I didn't know how I could live without it! After it began to make me sick and unable to eat, I forced myself to stop taking it. My strength continued to decline. When I looked in the mirror, I didn't recognize myself anymore.

I searched for another natural health practitioner after I learned, through my own research, that Lyme disease is drug-resistant if it isn't properly treated early. There was a facility, about two hours away, and the practitioner was frequently out of town. He was a Believer, sternly stating in popular Christian vernacular, *"I don't know what call you have on your life to be under this attack, but you have got to defeat the fear!"* And boy did I have a lot of fear! Nightmares and panic attacks gripped me as my mind ran wild from taunting voices suggesting that my leg would need to be cut off! This, along with the doctor's medications and the forty natural supplements from the first health practitioner, left me delirious. My body became confused and toxic from all the antibiotics and supplements.

The second natural health practitioner did not have a very good bed-side manner, to say the least. He was very tough on me, but looking back, I can say I needed it. I was so full of self-pity and fear that he was just trying to knock some sense into me, but I was unable to receive it. Part of his protocol was that I watch Curry Blake's *DHT (Divine Healing Technician Training)* on YouTube. He told me that I needed to watch it over and over again as many times as it took to learn how to receive healing for myself. I had never heard of Curry Blake, but I was eager to ditch all the false teachings about healing that I had learned over the many years of going to church. I was elated when I found out Curry's connection with John G. Lake. I had studied about Lake's life more than any other person that had walked in Christ's healing power effectively.

The second natural health practitioner helped me get off all the prescription medications from the Lyme Disease Specialist, which were causing shortness of breath, rashes, insomnia, and confusion in my body. He also took me off every supplement from the first natural health practitioner. He suggested a natural pain remedy that was just as effective as the prescription medication had been, but I had to stop seeing him because his office was just too far away. With so many strange, scary symptoms occurring in my body, I was driving him nuts from constantly calling him for help, *"Look, you're not my only patient!"* I needed to find someone, whose demeanor was not so abrasive, closer to where I lived. I was at the end of my rope.

I was driving my family, friends, and doctors crazy with my constant complaining, self-pity, pain, and confusion. Everyone was overwhelmed and tired of taking care of me as time seemed to drag on. I had homeschooled all of my five children for twenty-three years, teaching them Biblical principles. By this time they were all graduated and either married or working full-time jobs. All of my children looked to me as the spiritual influence in the family and it was very difficult for them to watch me go through my ups and downs. Homeschooling was one of the hardest challenges I had overcome up to that point. The thought of throwing away all of those years instilling God's truth and faithfulness into them, due to my own attitude, was more than I could bear! My second oldest son said to me, *"Mom, what is wrong with you? You were the one that taught us about God and faith and here you are acting this way?"* I realized I had allowed the disease to turn me into someone I didn't like—a delirious nut case! I had a hard talk with myself as I lay there, while tears of self-pity spilled over my cheeks for the last time, *"Michele, it's time you put on your big-girl pants and fight! What kind of testimony will you be to your children if you die? They will blame God and forsake Him!"* From that moment on, whatever it would take, I decided I would just refuse to die! After that decision, things began to change for the better.

The last natural health practitioner was awesome! She saw me once a month and, if I needed help, she was always available. By this time I had had a fever for four months straight, full body tremors, and I could only sleep for an hour each night. I had lost a lot of weight. I was such a mess physically, mentally, and emotionally when I came to her—but she was undaunted. I needed that!

On the spiritual side of things, I knew God was the Healer. I had prayed for the sick in the past and had seen miracles! I always believed that it was God's will to heal everyone *all* of the time, but I never knew how to live it for myself or see everyone I prayed for consistently healed. I remember sitting on a bench outdoors in a public place, full of pain and misery. I wondered why there was no one available to pray with me for healing, or at least give a word of encouragement. I knew in my heart that Jesus does not want people to suffer alone. I told the Lord, *"I don't know how to get through this cuz I'm in way over my head; but if You will help me, I'll dump everything I thought I knew about physical healing and teach others how to receive their healing."*

The Holy Spirit told me to watch my words. He told me not to speak about the pain or the symptoms. When I asked Him why, He said that the whole world functions by what people speak—like the news. People hear something on the news, believe what they heard, and repeat it, whether it is true or not. He taught me that death and life were in the power of my own mouth! I could not afford to be double-minded, speaking Scriptures one minute and complaining about symptoms later.

Next, the Holy Spirit told me to pray in the spirit for an hour every day. There is no Scripture that instructs us to pray in the spirit for an hour every day, but these were His directions for me because that is what I needed. When I asked Him why, He told me to purchase the book by Bill Hamon: *Seventy Reasons for Speaking in Tongues*; and *insisted* that I read it. You see, when I had been baptized in the spirit many years ago and received my prayer language, I was never taught what to use it for or why it was important. That book helped me to understand the power I had in my own mouth! I was obedient! I set an alarm on my cell phone to go off at the same time every day and set the timer for an hour, so I didn't need to watch the clock. And you know what happened? All that junk—the fear, the panic attacks, the voices—were purged from the inside as I prayed in the spirit! My inner man was being built up, as I replaced the barrage of emotions and thoughts bombarding my mind with God's love and peace! I was gaining spiritual strength, exactly as it is described in Jude 1:20-21!

The final directive Holy Spirit gave me was just as life-changing as the first two! Our family had previously come through several years of one difficult situation after another and it had torn us apart. I repeated the different situations that had happened over and over

MY STORY

in my mind, questioning God *"WHY?"* like a broken record. I wasn't able to move forward in my life because I kept looking back. I believed the lie that my best days were in the past. Holy Spirit gave me Philippians 3:13 *"...forgetting those things which are behind and reaching forward to those things which are ahead."* He told me that if I did not let go of the past and my constant questioning, I'd never be able to live the future He had prepared for me! He told me that I needed to *choose* to live! At that moment, I took every question, every fear, every shred of knowledge I thought I understood up to that point—and crumbled it up like a scrap of paper and threw it like a basket shot in the trash! *SWOOSH!*

I had to keep my heart guarded from *everyone*, and when I say *everyone*, I mean **everyone**! It was hard enough to sift through my own personal beliefs, thoughts, and emotions to keep myself from going off the deep end, let alone other Christians offering their well-meaning religious cliché's! I had to take into consideration that they just didn't understand. Church friends said things like, *"God is having you walk through this alone so you learn to trust Him."* WHAT? *"If I didn't trust Him, then who the heck did I trust?"* Another said, *"Oh, I watched a program on T.V. about Lyme disease. Did you know you could die from that?"* My response was, *"You're not helping me by saying that! You should be encouraging me, not stirring up fear when I'm fighting for my life!"* Yet another friend I had trusted tried to convince me, *"You better ask God what you did to open up the door for the enemy to get his hooks into you!"* I sat there several minutes examining my heart and asking Holy Spirit to search me! *"Hooks? What did I do, Lord?"* No answer came! Why? Because there wasn't any! I learned later that healing isn't based on my performance; it is based on Jesus' body that was broken for me!

While I was in the waiting room for an appointment, the nurses talked about their Lyme disease patients out loud in the hallway, *"This child had ten ticks on her body!"* and on and on about each new patient's symptoms. I literally stuck my fingers in my ears and read my pocket Bible out loud to drown out their voices and keep fear from getting a stronghold in my mind again. The other patients in the room shot nervous, glaring looks at me, but I didn't care—they weren't living my life.

When I was well enough to go to the store, my son had to drive. The first few times, it was refreshing to be out in the public again, doing normal activities. I was thankful to be able to go shopping, but I hated riding the scooter like an invalid. I was a reckless driver backing into displays, knocking them over in the aisles! Beeeep, Beeeep, Beeeep! *CRASH!*

I decided, *"Enough of this! No more crutches!"* So I walked limping with just the leg brace. Eventually, I wrapped both knees with bandages and forced myself to walk through Wal-Mart to get everything I needed, no matter how much it hurt. I began to pray for other people. You reap what you sow, right? I was learning that I needed to put my faith for healing into *action*! If I could heal others through Christ in me, I could certainly receive healing for myself! After six months, when I was finally able to drive again, I had to prop my leg up on the dash board to alleviate the swelling and throbbing pain! Try driving like that—it isn't easy!

I listened to solid Biblical teachings online about physical healing like Curry's *DHT, Tony Myers' Healing,* and *Two Guys and a Bible.* I saturated myself in Scripture for the next several years—day and night. No matter where I went, I always had a Bible with me. I honestly did not know there were so many verses in the Bible about physical healing—even in the Old Covenant. Oh, I knew there were a few, but now they were my life-line. I renewed my mind to truth, and as I did, my body began to change! Symptoms began to disappear! Fear no longer controlled me! My mind was being renewed!

I had this bright idea that I would buy a huge red magic marker and keep it in my purse. On the day I received the results of the final blood test, confirming that my blood was clean, I'd ask my health practitioner to write *HEALED* in big red letters across the page. That day finally came in March of 2019—exactly two years after the initial diagnosis! My blood test came back completely normal! And, yes, my health practitioner gladly wrote in big red letters *HEALED* with my magic marker, as we rejoiced together, hugging and crying at God's faithfulness!

Yes, there were moments of doubts due to the symptoms and emotions battling against the truth I was trying to reinforce. It was like a roller coaster ride—confident one minute approaching the top of the hill; slowly cresting the summit, then gaining lightning speed only to sink at the bottom. It seemed like my body and my mind formed an alliance against my spirit and my heart! It was a constant challenge to keep my mind stable, push negative thoughts aside, and act on the truth! It was a slow, steady process, but in time...

*His Word became **flesh**!—literally!* John 1:14 reveals Jesus as the Word of the Father made visible in the flesh. In the same way, His word became flesh in my body as it restored every cell! Jesus said that His words are spirit and they are life (John 6:63). When it looked like nothing was happening, I still clung with all of my might to what the Bible declared belonged to me. As I stated earlier—*I just refused to die!*

The supplements and treatments I used were limited in their power. They helped keep symptoms under control so that I could stay focused on truth instead of pain, but they could not provide permanent health. I learned that Jesus' finished work means *triune salvation* of my spirit, soul, and body. My spirit is not the only part of me that is complete. I don't have to make an effort to release the life contained in my spirit into my body—it's already there according to Romans 8:11! Jesus' redemption is a *complete* redemption of *every part* of my life! It's already done! I came to a knowledge of the truth about what He had already given me, how to live it for myself, and give it away to others! I discovered that the act of taking Communion is a powerful, symbolic reminder of *Christ in you*—you are an incarnation! I encourage you to take it regularly as a celebration, acknowledging Him living on the inside, imparting life to all of your flesh!

Holy Spirit directed me to write this Devotional when I was at my friend's house church. The speaker for the evening was sharing her newly published Prophetic Devotional. Her book was passed around the room, and the moment I received it into my hands, Holy Spirit spoke clearly on the inside, *"You will write a Healing Devotional."* I responded immediately, *"Ok! Yes! I will!"*

Beware! This is not your typical Devotional! *His Word Became* **Flesh** cuts to the core by removing common false beliefs, while enforcing solid Biblical truth about physical healing. I did not write out the Scriptures for you, so that you would grab your Bible for yourself. I am living proof that His Word ***works***! I have not spoon-fed you with prefabricated prayers to recite, so that you can create your own prayers from your own heart. You will discover the Holy Spirit on the *inside*, learn how to discern His voice for yourself, and gain the boldness to act on His instructions. Your relationship with the Him will be ignited! You will experience fresh revelation about the complete work of Christ's sacrifice for *you*! *Your confidence in Him for your own healing will explode!* When you reach the end of the year, you will look back and see how your mind and body have been transformed!

So feast, my friend! Laugh, cry, and rejoice as you read testimonies of healings, stories from my childhood, and lessons I learned directly from our Helper, The Holy Spirit! Most of all—BE HEALED!

God loves you and He wants you whole!

In Christ,

Michele

MEDICAL DIAGNOSTIC LABORATORIES L.L.C.
2439 KUSER ROAD
HAMILTON, NJ 08690-3303
TL: 609-570-1000 FX: 609-570-1050 TF: 877-269-0090
www.mdlab.com

Final Test Results

MDL#: 9039171

Patient Information:	SSN: N/A	DOB: [redacted]	Ordering Physician/Lab:	NPI: 1598831760
SNYDER, MICHELE [address redacted] LITITZ, PA [redacted]			ANY LAB TEST NOW-LITITZ CHRISTOPHER PORTER, DO 235 BLOOMFIELD DRIVE SUITE 110 LITITZ, PA 17543 Tel: (717) 207-7604 Fax: (717) 823-6787	

Patient ID: Date Received: 3/14/2019   Date Reported: 3/20/2019

Test Component	Specimen	Date Collected	Results Normal	Abnormal	Reference/Units/Comments
Bartonella henselae IgG/IgM by ELISA 355 Verified 3/19/2019	Serum - 1	3/13/2019		(Equivocal)	*IgM Index range: Neg: <= 0.89, Equivocal: 0.90 - 1.10, Pos: >= 1.11 * IgG Index range: Neg: <= 0.89, Equivocal: 0.90 - 1.10, Pos: >= 1.11
Anaplasma phagocytophilum IgG/IgM by IFA 439 Verified 3/20/2019	Serum - 1	3/13/2019	Negative		IgM:Negative; No significant level of detectable IgM antibodies (1:16 dilution negative). IgG:Negative; No significant level of detectable IgG antibodies (1:80 dilution negative).
Babesia microti IgG/IgM by IFA 440 Verified 3/19/2019	Serum - 1	3/13/2019	Negative		IgM:Negative; No significant level of detectable IgM antibodies (1:16 dilution negative). IgG:Negative; No significant level of detectable IgG antibodies (1:64 dilution negative).
Lyme disease (B. burgdorferi) DNA by Real-Time PCR 305 Verified 3/15/2019	Blood - 2	3/13/2019	Negative		
Mycoplasma pneumoniae by Real-Time PCR 336 Verified 3/15/2019	Blood - 2	3/13/2019	Negative		
Babesia microti by Real-Time PCR 410 Verified 3/15/2019	Blood - 2	3/13/2019	Negative		

*This test was developed and its performance characteristics determined by Medical Diagnostic Laboratories, L.L.C. It has not been cleared or approved by the U.S. Food and Drug Administration. The FDA has determined that such clearance or approval is not necessary.

Medical Director, Mats Sanden, M.D.

JANUARY 1

Everything Began With The Word

Read: John 1:1-2, Genesis 1:1-28

In the beginning was the Word...

These six simple words have such profound meaning! God demonstrated how everything on this earth was created with words—His words. Think about that for a moment and take a look out your window. Do you see trees or grass? Do you see birds or insects flying around? Do you see the sun shining? None of these things would exist today if God had not spoken them into being thousands of years ago. Go and look at yourself in the mirror right now, and think about where God said in Genesis 1:26, *"Let Us make man in Our image..."* You would not be here today if God hadn't first spoken about you! In fact, God made sure that you are here on this earth alive right now!

It seems far-fetched that words, which are just sounds and vibrations, can create physical things. But this is exactly what the Bible proves! God commanded, *"Light be!"* (Genesis 1:3), and it was so! *You* are the most important part and the ultimate reason He created everything we see. Every portion of His creation was made for you to enjoy!

JANUARY 2

You Are A Living Speaking Spirit

Read: John 1:3-5, Genesis 2:1-7

In the beginning...

God set His plan in motion by creating the earth with His words. We will take our cue from Him as the foundation for this entire Devotional. This will set us on the right course to build upon successfully for the rest of the year. We should desire for our words to align with His words so that we can experience all that belongs to us. Let's reread Genesis 2:7:

> *"And the Lord God formed man of the dust of the ground and breathed into his nostrils the breath of life; and man became a living being."*

A proper translation of this Scripture from the original Hebrew should state it this way:

> *"And man became a living, speaking spirit like God."*

You are a living, speaking spirit made in God's image to speak things into existence exactly the way He did! Be careful to speak only according to what the Bible says you are and what you have through Jesus—healing and life! You cannot speak out both sides of your mouth—positive one minute and negative the next, and expect that only the positive will come to pass. God ONLY spoke what He wanted to come into existence. Don't repeat a doctor's negative diagnoses or symptoms happening in your body. Speak life! Speak health!

JANUARY 3

Power In Your Mouth

Read: Proverbs 18:20-21

*M*aybe you are a lot like me. I didn't realize the power that my own words have! I used to believe they were merely a way for us to communicate—going in one ear and out the other. Yes, I knew they could influence people for good or for bad, but I didn't know my words literally carry life and death in them! I didn't realize how *my own words* affected *my* life! Our verse for today states that we will eat our own words!

During the late 1990s, a Japanese Scientist named Masaru Emoto performed experiments on frozen water. The purpose of this study was to prove the power of words and how they can impact and transform living things.

He tested the crystallization patterns of frozen water by speaking negative and positive words. To one group of water he spoke positive words, and to the second group he spoke negative words. After time, as the water froze, the negative group formed ugly, cloudy crystal patterns; while the positive group organized into beautiful, clear crystals!

We may not experience the effect our words have as quickly as Emoto observed, but look around you. Ask yourself what you have been speaking continually over time. Do you repeat the words your doctor said to your friends and relatives? The Bible says we will have what we say because we are created to have the same influence with our words that God had on Creation. Choose your words wisely and with care. The phrase, *"You will eat your words"* is not just a common expression—it's Biblical! You are not lying or being a hypocrite by saying things you don't yet see. You are just being like your Father who spoke and then it was so! (Source: thewellnessenterprise.com)

JANUARY 4

God's Final Report

Read: Matthew 18:16-20, 1 Peter 2:24

When I was sick and bedridden, I felt like I was in over my head. I had no idea how to get out of the mess I was in. Have you ever felt that way?

I asked the Holy Spirit to tell me what to do, because I knew that without His help, I would probably die. Do you want to know the first thing He told me to do? He told me to watch my words! At first, I thought that was too simple! *"Why, Lord?"* I asked. He responded,

> *"Do you see how the whole world is affected by words? Look at the news. People speak what they believe is happening politically across the world. Everyone who hears what the news said responds by believing what they heard and then repeating it to others, even if it isn't accurate. What about a doctor's diagnosis? Someone gets a diagnosis and then they tell everyone they know what the doctor said. I want you to speak ONLY what My Word says."*

I began to think about what the Lord told me. I thought about the influence words have on society, especially in governments. We hear what someone says on the news about a particular politician and within minutes everyone is talking about it via social media. Within a day or so later, we may find that it wasn't true but an opinion was already formed in people's minds. Sometimes this is done on purpose!

The wisest thing we can do is to agree with God's report about us! He says in 1 Peter 2:24 *"...by His stripes you were healed."* Speak only that. Choose to believe only that. Even though it may take some time, your mind will agree with the Word and your body will follow. The importance of transforming your mind to what God says in His

JANUARY 4

Word can literally mean life or death. No, it's not a magic incantation you walk around just repeating. And I'm not suggesting that you live in denial of your circumstances. The goal is a transformed mind (Romans 12:1-2) to think the way God thinks. The witness of your mouth, believing in your heart, and speaking God's Word will establish truth in your mind and will lead you to the physical reality of health in your body! These are some of the steps I took to experience my healing—and it worked!

JANUARY 5

Spiritual vs. Physical Realities

Read: John 1:14, Proverbs 4:20-22, Matthew 7:7

How can something spiritual become a physical reality? I've studied quantum physics a little, but I'm certainly no expert on the subject. The more we understand how physical and spiritual things co-exist; we can discover that science (when accurate information is utilized), actually proves the Bible rather than disproves it.

The science behind quantum physics is basically summed up in this idea, *"What you look for you will find."* Hmmm...that sounds a lot like what God said, doesn't it?

The more you give attention to something the more you empower it. What are you giving most of your attention to, symptoms in your body or the Word of God? I know the war of two worlds that goes on inside our minds saying: *"I feel this pain in my body, but the Word says that I'm healed."* It does take a concentrated effort to keep our focus on God's truth, which seems intangible and abstract verses a pain in the body we feel physically.

There is a choice we must make: I choose to believe in this pain or I choose to believe God's Word about the pain. We must settle it in our heart and mind to trust God at His Word as the final authority; not what the doctor says or what our body is trying to say. Sometimes it can be a slow process; a decision you may have to make again and again. But it doesn't have to be a slow process for you, like it was for me. I had to affirm God's Word to my body over and over again. Little by little, symptoms began to disappear! Over time, if you will stick with God and His Word, just like His Word became Jesus in the flesh, His Word will become healed flesh in your body!

JANUARY 6

Spirit And Life

Read: John 6:63, Matthew 5:33-42

Jesus said that His words are *spirit*. His Words are spirit and they are life! Remember our devotion on January 2nd? I stated that a proper translation of Genesis 2:7 says,

> *"...and man became a living, speaking spirit like God."*

If you are a born again Believer in Jesus Christ, your words are also spirit and life, because the Holy Spirit lives inside you. Of course, what you speak must be in alignment with what the Bible says. Jesus declared only what the Father wanted Him to say. It was guaranteed that when He spoke, whatever He said would happen!

When Jairus' daughter died, what did Jesus say to her? He said, *"Arise."* That word is so simple, yet it was enough to bring her back to life! That little word held the power of resurrection life, which caused her spirit to come back into her body. Immediately she got up, walked, and chowed down on her mother's cooking!

So speak life! And remember that as a believer in Jesus Christ, your words hold the *same power* as Jesus' words!

JANUARY 7

Prophecy Fulfilled

Read: Luke 1:26-38

Did you notice that before God ever did something, He spoke about it first? Even before Gabriel had visited Mary to proclaim Jesus' birth, there were many prophecies spoken about Him in the Old Testament, hundreds of years before He came!

If you carefully read the Gospels there are many references to Old Testament Scriptures that spoke about the Messiah and the works He would perform. Jesus fulfilled every one of those prophecies! But they had to be spoken so people would know who to look for and so that Scripture would be fulfilled.

When Jesus was on the cross, He was still in complete control. It may have looked like nothing but chaos when we read about the events that took place. The truth is, that over 300 prophecies were fulfilled about His life, death, burial, and resurrection! He fulfilled every prophecy about Himself, down to the very drink offered to Him on a stick while He hung on the cross! This was not a series of chaotic events. He chose to give His life, as He stated in John 10:17-18,

> *"Therefore My Father loves Me, because I lay down My life that I may take it again. No one takes it from Me, but I lay it down Myself. I have power to lay it down, and I have power to take it again."*

We would say in our modern-day vernacular: every "i" was dotted and every "t" was crossed.

And then there is Mary, Jesus' mother. She said to Gabriel, *"Let it be to me according to Your word."* Mary could have said, *"No, Lord, I cannot do this! What will people think of me?"* And God would have had to choose someone else. But she agreed with Gabriel's words

JANUARY 7 ───────

and received the greatest honor no other woman on the face of the earth would ever receive—to carry and give birth to Emmanuel, God with us. This is why, like Mary and Jesus, we can trust God at His word for our lives.

JANUARY 8

The Word Was Sent

Read: Psalm 107:19-20

*H*e sent His Word. Remember reading in John 1:1-2, *"and the Word was God?"* When He sent His Word in the flesh, He sent Jesus. Jesus was the full manifestation of God in the flesh. That is why many times Jesus said,

> *"The words that I speak to you I do not speak on My own authority."* (John 14:10)

Since Jesus was sent by the Father, He did the Father's works. What were the Father's works? To show us that God's Kingdom is a Kingdom of authority. Jesus had authority over every sickness, disease, and demon. There was never any person that He turned away, didn't heal, or set free. His Kingdom is a Kingdom of health and life. The Father sent His word to heal us—He sent Jesus!

In the world we live, there are few absolutes. We cannot take most people at their word. A handshake isn't a binding agreement any more like it was years ago. Our experience with life and interactions with people can easily affect how we relate to God.

Many people wonder whether or not it is God's will to heal us. It's easy to settle that question. Just look at Jesus! He was the perfect representation of the Father. He spoke exactly the same things the Father spoke and He did exactly the same works the Father did.

You will never see an example anywhere in the New Testament of Jesus saying one thing and doing another—Never. His actions always lined up with His words. That is why we can take Him at His word. Jesus was sent by the Father to heal and to restore. Period.

JANUARY 9

He Just Took!

Read: Matthew 8:16-17

*D*id you ever read a Scripture over and over, time and time again, but then in one particular instance, you read it and something you never saw before leaps off the page at you? That's what happened to me when I read today's Scripture. What leaped off the page was: *"He Himself took..."* That one word **took** said volumes to me. In a split second, thoughts came rushing through my mind!

Jesus didn't ask us if we wanted Him to take our sicknesses, He just took them! Before we knew we needed it, He took them upon Himself! What did He do with them? He became them and took them away, destroying all disease, sickness, and pain! We need no special qualifications. He doesn't pick favorites. What He did for one person, He did for everyone! He did it for you! Let us thank Him for laying down His life for us and taking it up again. He did it all to dwell in us by His life-giving Spirit! He took to give! Amen!

JANUARY 10

God, Are You Listening?

Read: Psalm 139:3, 1 John 5:14-15

I like the NASB version of Psalm 139:3,

"You are intimately acquainted with all my ways."

It is human nature to question whether or not God hears us when we pray. Does He know what is going on in our lives? Does He know what is happening in our physical bodies? These may be questions we have wondered about, but we cannot afford to remain in a place of repetitive questioning. There **has** to be an answer. That answer is never found on the side of human reasoning. Therefore, we must turn to someone more intelligent than ourselves for the answers we need—the Holy Spirit. He is always ready to help direct us to truth.

If you are born again, you are God's son or daughter and He lives inside you by His Spirit. If my best friend stayed by my side all day, every day and never left me, would she know what I was going through? She would probably eventually understand me better than I understand myself! This is just like the Lord. He is right here with us at all times, intimately acquainted with **all** our ways (Psalm 139).

Be assured that God is with you, in you, and around you. He knows everything you are feeling, physically and emotionally. He knows the answer you need and will give you what you ask. You can be confident of that! How do I know? I'm sure you can think of at least one time in your life that you asked God for help and He came through. Build on that. He proved Himself faithful then; He will do it again because that is who He is—Faithful!

JANUARY 11

No Regard

Read: Romans 13:13-14

*O*ne morning as I was walking my dog, I was praying in the spirit like usual. I asked the Holy Spirit how to live in Divine health. Immediately He responded, *"Have no regard for the flesh."*

As I pondered His words, I thought about how to apply them. You know as well as I do that the body is always screaming about something: *"I hurt." "I'm hungry." "I'm thirsty." "I'm tired." "I crave French fries."* The demands are constant and endless, and that's just the physical body!

Our emotions cry: *"I'm sad." "I'm angry." "They offended me." "I'm scared."*

For being a woman, I'm not a very emotional person. Most things I can shuck off and get over pretty quickly. I avoid drama like the plague. I wasn't always that way; when I was younger—I was quite a Drama Queen! The things I didn't like about myself I took to the Lord and asked Him to help me learn a better way to conduct myself. I wanted Him to work on my character so that I could be the person He wanted me to be—continually full of peace.

I realize that His answer about living in Divine Health is much the same as how we can approach building character and controlling our emotions. The same way I minimized drama and emotions and learned to replace those with peace by applying God's word (mostly using the book of Proverbs); I can minimize my body's signals by giving them *"no regard."*

To regard something means *to look at attentively or to observe closely, to have concern, to think or consider in a particular way.* Remember: *"What you focus on, you empower."* Whatever the situation is; whether it is physical or emotional, turning and churning

JANUARY 11

that thing over and over in our mind makes it look impossible to overcome. That approach is very damaging to the confidence we have in Christ. He emphasized that we are *more than conquerors through His love* (Romans 8:37). I like what Paul says in the *Mirror Bible's* translation of Romans 8:12-13,

> *"We owe flesh nothing. In the light of all this, to now continue to live under the sinful influences of the senses, is to reinstate the dominion of spiritual death. Instead, we are indebted to now exhibit the highest expression of life inspired by the Spirit. This life demonstrates **zero tolerance** to the habits and sinful patterns of the flesh."* (Emphasis added)

Zero tolerance! That empowers me! Just as we do not allow our emotions and thoughts to run wild and unchecked, casting down imaginations that exalt themselves against the knowledge of Christ (2 Corinthians 10:5), we should not allow our physical bodies to tell us how they feel. We give them no regard by minimizing pain and symptoms. We then magnify the truth in the Scriptures that says,

> *"...by His stripes we were healed."* (1 Peter 2:24)

I'm not telling you to ignore symptoms completely or to do nothing; I'm saying don't blow it up and make it bigger than it is. We don't tolerate the symptoms. Instead, we deal with them according to God's Word and regard what He says above the symptoms. This way, the discomfort fades away.

JANUARY 12

Immediately

Read: Mark 5:29, Mark 1:30-31

The word *immediately* is used about twenty-eight times in the book of Mark. I think it was the author's favorite word! As a result of studying the miracles, it has become one of my favorite words, too. Why? It brings the idea of *expectation* on the scene.

Change must take place in regard to our healing, so there HAS to be improvement. We are renewing our mind to the truth of the healing power of Jesus—God's Word. So there *has* to be a change. Check yourself out. Look for less pain; maybe even just 10% less. Try doing something you couldn't do before. Raise your level of expectation from healing coming over time to healing coming now! *Immediately!* Don't be discouraged even if you haven't seen it all yet. Remain confident that you will. Remember that we are looking to Jesus as our source of Life. We are not trying to get our healing. Because we have the Holy Spirit on the inside, He is giving health and life to our bodies. We have Jesus the Healer; we have everything we need in Him!

JANUARY 13

Marred

Read: Isaiah 52:14, 1 Peter 2:24

*T*he above verse says that when people saw Jesus after He had been whipped, beaten, mocked, and crucified, that He didn't even look like a human being! When I read the *Kenneth Wuest Translation* of 1 Peter 2:24 for the first time, I cried!

> "...who Himself carried up to the Cross our sins in His body and offered Himself there as on an altar, doing this in order that we, having died with respect to our sins, might live with respect to righteousness, by means of whose bleeding stripe [the word "stripe" is in the singular here; a picture of our Lord's back after the scourging, one mass of raw, quivering flesh with no skin remaining, trickling with blood] you were healed..."

With one mass of raw, quivering flesh with no skin remaining, trickling with blood, <u>you were healed</u>!

Imagine His entire body, not just his back, but His entire body and face—*all* of his skin ripped off; His flesh gorged from the pieces of metal and bone tied to the cords of the whip. There is no indication in Scripture that Jesus was only whipped thirty-nine times, as many of us have been taught.

Paul testified in 2 Corinthians 11:24, that he was whipped five times by the Jews with thirty-nine stripes. According to the Law of Moses, a man could only be whipped forty times as punishment (Deuteronomy 25:3). But Jesus wasn't whipped by the Jews. He was scourged by the Romans, who had no limit to the number of times a criminal could be beaten.

Generally, the Romans wanted the criminal's punishment to be just severe enough so that he could carry his own cross to his crucifixion.

JANUARY 13

But we know in Matthew 27:32, that they forced Simon of Cyrene to carry Jesus' cross for Him.

He was *marred* beyond that of a human being—they were astonished to look at Him! Yes! He suffered severely so that you could be healed! Thank Him for that!

JANUARY 14

Be Still, Be Healed

Read: Psalm 46:10

"Be still and know that I am God." Holy Spirit kept bringing this Scripture to my mind at least five different times within just a few days. *"Be still and know."* What was He trying to tell me? From previous studies of God's Word, I knew that the word *know* was probably the same Hebrew word in Genesis 4:1 that says, *"Now Adam **knew** Eve his wife and she conceived…"*

I looked up the word *knew* in my concordance. Yes, they are the same Hebrew word *yadah*, both in Psalm 46:10 and Genesis 4:1—*a type of knowing that produces intimacy.*

Then I looked up the words *be still*. That was the real shocker! The word *raw-faw* for *be still, is* related to the word *rapha*, the Hebrew word for *be healed, whole,* and *cured!* And if you're like me, you have gone many years believing that *be still* only meant that you are to just remain in quiet trust. Now, we know it means so much more!

By discovering the true meaning for the words *know* and *be still*, what was the Holy Spirit trying to say?

"I am the God who heals you by intimately knowing Me."

I was blown away by this revelation! Knowing this message from the Lord can draw us into deeper intimacy with Him! Every time we leave that place after seeking Him, we are changed; rearranged. We get to take another glimpse of who He is *in* us, and what He has done *for* us!

JANUARY 15

In The Name Of Jesus

Read: Acts 3:1-10

Verse six of Acts 3 says,

> *"but what I do have I give you: In the Name of Jesus Christ of Nazareth, rise up and walk."*

This was the first healing that occurred after 120 people were filled with the Holy Spirit on the Day of Pentecost. It was a natural outcome of being filled with the Spirit's power—the sound of a mighty rushing wind like a tornado bursting into the room—that forever changed those in attendance. They now received the capacity to work miracles exactly the same way Jesus had demonstrated!

Peter and John saw the paralyzed man in front of the gate begging. They did what they had seen Jesus do so many times before. *"I don't have any money, but I do have something better. Then you won't be a paralyzed beggar anymore! I give you the Name of Jesus!"* Peter reached out his hand to the man and pulled him to his feet, just like Jesus would have done! Immediately, the man's legs became strong! By the Name of Jesus, the man received the physical effects of the power in His Name!

Just by speaking that Name and by faith in that Name, creative miracles happen! There is miracle-working power released that changes physical bodies and makes them healthy and strong. This is the whole reason why we have been given the wonderful Name of Jesus!

JANUARY 16

Ask

Read: John 14:13-14

*S*ounds pretty simple, doesn't it? Jesus said *"Whatever you ask."* *Ask* in Greek means *"require, call for, request for one's self, demand."* But as I write this, I realize it is not God we are demanding or calling upon for something to be done. It is when we speak to disease in Jesus' Name; we are requiring and demanding it to obey!

Sickness and disease are living things that grow and consume. They hear you when you speak; and they also **must** obey the Name of Jesus when it is spoken by one of God's children. Disease and everything that has a name recognizes the Name of Jesus. It knows it has no choice **but** to obey that Name, because it is the highest Name in the universe!

Jesus promised that when we speak His Name, whatever we ask will be **DONE**. Look for that response; demand it. Treat disease like an annoying person you don't want hanging around. Remember, you aren't looking to yourself, but to Christ who lives inside of you. So trust His Name, trust the power He said is in His Name, and **ASK!**

JANUARY 17

The Wayside

Read: Luke 8:4-15

*A*s I read the parable of the soils, one word leapt off the page at me: *wayside*. It's the ground that isn't a part of the garden because it's located at the edge.

The types of soil Jesus described were different people and the condition of their hearts. As you can tell, most of them weren't fully committed followers. They were onlookers, standing at the side lines, but never completely entering in for one reason or another. That's where those thieving birds, the hard and dry soil, and the thorns and the rocks hung out—by the wayside. These spectators didn't have to stand there; the choice was entirely up to them.

The soil in the middle was the perfect condition. No rocks, no thieving birds, no dryness, no thorns. This soil represented people who heard the word of God and started doing what it says. These were people who grew steadily and consistently and, as a result, they produced fruit for the Kingdom of God—salvations, healings, and miracles.

Those on the wayside heard the same word, but they didn't incorporate it into their lives. They were too distracted by the cares and entanglements of life and they never became anchored in the Truth. Sadly, they never grew or matured to produce fruit in the Kingdom of God.

Everyone must decide for himself to either be "all in" or "all out." Some may think they are playing it safe by lingering on the outskirts, but really, the safest place anyone could ever be is fully committed to Christ. No matter what, step off the sidelines and submit yourself wholeheartedly to Christ. Hanging out on the edge, you will find nothing but an unproductive wasteland. When you completely abandon yourself to Him, you'll discover everything your heart has been longing for!

JANUARY 18

His Image

Read: 2 Corinthians 3:18, Colossians 3:10, Matthew 17:2, Psalm 119:130

In 2 Corinthians 3:18 the word *changed* is where we get the word *metamorphosis*, meaning *transformed*, or *transfigured* into the identical image of Christ. It's the same word used in Matthew 17:2, when Jesus is on the Mountain of Transfiguration with three of his closest disciples and Moses and Elijah.

Renewing our mind to the Word of God creates an image of who Christ is inside of us. His likeness is recognized and reflected through our spirit, and then mirrored onto our soul. This reflection of Christ changes the mental picture you have of yourself. A new image of Christ is formed, where it impresses first inside your mind then resonates to the outside of your flesh—the image of life more abundantly!

Your body becomes like a projection screen. People around you will sense Jesus' light and life emanating from you! See yourself as being full of bright, white glowing light on the inside, penetrating your flesh, and permeating the atmosphere around you!

JANUARY 19

Sin = Sickness

Read: Psalm 103, 1 Peter 2:24

*W*e must view sin and sickness as equal because this is the way God sees them. One does not have more power than the other. Sickness came about as a result of sin. Christ is the remedy for both. When Christ put away, or redeemed you (paid the price) for your sins, He redeemed your soul and your body at the same time.

Then why do we still experience both sin and sickness? Did you ever try to resist sinning? Did you ever wake up in the morning and promise yourself that you would go through the whole day without sinning one time? I used to do that! And it took me about fifteen minutes after making that promise to myself until I yelled at my kids for something. It didn't take much for a full-blown flesh fit! *"Well, I'll try again tomorrow,"* I'd console myself.

I was as free from sin then as I am now. The problem was that I didn't know that truth, so I lived under condemnation. It was like, the more I focused on not messing up, the more I did—which is exactly what I was trying to avoid! All I really needed was a proper understanding that Jesus had already set me free from sins, so I didn't have to try to get freedom for myself! Once the Lord showed me this truth, it was easy-peasy to live in the freedom He had made available!

Now, apply this same principle to sickness and disease. We don't have to accept sickness as a normal part of life any more than we should accept sin as a normal part of life—not as a Believer. It is no longer a problem for you when you know that it has been defeated! Sickness is not more powerful than sin. They both came into the world when Adam fell, and they were both defeated by Christ's shed blood. He took care of them with one fell swoop! With this understanding, we can resist sickness and pain the same way we

JANUARY 19

resist sin. We can treat sickness and pain like a criminal trying to rob our home. We can command it to get out! So speak to that body part and remind it that it is healed—the same way we can remind ourselves, *"No, I'm not going to give in to temptation because it goes against God's Word."*

I had a foot that was sore and swollen for about four months. It would go away and come back. Sometimes the swelling was so bad that it hurt to wear a shoe. I kept speaking to it with calm confidence, reminding my foot it was healed. Then my dog, who weighs about 80 lbs, would step on my foot and start the whole thing over again. This happened several times where my foot got injured again by my dog. I had other people pray over it because it was hard to walk. I persisted until it was completely healed. My healing was fully experienced because I expected it to be healthy, and then it was! No more pain or swelling! You can see that we don't have to put up with sickness anymore than putting up with a misdirected desire toward something sinful. *Amen to that!*

JANUARY 20

Getting Acquainted

Read: Isaiah 53:3

*T*his Scripture should be translated from the original Hebrew as follows:

> "He is despised and rejected by men, a man of **pain** and acquainted with **sickness**."

What is interesting to me is the word *acquainted*. When two people get acquainted, it means they get to know each other in a more meaningful way. The relationship develops beyond just casual talk about the weather—it gets personal.

This is exactly what the word *acquainted* means in the original Hebrew text. This word *acquainted* is the same word as *knew* that is used in Genesis 4:1,

> "Now Adam **knew** Eve his wife, and she conceived and bore Cain."

Jesus *knew* and became *acquainted* with all of our sicknesses, diseases, and pains. He literally BECAME one with them, like a husband knows his wife in all of her ways, inside and out!

Jesus didn't just carry disease and pain away, He literally became it! He became it, felt it, and then destroyed its power! When He said, *"It is finished!"* He meant it!

JANUARY 21

Be Whole

Read: Mathew 9:10-13, 1 Thessalonians 5:23

There is no doctor on this earth that is able to make us *whole*. Jesus said to the Pharisee,

> "*They that be whole need not a physician, but they that are sick.*"

The words *that be whole* Jesus spoke in the *Thayer's Greek English Lexicon of the New Testament*, is #2480, which means *"to be strong in body, to be robust, to be in sound health, be whole"*.

No doctor can do that. He may be able to help our body to some extent, but only Jesus can heal our hearts when they are broken. Only Jesus can deliver us, give us peace, and a sound mind. Only Jesus can completely heal our bodies and make them function perfectly. God's desire is for us to be whole—spirit, soul, and body. He knows what makes us tick! Of course! He is the One who created us!

JANUARY 22

Wholeness

Read: Matthew 9:20-22, Luke 7:36-50

Here we are introduced to two different women with two different problems; or were they?

The woman with the issue of blood desperately needed healing. She risked everything she had to seek Jesus and touch Him. What were the "strikes" against her? First, she was a woman, and culturally women weren't valued as much as men. Second, she had been bleeding for twelve years. According to the Law of Moses, she was unclean and an outcast of society. Third, if she had been discovered in public, she would have been stoned. All of her hopes and dreams, home, family, health, money, and friends were taken from her. No doubt she must have been dejected, emaciated, and anemic. When she heard about Jesus, she had nothing to lose.

The woman in Luke was identified as a sinner. The whole city knew her as a sinner. She, also being a woman, was an outcast in society. No doubt she risked her life entering the Pharisee's house. The Pharisee took the opportunity to test Jesus—he watched Him to see what He would do. He would never allow a woman like that to touch him, and he expected the same response from Jesus.

The woman broke an alabaster flask of perfume and rushed in behind Jesus, weeping uncontrollably. She doesn't even believe she is worthy to look Him in the eyes. Yet, somehow, Jesus knows who she is and He lets her kiss His feet, wash them with her tears, and wipe them with her hair. Immediately, the Pharisee who invited Jesus into his home began to judge Him in his heart, saying to himself,

> *"This Man, if He were a prophet, would know who and what manner of woman this is who is touching Him, for she is a sinner."*

JANUARY 22

Both of these women had a need only Jesus could meet. The woman with the issue of blood needed healing, while the woman who was a "sinner" needed forgiveness. Go back to the above Scriptures and compare the words Jesus spoke at the end of both stories to each of the women. Jesus declared to the woman with the issue of blood the EXACT SAME PRHASE He said to the woman desiring forgiveness of her sins. In the Greek, the phrase He spoke to both of them is:

"He pistis sou sesoken se" which, when translated to English is: *"The faith of thee has saved thee."*

Why is Jesus able to say the same exact words to both of the women, even though the one woman was seeking healing and the other woman was seeking forgiveness? When we understand that the word *saved* in the Greek means: *heal, deliver, protect, save, preserve, make whole*; we can easily see that forgiveness of sins and healing is *exactly* the same. Jesus paid the price for you to be whole in your spirit, soul, and body. Sickness and sin both came from the same source: the Fall of man. So, therefore, the cure is the same: Jesus! This proves that no matter what need you are facing right now, Jesus' answer to you is the same: *"The faith of thee has saved thee"* because you already have faith in Him!

JANUARY 23

Delegation Of Power

Read: Matthew 9:35-10:8, Revelation 12:11

Jesus demonstrated to His disciples how He wanted them to live. The Scripture says that in every city He went, that it was for the sole purpose to teach, preach the Gospel of the Kingdom, and to heal every disease.

He looked up and saw a multitude of people. Seeing the plight of humanity, He was moved with compassion—they were suffering with no one to lead them.

Jesus knew that He could be more effective if He could reach more people. He was ready to reproduce Himself by "deputizing" His disciples with the same authority He possessed. It was time for some "hands on" training for His disciples. They had seen Him perform many miracles up to this point, and now they were ready to apply what He had demonstrated to them.

If you need healing in your body, sow healing in others. Remember, the Bible says that we reap what we sow. The Holy Spirit is able to help you deliver healing to other people who need it. He has already equipped you with the same power and authority Jesus had given to the disciples.

Before my own healing was complete, I looked for people who needed healing everywhere I went. I'd testify to them how God had healed me and that He wanted to heal them too. Even though I still felt some physical symptoms in my body, I didn't let that stop me. I kept pushing myself beyond my comfort zone. I determined to keep myself full of the Word of God. I listened to solid, Biblical teaching about healing. I wanted to renew my mind to God's truth and not stay focused on what I was experiencing in my body. Then, I had to act on what I read in the Word and what I heard preached.

JANUARY 23

That was the challenging part for me. But before long, I received the results of the blood test confirming that I was completely healed!

"And they overcame him by the blood of the Lamb and by the word of their testimony; and they loved not their lives unto the death." (Revelation 12:11)

JANUARY 24

Grace Gave Us Everything (Part 1)

Read: Romans 3:21-26, Romans 8:32

If you read these verses in either the KJV or the NLKV Bible, there are some pretty big words such as: *righteousness, redemption, propitiation, and justification.* Of course, they are all good things we have been given through our faith in Jesus. His grace has made them automatically effective in our lives. But if we don't know what they mean, we may be unaware of just how good we have it!

To be *righteous* is to be set in proper relationship with God. There is nothing standing in the way between you and Him—not your sin, not your past, curses, nothing!

Redemption means to free someone from bondage by paying a ransom. We know that Jesus paid that ransom for our lives with His own blood.

Propitiation means turning away wrath by an offering and being reconciled to God. This is the New Testament word for *atonement.* We know that Jesus made atonement for us with His blood.

Justification means that God has declared you "not guilty."

Keeping all of these definitions in mind, we can now clearly see that the moment you were born again, this is the way God made you. You couldn't do any of this for yourself, so He put you in this position with Himself for you—*by grace*! Is there anything that can come between you and God that can keep you from this goodness? No! Is there any sin that can keep you from receiving His healing touch? No! Why? Because in Christ, God removed everything that you were and everything that you did in your past and totally wiped it away!

So come now with confidence, knowing that since He did all of these things: making you righteous, redeeming you, justifying you, and paying the ransom for your life—how shall He not, with Him, also freely give you all things—*including health!*

JANUARY 25

Grace Gave Us Everything (Part 2)

Read: Ephesians 2:4-10

*G*race gave us Jesus! And with Jesus, everything He is and everything He accomplished for us came with Him. Why? *Because God chose to love us!*

Mercy, kindness, grace, and love are all credited for the reasons why God shared His Son with us. He made us alive together with Christ. By His grace we are saved; remembering that *saved* means *sozo*, in the Greek: *saved, healed, delivered, protected,* and *made whole*—all by this wonderful gift!

From the moment Jesus set Himself to die, He took upon Himself our nature of sin and all of its yucky results: death, disease, and every evil force that was against us. When He was resurrected, He took us along with Him and *made* us sit together with Him in heavenly places.

It says in verse ten that we are His "workmanship," created in Christ. Father re-created us and all that was corrupted by sin. When I think of the word *workmanship*, it reminds me of the word *masterpiece*. I'm reflecting upon the feeling I get when painting a picture of scenery or decorating a birthday cake; declaring with pride, *"What a masterpiece!"* I'm sure Father had the same admiration for us once we arrived with Jesus and sat with Him on His throne. He must have smiled, nodded His head, and exclaimed, *"I done GOOOD!"*

The best part is—we didn't have to work for any of it! Our only work is to *believe*. That's pretty simple. Just believe in a grace so huge, that it swallowed up all our junk and gave us nothing but goodness in its place! One simple choice to believe and we get all the benefits Jesus purchased! Grace is not an ethereal vapor wafting around in the air. It was the power that possessed legal authority to

JANUARY 25 ———

carry Christ all the way through His suffering, picked us up, tucked us away inside, and then carried us to glory right next to our Father. *Free indeed!*

JANUARY 26

Do Unto Others

Read: Matthew 7:12

When I was very sick, I wondered where the Christians were that knew they had the power to lay hands on the sick to make them well. I remember sitting in a public place with people passing me by and no one ever stopped to reach out to me. I was in much pain and suffering and could hardly walk. I vowed that I would learn everything I could to pray for the sick so they could be healed. I'd be that person for them that no one was able to be for me.

Since I made that vow, I've met so many people who were very thankful that I took the time to pray with them. I found that it is very seldom that people refuse prayer. More often than not, they are appreciative that someone took the time to notice them and care about their pain. Someone once said to me, *"Who does that these days? Thank you!"*

A few times, I've seen someone who looks angry and thought, *"They will probably just cuss me out and tell me to get lost!"* When I take the time to talk to them and find out about their situation, they are more than happy to take my hand right there in Wal-Mart and pray in Jesus' Name. One woman I walked past was limping very noticeably. She looked pretty tough. She had pink hair, skulls, tattoos, and was dressed like a "motorcycle mama." I knew she was in pain. After introducing myself, she was surprised—her name was Michele too! She began to tell me her story. Her son had been killed twelve years ago and she missed him dearly. Her clothes were a constant reminder to keep him close in her memory because that was the way he had dressed. Michele was very appreciative that I took the time to listen and to pray for her hip and her broken heart.

JANUARY 26 ———

My friend, don't let appearances stop you. Things seldom are what they seem from the outside. Step out of your comfort zone and do for others what you would have them do for you!

JANUARY 27

Where'd That Old Body Go?

Read: Romans 6:6-14

"***K**nowing this*, that our old man is crucified with Him, that the **body of sin might be done away with** ..."

I'm expected to *know* this! My physical body and its inclination to feel crappy or sick like the rest of the world, was crucified. My old body is part of the old man. When Jesus' physical body was crucified, mine was crucified along with His!

Franklin Hall, in his book *Formula for Raising the Dead and Baptism of Fire* said,

> "*Faith looks for no visible sign from the senses. Faith people believe, preach, and declare what God hath said first, even when contrary to the senses, before manifestations come into existence.*"

This reminds me of old Abraham and Sarah. God quickened their bodies and made them youthful again so they could conceive. That little seed became the lineage of Jesus—not only physically, but it brought the lineage of spiritual sons by faith in Jesus! So right there is both the physical and the spiritual working side by side. They are not separate! Holy Spirit is in our flesh!

As Jesus' body was raised to life by Holy Spirit, my body was also raised to life by Holy Spirit. I got a new life! I got a new mind! I got a new body! This is a life of dominion—a life exactly like Jesus: spirit, soul, and body. Holy Spirit quickens and makes my body alive and full of life! I don't have to settle for the world's healthcare system. I've got a divine healthcare system straight from Holy Spirit, giving life to my flesh!

JANUARY 28

Reap What You Sow

Read: 1 Corinthians 4:1-7

"And what do you have that you did not receive?"

I heard the story of a man who had Crohn's disease. He was suffering terribly and was in need of healing. He believed that God was able to heal him. He decided that he would pray for others to be healed. He saw a lot of miracles take place. Even his wife had complications with their unborn baby, and when he laid hands on her belly, the baby was born perfectly well. Yet, he still had the symptoms of Crohn's. He didn't give up! He knew that the miracles he was able to give to others through the power of God, was the same power available to him. After quite some time, he finally received his complete healing. He had never given up!

That man knew that he was able to heal others because he possessed the Holy Spirit's power. And since he had healing to give away, he could also receive it for himself. What do we have within us that we did not receive from Jesus? Every good thing He has given to us we are able to give away!

JANUARY 29

Newness Of Life

Read: Romans 6:1-5

We received an entirely new life in Christ! But what exactly does that mean? What is all involved? For one, the desire to do evil is removed. No longer is there an *"I don't care"* or *"let the chips fall where they fall"* attitude; being dead to sin means that you don't intentionally live your life carelessly. From the moment you are born again, the nature of Jesus begins to give you new desires.

When we are baptized in water, it is symbolic of dying. It means that we were baptized into Jesus' death. It is symbolic of a funeral, and your testimony of the change in your life is your eulogy. The old you and your old ways of thinking and living are dead—gone forever! Yay!

Verse 4 says, that the same as Christ was raised up from the dead by Father's glory; we should walk in *newness of life*. I found that term a little odd: *Newness of life*. What exactly does that mean? *Newness* is #2538 in the *Strong's Concordance*. It means *freshness, new with respect to age, renewal, youthful, regenerate*. I like the sound of that! Our bodies were born again as well as our spirit when we came to Christ. Jesus isn't up there in heaven, hunched over and walking with a cane talking with a crackled voice. He is the ANCIENT OF DAYS, but He doesn't look like it! We don't have to either! Verse 5 says,

> "For if we have been united (made one, combined, made into a single entity) together in the likeness of His death, certainly we also shall be in the likeness of His resurrection." (Parenthesis added)

Since we died with Him, we are alive with Him the same way He is alive—healthy, youthful, and strong!

JANUARY 30

Emanating Life

Read: Matthew 14:34-36, John 6:38

Emanate means to flow out as from a source or origin.

Jesus' body and clothes emanated life. Life flowed out of Him because He is the source of life. When the multitudes of people touched His clothes, they were *"made perfectly whole."* This phrase comes from the word *diasozo* (related to *sozo*) which means: *to save thoroughly, to cure, preserve, rescue, heal, make perfectly whole.*

ALL that were diseased were made perfectly whole! There was no exception—**ALL** were cured. Jesus said that He came to do the will of His Father who sent Him. Clearly, we can see that it is the Father's will and desire for **ALL**-that includes you—to be "made perfectly whole."

JANUARY 31

The Promise Of The Father

Read: John 14:16-18, Luke 24:49-53

*W*hat is this "Promise of the Father" Jesus spoke about? Since Jesus gave specific instructions before His departure, it was of utmost importance that the disciples received this promise. Why was it so important for them to follow His instructions?

One morning as I was in prayer, I thought about Hebrews 12:2:

> *"Who for the joy that was set before Him endured the cross, despising the shame, and has sat down at the right hand of the throne of God."*

I said to Jesus, *"I can understand how keeping Your eyes on heaven and being re-clothed with the glory You left behind helped You to persevere through all of the torture You went through. I bet You were so glad to get out of this crappy place!"*

He gently responded,

> *"Michele, that thought never entered My mind. I wasn't thinking about Myself or how glad I was to leave a terrible earth. I was anticipating returning to My Father, so that I could send you His Promise of the Holy Spirit to come and live inside you and fill you with My power! I didn't want to leave My people powerless! I wanted to restore them fully back to the Father and finish His work!"*

WOW! His words really struck me! I realized that Jesus wasn't thinking about Himself—even though He certainly had a right to. He was more concerned about giving us the inheritance He paid for, reconnecting us back to our Father, and depositing the Holy Spirit inside of us so that heaven would be brought to earth! Thank you, Jesus!

FEBRUARY 1

Love

1 John 3:16-18 (ESV)

It's easy to say, *"God loves you."* We have heard it so many times that it sounds like a cliché', or it's just a nice thing to tell someone because we don't know what else to say when he or she is in a difficult situation. There is a whole lot more to this statement than just being nice. God's love for us is a perfect demonstration of sacrifice.

"By this we *know* love." *Know* love? What does it mean to "*know* love"? *Know* means *to perceive or understand as fact or truth; to apprehend clearly and with certainty.*

The Bible is very clear that Jesus demonstrated love perfectly by laying down His life for you and me. Yet sometimes circumstances come along that cause us to question, *"If God really loved me, then why did He allow this to happen to me?"* And the answer is quite simple: He didn't. Nor is it His method of trying to teach you something. The Holy Spirit is your Teacher. God gave you the solution: His Son. In Him is found the solution to every problem man could ever experience. Why? Because of His love for us, He laid down His life so that we could share in His! So cover yourself with this truth! See yourself wrapped in His blanket of love where all that has come against you is repelled. There you are safe and secure; nothing can touch you!

FEBRUARY 2

To Know And Believe

Read: Romans 5:8-9

*D*emonstration. The above Scripture tell us that God didn't just say, *"I love you."* He demonstrated it. He showed how much He loves us by taking all the sickness and disease man could ever experience, and allowed it to be put on His Son. Jesus took it to the grave with Him and eradicated it. Those stripes paid for **all** sickness and disease. He did this before you ever knew you would need it, *"while we were still sinners."*

Verse nine of the above Scripture goes on to say *"Even more than that..."* (My paraphrase) Even more than that, God demonstrated His love for us when we didn't know Him, He justified us—made us right with the Father through His blood. Did you know that to be justified and made right is not only for you spiritually? Justification is available for your mind and your body as well as your spirit!

Thank the Father for demonstrating His great love for you by making you righteous and justified in your spirit, soul, and body—*before you ever knew you needed it!*

FEBRUARY 3

Beloved

Read: 1 John 4:7

The word *beloved* is used nearly seventy times in the New Testament. It is used as a term of endearment to people in close relationship. Paul called Timothy his *"beloved son"* (2 Timothy 1:2). Paul also used this word to others who had labored with him for the Gospel. These were people who had traveled with him, sharing in his ministry; risking their lives for the sake of preaching Christ to the lost. This was not a term he used casually for people he didn't know in a personal way.

Paul also used this expression to address the churches he had planted. He corrected them, chastened them, and encouraged them as his *"beloved brothers"* (1 Corinthians 15:58).

John used this term exhorting the Believers in his letter (1 John 4:7).

We know that the Father referred to Jesus as His *"beloved Son in Whom He is well pleased"* (Matthew 3:17).

Jesus stated in John 15:9-17—*"As the Father has loved me, so I have loved you."* When we combine the words of Matthew with the words of John and Paul in the Scriptures I referenced, we can know for sure that we, too, are the *"beloved of God"*.

FEBRUARY 4

The Rock Of Offense

Read: Mark 6:1-6, 1 Peter 2:6-10

*O*ur Scripture reading in Mark records the events that occurred when Jesus was rejected by the entire town of Nazareth, where He grew up. Everyone knew Him and His family. He began His ministry when He was thirty years old (Luke 3:23). At this age, He revealed Himself as the Son of God and began to teach in the synagogues. Many were offended at Him, even though He proved through the miracles He performed, that He was the Son of God.

1 Peter states that some will regard Jesus as a *"rock of offense."* Those who are offended at Him won't see Him as He truly is, so they throw Him out like a worthless stone. Those who regard Him as a precious stone (or jewel) will build their lives on Him and His words of Truth. They will become His family and a nation of people holy unto the Lord.

Sometimes the truths we learn in the Bible "offend" our beliefs because we have been taught wrong doctrines. We are hindered from living the abundant life Christ purchased for us because we don't have a thorough understanding. I gave the Lord permission to "offend" me in any area that I believe incorrectly. Do you want to be like the people in Jesus' home town, who were unable to receive everything He could give them, because of a stubborn mindset? Let's allow the Holy Spirit to "tweak" any areas where we don't see the whole truth clearly. Decide to keep your heart pliable, so that He can expose any shortsightedness you may have—even if it offends you!

FEBRUARY 5

The Language Of The Spirit

Luke 5:16-26

Look at all of those Pharisees! They came from Galilee, Judea, and Jerusalem just to hear Jesus! They considered Him their enemy, didn't they? They were jealous that the multitudes were listening to Him. They were dumbfounded that He didn't re-enforce their teachings! Yet *"the power of the Lord was present to heal them."*

Jesus told the paralytic, *"Man, your sins are forgiven you."* It says that the Pharisees began to reason in their minds, *"Who is this who speaks blasphemies? Who can forgive sins but God alone?"* Verse 22 says that Jesus *perceived their thoughts*. This is what all of them were thinking at the same time! Jesus read their minds! How? The Holy Spirit inside of Him gave Him the knowledge to survey what He was up against—a religious mindset. He was trying to help them to know who He really was. In verse 24 Jesus says,

> *"But that you may know that the Son of Man has power on earth to forgive sins"*—*He said to the man who was paralyzed, "I say to you, arise, take up your bed and go to your house."*

Jesus was able to discern what was in the hearts of these Pharisees. He didn't have to have a conversation with them to know what was going on in their hearts. He didn't need to, because the Holy Spirit told Him. He was able to perceive like it was a natural, common thing to know what was in people's hearts. It wasn't to condemn them, but to help them come out of their religious mindset and embrace healing and truth!

Have you ever had an experience where you just *know* something? Sometimes it's a heart issue a person is carrying without them saying a word. You can sense that they are struggling with something. That's one of the ways that the Holy Spirit communicates with us! It may be more technically called, *"a word of knowledge"* as

FEBRUARY 5

spoken of in 1 Corinthians 12. It's always wise to pay attention to that *knowing* inside. There is a reason the Holy Spirit is showing you something. Many times, it is just to pray for someone when their name comes to your mind out of the blue. Sometimes, it may be discerning something about yourself or a situation you are in. Ask the Lord what to do with the information He is entrusting you with. But whatever the reason, it is never to condemn. God always reveals to heal. So pay close attention to the language of the Spirit, the language of *knowing*.

FEBRUARY 6

120 And Strong

Read: Deuteronomy 34:1-7, 2 Corinthians 3:7-13

*M*oses had discovered the "Fountain of Youth!" Boy, what Maybelline® would give for that, right? Moses was 120 years old and climbed to the top of a mountain. There, he was able to see a great distance north, south, east, and west—the treasured Promised Land!

Imagine being 120 years old and still able to climb a mountain without losing your breath! Imagine, at that age, standing on that mountain top and being able to see miles in every direction without glasses! Get a group of older people around each other today and their conversation quickly turns to their aches, pains, and all the medications their doctors prescribed. But not Moses!

What was so special about him? Did he really discover the "Fountain of Youth?" Yes! He did! It was simply hanging out with God! Remember how his face glowed with the glory of God? His physical body was affected by the glory of God Himself because he spent more time hanging out with God than anyone else—and that was under the Old Covenant! Moses did not have salvation like we do through Jesus. God affected him from the outside in, not from the inside out like we can have today by the Holy Spirit living inside of us.

So, why do we think we have to accept aches, pains, and disease just because we are getting older? We have a New Covenant established on better promises, don't we (Hebrews 8:6)? We have the Holy Spirit—the SAME Holy Spirit that raised Jesus from the dead—living inside of us! I like the *Peshitta Bible's* translation of Deut. 34:7,

> "And Moses was a hundred and twenty years old when he died; but his eye was not dim, nor the skin of his cheeks wrinkled."

FEBRUARY 6

Move over anti-wrinkle creams! Note that Moses didn't die because he was old or because he was sick. God took his spirit home with Him and buried his body there on that mountain because he was not going into the Promised Land with children of Israel.

I have heard many accounts of men of God not dying because they were old or sick. They died because they longed to go home to be with Jesus: Kenneth Hagin, Charles Capps, and F.F. Bosworth, to name a few. We can believe God just like these men of our time who preached life and healed the sick. How? Just hang out with Jesus! Make it a habit to be strong in the Word. Keep your connection with Him open all day, every day; fellowshipping with Him, acknowledging His presence giving life to your body, and sharing your life with Him! You too can stay vigorous and strong to 120 with wrinkle-free cheeks!

FEBRUARY 7

What's Love Got To Do With It?

Read: 1 John 4

*T*his chapter in 1 John speaks a lot about love: the love of the Father and the Son, the love we have for other Believers, and the love God has toward us. The author even goes on to say that love is so powerful that fear is thrown out in its presence.

We know that Scripture tells us that God doesn't just love us, but that He actually *is* love. He is a special kind of love called "agape" that loves us unconditionally and qualifies us to be His own sons.

I've heard it preached many times that verse 18 means that you must know that God loves you in order to be free of fear. Once you are free from fear, you can receive the truth that God loves you, and as a result, you can be healed. The focus becomes getting rid of fear and trying to convince ourselves that we are loved. Anyone been there?

So what is the hang up with this perspective? This type of mindset keeps us in a perpetual state of thinking we need to *do* something in order to *get* something from God. It's like walking on a treadmill—you can walk fast or run but still not go anywhere. Religion is always trying to *get*. A son knows what he already *has*. This perspective sure takes the pressure off, doesn't it? Verse 17 in the *Amplified Bible* says,

> *"In this [union and fellowship with Him], love is completed and perfected with us, so that we may have confidence in the Day of Judgment [with assurance and boldness to face Him]; because as He is, so are we in this world."*

Now taking a closer look at this verse, we can see that our love in Christ is a compilation of several things:

FEBRUARY 7 ———

1. Understanding the complete union we were given in Christ
2. Confidence is equal to boldness so we can stand equal with Him
3. We are on earth as He is *now* in heaven, not as He was when He was on earth
4. His love is completed, perfected, and matured; not needing anything else added to make it affective toward us

When we put these four things together we recognize that these are in the *past tense*! This is already what we have! The work is DONE! Fear isn't part of the package! Love is perfected in us through Christ, so healing is already yours! You are already made perfect in His love! You have your healing because you have the Healer!

FEBRUARY 8

The Abiding One

Read: John 15

Abide means to *stay, continue, dwell, endure, be present, remain, stand, tarry, to sink deeper, to settle.* The relationship between God the Father and His Son Jesus is a continuing state of oneness. The relationship we have in Jesus is the same relationship Jesus has with the Father; which in turn, makes us one with the Father as well.

It is much like cutting a branch off of one tree and splicing it into a branch on another tree. All of the branches grow together as one, nourished from the same source. The grafted branch is now a living, fruit-producing extension of that tree.

The Word of God is the nourishment that feeds us as a result of being grafted into Jesus. Its replenishing power makes us just as much a part of Him as He is of Himself. When we bring a request to the Father, He hears us as though Jesus were asking for Himself—because He is! We are one with Him, dwelling in His Word, fed by His Word, and strengthened by His Word. We will know His will by the Word dwelling in us! That's why we can ask anything according to His will and it will be given!

His love awakens inside you, and you are able to manifest that love to others. You're connected to Jesus—His living extension! Everything that is in Him is in you, feeding you, making you alive just like Him!

FEBRUARY 9

Love Poured Out

Read: 1 John 3:1-3 (NIV)

God poured out His love in us by sending the Holy Spirit. The Holy Spirit imparts the character and nature of God and compels us to live like Jesus. He accomplished all of this before we ever knew we needed it—while we were still His enemies! He rescued us from ourselves and delivered us from the effects of the world!

I don't know about you, but I like myself a lot more now than I did before I knew Jesus! He saved me from myself! And the more I know Him, the more I realize that I don't have to put up with the stuff that the world dishes out to me either! *Talk about love!* I like the way the NIV expresses John 3:1,

> *"See what great love the Father has **lavished** on us, that we should be called children of God! And that is what we are!"*

God's love made us know Him as Father, revealed us as His children, and made us like Him. His love made us holy as He is holy!

The thought that He *lavished* His love on me makes me feel full and satisfied! To *pour out* implies that He is brimming over with so much love that He can just slop it all over us! That reminds me of the song "He Loves Us" by John Crowder. The original lyrics where he sings *"Heaven meets earth like a sloppy, wet kiss and my heart turns violently inside of my chest"* convey His overwhelming affection. Is it any wonder that God's love satiates the deepest desires of our heart?

FEBRUARY 10

Bondservants

Read: Romans 1:1-7, Romans 8:38-39, Philippians 2:5-8

The opening greeting of Romans Chapter 1 is a masterpiece. Paul magnifies Jesus at least four times! He also glorifies Jesus' resurrection. Paul himself proved Christ by preaching the Word and then he backed it up with miracles, signs, and wonders to bear witness that God wanted people set free.

Romans 1:1 in the KJV says: *"Paul, a **servant** of Jesus Christ..."* or the NKJV uses the word **bondservant**. In the Greek, the word *servant* literally means *slave*. Philippians 2:7 decrees that Jesus *"...made Himself of no reputation, taking the form of a bondservant (**slave**) and coming in the likeness of men..."* (Emphasis added)

A note in *The Passion Translation* says that a *bondservant* is *"One who has chosen to serve a master out of love, bound with cords so strong that it could only be severed by death."* But we know that the love God has for us cannot even be severed by death!

Paul states emphatically that he separated himself as a slave unto Christ for the sake of the Gospel. By choice, his life was no longer his own. Paul made note of Christ's humility when He laid down His life to liberate the entire human race! I think it's pretty darn amazing that God made Himself a slave so that He could free us from bondage, including everything the world can dish out: hatred, lack, disease, addictions, oppression, death—all of it!

FEBRUARY 11

In As Much

Read: Hebrews 2:14-15

"*Inasmuch*" used in the NKJV are three powerful words when put together. This means that in *exactly* the same way that we are flesh and blood, Jesus became *exactly* as we are, so that He could make us *exactly* as He is now in heaven—resurrected, alive, and free! We don't have to wait until we die someday to experience it either. We can have resurrection life right now!

The above Scripture states that through His death, Jesus destroyed the enemy of death and delivered us from all of its power. Not only was everything that could cause death destroyed, but even the fear of it! He liberated us from its bondage!

Many Bible-believing Christians don't know that these truths are available. Some still see themselves in bondage, trying to break free. We have been taught inaccurately that we need a special "breakthrough" in order to be completely loosed. We can see the proof, in these two Scriptures, that Jesus paid the price by becoming human and dying our death! You don't need a special breakthrough! You don't need a special move of God! You don't need to keep repenting over and over again! Just begin to thank Him that it's already done—whatever the necessity! I guarantee that, when you begin to see yourself the way Jesus already made you, all of these hindrances will fall away—even disease will lose its grip on you!

FEBRUARY 12

The Word Prevailed

Read: Acts 19

Acts 19 is chock full of the miracles Paul ministered. He baptized new Believers in the Holy Spirit, preached the Word, and God worked *"unusual miracles by the hands of Paul"* confirming the message of the Gospel.

In verses 16 and 20, the word *prevailed* is used. In verse 16, the evil spirits prevailed over the seven sons of Sceva because did not have authority in Jesus' Name. They wanted the power Paul had, but they weren't willing to be born again so that they had the right to use that Name. The evil spirits disgraced them publically by giving them a beating they'd never forget! This brought a fear of the Lord on the people who lived in Ephesus. It says that the Name of Jesus was magnified. Many people believed in Jesus as a result.

Verse 20 says that *"...the Word of the Lord grew mightily and prevailed."* These pagans tossed their books containing witchcraft into the fire and confessed their wicked deeds. Strongholds were broken off of the people and many were born again. The Word of God will always prevail in the face of evil. Nothing can stand against it.

FEBRUARY 13

Life, Light & Love

Read: John 1:1-18, Mark 11:12-24 (KJV)

The first few verses of John chapter one can be separated in to three sections: Life (John 1:1-4), Light (John 1:5-11), and Love (John 1:12-18).

In verse 5 it says that darkness did not comprehend the light. The Greek here has a double meaning. Not only could the darkness not comprehend or understand the light, but it could not overpower or diminish it either.

We know the world was created through Jesus. All of creation knows His name and will respond to His name. Remember when Jesus spoke to the fig tree? Jesus was hungry and expected it to produce fruit for Him. He seemed to be having a conversation with this tree! It says in verse 14, in the KJV, that Jesus *answered* it and said, *"No man eat fruit of thee hereafter forever,"* as though the tree was giving Him a reason why it had no fruit. Did the tree have ears? Did the tree have a mouth? Physically, no, it had neither. So why did Jesus speak to it as though it could hear Him? What if all of Creation has "ears" and can hear us when we speak? What about diseases? Do they have ears? I believe they do! They must leave when we command them to *"GO!"* in the Name of Jesus because they know that Name!

I know from experience that mosquitoes can hear me when I speak. In the summertime, when one of those buggers comes to sing me a song, I tell her that I am not her lunch, and if she tries to bite me, she will die. Most of them are smart and stay away, but once in a while one thinks it is brave and "SMACK!"—it's a goner! The world is held in darkness and bondage till there is someone who comes along in Jesus' Name and sets it free! If more people walked in the Truth: Life, Light, and Love, this earth would be a different place, that's for sure!

FEBRUARY 14

Miraculous Power

Luke 10:1-9, 17-20

*R*ecently, I was staying at a hotel. They served a continental breakfast buffet. I went downstairs to the buffet to get some oatmeal and saw a man with a cane. The thought came to my mind that I should pray for him, but I didn't. I wrestled with myself, made some excuses, and went back to my room with my oatmeal. Once I returned to my room, I was reminded that living for Jesus isn't a democracy. We don't get to choose which commands we want to obey and the ones we don't. It's not about our lives or our own comfortability. People are suffering in the world, and having the answer to their problem may sometimes require putting ourselves in uncomfortable situations.

If I want to experience the miraculous power of Jesus in my life, then I must step out and pray for people who need help. Did Jesus sit around with a group of people and say, *"Just listen to what I say because I'm the Son of God?"* No, He didn't. He demonstrated that He was the Son of God by the miracles He did. Then, He sent out the seventy with the same authority He had to do the same miracles He did.

Notice that He sent them OUT. They didn't sit around and wait for the people to come to them. So, wherever you go, step out of your comfort zone and give away the power that Jesus freely gave to you. If you want to see miracles in your own life, you have to actually DO something. I think that's where a lot of us miss it. We've been conditioned to sit in church to learn, but once we leave, we forget what we heard and don't do anything with it. The basics of the Christian life are: "hear and then do." Otherwise, we will not produce much fruit for the Kingdom of God.

FEBRUARY 15

Perfect Love

Read: Romans 8:15

When Jesus came into your life, so did His power. When Holy Spirit filled you, He did not bring a spirit of bondage. His love came in and kicked fear out! He brought freedom and identification. His Spirit within you cries out, *"You are my Daddy! I belong to you!"*

When Holy Spirit was poured out, He came to live inside and fill us with love—perfect love. You are not a step-child. You are not a backwards kid or the "black sheep" of His family. His blood fixed all of that. He kicked bondage out because when His love came in, there was no more room for anything else! His love brought peace. His love brought a sound mind. His love brought identity, power, security, confidence, and an inheritance that we could never exhaust in our lifetime. His love perfected you.

Christ in us = His love in us. God's not angry; the fear of His disapproval was cast out!

FEBRUARY 16

Invisible Becomes Visible

Read: Hebrews 1:1-4, John 15:1-5

Jesus was the visible image of the invisible God while He was here on the earth. Now we, the church which is His body, are the visible image of the invisible God. The church—that's you and me—are to make Him known by doing His works. Jesus said, *"As you've seen Me, you've seen the Father. It's the Father's works that I do..."*

You and I are the visible image of the invisible Christ. There is *interdependence*. The vine (Jesus) cannot bear fruit (works) without the branches (us). The works that we do are the same works Jesus did. Jesus said to the men sent by John the Baptist to question if He was the Messiah:

> *"Go and tell John the things you have seen and heard: that the blind see, the lame walk, the lepers are cleansed, the deaf hear, the dead are raised, the poor have the Gospel preached to them."* (Luke 7:22)

These are the same works that Jesus told us to do before He went back to the Father:

> *"Most assuredly I say to you, he who believes in Me, the works that I do he will do also; and greater works than these he will do, because I go to My Father."* (John 14:12)

I believe that we are living in days where the general population has heard enough of the church flapping their gums. They have heard about Jesus in one way or another. We haven't had a very good track record because we have said a lot and demonstrated little, even with our attitude. We are reminded of the awesome privilege of being made in the image of Christ and the resoluteness of His words to do the same works He did. People believed the words He spoke because He had the power to make the invisible visible. My

FEBRUARY 16

friends, we have been given the same mandate that Jesus was given by the Father. When we do His works and set people free, we are making the invisible Jesus visible to a world that desperately needs to see Him!

FEBRUARY 17

Putting Off The Old Man

Read: Ephesians 4:17-24

*W*ilford Reidt said in his book, *John G. Lake: The Man and His Message—*

> *"Putting off the old man is not a lifetime process. Jesus' crucifixion did not take a lifetime. He took you out of the world and now He takes the world out of you."*

Jesus said in John 14:30, *"For the prince of this world cometh, and hath nothing in Me."* We were crucified to sin and sickness when Jesus took all of its power to the cross and finished it off. There was nothing that could add to His crucifixion or take away from it. It was a done deal, PERIOD.

Then why do we still experience sin and its effects? Most of us have been taught that someday we'll be holy and good enough for God to use for His glory when we can get our act together. Some spend their time striving to do right, believing that they still miss it every day. When we take this approach, we never see ourselves arriving, but just muddling along life until, someday, when we get to heaven.

Verses 17-24 in Ephesians are full of commands. *We* put off our old lifestyle. *We* renew our mind and put on the new man. Nothing happens by osmosis. Yes, Christ made us a new Creation, but in order for what He has given to be effective, we must cooperate with the Holy Spirit. Once we are born again, we are required to change the way we live. Having one foot in the world and one foot in the Kingdom brings a person much confusion and heartache. This is the main reason there are "carnal Christians."

We don't have to try to accomplish a sinless life. The moment you came to Christ, as Wilford Reidt stated, He took the world out of you. Our nature and desire for sin has been obliterated. We now act in response to what Christ has provided.

FEBRUARY 18

This Resurrection Realm

Read: Acts 9:1-22

After Paul had a miraculous conversion, he didn't sit around. His sight was restored; he was baptized in water, and then immersed in the Holy Spirit. He was fully equipped to preach that Jesus was the Messiah. He had just experienced Jesus' power! Acts 9:20 says, *"Immediately he preached the Christ in the synagogues, that He is the Son of God."* Paul didn't waste any time! He told everyone he knew about Jesus! I remember the excitement I had when I first came to Jesus. I wanted to get everyone I met saved too!

The most important part of the message Paul preached was Christ's resurrection from the dead. Everywhere he went, He preached *"Christ crucified and resurrected."* The scribes and the Pharisees opposed what Paul preached. They had him imprisoned and whipped five separate times because he proclaimed that Jesus was the resurrected Son of God.

Paul even went as far to say that he wanted to experience Christ's resurrection power for himself. He wanted to be so much like Jesus that he wanted to participate in everything Jesus experienced—even if it meant suffering for Him (Philippians 3:10-11).

Jesus said in John 11:25, *"I am the resurrection and the life,"* when He raised Lazarus from the dead. It wasn't gold dust and diamonds that revealed God's glory. It was Jesus' power over sickness and death that displayed His glory. E.W. Kenyon said,

> *"If our minds could only grasp the fact that satan is paralyzed, stripped of his armor by the Lord Jesus, and that disease and sickness are servants of this Man; that at His voice, they must depart, it would be easy to live in this resurrection realm."*

FEBRUARY 18

Did Kenyon say *"EASY?"* Did he say it can be *EASY* to live in Christ's resurrection realm? Yes! He did! I learned from studying the life of E.W. Kenyon, that he taught his entire congregation how to live free from disease. No one died under the age of seventy for the forty years he pastored. Kenyon knew what he was talking about when he said we can live in Christ's resurrection realm when we understand that diseases must obey the Name of Jesus.

Just like Paul, E.W. Kenyon, and many other examples in our time, we too can live in the resurrection realm of Christ—knowing that our enemies are a completely defeated foe!

FEBRUARY 19

That You May Marvel

Read: John 5:19-21

To marvel means *to gaze at with wide-open eyes at something remarkable.* Jesus confidently stated that He would make men marvel by the works He did— specifically raising the dead. He said that He could do nothing of Himself, but only what He saw the Father do. He never did anything His own way. He was a man full of the Holy Spirit, completely surrendered to His Father's will.

How was Jesus able to do this? Verse 20 states that Jesus knew His Father loved Him. He had developed a relationship based on love with His Father, and out of this relationship, He knew the Father would never lead Him down a wrong path. Jesus still had His own will as a man, but He chose a life of submission. Knowing that He could trust His Father was the foundation for doing whatever He was told to do, so the idea of making a mistake was never a consideration. He proved that the Father was in Him and that He was in the Father—that they were one in heart, mind, and purpose. Verse 20-21 says in the *Message Bible*,

> *"But you haven't seen the half of it yet, for in the same way that the Father raises the dead and creates life, so does the Son. The Son gives life to anyone He chooses. Neither He nor the Father shuts anyone out."*

I've heard of many testimonies from people who have raised the dead. These opportunities come when you least expect! For me, the first time was over the phone. My friend's son had overdosed on drugs and passed out upstairs in his room. When his mother heard a loud thud, she immediately searched for him to find out what had happened. She found her son lying on the floor, unresponsive. After realizing what he had done, she called me on the phone. She said that he had stopped breathing; his face and lips were turning blue.

FEBRUARY 19

Dazed by the information, my super-spiritual mind thought, *"What the heck are you calling me for? You should be calling 911!"* Then I thought, *"Wait! Get a hold of yourself! This is what she is supposed to do—call someone who can help!"* Then I asked if she had called for an ambulance. She was calm but straightforward, *"The paramedics are on the way, but I don't have anyone else I can call who believes like I do. I need you to pray while I give my son CPR."* I snapped out of shock and responded, *"Put your phone on his chest. I'll pray while you do CPR!"* I began to command her son to live and not die in Jesus' Name! I commanded life to come back into his body. After a few minutes, like a methodical team—as she worked on him and I spoke life—her son started to respond! By the time the paramedics arrived, he was breathing on his own, color was returning to his face, and he was able to sit up. Within a few minutes he stood up and began pacing around the room. After an examination and checking his vital signs, the paramedics said that he was fine and that there was nothing else they could do for him!

I was pretty shaken after I got off the phone with her. To help save her son's life, for me, was quite overwhelming. She was a rock the whole time—very calm and focused! If it were my son, I honestly don't know if I would be able to do the same. I had to get a grip on my thoughts and push all of my emotions aside. This was life or death!

I praise God that He had taught me what to do in a situation like that. The fact that it was over the phone was a blessing; it kept me from seeing the signs of death and my mind from running away with *"What if"* scenarios, so I could stay focused.

Jesus raises the dead! He loves us so much that He gives us His resurrection life to share His dead-raising power...*that you may marvel!*

FEBRUARY 20

Full Of Faith And Power

Read: Acts 6, Acts 7

*A*s the Gospel was spread, the number of disciples multiplied greatly. We're talking "instant mega-church!" They numbered from 120 in the upper room to a multitude of people who needed to be discipled. The apostles listed several critical qualifications to fill the position of leadership. Verse 3 says, *"...seek out from among you seven men of good reputation, full of the Holy Spirit and wisdom..."*

Stephen was among the seven who were chosen. He met the specifications as a man *full* of faith and the Holy Spirit—admirable qualities to be noted for! Verse 8 says, *"And Stephen, full of faith and power, did great wonders and signs among the people."* I'm sure it is safe to say, that among this vast number of people, there were an enormous amount of issues that needed attention. Stephen was easily able to step up to the plate. He had the faith and the power. Take notice that it is mentioned three separate times that Stephen was *full* of the Holy Spirit!

When Stephen started to attract attention from the religious leaders, he didn't back down one bit! As a matter of fact, he got bolder! And as he was emboldened, the Spirit in him was displayed even more mightily! This only incited their anger! The Bible says, *"...they were not able to resist the wisdom and the Spirit by which he spoke."* The Jewish elders dragged him to a ruling council and staged false witnesses against him. Still, religion was no match against Stephen's wisdom. As he testified about Jesus, his face began to radiate like the face of an angel!

Stephen really socked it to them! When he evangelized with undisputable proof that Jesus was the Messiah, they were cut to the heart and gnashed their teeth at him. They screamed, covering their ears like a bunch of petulant children. The enraged mob didn't want to

FEBRUARY 20

hear that they were guilty of murdering Jesus—talk about conviction! They became delirious, bashing him to death with rocks. Stephen, full of the Holy Spirit, gazed upward as the curtains of heaven were peeled open, staring face to face with Jesus while glory beamed from his countenance.

This was one rare occasion when Jesus was *standing* next to the Father. I bet He stood there cheering Stephen on; clapping, shaking His fist in the air, shouting, *"Come on Stephen! Atta boy! You got this! You tell them!"* Stephen called back, *"Lord Jesus, receive my spirit."* Of course, Jesus would welcome him—they belonged to each other; they had the same Spirit! Talk about going out in a blaze of glory! Jon Bon Jovi has nothing on him! I want to be remembered as a person having these same qualities, don't you? Stephen was:

1. Full of faith
2. Full of the Holy Spirit
3. Full of power
4. Full of wisdom
5. Preached Jesus was the Messiah
6. Did great signs
7. Did great wonders
8. Face shined like an angel's
9. Saw heaven opened
10. Saw the glory of God
11. Saw Jesus standing next to the Father

FEBRUARY 21

A Legacy Of Power

Read: Acts 8:4-40

Philip was among those chosen for leadership in the new, thriving church, as a man full of faith and the Holy Spirit (Acts 6:5). After Stephen was martyred, the church dispersed to evangelize the surrounding regions. *Everywhere* those who were scattered went, they preached Christ. History tells us that this happened about five years after Pentecost, and we can see the church was still going strong, multiplying Believers with a demonstration of signs and wonders.

Philip was a lot like Stephen—he was fearless when he preached! He also demonstrated Jesus was the Christ by the miracles he did using the power of the Holy Spirit. Multitudes of people were delivered of unclean spirits, the paralyzed walked, and joy flooded the city of Samaria as a result. Peter and John followed up by going to Samaria to make sure every new Believer was baptized in the Holy Spirit.

Philip traveled on to Gaza, where a man was sitting in a chariot reading the book of Isaiah—talk about a Holy Spirit set-up! Philip explained that the Scriptures prophesied about Jesus. The man put his faith in Christ and was compelled to be baptized. Philip suddenly disappeared—transported to another place so that he could preach to more people! The Holy Spirit was certainly affirming his message with signs and wonders! Philip had many awesome experiences with God. His phenomenal characteristics include:

1. Full of faith
2. Full of the Holy Spirit
3. Preached Jesus was the Messiah
4. Led people to Christ

FEBRUARY 21

5. Did miracles—delivered people from demons, healed the sick
6. Brought joy to the people by setting them free
7. Baptized Believers
8. Was transported

He was known as "Philip the Evangelist." (Acts 21:9) Evidently, Paul and his traveling companions stopped to visit him and his family. We can learn a few things from Philip's life. He hung around like-minded people. He was known as one of the seven, along with Stephen, as a man full of wisdom and the Holy Spirit. He raised his children in the faith, having four unmarried daughters who prophesied. He left a legacy of character, wisdom, and power for those who would come after him.

FEBRUARY 22

It's All In The Knowing

Read: Isaiah 53:3, Hosea 13:4, Psalm 100:3

*T*here is one word all of the above Scriptures have in common, and that is the verb *know*. It is #3045 in the *Strong's Concordance*. Isaiah uses the expression *acquainted*, but it is still the same word. This little word is also the same Hebrew term used in Genesis 4:1 where it says, *"Adam knew Eve his wife; and she conceived and bare Cain..."*

This describes much more than a casual relationship—it is intimacy in the deepest sense. The marriage between a husband and wife is the closest human bond possible. One purpose for that intimacy is to bring forth children in their own likeness, as God had done at Creation with Adam and Eve. It is certainly remarkable that He knows us inside and out; after all, He created our organs and tissues.

Consider what it means for Christ to *know* or be *acquainted* with our sickness and pain. The words *sorrows* and *grief* in Isaiah 53:3 should be translated as *pain* and *sickness*. The verse should be stated this way: *"He is despised and rejected of men; a man of pain and intimately acquainted with sickness..."* We have assumed that Jesus merely stuffed our diseases in a huge bag and just dumped them off in the trash somewhere. But this verse tells us that He literally **became** sickness and disease. He experienced all of their effects in His own body. He took our afflictions to the grave with Him and destroyed their power!

When we have clearer understanding of what it meant for Jesus to *know* sickness and pain, and that He *became* every evil disease that we might experience, the reality of healing now seems attainable. How? We discovered that we don't have to put up with lying symptoms anymore! We can declare that we are healed. Don't move off this truth, and watch the symptoms disappear!

FEBRUARY 23

Keep Knowing

Read: Psalm 103:7, Daniel 11:32

Building upon our understanding of the word *know* in our devotion from yesterday; let's take a look at these other verses that use the word *know* as well. This is still the same Hebrew word we learned about that describes a personal, intimate relationship.

Psalm 103:7 declares that God made His ways *known* to Moses. We recall many of the extraordinary things Moses experienced, particularly when he requested to see God's glory. Moses spent more time with God than with the children of Israel. In Exodus 34:29, when Moses came down from Mt. Sinai, his face shone so brightly he had to put a veil over his face because the radiance of God's glory! The Lord even said in Exodus 33:17,

> *"for thou hast found grace in My sight, and I know thee by name."*

Here lies the key to knowing God's ways: Hang out with Him! We don't go into our prayer closet because God is only in there. We go into a secret place because that's where other people aren't. There are times when we need to seclude ourselves from distractions so we can just sit and listen. If we want to know His ways, we should do what Moses did to get the results Moses got! However, remember that the moment you leave that place, God is still with you as much as He was a few minutes ago. Don't allow the cares of daily life to interrupt your awareness of Him. Keep the communication flowing.

Daniel is another perfect example. He prayed three times a day, even though it almost cost him his life! Did Daniel do great exploits for God? Absolutely! He interpreted the king's dreams, saw visions of future governments, interacted with angels, shut the mouths

FEBRUARY 23

of lions, and had great wisdom above all the other wise men in Babylon! Why? Because he knew God and God knew him.

It is obvious that it's all in the *knowing*. We can know God's ways, His thoughts, and His desires by spending time with Him without distractions. Communication is a key to build any meaningful relationship, if you want that relationship to amount to anything. We all know that from our experiences with family and friends. Some Believers search for methods to "go deeper" with God, as they say. But if we want to know Him more intimately, if we want to do great exploits like Daniel, than hang out with Jesus! We become like those we hang around!

FEBRUARY 24

The Name Above All Names

Read: Philippians 2:5-11

*E*verything has a name. Names give someone or something its identity. The word *chair* is the name of a piece of furniture to sit on. *Dog* is the name of an animal. *Sue* is the name of a woman. Everything living or not living has been given a name, even if it is an abstract thing like *love* or *faith*.

The Bible tells us that Jesus is the Name that is above **every** name. Every Name? Yes, **Every** name! No matter how large or small, rich or poor, weak or powerful, Jesus' Name is higher than any other name. Higher? Yes, meaning having authority above all things that have a name. Jesus' Name is above **All** names and at the mention of His Name, **ALL** other names must submit. What about cancer? How about a virus, though it is small and can only be seen by a microscope? Aren't those just names?

Several years ago I had terrible, excruciating pain and inflammation in my left knee due to Lyme disease. The joint was the size of a grapefruit! It was very hot, and I could not bend or walk on it for about five months. I found the Scripture in Philippians that says every knee will bow in heaven, on earth, and under the earth—to the Name of Jesus! That meant my knee too! At the time, the reality of getting on my knees to pray and worship in that condition wasn't possible. I began to speak to my knee and command it to bow and bend to the Name of Jesus. In time, as I kept consistently commanding my knee to bend, I was able use it little by little! Eventually I got back full mobility of my knee!

So don't let anything tell you otherwise, no matter what situation is staring you down, you too can make it bow to the Name of Jesus!

FEBRUARY 25

Peace Is War

Read: Exodus 14

*T*his is an awe-inspiring account of God fighting for the children of Israel. They had to learn for themselves who God was on a personal level. Israel was headed toward a life of freedom that they had never experienced before. These were not battle-trained warriors—they were frightened slaves, with no one to defend them but God.

Don't we sometimes feel this way: *"God, where are you? Don't you see what is happening to me? Don't you care?"* Where was God when the children of Israel fled from Egypt? He was right there, in the midst of trouble, protecting them from the Egyptian army. When the children of Israel came to the Red Sea, they were shaking in their shoes! They weren't armed for war; they had no way to contend for themselves. Moses answered the people, *"The Lord will fight for you, and you shall hold your peace."* I like the way the NKJV translated Exodus 14:24,

> *"Now it came to pass, in the morning watch, that the Lord looked down upon the army of the Egyptians through the pillar of fire and cloud, and He troubled the army of the Egyptians."*

Imagine what the Egyptians saw. Can you envision God's eyes staring down at them through the pillar of fire and smoke? That would freak me out too! I can almost hear them screaming in stark terror, *"Let's get out of here!"* They were struck with total chaos as the horses reared and the wheels of their chariots fell off!

Israel didn't have to fight, nor did they have to cry out for help. God didn't allow their enemies to lay one finger on them, proving that He was their protector! All they needed to do was hold their peace and walk into freedom.

FEBRUARY 25

How does this story apply to those who desire to be healed? We may be doing everything we should: renewing our mind, making decrees based on the Word, receiving prayer from others, etc. When we don't see instant results, what should we do? We may be tempted to say, *"This ain't working!"* But don't! Once you do that, it's almost like retracting all the good things you've been believing for! Hold your peace! Don't start speaking the opposite. Look for improvements, no matter how small they may be, and build on them. If God will do the little, He will do the much!

Recently, my four year old grandson had a bad tummy ache. He was in so much pain that he didn't want to move. His little belly was bloated, making his ribs stick out; his tiny face grew pale. I prayed over him several times. I did everything I could to help him: I gave him a warm bath to help him relax, natural remedies and medicine for an upset stomach. He still just wanted to lie in bed, writhing in pain, holding his belly, groaning. My daughter prayed over him several times and a friend had also prayed with us over the phone.

Frustrated, I was like, *"What the heck, Lord? This is my baby! This should have been gone the first time I prayed! How dare it persist!"* Later that evening, as I was driving to church while praying in the spirit, I sensed a heaviness lift off. Then I started laughing! Come on—this was nothing for God! I reminded myself that I am in covenant with Christ and that it extends to my children and grandchildren!

Later that night, my daughter said that my grandson was up and out of bed, acting normal and laughing! In fact, he got up out of bed, healed, at the exact same time I was praying in the spirit! I was so thankful and relieved. The Holy Spirit reminded me that every time I prayed, it was working! Even if I didn't see instant results, it WAS working! I held my peace and I didn't say anything other than insisting that is had to leave. And it did! God was right there in the midst of it all, working!

FEBRUARY 26

The Dangling Carrot

Romans 8:26-27, John 14:25-27

Did you ever feel like the promises of God are just a carrot dangling in front of your face? You believe that you are doing all the right things, and healing still seems to evade you? You hear other people's testimonies of how they were instantaneously, miraculously healed, but you find yourself another day with the same old pain, and the same old crap? You wonder if there is something wrong with you, or if God favors others more than you? Am I speaking to anyone out there?

I get it. I've wrestled with all of those thoughts and feelings myself. I even once questioned Jesus,

> *"Lord, what good is what You did if I can't experience the manifestation of it right here and right now in my body? You didn't go through everything for nothing! You did it so we could experience it! So, where is it? You said that You would manifest Yourself to me. So, where are You?"*

Thank goodness that He doesn't get mad or frustrated with us when we ask Him questions or share our true feelings with Him. Let's get down to the nitty-gritty! It's not that we don't believe—that's not the issue. Then what is it?

The Lord pointed out that He had already manifested Himself by sending the Comforter, the Holy Spirit, to live inside me. Our understanding of the term *"comforter"* has lost its original meaning. For most Believers, we think that it refers to feeling warm and cozy, snuggled up in a blanket. But the original meaning of *"Comforter"* means: *"One called alongside to help."* An accurate description would be to put someone right in the middle of a battle and give them the strength they need to face it! *Comfort* means: *to fortify, equip, fashion,* and *overcome to win!*

FEBRUARY 26

Once I understood that I was not alone, and that Jesus had already manifested Himself in me, I began to see myself quite differently. I was not a weakling; I was not a beggar, and He was not dangling promises in front of me that I could never attain. He was right there in the thick of it, empowering me to overcome!

The Holy Spirit instructed me to pray in the spirit as often as I could throughout the day. I became fortified on the inside; stronger mentally and physically. This helped me to understand the Word more accurately and see things from a perspective that I never saw before. Was it awkward at first? Yes, honestly, it was. I knew how to pray in the spirit, but I never really practiced it very much because I didn't understand the dynamo that it is. How can we go wrong praying perfect prayers with our spirit language?

As I was building myself up in faith (Jude 20), all the negative thoughts and wrong beliefs fell away. Symptoms began to disappear because I was more focused on Jesus, instead of what I felt in my body. My awareness of the Holy Spirit on the inside brought clarity, wisdom and discipline. As a result, I became stronger spiritually, mentally, emotionally, and physically! Honestly, I felt like Rip Van Winkle waking up from a twenty-year nap!

Remember, that the Holy Spirit is right there with you—on the inside—taking hold against sickness; supplying you with the power to overcome!

FEBRUARY 27

Stuck Like Cement

Read: 1 Corinthians 6:12-20

The word *joined* in verse 17, defined in the Greek, means a lot more than just being connected, like a chain linked together. *"But he who is **joined** to the Lord is one spirit with Him."* It means *"to glue together, stick, cement, cleave to form an intimate connection with, enter into closest relations with, unite one's self to."*

It further goes on to say in verse 19, *"Or do you not know that your body is the temple of the Holy Spirit, **who is in you**, whom you have from God, and you are not your own?"* (Emphasis added) Picture yourself like Jesus with skin on, because that's exactly who you are! Your body is the wrapper for the Holy Spirit to live in.

We are not merely muddling through life while Jesus is sitting up there, perched on His throne, disconnected from what's going on. Our relationship is not reduced to calling up to Him, trying to get Him to come down. We do not need an "open heaven" to convince Him to rain down His favor upon us. Many songs we sing in church are about crying out to get more of God, more power, or begging Him to show up. The truth is—He's already here! He sent the Holy Spirit to live inside you the moment you decided to make Him Lord. I had to change the way I believed in order to experience a thriving moment by moment relationship with Holy Spirit. I had to retrain myself to stop thinking of Jesus only being with me on the outside, to Him living on the inside. An important truth my mentor stated quite frequently, when I was new in Christ that I never forgot: *"The Holy Spirit is never silent and He's never still. He's always working."*

We have been conditioned to look for the big stuff, the miraculous, that we miss the little things, when Holy Spirit speaks in simple ways. Sometimes, it can be the quick flash of a picture, or someone's

FEBRUARY 27

name coming to your mind that you haven't thought about for a long time. It may be when you're driving down the road, and you feel prompted to go another direction to arrive at your destination, only to find later the road was closed, and it saved you from being late. There are ways that the Holy Spirit is directing you which require little effort. It's just as vital to hear His voice when it seems unimportant, because you are training yourself to listen when the big issues roll in. Holy Spirit is living inside of your body. He will never remove Himself from you. As I say to my husband, *"You're stuck with me forever!"* Holy Spirit chooses to be stuck inside you—like cement!

FEBRUARY 28

Are You Paying Attention?

Read: Proverbs 4:20-27, Hebrews 4:12

In order to give something your full attention, it requires blocking out all distractions. It requires valuing that information above all other things. The importance of putting God first in every area of our lives cannot be over emphasized. It means that, regardless of what anyone else says, what God says goes. Yes, there are many situations that come along in life that challenge our commitment to handle them biblically verses with a worldly solution. The top three are health, finances, and relationships.

What are the benefits of adhering to the Scriptures above all other methods? Hebrews 4:12 is a great example. Look at the details provided in the *Amplified Classic Bible*:

> *"For the Word that God speaks is alive and full of power [making it active, operative, energizing, and effective]; it is sharper than any two-edged sword, penetrating to the dividing line of the breath of life (soul) and [the immortal] spirit, and of joints and marrow [of the deepest parts of our nature], exposing and sifting, and analyzing and judging the very thoughts and purposes of the heart."*

Can you imagine anything that could be more effective and long-lasting than what these verses claim to provide—we're talking as deep as the mitochondria of every cell in our body! When we partner the verses in Proverbs with the above Scripture for physical healing, we experience the effects that the Word of God produces—life and health to all our flesh! Are you giving your undivided attention?

FEBRUARY 29

I Wanna Hold Your Hand

Read: Isaiah 41:10-13, Psalm 34:4-7

When you read Isaiah, did you recognize that it used the term *"right hand"* two separate times? God says He will uphold you with His righteous right hand, and further on it says He will hold *you* by your right hand. If you think about that for a minute, there is no way anyone can hold your right hand with their right hand unless you are standing face to face. In order for Jesus to hold your right hand, He has to be looking you right in the eye, standing toe to toe.

Today's verse in Psalms says that those who look to Him are radiant. All their shame was blasted away by the glory on His face! Imagine yourself standing face to face with Jesus, your right hands taking hold as your arms cross over, as you stare directly into His beautiful eyes. There is something about His eyes that makes all of your troubles dissipate. Fear is exchanged for His love and security. You can feel the strength of His countenance. Jesus is right there, holding your right hand with His right hand, your faces are beaming with light as you are lost in each other's gaze!

MARCH 1

Strong In The Word

Read: 1 John 2:12-17

Whether we are young or old in age, or in our faith in Christ, we can become indomitable. These verses show us clearly how fortifying yourself in the Word keeps you abiding in God and overcoming every enemy. Even though there are adversarial forces and temptations in the world, we can guard against being lured away. I like the way the *New Living Translation* states verse 14:

> *"I have written to you who are God's children because you know the Father. I have written to you who are mature in the faith because you know Christ, who existed from the beginning. I have written to you who are young in the faith because you are strong. God's Word lives in your hearts, and you have won your battle with the evil one."*

It reminds me of the bumper sticker with a school of fish and one fish out of the group is the oddball, swimming the opposite direction. The Word keeps us from going the same direction as the rest of the world. Notice two important points: as God's children we can *know* the Father and *know* Christ. Whether young or mature in the faith, strength and endurance are part of our inheritance. Why? Because God's Word is *living* inside you!

MARCH 2

Flip Flop

Read: 2 Corinthians 1:17-22, 1 John 2:26-27

*O*ur mind can say *"Yes"* and *"No"* at the same time. When that happens, it's very difficult to decide what is right. This duality keeps us unsure, wavering back and forth and double-minded, flip-flopping around. The good news is that God never says *"Yes"* and *"No."* He only ever says *"Yes!"* He even adds *"Amen! So be it!"* We have been anointed with Holy Spirit as a guarantee of His promises.

Our mind tries to make sense of what we see. Yet, there is nothing sensible about this world and its ways. They may seem logical at first, but in time we may find ourselves further down the road of confusion. One day the Lord told me that if I kept looking at myself, I would only see impossibility. He told me to not look at what seemed right in the natural and to look completely into His face.

One example how I put that into practice was at my natural health practitioner's office. There were videos playing in the waiting room over and over on a cycle ad nauseam, of the different treatments available. At the same time, the nurses were talking loudly in the hallway about the same disease I was experiencing and how horrible it was for several of their patients. This was too much negativity for me! I got out my pocket Bible and started to read the verses out loud. I literally stuck my fingers in my ears so that I could drown out their voices. I didn't care that other patients in the waiting room were looking at me weird. The Word brought comfort to me and chased all the fear away. You know, it doesn't take much for your mind to start running in a million different directions with *"What if's."*

The Lord had told me to be careful what I listened to and to be careful what I spoke. I know that was a rather extreme way to do it, but, hey, ya gotta do what you gotta do!

MARCH 2

I believe that keeping His Word in my face, literally, and stopping up my ears was making His Word become new flesh in my body and restoring my immune system. No one knew what I was going through. They weren't living my life, so "phooey" on what others may have thought! God gave me His *"Yes and so be it!"* and that is good enough for me!

MARCH 3

Shine On!

Read: 2 Corinthians 3:17-18, 4:6-11

*W*here the Spirit of the Lord is, there is liberty! Where is the Spirit of the Lord? He is inside of you! *"Well, I don't feel free!"* you might be thinking, *"I've got this, this, and this, going on right now."* When do problems ever go away? This life is full of distractions that are designed to pull you into them. These issues may cover your countenance with a dark veil. Focusing on circumstances makes them look huge and makes God look small. Why? We toss them around again and again; entertaining thoughts with every possible outcome we can imagine. Did you ever have a silent conversation in your mind about a particular situation? Then you may realize you have wasted the whole day consumed with various scenarios that will probably never happen.

The above Scriptures talk about being transformed into the same image of Christ by the Spirit of the Lord, from glory to glory. The treasure is inside of us—it's the Holy Spirit transforming these earthly bodies into fully cocked and loaded vessels of miraculous power! How do we go from a common, earthly vessel to a radiant, powerful vessel? It all depends on what you look at and how you perceive yourself and your circumstances.

Did you ever hear the term, *"Perception is reality?"* Do you want the life of Jesus manifested in your mortal flesh? Your perception is the key to experiencing it. In 2 Corinthians 4:10, the last part of this verse says, *"that the life of Jesus also may be manifested in our body."* How is that possible? Refer back to 2 Corinthians 3:18 which describe how: *"beholding His face as in a mirror."* Now, I don't know about you, but in the morning when I'm getting ready for the day, I spend quite a bit of time in front of the mirror, especially if I'm putting on makeup and doing my hair to go somewhere. I make sure I plaster all the primer, makeup, and hair spray necessary to

MARCH 3

keep everything looking as good as it does from the moment I put it on!

What if we looked into the Word of God that way—in a way that transforms us from a tired, baggy-eyed person with sleepy dirt in her eyes, to a face that is radiant with the life of Christ shining through? In a way that brings life to our flesh and manifests Christ to all who look at our face? Take the necessary time and purpose yourself to behold His face as in a mirror and shine on!

MARCH 4

Not One Iota!

Galatians 2:1-10

I love Paul's boldness and his attitude. He says in verses 4 and 5 that these pseudo-Christians were trying to infiltrate the church of Galatia secretly and make them conform to the Law. He says that these "false brethren" were secretly brought in to spy on them! They were so religious that they hated the freedom Paul taught through the Gospel of Jesus Christ. But Paul wasn't about to fall for it. He probably remembered the bondage of living the life of a Pharisee and how it had oppressed him. It wasn't a temptation for him to add a little bit of the law back into what he lived and preached.

Paul says that he didn't give into those religious gurus even for one hour! He wanted to keep the Gospel pure as he had taught them from the beginning. I ask Holy Spirit often to let me know if I'm wasting time thinking about things that don't matter. I want to keep my mind on Him and I want to be listening for the Holy Spirit to talk to me, even if it isn't something that is really important. That's what relationship is all about. I want my life with the Lord to be fun and enjoyable, not always talking about problems and needs—that's a real drag!

I have found, more than anything, that striving in my relationship with the Lord is exhausting and boring. And let me tell you, if anyone can strive—it's me! I wear myself out sometimes! Striving is like a dripping wet blanket put on a hot fire. Don't let it destroy the freedom you have in Christ.

I remember John G. Lake once said that having a relationship with God is not something we have to work up, but it is a "settling down." I have found that to be very true. So, relax, and don't give one iota to anything that tries to steal the joy you have in Jesus!

MARCH 5

The ABC's Of Faith

Read: Ephesians 3:12

*O*nce a child learns his ABC's, it is the foundation for learning how to read. His world opens up to a whole new experience. He can learn how to do just about anything! It is the same with our relationship with Jesus. Once we learn the ABC's of faith, we can experience anything!

The above Scripture is preceded by some valuable and powerful truths for us as Believers. Paul talks about how the mystery of Christ was hidden in ages past, but has now been revealed to the whole world. God intentionally and purposefully chose to manifest Christ to everyone, even the evil cohorts of darkness. Why? So everyone would know their place, and so that everyone would know what they have been given in Christ.

Verse 12 says *"...in whom we have boldness and access with confidence through faith in Him."* Right there are the ABC's of faith! We have **A**ccess, **B**oldness, and **C**onfidence for whatever we need because of our relationship with Christ.

What is God saying?

> *"Come get it. It's already yours. You don't have to beg or cry. You don't have to perform or pay tithes. Just come with boldness because I've already given you access thorough Christ. It's no longer a mystery. I'm not hiding anything. It's yours for the taking!"*

MARCH 6

One Single Stroke!

Read: Hebrew 4:12 (Amplified Bible)

*T*he word *penetrate* in the dictionary means *"to pass into or through something."* This Scripture is so powerful because when there is sickness in the body, we can imagine God's Word penetrating and seeping into the bones, all the way into the marrow—every cell right down to the nucleus! I love that!

I imagine God's Word being sharper and more precise than a doctor's scalpel or laser beam that separates all disease from every part of our flesh! The Word of God is alive! It's actively seeking the wrong and making it right.

I did a word study on Hebrews 4 and then I took the words I had looked up in the *Strong's Concordance* and I substituted the definitions for the words in this Scripture. Here is my version of Hebrews 4:12:

> *"The Word of God is alive and moving. It has such great power and strength that is cuts with one single stroke and penetrates to separate even the deepest hidden places. The Word operates so effectively because it has legal power wielded to succeed and accomplish transformation. The Word of God is constantly in motion and diligent to accomplish everything it is sent to do."*

I love the part where it says it cuts with one single stroke, like it opens up the way for it to sink in and go to work. You don't have to walk around shouting, hacking at it over and over again with decrees. I also love where it says the Word has *legal power* to succeed! That's Covenant talk! There isn't anything that can stop God's Word once it is spoken by a Believer! One single stroke baby, and....**boom!**

MARCH 7

A Perfect Man

Read: Ephesians 4:11-16, 1 Thessalonians 5:23-24

*B*elievers becoming equipped and mature are two important components for the body of Christ coming into unity. Unity of the faith may not merely require people getting along in relationships, but individually within their own spirit, soul, and body. It is the knowledge of the Son and His Word that teaches us who we are—a perfect, complete man in every part. This is the fullness Christ manifested and demonstrated.

A man that is renewed in his spirit, soul, and body is one that is living in the full stature of Christ. It's an individual responsibility and a corporate responsibility. Imagine a church where no one is sick or lacking and everyone is out there daily ministering to the lost! That's what Jesus demonstrated. That's what Jesus wants. Many Believers sitting in the church are just as sick and needy as the world around them. God doesn't want His sons and daughters sick and oppressed. They cannot be as effective as they should be in the Kingdom.

So what do we do? What is your part? Start taking personal responsibility for your own situation. Don't let it roll all over you. Decide to believe the Word and not back off. Then, get up and go! Start praying for others and begin to bear fruit for the Kingdom. Use the gifts, talents, and desires that are already in your heart to do for the Lord. Most people are sitting around waiting for God to set everything in order before they will step out, but I have seldom seen things work that way. Once you get going, Holy Spirit will be right there to assist you.

For me, writing this book was a huge step. I also started a YouTube channel called *Kingdom Dominion* (now **East Coast Healing Center**) to record and share my teachings. All the other opportunities I had dried up. I didn't want to become stagnant, so I stepped

MARCH 7

out to bless the world with the little I have. It doesn't have to be anything monumental. Just taking the risk to talk to a stranger at Wal-Mart and tell them that God loves them is a good place to start. You will find the courage to do the things you have always had in your heart to do. And that, my friend, will bring you into maturity along the way.

MARCH 8

His Good Pleasure

Read: Luke 12:22-34

What describes God's good pleasure? Jesus said that living in the provision of the Father is receiving His good pleasure. What does that mean? Kingdom living! For one thing, He doesn't want us to worry or fear about our daily needs. This is the main problem that interferes with living freely and powerfully in the Kingdom. Demonstrating the works of God is the last thing on our mind if we are loaded down with daily nuisances.

The world is so encumbered with daily provisions that do nothing but create anxiety. When Jesus said that we should "seek" the Kingdom, He meant that we are to do things God's way. His way is to *"GO!"* and as we go, we meet the needs of others. He supplies what we need along the way so that we can keep going, advancing the Kingdom.

There are heavenly treasures waiting for us that I don't believe we have to wait until we die and go to heaven to experience. For example, divine health is something we do not have to wait to experience. Provision is another. Even more than all of this, the Kingdom of God is His realm. It's His way of doing things, like setting the oppressed free, healing the sick, and raising the dead! I don't think there is any greater experience than when God steps through us and uses us to heal someone! That never gets old for me!

Jesus was the perfect demonstration of living in the Kingdom. Everything He needed was there when He needed it. Sometimes it came through other people, such as eating a meal at someone's house. Other times the need was met supernaturally, like when He told Peter to go fishing and use the coin in the fish's mouth to pay His and Peter's taxes; or when He walked on the sea to catch up to the disciples because He didn't have a boat. He's the Creator! It was nothing for Him to create what was needed; even for someone else, such as the man who was born blind. Jesus used dirt and spit to create some eyes. That's the Kingdom—whatever you need is there when you need it; and it's His good pleasure to give it to you!

MARCH 9

Cherish Liberty

Read Galatians 5:1

I love the *Passion Translation* of Galatians 5:1,

> "Let me be clear, the Anointed One has set us free—not partially, but completely and wonderfully free! We must always cherish this truth and stubbornly refuse to go back into the bondage of our past."

When I was sick and suffering and I read the *Passion Translation* of this verse, it gave me the gumption to refuse to settle for pain and disease or go backward. I set myself to moving forward in my healing and I wasn't about to let anything or anyone push me back into bondage. Sometimes, it didn't seem like I was making much progress. But when a friend told me to make a list of all of the improvements I had received in my body up to that point, it gave me the confidence I needed that proved God was still actively working. I had a list of at least two pages of things the Lord had already healed! Then, I became more stubborn and refused to back off. I knew that if I got lazy, my mind would wander about all the wrong things. It's not easy to stay focused on things you cannot see when pain is constantly slapping you in the face and demanding your attention.

I did use a few natural remedies to help manage the pain so that I could stay focused on the Lord and keep my mind in the Word. And sometimes I'd reach a point and say, "OK, Lord, enough of this. It's time to eliminate dependence on this."

You probably have experienced the financial strain sickness brings. It's a royal pain in the keister to not only deal with the physical problems, but the financial is an additional strain that robs us as well. So, little by little, I began to eliminate the supplements I was taking with the Lord's help. That was just my approach to things,

MARCH 9

but I am not suggesting you do this. Sometimes, it was a physical action, like forcing myself to walk instead of riding the scooter at the store. I refused to go backward. I chose to move forward into freedom, physically, mentally and financially. The Anointed One had set me free, not partially, but completely and wonderfully free! So, don't quit! Don't give up! Keep moving forward!

MARCH 10

Have Confidence

Read: Philippians 3:1-9

*P*aul interestingly calls circumcision under the law "the mutilation." He was so tired of hearing about the argument from the Pharisees that taught men needed to be circumcised in the flesh to follow Christ. He knew better than all of them that they couldn't have it both ways, being a former Pharisee himself. It was Christ and Christ alone. So he had to leave it up to them: *"Are you going to follow Christ or the law?"*

In relating to this situation in our day, we are far removed from that argument, so it is kind of hard for us to understand the gravity it held back then. For us, we don't have specific "laws" that were written down that we were forced to follow like they did. Yet, there is a very similar issue we face. Do we trust in an outward sign in our flesh or the inward testimony of the Holy Spirit when we face disease? In other words, where do we put our confidence? Do we put our confidence in what we see and feel or in Christ's finished work by His stripes? We, like the Pharisees of old, have to make the same choice: trust the flesh or Christ.

The above Scripture tells that those who worship Jesus don't have any confidence in the flesh. One day the body acts one way and the next day something totally different, and sometimes there is no reason for it. It can act like this rogue entity with a mind of its own! One helpful thing we can do is to minimize the situation. Jesus didn't look at healing Peter's mother-in-law suffering from a fever any different than raising the widow's son from the dead. In this way we are taking the focus off the pain or sickness and putting it in its proper place—defeated.

We can then shift our focus to Christ where He suffered in His body to deliver our bodies, whatever is going on. Magnify Christ.

MARCH 10

Minimize the symptoms by reminding yourself that whatever you are facing is small compared to Jesus' sacrifice. Thank Him for what He has already provided. This will build up your confidence and grow your expectation to see that disease or pain disappear!

MARCH 11

What Are You Fighting For?

Read: Isaiah 30:15, 1 Corinthians 4:7-8

"Are you seated in heavenly places or are you warring in heavenly places?" Holy Spirit asked me in response on one of my questions. *"I'm seated. That is what Your Word says."* I responded. *"Then what are you fighting for?"* He replied.

Religion has taught us that we are in a war and that we must fight, fight, and fight. So we spend much time and energy fighting and warring against our enemies. After a while, we are drained physically, emotionally, and mentally. We've bound and loosed everything we can think of. We've spoken to the mountain. We've forgiven everybody and their brother who offended us in our entire lifetime. Still, the results we desire seem to evade us. Frustration sets in, then anger at the circumstances and maybe even anger toward God. *"Why isn't He doing anything? Why isn't He keeping His Word?"* we may question.

If I haven't been there myself, I wouldn't be able to write about it, so you are not alone. Trust me—been there, bought the t-shirt! But more importantly, *"What is the answer?"* The conversation above is a real conversation I had with Holy Spirit. I was frustrated. It should be cut and dry: He said this in His Word and I believe and trust Him, still nothing happened.

The work of Christ is finished, right? We know that much, right? Where is Jesus? He is seated at the right hand of the Father. Where are we? We are seated in Christ at the right hand of the Father. *Seated.* So what are we fighting for? Since we received all things, we don't have to fight for anything. We already have it.

Isaiah 30:15 says that, *"quietness and confidence is our strength;"* which may be paraphrased as *"utter trust."* In verse two, the Lord says they are trusting in the *"shadow of Egypt;"* which is contrary to

MARCH 11

trusting in the *"shadow of the Almighty"* we are familiar with from Psalm 91. The whole chapter of Isaiah 30 is about Israel making an alliance with Egypt to protect them against the Assyrians, because Egypt had horses and iron chariots. The Assyrians were fierce, war-like people. No doubt they were intimidated by them. God was not thrilled with Israel's decision to join with Egypt for their protection instead of trusting Him for help.

But don't we do the same thing? We try our own ways first, and when it doesn't go well, we turn to God as our last resort. And we even think we are doing things God's way when we do certain things Scripture says we should do. We can get in our own way. Striving and fighting always does the opposite of getting us what we need. Somehow, it's like Holy Spirit is pushed away when we handle things this way.

Confidence in all of God's ability, in which He is for us and not against us—this is entering into Christ's finished work. Settle down. No really, settle down and sit down, mentally, emotionally, spiritually. Enter His rest. Take a deep breath. See yourself sitting inside of Jesus. He knows. He's got this. He's got you! Just thank Him!

MARCH 12

Diplomatic Immunity

2 Corinthians 5:12-20

When my family and I lived in Kenya, we went to visit the U.S. embassy. We even got to meet the ambassador to the U.S. Even though we were in Kenya, it was like stepping on our homeland's soil because all the laws and blessings we have in the U.S. were right there in city of Nairobi! Drive down the road a little further, and we realized we were still in Kenya. Though the country is very beautiful, their government had not advanced their country as much as ours in the U.S.

A child of God living on the earth is much the same as an ambassador sent to live and govern in a foreign country. We are ambassadors sent by Christ from heaven to bring heaven's realm, rule and authority here on earth. The benefits of heaven far outweigh any benefits we have on earth, no matter what country you live in. Jesus was given all authority in heaven, on earth, and under the earth. He, in turn, told us to go do the same works He did. I'm sure you remember the Lord's Prayer:

> *"Thy kingdom come. Thy will be done in earth, as it is in heaven."* (Matthew 6:10)

There is no sickness, disease, pain or death in heaven. There is no poverty or sorrow. There is no depression or lack. Wherever there was a need, Jesus supplied that need. He never qualified anyone who received from Him, He just freely provided because He was demonstrating the ways of His Father and His Father's Kingdom.

We are Christ's ambassadors, sent by Him to demonstrate the works of the Kingdom. Jesus said that the Kingdom of God is inside of us (Luke 17:21). That also means that everything Jesus has, we have. Did Jesus ever get sick, even after He laid hands on the leper? No! Was Jesus limited by the laws of nature, like gravity? No! He

MARCH 12

walked on water without sinking. He also changed the molecular structure of water into wine! Jesus had diplomatic immunity to the laws of nature and the law of sin and death. So do we! We represent the Kingdom of our Father in the same way Jesus did with the same authority Jesus has!

MARCH 13

From The Inside Out

Read: Romans 8:11

Physical healing occurs from the inside out. The Kingdom of God is inside of us because we have the power of the Holy Spirit giving His life to all of our flesh. We can also receive healing when another Believer in Christ lays hands on us. In this instance, the power of the Holy Spirit in the other person is affecting our flesh from the outside in.

How did Jesus stay healthy? He never contracted any disease, no matter how contagious the disease was. The life of the Holy Spirit in Him destroyed sicknesses in other people as well as kept Him immune from the effects of disease. It was never even a temptation for Him to feel sick! He lived in divine health. Not because He was the Son of God, but because He was a man full of the power and presence of the Holy Spirit.

Did you know that you can resist the temptation to feel sick the same way that you can resist sin? Sin and sickness originate from the same place, don't they? So, we can resist sickness and symptoms the same way we choose not to steal or talk trash about someone. We can also live free from all symptoms and live in divine health exactly the same way Jesus did. Jesus declared, *"Believe Me that I am in the Father and the Father in Me..."* (John 14:11) Jesus kept an awareness and connection open to the Holy Spirit, speaking and listening to Him constantly. He was continuously aware of the life, energy, and power of the Holy Spirit working inside of Him, through Him, and all around Him. If we keep a sharp awareness of Holy Spirit's miraculous power flowing inside our body, we can stay free of symptoms and disease the same way Jesus did!

MARCH 14

Bread Of Life

Read: John 6

This chapter begins with Jesus feeding the 5,000. The people followed Jesus because they wanted to get a free meal ticket for life. What is interesting to me is that they had originally come to Jesus because they saw the signs He performed on those who were diseased. A tradition that the people believed back then was that the Messiah would rain down bread from heaven, the same way Moses did. If you're like me, being healed is way more important to you than food.

When the multitude of people searched to find Jesus for their lifetime of free meals, Jesus began to try to shift their understanding to eternal life. He explained to them that when they put their belief in Him as their true source for life, He would give them the same life (Holy Spirit) He had inside of Him—eternal life. They could have it all: health, food, and eternal life!

What was Jesus trying to tell them? *"Stop looking for physical bread. I am the Bread of Life which came down from heaven."* Bread was a necessary part their everyday meals back then. For us today, we try to avoid it because we believe that carbs make us fat! Shows you how far we have come as a society! Bread is no longer the staple of our diets, so Jesus' concept is difficult for us to understand.

Jesus even takes things a bit farther and tells them that they must eat His flesh and drink His blood to have His life in them. Once again, the people were thinking in the natural and they were like, *"Ew, gross, we're not cannibals! If that's what it means to be Your disciple, then I'm outta here!"* Jesus was trying to show them the New Covenant. Whenever a covenant was cut in their culture, a meal was eaten together.

MARCH 14

In verse four it says, *"Now the Passover Feast of the Jews was near."* What did Jesus do at the Passover meal before He went to the cross? He ate His last meal with His disciples. He showed them that His body was their bread which would be broken for their healing. He showed them that His blood was life and cleansing from sin once for all. It was a spiritual, prophetic act that brought literal physical and spiritual benefits. He is the living Bread that came down from heaven! Taste and see that the Lord is good!

MARCH 15

Incorruptibles

Read: Matthew 23:1-22, 1 Peter 1:13-23

The Holy Spirit is HOLY. Well, of course He is, or He wouldn't be called the *Holy* Spirit! When Holy Spirit takes up residence inside of us, He doesn't become the *dirty* Spirit. He removes our iniquitous bloodline and sins. He makes us just as pure and holy as He is!

Jesus attempted to wake up the Pharisees, who were blinded by their traditions. He tried to show them that the temple was holy because God was there, not because of its beauty or the sacrifices.

In the same way that God resided in the temple building and made it holy, Holy Spirit now lives inside us and makes us holy. We have become born again. The physical birth we experienced as babies made us slaves of a corrupted world. When we became born again, or born from above by believing in Jesus, He literally came to live inside our body, making us incorruptible!

Now, think for a minute. He would have had to prepare our body to be a suitable place for a holy God to live in, right? When you gave your life to Jesus, in an instant you were cleansed and born from God's incorruptible seed. We know that any seed reproduces after its own kind, right? God is incorruptible, so that means you no can longer be corrupted with sin or sickness! You are as holy as He is holy!

MARCH 16

A Covenant For All Generations

Read: Isaiah 59:21

I want to see the covenant blessings that the Lord has given to me upon my children, grandchildren, great grandchildren, and all the generations that are born after me. The Lord has been so faithful to my family. Many times I have prayed the above Scripture for my children over the years. Even though I did the best I knew in raising them, I couldn't choose Jesus for them. I realized it was my responsibility to teach them the best I could and then I had to leave the results up to God. Sometimes that wasn't easy when I saw them making the wrong decisions.

Today, on the other side of parenting and now being a grandparent, I'm so thankful that God's grace was there even when I fell short. I always desired that everything the Lord has taught me, my children would begin to walk in it for themselves and even go farther than I have. I can say that God has been faithful to do just that.

The truth the Lord has taught us, the covenant that we have with Him extends to all of our children—forever. The inheritance we have in Jesus is freely theirs as well. I know that the difficult things we have gone through in life, our children can be spared from those hardships because of God's help and grace.

His promise is that the same Spirit in us is in our children. The same gifts of the Holy Spirit in us, is for our children. And the same blessings upon our lives are being passed down to our grandchildren. Forever. Amen!

MARCH 17

The Recompense Of Reward

Read: Hebrews 10:35-36, 2 Corinthians 4:13

*C*onfidence = boldness. The Greek definition of confidence means *all out spokenness that is frankness, bluntness, and assurance.* When I have confidence in something, I want to share it with all of my friends and family, like shouting it from the rooftops! I can have a "matter-of-fact" attitude about it. If someone tries to get snarky with me, I've got the proof to back up what I'm saying.

The Lord is saying, *"Don't throw away your confidence in Me! It contains a great reward!"* What is the reward of not giving up? Receiving the answer you've been trusting in Him for!

When I was sick with Lyme disease, this was one of the first Scriptures the Holy Spirit brought to my mind. It encouraged me that the promises Jesus gave to me for healing were mine. I learned that confidence = faith. Faith is fearless. Faith brings the reward, the recompense.

I also learned that I did not have to try to find faith and confidence; I already had it. I believe in Jesus. I didn't have to try to get faith, I already had it. 2 Corinthians 4:13 says that I have the same Spirit of faith as Jesus. I can speak what I believe and have it, just like Jesus. That was a relief for me. If I had to spend hours and hours reading the Word and hope I got a hold of some faith and then try to apply it for healing, I don't think that would have had the results I was looking for. That sure is a roundabout way to walk in what is already mine. Believing I have the same Spirit of faith and using it with confidence in Jesus took a lot of the guesswork out of healing!

MARCH 18

Stout

Read: 1 Corinthians 16:13, 2 Timothy 1:6-7

*S*tout has a better meaning than a cute way of saying something is fat, like the childhood song about the teapot. *Stout* means *to be determined, steadfast, unyielding, brave, bold, courageous, valiant, and fearless.*

Faith is fearless. It has absolutely no fear—not even of death! Holy Spirit makes us stout in the spirit. The confidence we have in Jesus that He loves us, fortifies us in the spirit.

When we turn inward, where Holy Spirit is dwelling inside of us, we are more in tune with what He wants to do, the way He wants to do things. We can hear His voice easier when we always keep an ear out to listen for Him. Holy Spirit speaks to us Spirit to spirit; yet the purpose of this relationship is to bring spiritual things into the physical realm.

Paul told Timothy, his son in the faith, to stir up the gift of the Holy Spirit inside of himself. The most effective way to do that is to pray in the spirit. Paul taught Timothy that stirring up the Holy Spirit in himself would stir up miracle-working power, release the unconditional love of God, and give him a sound and self-disciplined mind.

Timothy was up against some persecution in the church. The elders didn't want to listen to his instruction because he was a young man. Paul encouraged Timothy to not back down and to remember his roots of faith not only from his grandmother and mother, but as his son in the faith.

History tells us that Timothy was fearless and bold; not only against the other leaders in the church, but against persecution from the people he tried to lead to Christ. In the year 97 AD Timothy was eighty years old. He attempted to stop a procession in honor of

MARCH 18

the goddess Diana by preaching the Gospel. The angry pagans beat him, dragged him through the streets, and then stoned him to death.

Apparently, Paul's letter of encouragement worked! Timothy must have followed Paul's advice. The stirring of his faith was able to make him stout in the spirit to the end!

MARCH 19

Christ Crucified

Read: 1 Corinthians 1:20-2:8

*P*aul's rock-solid conviction of Christ was centered in Christ alone and Him crucified. He didn't compromise this message for any reason. It is proof that his message of Christ was the truth because the Holy Spirit was right there confirming the word that was preached with *"a demonstration of the Spirit's power."*

Paul was reasoning with men of worldly wisdom. What they heard was foreign to them at first. He didn't try to persuade them with fancy words; he preached Christ, a stumbling block and foolishness to those who heard. He preached the wisdom of God: Christ, our righteousness, sanctification, and redemption (verse 1:30).

Maybe he sounded like a bumbling idiot. But when he was able to show the works of God by doing miracles, well, as they say, the proof is in the pudding. There was no denying that what Paul was saying was the truth.

Paul said the mystery of God was hidden for the day when Christ was revealed, and His Spirit was sent to live inside of those He redeemed. Such a profound mystery kept secret from the beginning of time until the crucifixion, and shortly after completed, by pouring out His Spirit upon all flesh.

Do we have the same Holy Spirit Paul had? Should we expect lesser results when we share Christ with others? Shouldn't a demonstration of the Spirit's power accompany us the same way the Holy Spirit confirmed Paul's preaching? Christ crucified. Man redeemed and full of the Spirit of God! Many call it foolish, but God calls it wisdom!

MARCH 20

Faith—I Have It!

Read: 2 Corinthians 4:13-14

I've heard a variety of teachings on faith in the past that I got so frustrated I didn't want to hear that subject preached anymore. Teaching about faith has been so hyped, most Christians don't even know whether they have faith or not. We've also had the Scripture, *"Without faith it is impossible to please God."* (Hebrews 11:6) shoved down our throats.

We've been taught that Jesus commended "great faith" like the Centurion who asked Jesus to heal his paralyzed soldier. We've been taught that Jesus scorned the disciples for having "little faith" in the midst of a storm. The woman with the issue of blood just decided she would be healed if she touched His robe, and she created the circumstances for her own healing. Jesus told her that "her faith" made her well. And we can also quote Jesus saying that we only need "faith the size of a mustard seed" to move a mountain. So which is it? What type of faith works?

It is vital to recognize that all of these events happened before Jesus went to the cross, so none of these people were born again. They didn't have the Holy Spirit, which is the Spirit of faith, living inside of them. They could only go by what they heard about Jesus or what they saw. Did Jesus ever walk up to anyone and say, *"Well, I can see you don't have any faith that I can heal you, so tough noogies."* No! Of course not! Why? He had the faith for them to be healed.

Now, think about our relationship with Jesus on this side of the cross. You believe in Jesus, right? If you didn't believe in Jesus, you couldn't have gotten saved in the first place. You have the Holy Spirit living inside of you! Our Scripture reading for today affirms that we have the *same spirit of faith* that raised Jesus from the dead!

MARCH 20

That's resurrection power! So here's the clincher: YOU ALREADY HAVE FAITH!!

You already have the faith to be healed because you have the Spirit of faith inside of you! He's not the spirit of doubt and unbelief! He is the Spirit of faith! We don't have to try to find faith or even a greater level of faith to be healed. You have already been using your faith by believing in Jesus. You know He is your Healer just as much as He is your Savior. The faith you need is the faith you already have! Whew! That saves us a lot of frustration!

MARCH 21

Faith Sees

Read: 2 Corinthians 5:7

*F*aith sees the end result. What that means is that we see certain circumstances in our face every day, yet we are able to look past them and declare, *"You will become what I say."*

One day when I was talking to the Lord about something He said, *"Michele, I don't do anything without expectation."* I thought about Creation. God had in mind exactly what He wanted to create. He had the image of the end result first before He spoke it. Then He inspected everything piece by piece to make sure it was exactly like what He had in mind. He nodded his head and announced, *"It is good!"*

It is important for us to look at the end result when we are standing for our healing or praying for someone else to be healed. What we think about a situation is just as important as what we say about it. The thoughts we think are a true reflection of what is in our heart. Sometimes it's easier to control what we allow to come out of our mouths than it is to guard our mind from running wild.

I remember when my leg was so swollen that wearing a shoe was impossible. My daughter bought me a new blouse, skirt, and high-heeled shoes to match. At that time there was no way I could wear those shoes, but I kept them near my bed where I could see them every day. Each time I looked at them I said, *"I'm going to wear you soon with no problems."* I thought about wearing them too; what it would feel like to walk normal like I used to? And you know what? While I was recovering I decided to work on a book I had written years ago and publish it. After the book was published, my pastor was going away on a trip and asked if I would like to preach in his place. He said I could share from my book. And I did! I guess you can figure out what I wore that day! Yep! I wore that

MARCH 21 ———

outfit and those high-heeled shoes—with no problem! That was the first time I had preached in a few years, and it was great to be back at it! I haven't stopped since! Faith sees and then faith experiences the end result!

MARCH 22

Two Heads

Read: Romans 8:5-8, Ephesians 1:22-23

*M*ost of us have heard the saying: *"Two heads are better than one."* In the case of healing, there is not much that can be farther from the truth. When we live by what we see, hear, and feel, it is not living by the Spirit—it is living by our old nature. Yes, renewing our mind to the Word of God is very essential, but it should not take us years and years to live in our bodies what God had promised and made available through Jesus now. At what point is your mind renewed? When you are experiencing every day what the Word says you have been given.

What does this require? Recognize that Jesus is the head or supreme authority over your body through the life of the Holy Spirit living in you and giving life to your flesh. Did you ever notice that when you start feeling a pain somewhere in your body, your mind simultaneously tells you about that pain? For example: A person starts to feel pain in their head and immediately the mind thinks, *"I have a headache!"* Has that ever happened to you? At that moment we have the choice: Do I listen to the thought and the pain, or do I agree with the Word that says I was healed by Jesus' stripes? If we catch it right away and resist the thoughts and say, *"No, head, you cannot have pain because you are healed!"* More often than not, the pain will leave immediately.

At times, when I feel a new symptom I think, *"Oh, what are you doing there?"* and I just keep going on with life. When the symptoms start to nag me after a few days it's like an epiphany, *"Why am I putting up with this?"* Then I go after it by telling that part of my body it is healed. Immediately I begin declaring, *"Thank You, Jesus!"* for the price He paid for me to be whole. Sometimes things don't leave right away like they should, but they always do leave. They have to because I'm already healed!

MARCH 23

Effective

Read: Galatians 2:6-8, 1 Thessalonians 2:10-13

*W*e all want to be effective in everything we do, especially in the Kingdom and our position of sonship. To be *effective* means *to be active, operative, effectual, and powerful.* It is derived from another word that means *"to be mighty in and show forth self-work."*

In the book of Galatians, Paul described the Holy Spirit as working *effectively* in his ministry to the Gentiles. In Thessalonians, Paul referred to the Word of God being *effective* as he preached the Gospel to bring people to Christ. Notice that Paul gave credit to both the Spirit and the Word together as being effective in his life to produce the results he had demonstrated. We know that Paul was effortlessly always doing the miraculous by the power of the Holy Spirit.

It is interesting that the word *effective* is also used in Hebrews 4:12 describing the Word of God as being *powerful* (they are the same two Greek words). Our experience with what has been effective, especially when we are referring to physical healing, may be subjective. We can hop from one thing to another trying to get our healing till we find ourselves years down the road dealing with the same limitations. I know I'm talking to someone out there right now.

What do we do? We know the healing Scriptures inside and out, backward and forward. We may even pray for other people and they get healed, but we still experience the same symptoms. For one thing...there...*one thing*. Keep it right there, with this *one thing*. That's what the Lord is saying to you right now. Then take a deep breath and relax. Stay there, with this *one thing*: He is Healer. His Word is true because He is that Word. That is who He is, not just something He does. Don't move on to one more thing, not one more prayer from yet another person. Decide it has to be done

MARCH 23

and don't move on to another possible thing to try. Settle it. All those prayers, the verses you've quoted over and over...all of it, it is enough. Now, rest. No more fighting, no more praying in tongues or whatever. Don't keep checking and looking for any symptoms. It is done. His Spirit has been working in you *effectively*. His Word has been working in you *effectively* all of this time. Now just expect the results and thank Him for your healing.

MARCH 24

Supplied

Read: Galatians 3:1-9, Philippians 1:12-26

The NKJV uses the word *supplies* and *supply* in each of the verses in Galatians 3:5 and Philippians 1:19. The definition of these words means: *to furnish, supply, aid or contribute, add, minister, or nourishment.* The word *minister* is used in the KJV for Galatians 3:5. *Supply* is derived from the word *minister*. It is interesting that in these two separate occasions; Paul is referring to the Spirit producing miraculous works by ministering life and righteousness to those in Galatia, and the other end of the spectrum, where he refers to the Spirit supplying the strength to live in the midst of persecution to those in Philippi.

Sometimes we may think of Paul as some super-saint that had been given special inside knowledge the rest of us aren't privy to; that God gave him an extraordinary anointing just to "jump start" the church to keep it growing in those early days. Then my question is: What would be the purpose for God preserving the Bible for us to read today? So it could make us passive admirers? Or could it be so that we were able to see ourselves supplied with the same Spirit Paul possessed; to preach the Gospel with the same effectiveness, and live the same type of miraculous life? I believe the latter is true. God doesn't do something for nothing. We are all equal at the foot of the cross. There are no favorites. We know He is no respecter of persons.

What if we began to see ourselves as supplied with every need? Practice seeing yourself as whole, full and not lacking any good thing; even though that may not be what you are experiencing right now. Expect it to change. The truth will begin to transform what you see and how you see it. You will begin to have fresh eyes and a different view. You will begin to see things the way God sees them: both the Spirit and the Word *effectively* working, empowering you to minister the miraculous with unending supply!

MARCH 25

When Is Impossible Possible?

Read: Jeremiah 32:17, 27, John 9:1-11

God is the God of all flesh because He created it. Some people claim to be atheists, but if anyone would take the time to even study the human eye and how it works, he would be so astonished he would have to claim there has to be a God!

Jesus did a creative miracle for the man that was born blind. Although it doesn't specifically say this in the Scripture, I believe the man was born without eyes. Either way, it was a notable miracle that proved He was the Messiah. When Jesus made the clay from His spit and dirt, I like to think of it like the day he molded Adam from dirt at Creation. He knows how every part works because He created them.

Jesus proclaimed that He was sent to open the eyes of the blind (Luke 4:18), and he told those who believed in Him to do the same works that He did (Mark 16:17-18).

So, is impossible *really* impossible? God is on the scene because He is present inside every Believer. Is it too difficult for Him to heal your hurting back? No, He created it. Is it too difficult for Him to heal your broken leg? No, He created it. What about your liver? Nope, not that either. Why? He is God Almighty, The Lord and The Master Creator of all of your flesh!

MARCH 26

Sealed

Read: Song of Solomon 8:6

Many of us have been taught that God's name is never mentioned in the *Song of Solomon*. In further study of the original words here in our reading for today, we are going to take a deeper look.

The word *seal* means, in the Hebrew, *signet ring*. We know how important signet rings were to the ancient world. Only kings and those in a position of authority could use them to seal important documents. It was equivalent to signing their name to enforce a law; carrying with it legal authority.

This Scripture infers that we are sealed with God's signet ring as a symbol of His love. While *Song of Solomon* may be a bit too mushy for some to refer to our relationship with the Lord with this type of symbolism, we can still gain some spiritual truths that apply to our lives. Personally, I love the passionate language used here. The woman is being marked in her spirit and flesh with the symbol of her beloved. Two examples in the New Testament also reveal the Holy Spirit sealing us for the day of salvation: Ephesians 1:13-14 as well as Revelation 22:4 describing the redeemed of the Lord engraving His Name upon their foreheads.

The last line in verse six is describing love as flames of fire being *"a most vehement flame."* First, let's take a look at the word *vehement*. It means *to be fervent, very ardent, or passionate, acting with great force or energy*. Another way to phrase it is *a mighty flash of fire*. There are two Hebrew words that make up this term *"vehement flame."* The two Hebrew words are "shalhebet-yah." This is the sacred name of God Himself that means *"Mighty flame of the Lord most passionate."* We can see God is mentioned here in a very specific way, unlike what we may have been previously taught.

MARCH 26

Since God has put His love as a seal upon us and His life sacrificed for us is referred to as *"His Passion,"* we can be certain that, no matter what life may throw at us, He has sealed our hearts with His signet ring of such strong love—a most vehement flame—and with the Holy Spirit for the Day of His coming.

MARCH 27

He Sent His Word

Read: Psalm 107:19-20

"A continual affirmation of God's Word in faith will build into your immune system a supernatural anointing that is capable of eliminating sickness and disease in a natural manner." – Charles Capps

God's Word carries within it the power to heal, deliver, and restore life to infirmed tissue. We have many examples in the Old Testament where God sent His Word to heal and deliver Israel when they were in trouble. When they came to the edge of the Red Sea, it was imminent destruction until the Lord delivered them with a mighty wind that divided the waters and held them back. When they came to the waters of Marah, Moses flung a piece of wood in the water and it was healed. It was there the Lord God entered into a covenant with His people. He promised to keep them from all disease if they would agree to listen to His voice and obey His commandments. Not a bad exchange! God healed the water *before* they drank it! He had promised to protect them from physical harm.

The covenant God offered to them was made with a vow and an exchange of words. How binding were those words? God expected Israel to honor their promise to obey Him and He promised to keep the safe from harm, keep their bodies free from disease, keep their food and water healthy, keep their clothes from wearing out, and to keep their enemies at peace with them. That's some promise-keeping!

What about today on this side of the cross? Anyone who believes that God is only interested in spiritual things and taking our spirit with Him to heaven when we die has really missed the big picture. Jesus offered His physical body for our physical healing. Can I prove it? He sent His Word, Jesus. Jesus is the manifestation of

MARCH 27 ———

God's Word in a man. He is the Father, the Spirit, and the Word living all in one place—inside you and me! We can have all the benefits of God's healing promises by learning what they are by reading the Bible. We can receive healing through Christ's brutal stripes. And we can apply all of the benefits by the power of the Holy Spirit giving life to our bodies through our faith in Jesus today. God has never changed His plan from the beginning. When He said He sent His Word and healed us, it was more than just "hot air." He proved it.

MARCH 28

Nope, Never!

Read: John 8:12, Hebrews 13:5-6

In both of these Scriptures a form of the word *not* is used. The word *not* in John 8:12 and *never* in Hebrews 13:5 are the same Greek word # 3364 in the *Strong's Concordance*. It is a "double negative" which emphasizes the Lord's emphatic sincerity that we will never, ever walk in darkness and that He will never, ever, leave us, under any circumstances.

Those are two very comforting promises, especially during difficult times. Isn't that when we need to be reminded the most? Sometimes it may seem like God is far way, but He isn't. Sometimes we may wonder if He knows what's going on in our lives. I can assure you that He does. When it comes to God, a promise made is a promise kept. You can bet your life on it! He will never, ever leave you!

Nope, never!

MARCH 29

Enriched

Read: 1 Corinthians 1:4-9, 2 Corinthians 9:6-11

When food companies make bread, they use *enriched* flour. This means that in the processing, most of the nutrients are removed so it has a longer shelf life. Then they add some of the vitamins and minerals back in to try to match some of the nutritional benefits of the original product.

I'm glad God isn't like that! He guards all the good things He provides for us. His blessings never need to be *enriched* because they stay fortified. The word *enriched* in 1 Corinthians 1:5 is #4148 in the *Strong's Concordance*. It is also the same word in 2 Corinthians 9:11. It means *to be made wealthy*. We were *enriched* or *made wealthy* with every benefit because of Christ. It says we come short in nothing. God held nothing back when He gave us Jesus.

Have you ever noticed when we read the New Testament it uses such adjectives as *abounding, exceeding, abundant, enriched,* etc. concerning everything we need? God doesn't need to take something and make it better. He starts from the beginning with everything good and preserves it for you until you need it. It is a never-ending supply!

MARCH 30

Stable

Read: Psalm 112

This Psalm talks about two kinds of fear: *the fear of the Lord* and *the fear of bad news*. To have a fear of the Lord means to morally revere Him. The fear of receiving bad news means to be dreadful of possible future events.

Because a person fears the Lord, he can be emotionally stable and keep his heart at rest. It's the opposite of being double-minded. I like that verse two says that a person who fears the Lord builds a generation of mighty men and women that are blessed! They have learned to give graciously to those in need and use wisdom in governing their lives. They aren't wishy-washy like the rest of the world. Their heart is steadfast and immovable. They know that God will deal with their enemies.

The generations of the upright fear the Lord more than the treasures of the earth. To me, that is a greater possession than having a lot of fancy things or spending my time here on this earth gathering up stuff I'll never be able to use. The reward of raising up a godly generation will always, by far, be our greatest contribution to society, our country, and the Kingdom. To remain in the fear of the Lord and walk in His ways is the greatest inheritance we can give to our descendants: stable, steadfast, immovable.

MARCH 31

Resurrection Life

Read: Colossians 3:1-4

"*Christ's resurrection is your resurrection too. This is why we are to yearn for all that is above, for that's where Christ sits enthroned at the place of all power, honor, and authority. Yes, feast on all the treasures of the heavenly realm and fill your thoughts with heavenly realities, and not with the distractions of the natural realm.*" (Colossians 3:1-2, *The Passion Translation*)

Don't you love *The Passion Translation* of this verse! It reminds me that when Christ died, we died with Him. When He was buried, we were buried. When He was resurrected, we were resurrected with Him into a new life. When He was raised to the right hand of the Father, we were raised to the right hand of the Father. Our life is completely hidden in His! Jesus didn't die *for* us. He died *as* us.

What does all of this mean? It means that His resurrection life is as much ours as it is His. We don't have to succumb to the kind of life this world dishes out. The evils of this generation are enough to send someone to the loony bin if they don't know Christ. But that is not our inheritance. We don't have to live without Him! He gave us His very life so we can share in all the treasures of heaven now, not just for some day when we get to heaven. We don't have to be broke or sick or lonely. Christ's resurrection is our resurrection too; far above the limitations of this world's system!

Several years ago, my family and I were living with some friends in Oklahoma. We didn't have a lot of resources at the time. One morning, a tractor trailer truck full of fresh chicken overturned at the side of the road near our house. They had to get rid of all the chicken or it would spoil. We were given over $800 of fresh meat for free that fed us for several months! It was the *best* kind—pre-sliced

MARCH 31 ─────

boneless, skinless chicken tenders! How's that for divine provision? When we didn't know how we were going to make it, we received an abundance of food at just the right time. God is always good like that!

APRIL 1

What I Believe Hinders How I Receive

Read: Colossians 2:13-15

"A Christian will never experience the victory of the Lord Jesus Christ until he first recognizes that the enemy is a completely vanquished foe." –John G. Lake

The above Scripture says that Jesus *disarmed* the principalities and powers of the evil realm. If the enemy is *disarmed* and *defeated*, why are so many Christians afraid of an enemy that has no arms and no feet? I'll give you a minute to get that...LOL!

So many Christians believe they have to stay in a place of attack mode or the devil is going to jump out any minute and steal, kill, and destroy everything they've got in an instant. All they talk about is, *"The devil this, and the devil that."* They talk about the devil more than they do Jesus. I've even met some people who would say they are a Christian when asked, but the next minute they aren't really sure if they are saved! Sadly, this is the cycle some people live in.

I've met a few people when I've been out ministering on the streets that are so confused about what they believe it is alarming. One lady I met said she was a Christian in the past, but became a Muslim. She was not born of a certain ethnicity that is normally associated with that religion. As I talked to her, she was very confused. She mixed some Scripture she knew with other religious beliefs. The only way I could relate to her was on the basis that God loves her and He knows her every thought. Otherwise, she would have stood there trying to argue with me the entire time. Thank God I was able to get through a little to remind her of truth. Unfortunately, I was unable to help her see herself as God sees her before the bus arrived. What she believed hindered what she could receive. I'm

APRIL 1

sure that the Lord will send other people to minister to her in the future. He never gives up on us!

When we know that Christ is seated next to the Father and we are hidden in Him, there is nothing that is above Him and therefore nothing that is above us. We are not under principalities and powers here on earth. We are above them seated with Christ in heaven according to the Word of God. So, to spend our time constantly warring after the devil is a complete exhausting waste of time and energy. Knowing our position of authority in Christ and the power given to us through the Holy Spirit while standing immoveable, is the way we enforce Christ's finished work.

APRIL 2

Legal Union

Read: Galatians 3:13-29

*T*o be baptized *into* Christ means that when you were baptized, you were *immersed into* Jesus, just like you were submerged under the water—no sprinkling here! The *Amplified Bible* says in Galatians 3:27,

> "For all of you who were baptized into Christ [into a spiritual union with the Christ, the Anointed] have clothed yourselves with Christ [that is, you have taken on His characteristics and values]."

In other words, you don't exist anymore. You became an entirely new person. So many people would be free of themselves if they only knew what it truly means to be born again. We can try any number of things to rid ourselves of the pain we have experienced from our past, but nothing can give us a brand new life like Jesus can.

I like how E.W. Kenyon describes our new life in Christ. Regarding the above Scripture he says, *"Baptism here is equivalent to marriage, as a wife puts on marriage and takes her husband's name and enters his possessions and has legal rights in his home, Believers so put on Christ. We take on all this union means!"*

This is a beautiful expression of our complete union with Christ. It is legal in the spirit and binds us to Him in the natural realm just as effectively. He took care of both sides. Nothing was left undone. It's a blood covenant that cannot be broken and a union legally binding, leaving a legacy of both physical and spiritual benefits!

APRIL 3

To Be Known

Read: Ezekiel 1

One night, while I was in prayer, I asked the Lord, *"What is Your greatest desire?"* His answer took me by surprise! He said simply, *"To be known."* I was reminded of the theme in the book of Ezekiel. The first chapter displays an open vision the prophet saw—a pure array of the Spirit and the spiritual beings that dwell in the heavenly realm! Awestruck, he fell on his face! God disclosed Himself to Ezekiel and commissioned him as a messenger to rebellious Israel. He involved Himself in the affairs of His people with the intent that, *"Then you will know that I am the Lord."* God repeated that phrase frequently throughout the book of Ezekiel, desiring to prevent them from self-destruction!

Have you ever heard the teaching that God hides himself and that we have to "chase" after Him to catch Him? I used to believe that. Now I know better. There are certain things that God did hide until an appointed time, like the specific time for Jesus to come as Savior. But God wasn't hiding Jesus and all of the things He wanted to give *from* us. He hid them *for* us for this present time. If He had told everyone His plans, evil would have tried to mess it up. But now, all of these things have been revealed!

People get stuck on the Scripture that says, *"No eye has seen, no ear has heard, and no mind has imagined what God has prepared for those who love Him."* (1 Corinthians 2:9, NLT) But just like Believers do many times, they stop short of the rest of the chapter and make a doctrine out of one verse that leads people astray. Continuing in verse 10, **"BUT God has revealed them to us through His Spirit..."**

Why would Jesus have suffered so incredibly and then hide it all from us, or make us play hide and seek just to prove that we want to have a relationship with Him? Sounds silly, doesn't it? Because

APRIL 3

it is! If God really wanted to hide from us, then forget it! You would never even know He existed! But He made Himself known— even in Creation, so that men are without excuse (Romans 1:20).

Ezekiel was able to peer into the spiritual realm and see the glories of heaven, and that was under the Old Covenant. Would God withhold such wonders from us now? God does not play hide and seek! He stated that when you seek Him with all of your heart, you will find Him! And obviously you did, because you are born again. So, remember that your relationship with Him is not just one-sided. His greatest desire is for you to *know* Him!

APRIL 4

Slaves Unto Righteousness

Read: Romans 6

God chose Abraham and his descendants so that Jesus could come through his lineage. He made a promise to Jesus through Abraham and then He put us into Christ as an heir or the "seed in the Seed." This way God could legally destroy all sin, sickness... well, everything that came about as a result of the Fall.

God restored mankind, making him able to walk in the Spirit with our Father, instead of living controlled like a slave driven by an evil nature. We can be a *bondservant*, which means to be a slave unto righteousness by our own choosing, or we can choose to be a slave sold as a prisoner under the sin nature. The offer is always extended for us live as a God-man like Jesus.

The Holy Spirit never drives us or forces us to do anything. He always leaves an open invitation for us to be involved in His life as much or as little as we want. When we choose to walk with Him every day, we get to experience more of who He is. It's not quite the same as knowing another human being. It goes beyond the surface, right to the heart. I believe that every human being has the longing to know God this way and to be known by Him; they just don't know it is possible.

I'd rather accept the open invitation to be a slave unto righteousness than a forced slave of evil desires I cannot control. The freedom we have in Christ because of a changed nature draws us to want more of what is good and to turn away more and more from evil.

I believe this is why sickness attacks our body. It is like an evil intention from an enemy assaulting our bodies, when they are meant to be pure and holy. Sickness goes against everything within us and we want to throw it off as quickly as possible. We can and we should throw it off A.S.A.P! The sooner we resist the

APRIL 4

symptoms and refuse them the right to hang around, the sooner we can protect our bodies from being violated by foreign invaders. Our bodies were made righteous the moment we came to Jesus. He moved in and the old nature got evicted—all of it! So don't let sickness fool you. You are the righteousness of God in Christ Jesus; spirit, soul, and body.

APRIL 5

The Last Supper

Read: Luke 22:14-20

Most of us who grew up going to church took Communion, otherwise known as *The Lord's Supper* or *The Last Supper*. In many traditional churches like mine, we had to be at least twelve years old. We had to attend Confirmation classes and then we were allowed to take Communion. We also officially became a member of the church.

Communion was usually only offered during special occasions like Easter and Christmas. Although there are two elements, the bread and the juice, the emphasis was more about the juice representing the blood of Jesus for the forgiveness of our sins. They entirely missed the part about His body being broken so that we could be healed.

From this monumental moment in Jesus' life when He ate the Last Supper with His disciples, He stated in Luke 22:15, *"With fervent desire I have desired to eat this Passover with you before I suffer."* It is interesting to me that He was eager to eat this meal, since immediately following, He would suffer greater than any human being would ever endure.

What was special about this time more than any of the other times He ate with His disciples? He was enacting the New Covenant. His body was represented by the bread and His blood was represented by the wine. This time when the disciples ate of it, they were entering into this Covenant with the Father as much as with Jesus. They would become a part of Him, and He a part of them.

From the moment they shared this meal with Him, it set in motion a series of events that would fulfill many prophecies. It is recorded that Jesus fulfilled at least 300 prophecies in His lifetime and about twenty-eight of them alone on the day of His crucifixion!

APRIL 6

One Loaf, One Body

Read: Matthew 26:26-29

When I was a teenager at my church, I sat up on the balcony and I was able to see everything that went on from a higher view. It was always intriguing to me whenever we took Communion because I envisioned this one loaf of bread being cut up into little pieces. When everyone ate a piece of that bread, it literally became a physical part of their body. I imagined all of us being a part of each other, just like the pieces of bread made up the whole loaf. Pretty deep revelation for just a kid! But it was a true depiction of exactly what was happening. We were all a part of each other. And one thing I can say about that church, they loved each other and they cared about people's salvation...even a backwards little girl like me!

How serious is taking Communion? This was entering into a Covenant that meant life and death. Paul was teaching the Corinthians the importance of this meal. He clearly explains the purpose for the bread and the wine. Jesus had instructed each of His disciples to eat a piece of bread all from the same loaf. That meant that they were all one. They were entering into this Covenant together. From this moment on Jesus' time with them was short. He needed them to be committed to each other as one body caring for the other parts, especially as the early church grew.

These uneducated disciples had spent the past three and one-half years with Jesus. They had left their businesses, families, and lost their reputations. Now they needed to band together and watch each other's back. They had been through a lot with each other; their lives were turned upside down. Yet, this was only the beginning! The Lord's Supper would be an indentifying mark of the new Believer's fellowship with each other, house to house. The revelation of Jesus' death, burial, and resurrection was the message God would use to send them out to change the world!

APRIL 7

God's Revenge On Sickness

Read: Mark 15:15-39

From the moment of the Fall of man through Adam, God set in motion the anticipation of sending His Son, Jesus—Emmanuel, God with us, to make everything right again (Genesis 3:15). God Revealed Himself as Healer to a pagan king named Abimelech as early as the book of Genesis (Genesis 20:17) and to Abraham and Sarah, so they could give birth to Isaac in their old age. Moses even prophesied of the coming Messiah in Deuteronomy 18:15,

> "The Lord your God will raise up for you a Prophet like me from your midst, from your brethren. Him shall you hear..."

God was committed from the beginning to see His people free from the vices of evil. He involved Himself in every detail of mankind's condition. In Isaiah 52:13-53:12, the prophet foretold of Jesus as the *Suffering Servant* that would pay the price for our all our sins and diseases. All of humanity would live forever affected by the advent of Christ. Two eras now exist: BC—before Christ, and then a "restart" in history AD—where time itself was forever altered by the coming of the Messiah.

We can see how much our Father hated disease, and as a result He immersed Himself in the plight of mankind by placing all sickness upon His own Son. There was no disease in the beginning at Creation. The idea of freeing mankind from sickness and disease was His idea. He even called Himself "Jehovah Rapha—The Lord who heals you." Healer is who He *is*, not just something He *does*. The Father is fully involved in the eradication of disease by the sacrificial work of Christ, the Lamb of God, who takes away the sins of the world and *all* of its effects!

APRIL 8

This Is My Body

Read: 1 Corinthians 11:23-32

*P*aul, not being one of the original twelve present at *The Last Supper*, had the greatest understanding of the purpose for taking Communion because he had received it by revelation. He was able to explain to the Corinthians the purpose for each of the elements: the bread and the wine.

For most of us who have attended a more traditional church, we usually only took Communion on special occasions like Christmas and Easter. Holidays were considered the best time to do it because it drew the biggest crowds. The emphasis was usually more focused on the wine, which represents the remission or washing away, of all of our sins by Jesus' shed blood. We were given time to search our heart and self-reflect to examine whether we had any hidden sin in our lives. Then we all ate the bread and drank the juice as the pastor instructed. After that, we moved on to the next part of the service. This was my experience with Communion growing up, and I never questioned otherwise.

Having my own relationship with the Lord and reading the Bible for myself has opened up my eyes to greater truths I was never taught before; or maybe I just wasn't listening. Either way, once I found myself in the need of healing, I turned to the Word of God for the answers. The Word had never let me down in past experiences. The Lord always gave me Scriptures that guided me through many challenging things in the past, and I knew He'd be faithful once again.

Taking Communion does not need to be limited to a corporate church setting or to special holidays. We do not need a pastor to instruct us. Jesus clearly said, *"As often as you do this, do it in*

APRIL 8

remembrance of Me." So, if you want to take Communion every day at home by yourself, you have the freedom to do that.

In 1 Corinthians 11:23-32, it is very obvious that Jesus said the bread represented His body that was broken for our body. He said that the wine represented His blood that would wash away all of our sins. We know that when we partake of drinking the wine (or juice) that it represents His blood. We share in the victory He purchased for us to deliver us from *all* of our sins—no matter how bad they are; there is no sin His blood cannot wash away. What about the bread that represents His body when He was whipped and beaten for our bodies to heal every disease? It is His blood for our blood and His body for our body, is it not?

If we can agree that His blood is powerful enough to cleanse the worst sinner who truly repents, can we agree that His body can cure the most horrible diseases? *All* diseases? Yes, we can and we must!

APRIL 9

From Desert To Dessert

Read: Numbers 14, Psalm 103:1-5

When I was young in the Lord, I was taught that I should expect to go through wilderness seasons, where I'd feel dry and not be able to sense God's presence. This was compared to Israel wandering around in the wilderness for their disobedience. So, every time I "felt" alone, I thought I was just going through a dry time; and when things were really bad, I believed I was in a "wilderness"— that God had put me there to teach me something.

One particular time, when things were very rough and my kids were little, I didn't have much prayer time. I felt alone. I was in a house church meeting and my friends prayed for me. I'll never forget what this one girl said to me. She said I was not in a wilderness; that I was on a golf course stuck in a sand pit with green grass all around. All I had to do was walk out of the sand pit unto the green grass and start enjoying everything the Lord wanted me to have. Well, I didn't receive what she said and I got hacked off! How dare she make my plight seem so silly! She didn't know what I was going through! Looking back now, I wish I would have listened. It would have saved me many years of yo-yo, up and down frustration because I was living by my emotions.

I didn't understand that the wilderness time was for Israel under the Old Covenant. I didn't have to cross any "Jordan Rivers" to get to my promised land. Jesus went to the wilderness for me, defeated every temptation where Adam had failed, and gave me His Promised Land: freedom from all of the world's system of evil. He sent heaven inside of me through the Holy Spirit.

We don't ever have to be dry because the Holy Spirit is a river of life inside of us. He isn't a stagnant pool of muck, or a dry river bed. He's a river of *living* water! He does not lead us into trials, temptations and dry seasons. He satisfies us with good things, like dessert finishes off the perfect meal!

APRIL 10

Seasons

Read: Malachi 3:6, Psalm 102:25-27

When we were in grade school, we learned about the four seasons: spring, summer, winter, and fall. We are taught about the changes in the weather and how we need to dress appropriately.

Today, we've got a season for everything. Every time we go into a store the new products for sicknesses are on display in the front of the aisles. Spring isn't spring anymore without allergy season. Fall isn't fall anymore, it's cold and flu season. And grocery stores have the diabetic medicines on display right behind the doughnuts. They don't care, it's just what sells. They want to make it convenient for us to remember to stock up for when those sniffles come. Or grab your doughnut and a new cane when the bakery and the pharmacy are right next to each other. Think that's just a coincidence? The world has conditioned people to be sick. Sickness sells. Somewhere along the way they forgot about the natural seasons: spring, summer, winter and fall.

The church is not much different. We've got dry seasons, wilderness seasons, seasons of oppression and depression, and of course, seasons of blessings. We've got mountain tops and valleys; hills to climb, windy roads to travel. It's what keeps people coming back to pay their tithes. Ouch! Did I just step on somebody's toes? Oops!

Well, I'm so glad that God is forever constant. You can read His Word twenty years from now and it will still say the same thing. God will still honor His Word above His own Name. That's why He says, *"I am the Lord, I change not..."*

So, grab your doughnut, be happy and smile in the sunshine God created. Free yourself from the mumbo jumbo of this ever-changing up and down world. Don't get hung up on seasons of sickness, wilderness wanderings, or religious jargon. Live in the grace and freedom God has freely given you in His Son!

APRIL 11

Dichotomy

Read: John 14:6-27

A dichotomy is a contrast between two things.

If you haven't realized by now, this world and the Kingdom of God are totally opposite each other. All our lives, from childhood unto adulthood, we are taught to become independent and learn to do things for ourselves without needing the assistance of others. It's a sign of maturity. There's nothing more annoying than an adult who refuses to grow up and take responsibility for himself.

Yet the Kingdom of God is exactly the opposite. Jesus told us that if we want to enter the Kingdom of God, we must become like little children. In fact, the more *dependent* we are upon God, the more mature we are. Children don't question very much; they just trust and accept what adults tell them. Under normal circumstances, children don't worry about whether they will eat their next meal, where they will sleep, or what clothes they will wear.

The Bible says that we must die to live, give to gain, and that rest is work. This is totally opposite of the way the world functions, isn't it? This is precisely why we cannot operate in the Kingdom effectively by using worldly understanding. We must renew our minds to how the Kingdom of God functions.

The world says that *seeing is believing*. The Bible says that *believing is seeing*. Having this knowledge is very helpful when it comes to physical healing. Casting down imaginations that exalt themselves against the knowledge of Christ is an effective way to destroy a stronghold in the mind. Contrarily, it is helpful to entertain imaginations that exalt Christ. Knowing that 1 Peter 2:24 says, *"by His stripes you were healed,"* even though your leg may be in pain or swollen, imagining yourself riding a bicycle is more advantageous than just sitting around thinking about having surgery. Seeing

APRIL 11

yourself doing something you cannot do is Biblical. Jesus did it all the time. He told the man with the withered hand to stretch it out. The man could've said, *"But I can't, its withered!"* Instead, he obeyed and his hand was healed.

Encourage yourself in the Lord. Start by imagining yourself doing the things you want to do, maybe even for the first time. Even if it takes some time, encouraging yourself in the Word and in your imaginations gives you hope and a "can do" attitude. Before long, you'll be riding that bike or walking without that cane. You will find that believing *is* seeing!

APRIL 12

Bruised

Read: Isaiah 53:10

I recently went shopping at a Christian thrift store. It's one of my favorite things to do. I'm blessed to have at least four of them in my area. The first time I went into this particular thrift store, I noticed the lady at the counter was limping severely. I don't know what it is with legs, but it seems like I meet more people with leg issues than anything else. I asked the lady, assuming she was a Christian, if she had a problem with her legs. *"Oh yes, I have stage four osteoarthritis. I just got my diagnosis last week."* I offered to pray for her and she willingly took my hand. I commanded her legs to be strong and have stability. I commanded the pain and swelling to leave, and I spoke to her entire body to be filled with life. I felt the Spirit stir up inside me as I held her hand. I know life went into her!

I realized at the beginning of our conversation, when she confessed her doctor's diagnosis as her lot in life, it was a clue where she was at in her understanding of Scripture. Even *after* praying for her, she said, "Well, the Lord keeps bringing me to my knees with this pain to get me to listen, and I just keep missing it, and He says, 'My child, my child!'" as she shook her head. That stung me on the inside and I cringed when she said those words! She actually believed that Jesus was giving her that disease and pain! She said next week she was going to pursue surgery because the arthritis doctor said there was nothing else he could do for her.

I told her Jesus will help her. I told her that Jesus healed everyone, regardless of who they were or what the problem was. She told me she believed in healing. I'm thinkin' *Really??* Jesus doesn't have sickness and pain, so how could He give it to her? I couldn't get her to see that Jesus wasn't the one making her sick.

APRIL 12 ———

You know, the fact that this is actually taught and believed by people is a great travesty! She should have been free and walking without limping or pain. Instead, she was planning her next appointment. This story is TBC (To Be Continued) because I will certainly be visiting that store in the future to minister to her again!

APRIL 13

Zombie Apocalypse

Read: Matthew 27:50-54

This biblical account is not our modern-day description of zombies coming back from the dead and stomping stiff-legged, arms stretched out, looking for live humans to feast on! No! No! No!

Jesus, the First-born among many brethren, gave up His Spirit and then the graves of saints who had passed away were opened! Imagine: Uncle Bob, a devout Believer who had passed away, came out of his grave and went home to his family! Aunt Martha fainted because she could hardly believe her eyes!

These were not people who no one knew. These people were contemporaries that had been alive and had somewhat recently had passed away. These were people known and recognized by others—not saints of the Old Testament.

What was the message God was sending to the earth? Resurrection Life is here! Imagine that the first miracle immediately after Jesus gave up His Spirit was resurrecting other people's bodies from decay and disease (or whatever had killed them) and giving these people a new, healed body! Families were restored—well, after Aunt Martha awoke from fainting and got up off the floor!

There were MANY people who once were dead and were now alive standing in the city appearing to others. Imagine the commotion stirring in the city! Picture the Roman guards at the tombs watching dead people come out of their graves! There must have been a great flash of light when the earth shook and SHAZAAM! BOOM! Rocks split! Stones rolled away from select tombs—not just anybody, but saints! Resurrection Life came on the earth and has never left.

APRIL 13

As the disciples of Jesus saw His resurrected body and Uncle Bob among the others who came out of their tombs, they had no problem raising other people from the dead. Just as Jesus had taught them, and as they believed that He was *"The Resurrection and the Life,"* they went in the power of the same Holy Spirit and brought resurrection life to others! We are those who believe as a result of their message (John 17:20-26). We have the same Holy Spirit to keep us full of life—so much life, we can give it away to others!

APRIL 14

Fully Convinced

Read: Romans 4:13-22

The life of Abraham always amazes me. Paul, influenced by the Holy Spirit, wrote that Abraham never considered his own body being as good as dead or even Sarah's barren womb. Yet, when I read the story as it took place in the Old Testament, those details seem to be missing. It's like Paul is giving this spiritual perspective about what had happened, but it looked like Abraham was missing it big time in the natural. Even so, both Abraham and Sarah made it into the "Great Hall of Faith" in Hebrews chapter 11.

Did Abraham and Sarah make mistakes along the way? Oh yes, they did! Twenty-five years is a very long time to wait for a promise to be fulfilled! But God never looked at them as failures. He discounted their mistakes and called them righteous. They became the father and mother of our faith!

Many times when we are expecting a promise to come, we get frustrated and say or do things that we normally wouldn't do, just like Abraham and Sarah. Now that we are in the New Covenant, we are not "in the waiting" like they were for God's promises. There are still times when we are challenged to believe the Word doesn't work or that God hasn't kept His promise. Fortunately, God doesn't look at us as failures. He's sees something deeper—a heart that believes, a heart full of faith, and a heart that is fully convinced just like believing Abraham!

APRIL 15

A Blessed House

Read: 2 Samuel 6:11-12

This account of the Ark of the Covenant is fascinating! Here is this box made of wood and covered in gold with two open-winged angels on the lid, all crafted by humans hands. Inside was a jar of manna, Aaron's rod (which became alive and budded although it was previously just a dead twig), and the two tablets of stone with the Ten Commandments written on them.

After the tabernacle and all the items were made, the Spirit of God came down and filled that box. There, God remained in the center of His people. In the story we read for today, David wanted the presence of God in Jerusalem, so he set out to move the Ark. He discovered he was going about it in the wrong way, so he temporarily put the Ark in Obed-Edom's house.

The Ark remained there for only three months. In that short time, it says that Obed-Edom's house and *all* that belonged to him became blessed! When David heard the news of the blessing that came to Obed-Edom's household as a result of the Ark residing there, he was stirred in his heart to move it once again to Jerusalem so that all the people of God would be blessed.

All of this got me thinking: God's Spirit now dwells inside of you and me, right? Shouldn't everything that is mine be even more blessed as a result of Christ who lives in me right now? If the effect of God's Spirit inhabiting a wooden box was a blessing upon everything Obed-Edom owned, shouldn't we as well be experiencing such blessings? Aren't we the Ark of the New Covenant?

Picture that beautiful gold box surrounded by a cloud of God's glory. Imagine the financial blessings that came to Obed-Edom. Maybe his flocks of sheep began multiplying, the health of his family improved—whatever could be blessed was blessed! Now

APRIL 15

imagine yourself filled with the Spirit of God emanating out from where you are right now. Imagine every person in your household, blessed and healthy, because God lives there—right inside you!

My friend, if God would do all of that as the result of living in a man-made box, aren't you the one worth the price of His Son? Would He not extend the same blessings and more? Scripture says, *"...Since He did not spare even His own Son but gave Him up for us all, won't He also give us everything else?"* (Roman 8:32, NLT). YOU! Yes, YOU are the Ark now! Imagine your body, everyone, and everything in your house blessed. This is what God sees. When we begin to see imagine this, it will become our reality too, and others will experience the blessings!

APRIL 16

Christ In You

Read: Galatians 2:20-21

"With Christ I have been crucified, and it is no longer I who live, but there lives in me Christ. And that life which now I live in the sphere of the flesh, by faith I live it, which faith is in the Son of God who loved me and gave Himself on my behalf. I do not thwart the efficacy of the grace of God. For if through the law comes righteousness, then Christ died to no purpose."
(Galatians 2:20-21, *Wuest Translation*)

I like the way the *Wuest* translated this popular Scripture. We can read a verse so many times, and even quote it from memory, but as the old saying goes, *"Familiarity breeds contempt."* We can easily miss the heart of what this Scripture is saying. Reading it is one thing, but what does it look like to actually LIVE this way? Think about that! What does it mean to live dead as yourself, and now live through Christ? How would you speak differently? How would you act differently? What things would be different in your life if Jesus was sitting next to you right now, or if He was physically walking next to you everywhere you went?

"Well, for one thing, I'd be healed," you might think to yourself. Now wait a minute...

We have this modern terminology where we talk about *the presence of God*. Many say, *"Wow, the presence of God was so strong in church during the worship today that I could feel Him!"* And usually that means they felt Him on the outside of their body and in the atmosphere in the room. It usually means they felt joy or peace. But after the service is over, everything goes back to "normal" and they go on with life hoping next Sunday they can *feel* His presence again. It's just enough to satisfy until next time. His presence comes, then leaves—almost every Sunday, if the worship is good and ushers in the presence of God to "set the atmosphere."

APRIL 16

I used to live that way, so I know what I'm talking about. I was there every time the church doors were open so I could just "get in His presence," at least for a little while. But then He would leave, or so I thought.

The game changer for me was realizing that He *never* left; that it was me who was distracted, trying to fix myself all the time. I finally had the revelation that He is *inside* of me, right here *all* the time; that I can talk to Him spirit to Spirit every minute of every day. He is not a mere feeling, but His actual nature, character, ability, power—*all of Him* had made His home in me! Whoa! Life became a lot more interesting!

I finally understood that I didn't have to try to fix myself, get healed myself...any of those exhausting things anymore! He didn't make His home in me to "fix" me. He killed me off; then I received His life! Whew! No more griping, whiny, sarcastic, sick, manipulative....ok I'll stop there, you get the picture...I'm dead, done, crucified when He was crucified!

He came to *live* His life in me, and I live my life through Him. He gave me His resurrection life and now, because He is living in and through me, I have His life in my spirit, in my soul, and in my body! He's in every cell of my flesh! What an exchange! It is the same for you too! The day you were born again, your old self died and Jesus came to live His life inside of your body. He gave you His life for yours, His health for your health, His character and nature for yours.

So, what if He was physically sitting next to you right now holding your hand? You would be healed. Well, my friend, He's doing more than that right now! He's touching and permeating every cell of your body from the inside out! He's not a floaty feeling in the atmosphere around you, He's a real person that exchanged His life for yours! He's tangible from the inside out! He's always with you because He is infused into your very being! Think about that! Imagine His life constantly touching you from the inside out! This is your reality: CHRIST IN YOU!

APRIL 17

Order Your Life

Read: Romans 8:1-4

*W*e have heard this Scripture so many times—that there is no condemnation to those who are in Christ Jesus. But what does that really mean? Did you know that this statement is actually *legal* terminology? It means that there is no indictment or guilty charge against you because Christ paid the requirements to set you free.

That doesn't merely include sin. That includes sin *and all of its effects*! Disease, pain, and lack are all results of sin in the earth. That's where every evil thing came from. We know this because everything was perfect in the Garden after Creation.

Before we were in Christ, we couldn't help ourselves. We don't have to teach children to act wrongly, it just comes natural; and to a child, it's hard to share. We were born with a selfish nature screaming, *"Gimme that, I had it first!"* We have to teach children to share, be kind, and not to be selfish, but it seldom sticks until they are older.

Romans informs us that Jesus freed us once and for all from that sinful nature, to the point that sin and all of its effects became the guilty party instead of us! The *Wuest Translation* says in verse 4:

> *"in order that the righteous requirement of the law may be brought to completion in us who, not as dominated by the sinful nature* **are ordering our behavior but as dominated by the Spirit.***"* (Emphasis added)

We order our behavior. You can look at this two different ways. You can think of it as the way you go about your life, or you can look at this as more of taking charge and ordering your flesh (senses) to obey Holy Spirit (not in a religious/legalistic way, just not being willy-nilly). We order our life to be dominated by Holy Spirit.

APRIL 17

When we are free once and for all from the sinful nature, we don't have to keep trying to get free from this thing and that thing over and over again! That's good news!

If Holy Spirit was allowed to be in control; if we fully submitted to the way He lives life, what would that look like?

It'd be pretty darn good!

APRIL 18

Made Righteous

Read: 2 Corinthians 5:21

The *Peshitta Bible* gives us a fresh perspective of 2 Corinthians 5:21:

> *"For He who did not know sin, for your sakes made Himself sin, that we may through Him be made the righteousness of God."*

Jesus *made* Himself sin! Did you ever think of Him that way? As a result, He *made* us righteous! We didn't know we needed it. We didn't know that righteousness had to be a legal transaction Jesus became for us to reconcile us with His Father. Everything that stood in the way of having a close, intimate relationship with our Father, Jesus cleared out of the way by His sacrifice!

Most of us have heard that *righteousness* means "right-standing" with God, but have you ever stopped and thought about what that means for you as a Believer? Is it really that important?

The *Thayer's Concordance* defines righteousness as *"the state acceptable to God which becomes a sinner's possession through faith by which he embraces the grace of God offered him in the expiatory (atonement) death of Jesus Christ."* Thayer's also defines righteousness as *judicial justice*, meaning that every requirement that was needed to make us right with God was legally met through Christ.

The dictionary defines righteousness as *"a coming into spiritual oneness with God, because for Christ's sake the Believer in Christ is treated as righteousness."* Righteousness also means *to be free from guilt, sin and all its effects*. It is the polar opposite of sin and everything that we were when we lived in darkness in the world.

What does that mean for Believers? There is absolutely NOTHING standing between us and God anymore! Whatever the need is:

APRIL 18

healing, a relationship restored, financial provision—whatever it is, Jesus opened up the way to receiving everything we need from our Father by making us just as righteous as He is! I don't know about you, but I think this is pretty phenomenal! I encourage you to meditate on this all day today. Allow the understanding of being made right with your Father supercharge your connection with Him in fresh communion!

APRIL 19

Righteous & Mature

Read: Hebrews 5:12-14

We should take the Scripture reading for today very seriously. Understanding the teaching of *righteousness* means the difference between remaining a spiritual infant verses becoming a mature Believer. This verse is clearly an important key in understanding our maturity in Christ.

As Believers, there are certain things that are acceptable in our conduct and way of thinking, and obviously things that are unacceptable. The world's way of thinking and acting is by taking information into our lives from the outside and internalizing it on the inside of our hearts. The way of righteousness in the Kingdom of God is the opposite. We live from the truths and information deposited inside of us by Holy Spirit and bring them to the outside. This requires a firm control of our thought life, since we do not act without something beginning as a thought in our mind first.

A Believer that is unskilled in the word of righteousness is unable to fully experience the righteousness we have received in Christ. They may not know what righteousness means and they may not know how to live out the benefits that being righteous has given to us. Because of this, they may continue to go in circles, needing to be taught again and again the truths that are laid out in Scripture. This is what is defined as the "milk" of the Word. They don't know how important it is to discipline their senses and practice self-control. In fact, they are unable to discern between what is acceptable and what is unacceptable for themselves.

If we cannot enforce discipline over our own thought life and actions, it becomes more challenging to enforce the authority Christ has given over diseases, pain, or any other trial that may come against us. Strongholds can be built in our minds that are

APRIL 19

contrary to the Word of God if we do not constantly keep our thought life in check. I cannot emphasize enough how important it is to make every thought obedient to what the Word says. Understanding righteousness helps us plow through the lies and throw them out. When you are *skilled* in righteousness, you are living from your spirit; not your emotions, nor your senses.

A person who has been a Believer for a number of years is expected to be mature and take responsibility to disciple others. Just start right where you are. Begin to step out and share with others what you know. The more you spend yourself on behalf of others, the quicker you will grow yourself!

APRIL 20

Righteous & Healed

Read: 1 Peter 2:24

If we take this verse and separate it into parts, it's easier to glean the important truths. Let's look at the first part:

"who Himself bore our sins in His own body on the tree"

In the English language, when we see two pronouns together that refer to the same person, the writer is purposely bringing extra added emphasis to that person. The words *"who Himself"* is adding emphasis on Jesus. He was the only One who could bear our sins, and He did it by His own choice. Peter is making a reference to Isaiah 53. The word *bore* in Isaiah 53:12 means in Hebrew: *to bear as punishment for another so we don't have to bear it ourselves."* Jesus didn't merely take our sins upon Himself, He bore them. He literally *became* sin because that is what we were. In the next part of this verse it says:

"that we, having died to sins, might live for righteousness"

When Jesus was crucified and died because of our sins, we died along with Him and we died to sin and all of its effects. Because Jesus is righteous, He made us His righteousness. Now we can share in all that He is. He re-positioned us in right relationship with our Father. Now nothing is standing in the way of receiving the fullness of who Jesus is for our own lives too. We live in righteousness, or in right-standing with our Father. The last part of this verse says

"by whose stripes you <u>were</u> healed"

Again, Peter is referring to Isaiah 53 where in verse 5 it says *"And by His stripes we **are** healed."* Notice that the verb *are* is changed to *were*; from present tense to past tense. Because of Jesus' death on the cross, *healed* is now past tense, meaning healing is already finished. Why? Because He made us righteous by removing sin and

APRIL 20

all the garbage like disease, hatred, envy and death that came with it! By making us as righteous as He is, we are able to stand before our Father free, healed, and whole—nothing blocking the way!

APRIL 21

The Breastplate Of Righteousness

Read: Ephesians 6:14

*T*his verse tells us to put on righteousness as a breastplate. When Paul wrote these verses, it is interesting to think about why he chose to name each part of the armor they way he did. We can clearly see that having the main part of our bodies protected with righteousness, Paul, being guided by the Holy Spirit, was very wise. Our righteousness in Christ is protection for the heart and vital organs—the deepest parts of who we are.

We know that it says in Proverbs 4:23 that we should guard our heart because everything we do flows from it and determines our course of life—down to every decision we make. Righteousness can guard our heart by helping us to choose wisely and to think according to the Word of God instead of relying on our own wisdom, which can easily lead to trouble.

The more I learn about our righteousness in Christ, the more amazed I am at the things I discover that belong to us. For example, when we read in the Psalms & Proverbs about righteousness, we can now look at these benefits through Christ! This is such an advantage over what the people had under the Old Covenant. They had to *earn* their righteousness by keeping the law, compared to us being *made* righteous when we were born again.

Proverbs 10:2 and Proverbs 11:4 both say, *"righteousness delivers from death."* There are two ways we can apply this truth; both physically and spiritually. Either way our righteousness keeps us in Christ! Proverbs also says that righteousness delivers from trouble while leading us to life! Knowing that being clothed with God's armor protects us from any destruction this world tries to bring, helps us have a lot more confidence knowing who we are in Christ!

APRIL 22

A Righteous Man's Prayer

Read: James 5:16, John 16:23, 26

*W*e read that a righteous man's prayer is powerful and effective, but have you ever stopped to ask yourself why? The simplest answer is: because we are IN Christ!

In both of the verses in John 16, Jesus says, *"In that day..."* What day was He referring to? The day when He would be taken up to heaven after His resurrection and the disciples would have to ask the Father for what they needed for themselves. They would need to develop their own relationship with the Father; because that was the reason He came. Jesus said that whatever they asked of the Father, He would hear, answer, and give them whatever they asked. This is what makes a righteous man's prayer powerful and effective—now that we are IN Christ. Because of the authority we have in His Name, our prayers are heard and answered.

"Well, then why do I still have pain or sickness? I've been asking and asking and asking and here I am in the same situation!" Many times we wonder if God even heard us in the first place. But I can assure you that He heard you the first time you asked. Is His arm too short to save and His ear too dull to hear (Isaiah 59:1)?

There comes a point where we must start thanking our Father for hearing and answering us because He promised that He would. Read Hebrews 4:13-16 and be confident that He has heard, and many times He has already answered. We may need to quiet ourselves and just listen and expect. It may be the quick flash of a picture that you see in your mind, or a verse of Scripture you think about. It may be something you read that leaps out at you, or He may just flat out speak to you through words that come to your mind. In whatever way He may communicate to you, act on whatever it is. In this way, you are showing that you acknowledge Him and believe what He

APRIL 22

told you. Then thank Him and write down the date and whatever He showed you. Remember how stirred you felt inside. In this way you can reread what He said and encourage yourself in the Lord. Remember that because He made you righteous, your prayers have been heard and they are powerful and effective!

APRIL 23

Free For All

Read: Romans 5:17

It's a "Free for All" kinda deal! This is the best kind! I like the way the ESV states this verse:

> *"For if, because of one man's trespass, death reigned through that one man, much more will those who receive the abundance of grace and the free gift of righteousness reign in life through the one man, Jesus Christ!"*

Man oh man! That says it all, doesn't it? Mmmm, Mmmm! This is so good! I'm in the "much more" crowd, how about you? We've got an abundance of grace, and as a result, we have received the free gift of righteousness through our relationship with Jesus.

You didn't ask for righteousness. You couldn't earn it. You didn't even know you needed it. But He gave it to you because He knew you needed it. Isn't it remarkable when we learn that Jesus provided everything we needed before we knew we needed it? We can go to Him for healing and say, *"Thanks, Lord! You've got me covered!"*

Righteousness means that nothing, absolutely *nothing* is blocking you from accessing everything Father has for you. Jesus made you His equal to share in His inheritance. What are His benefits? We know Psalm 103:1-2 says that forgiveness and healing are part of His benefits. Life is yours, health is yours, deliverance is yours, joy is yours, peace is yours—all of it—free for everyone for righteousness' sake!

APRIL 24

Righteousness Releases Authority

Read: Romans 5:17-21

*L*et's read the *Wuest Translation* for verse twenty:

> *"For in view of the fact that by means of the transgression of the one death reigned as king through that one, much more those who receive the abundance of grace and the gift of righteousness, in life will reign as kings through the One, Jesus Christ."*

This is talking about Adam and how death reigned (and everything that came with it) as king in our lives because of his disobedience, but now we reign as kings because we have received the grace and the gift of righteousness through Christ's obedience.

In order to reign as a king, there must be a kingdom and subjects to rule over. Jesus is the King of kings. We are kings and He is our King. He rules over us, but He has given us His authority to use in His Name against sickness and disease, poverty, and anything that has not been submitted to the Kingdom of God.

Almost EVERY preacher I have heard regularly teaches that there is a "Kingdom of Darkness." To tell you the truth, my friend, there is NO Scripture ANYWHERE in the Bible that mentions the words *Kingdom of Darkness*. In order for there to be a Kingdom of Darkness, there would have to be a king and its kingdom. Satan is never mentioned in the Bible as a king having a kingdom of darkness. Go look it up for yourself. There is only the Kingdom of God and the Kingdom of Heaven. That's it! Period!

It is crucial to realize that the only way evil can work in our lives is when a suggestion comes to us in the form of a thought. How we interact with that suggestion determines whether or not it has any power to influence our decisions. We have a choice to make:

APRIL 24

1. We let the thought repeat itself and ponder it over and over until we react in fear or accept it as truth. Then we start thinking of plans how we will deal with that possibility, such as to call and make a doctor appointment, call some friends and ask their opinion, or Google it and check to see if our symptoms are possibly a certain disease.

OR

2. We grab it by the jugular and cast that thought down where it belongs and say, *"NO! This is not what the Word of God says! The Bible says that by His stripes I was healed!"* Then we enforce God's truth into those symptoms and expect them to leave, confident that something changed, no matter how subtle. Knowing the authority Jesus gave us over all disease—we thank Him that it is finished!

Sometimes we don't *feel* very authoritative, but what we feel doesn't matter. Jesus said that we are MORE than conquerors. When we make the choice to trust Him and not what we feel in our bodies, what we feel in our emotions or what seems logical to our natural mind, we will experience the results of taking the authority Jesus gave to us. Because we are righteous in Him—it's a done deal!

APRIL 25

Righteousness Connected To Life

Read: Philippians 3:7-12

*P*aul connected his righteousness through faith in Christ as the catalyst to acquire Jesus' resurrection life and power. He so fervently desired to obtain resurrection life that we can sense his zeal for the experience—not only someday when he died, but presently while he was alive.

I encourage you to read 1 Corinthians 15, where Paul defends Christ's resurrection throughout the entire chapter. He goes on to say that if Christ was not raised from the dead, our faith is futile and we are still dead in our sins! Later on in verse 34, Paul says, *"Awake to righteousness."* In other words,

> *"Wake up! Stop acting like a man in a drunken stupor and realize that because of Christ's resurrection, you are resurrected too; free from all bondage, now that you are in right-standing with Him!"* (My paraphrase)

Christ's crucifixion is your crucifixion too! Christ's resurrection is your resurrection too! You are a completely new creation and the things that belonged to your old life no longer apply to your new life in Jesus! What you see in the world doesn't apply to you any more than it applies to Jesus! Just as Jesus was raised to life by the Holy Spirit, so were you and now Holy Spirit is keeping your body alive (Romans 8:11).

I like to think about His resurrection power as a pure blue-ish white light, like a ball of endless energy stationed in my abdomen area and pulsating outward into my head, arms, and legs, even in the atmosphere all around me. I remember several years ago, when I had spent many hours every morning hanging out with Jesus, every time I quieted myself, my entire body would shake because of recognizing Holy Spirit inside me! He's still there in that same

APRIL 25

strength and ability, even though I'm not shaking now like I was then. It really comes down to hanging out with Him in everything you do and inviting Him to interact with you everywhere you go. The understanding of His resurrection life inside of me is like this ball of fire that is able to bring life to everything I come near to! We too can be like Paul, setting our sights on Jesus' resurrection life by ordering our lives so that we can experience His power for ourselves and give it away to others!

APRIL 26

Righteousness Releases Boldness

Read: Proverbs 28:1

*R*ighteousness gives us boldness, confidence, and freedom from fear. Proverbs 28:1 says:

> *"The wicked flee when no one pursues, but the righteous are as bold as a lion."*

Fear is a tormenting force, largely brought on by thinking about things that haven't even happened yet. The more one dwells on bad thoughts concerning their circumstances, the larger that problem becomes in his mind. Those thoughts begin to consume him, so he starts making plans to accommodate the "what-if's" just in case.

This Scripture says that no one is pursuing, yet the person is running in paranoia, fearful of being attacked. A good habit to form is separating our emotions and thoughts from reality. This is extremely effective for living with a stable and sound mind. I had to practice this myself when my knee was hot and swollen larger than a grapefruit. I couldn't walk and at times I had to lift my leg with my hands to step over something. Many times fear rose up in me and spoke, *"They're gonna cut your leg off!"* And even though the thought of such a thing was quite terrifying, I refused to entertain it. I'd say right back, *"Oh, no you won't, it's not your leg, so get lost!"* This happened quite a few times, and I answered the same way every time, then that was the end of it.

You see, we have to keep our mind rational and stable with God's Word. Knowing that our bodies belong to Jesus; that we are a container for the Holy Spirit here on the earth just as Jesus' body was for Him, we can stand bold like a lion guards his territory. We have boldness because we have access to everything Jesus has access to in order to deliver us. So don't allow your mind and thoughts of fear to get the best of you. Stand boldly in the righteousness Jesus

APRIL 26

put in you—the position of a son/daughter that is accepted before our Father.

APRIL 27

God's Throne

Read: Psalm 89:14, Hebrews 1:8

*V*erse fourteen of Psalm 89 in the *Peshitta Bible* proclaims:

> *"Thy throne is built on righteousness and judgment; mercy and truth go before thy face."*

How important is righteousness to God? It is so important that He rules by it! I love the picture Hebrews 1:8 describes! We can imagine Jesus sitting on His throne in heaven holding a scepter with the word RIGHTEOUSNESS written on it.

Righteousness is not a way of acting, but is a result of being placed in the position of "right-standing" with the Father. Righteousness itself isn't holiness. It is the relationship restored through Christ; producing the desire to live a holy, upright life because that is the nature and character of God.

It is marvelous when we become aware that, along with righteousness, Jesus made us everything in the character and nature of the Father. That includes being whole in our spirit, soul, and body. We are delivered from every evil force in this world and translated into God's Kingdom. What He says goes, now that we belong to Him.

Our Father is right, just, and fair. This is how He rules; it's the foundation for everything He does. Nobody is getting away with anything—it always catches up to them one way or another. I'm glad He is merciful, kind, and good. We know that it is His kindness and goodness that draws us to Him.

Within the understanding of righteousness, we read in Proverbs 11:19 that *"righteousness leads to life."* In Proverbs 12:28 is says that *"in its (righteousness) pathway there is no death."* This causes us to realize that, because there is nothing but life in Jesus, there can be nothing but life in us!

APRIL 28

The Benefits Of Righteousness

Read: Psalm 103:1-8

The beginning of the Psalm lists some noteworthy benefits when we apply them through the understanding of being one with Jesus! Here is a list:

1. Forgiven of all iniquities—even the ones from past generations, implying that there are no longer any generational curses

2. Healed of all diseases

3. Jesus paid the price to deliver us from destruction

4. He showered us with His loving-kindness and tender mercies (Notice that mercy is plural! This means He never runs out of His mercy toward us)

5. He feeds us with every good thing that keeps us young and refreshed—We never have to dry up like a wrinkly old prune! LOL!

6. He gave us righteousness and justice in the place of oppression and depression

7. He shows us the way He does things and acts on our behalf

8. He gives us mercy, not anger; patience instead of harshness

In the light of understanding the Covenant we have in Christ, righteousness is the gateway that has opened the floodgates for us to stand under this shower of goodness and be bathed and cleansed in His love.

When we look at all of these benefits given to us as a result of being made the righteousness of God in Christ, we also must choose to unlearn quite a few things that we may have been taught that

APRIL 28 ———

are opposite of what we see here. We must be intentional about replacing lies with the truth. When we look into the light of His righteousness, all of the other worldly things disappear.

APRIL 29

Favor

Genesis 39:1-6, Luke 4:19 (AMP)

From the time he was born, Joseph had favor. It began with his father. Even though his brothers were jealous of him and sold him into slavery, favor followed Joseph everywhere he went—even in prison. Wouldn't it be wonderful to know that you would always rise to the top no matter where you ended up?

I heard this quote several years ago, *"A moment of favor is worth a lifetime of labor."* What really bothers me about this statement is the fact that, if we try to live like this, we will always be chasing favor. I have also heard it taught that favor is linked to obedience.

While Joseph certainly honored God with his life regardless of what other people did to him, we do not stand in the same position with God that Joseph did. As a matter of fact, we have it much better because of the New Covenant we have in Christ. Now, don't misunderstand me. I'm not saying that you can just live any way you want to. But what I am saying is that you do not have to work yourself into a frenzy so that you have favor with God. Why? Because you already have it!

The *Amplified Bible* in Luke 4:19, says that Jesus came to proclaim the *"favorable year of the Lord."* This is referring to the year of Jubilee in Leviticus 25 when Israel had everything restored back to them and all debts were erased. Jesus was proclaiming that He is the Jubilee that restores everything the enemy has stolen from us and He has cancelled every debt that sin brought upon us! Talk about favor! We're totally free! We can't earn that, but by putting our trust in Jesus we receive favor that restores us to a better than Pre-Fall condition! The Bible also says that Jesus grew in favor with God and with man (Luke 2:52). Since Jesus had the favor of God, He simply gave it to us when we were born again.

APRIL 29 ———

If we try to work for favor when we already have it, we will just be exhausting ourselves for nothing. This is how the Kingdom of God works—by simply recognizing what we have been given, thank Jesus for giving it to us, and live like you already have it, cuz you do!

APRIL 30

Not Guilty

Read: Colossians 1:21-22 (The Passion Translation)

When I remember the person I was before I came to Christ, it's like talking about somebody else. Want to know why? It is because I'm no longer that person. She is long dead and gone, thank God! Trust me; you wouldn't have liked me very much. I was very sarcastic and insecure. If there was something sneaky to do, I did it and let the chips fall where they may. Jesus freed me from myself!

I met a woman a while ago who had been born again for many years. She said she was a Christian, but she kept questioning her salvation. As a result, she never felt good enough. She was on a roller coaster ride in her relationship with Jesus. It really was sad to watch. No one could convince her otherwise.

Sometimes there are particular areas in our lives that we yo-yo up and down about. Healing is certainly one of those subjects. How do you really settle the fact that, *"by His stripes you were healed"*?

Most of us know someone who has been healed of a major disease and we think that they must know a secret that we haven't been privy to, or that God just has favor on some people, while others just have to suck it up. While it is true that healing may happen easier for some people than for others, it isn't because God is holding back or that there a few extra hoops you must jump through to receive it.

In fact, many people I know who received a miraculous healing found themselves a short while later with the same symptoms again. Some of them went to the Lord and asked for help and He showed them what to do. Others just figured they lost their healing. I've seen both ends of the spectrum.

The bottom line is that Jesus paid for our salvation and our healing at the same time. We must make the choice to trust that He took

APRIL 30

care of it and there is *nothing* standing between you and Him anymore. No guilty charge means nothing is standing in the way of receiving what He has provided through His Body and His Blood. Finalize it in your mind and in your heart. Choose not to back off this truth and your body will follow.

MAY 1

Holy Spit

Read: John 9

*I*magine if you could spit on someone and they would be healed, or if they just touched your clothes diseases were cured! I think that would be pretty cool, don't you?

Using spit is a pretty strange way to heal someone. I believe that this man either didn't have eyes, or they weren't fully developed. Jesus used His spit and some dirt to do a creative miracle, like when Adam was formed from the dust of the earth and made into a man. The blind man had a part to play. Jesus told him to go wash. He obeyed and got a new set of eyes! No matter how strange the Holy Spirit's instructions may be, it's always best to comply.

When I was in Kenya several years ago, an apostle from the congregation was leaving on a mission trip from Kenya to Nigeria to lead a yearly conference. During the service before his departure I was told, *"Michele, you have the word of the Lord! Prophesy over Apostle for his trip!"*

I was sitting there thinking, *"Do you know something I don't know, cuz I ain't got nothin'!"* A microphone was shoved in my hand and I was expected to stand up and prophesy over this powerful man of God who was highly honored and respected! Little ol' me had to give a word from the Lord about this man's trip to help guide him. I stood there in front of about 200 people, and I said to the Lord inside, *"Help!"*

I opened my mouth to speak, and the following words came out that never had time to come to my mind, *"I see darkness coming against you..."* and in my head I'm saying to the Lord, *"Oh great, thanks! Not only am I up here but You have to give me a doom and gloom word for this man of God!"* I finished by saying that even

MAY 1

though darkness would come and try to interfere with the conference, he should stay strong and God would see him through.

It was probably a month later until that man had returned to Kenya and I saw him again. He said, *"Michele, I have to tell you, everything you prophesied happened to me and the Lord kept His promise."* I'm like, *"Okay, I don't really remember anyway."* Initially, once I spoke that word, it came out and it was gone. I never gave it another thought. But then the man shared with the whole congregation that he had taken his son, who was in his early twenties, with him on the trip to Nigeria for the conference.

During the several days of the conference, the boy became very sick. The Pastor hosting the conference said to the Apostle, *"You have to stop these conferences and get this boy home to his mother or he may die!"* This was not an easy trip! They were somewhere in the African bush in Nigeria, nine hours by jeep from the airport, (let me tell you, their roads are dirt and have holes so huge they can almost swallow a car! Kenya is located on the far East coast of Africa, Nigeria is on the west side of Africa). My friend said, *"No! I will stay the course, I have the word of the Lord that darkness would try to stop this conference, but the Lord would see us through!"* The man prayed, the son became well, and he finished the entire conference!

Now, let me tell you, when he returned to share his story, I almost fell off my chair! The fact that the Lord gave me that word when I had nothing but a complete blank in my mind astounded me! Even more amazing was that God was faithful and healed his son as a result of his father's trust because of that prophecy. Honestly, when he shared the story, I was thinking, *"You did WHAT because of the word I gave you!!??"* But I just kept on my "poker face" and said to the Lord, *"Wow, Lord, thanks for backing me up! Cuz if that would have been me me, I don't know if I could have pressed through like he did and finished that conference at the possibility of losing my son's*

MAY 1 ―――――

life!" I had to realize that it was the word of the Lord, not mine. I was just the messenger.

So, no matter what the Lord tells you to do, even if it sounds strange, just do it! He will back you up and you will see how faithful He works, even when a situation looks impossible!

MAY 2

God's Wish List

Read: 3 John

*T*rue prosperity means more than just a jingle in your pocket. John says that he prays, desires, or wishes (depending on which translation you are reading) that his friend Gaius would prosper in all areas of his life. This is the full meaning of Biblical prosperity. It is also God's "Wish List" for us.

Gaius was a faithful, loving servant to the church. John was commending him for the work he was doing as a leader. Even though this was John's prayer for his beloved friend he longed to visit, it is also God's desire for us.

How can a person prosper in their soul? This seems to be the key to experiencing the benefits of prosperity in health and all the other areas of life. One of the most important habits a Believer can do is to train their thought life. I cannot emphasize this enough!

Think about it: if Biblical prosperity and our ability to experience it are directly related to the condition of our thoughts and emotions, we need to stop and take constant inventory on what we think about. Our thoughts have a direct affect on how we experience life, for the good or the bad. In turn, these thoughts can have a direct effect on our health. Jesus gives the opportunity for us to prosper in every area, but if we are haphazard about the way we go about life, we will not experience what He has made available as much as we should.

It is important to have a disciplined thought life. We must make it a habit to think on things that are pure and of a good report and not participate in the type of conduct this man Diotrephes was doing, causing strife. He was spreading lies and causing division. We have to remember that we do not live on an island alone. The way we think and our actions affect the people we love around us. We must

MAY 2 ———

regularly read God's word and talk with the Holy Spirit every day, all day—as much as possible (praying without ceasing).

Recognize that the Holy Spirit is right there inside of you, communicating with you. When you keep an ear out for Him all the time to listen for His voice like you would your husband or wife, you will enjoy life to its fullest. His Spirit is supplying you constantly with everything you need, and He's always right there with you in the daily grind of life. That's where He wants to be, helping you to prosper in every way!

MAY 3

God's Health Care Plan

Read: John 14:29-30

There's no fee to pay to enter into God's health care plan. Jesus already paid it; all you have to do is believe in Him—it's that simple. The Kingdom of God comes with so many benefits that the world's system can never come close.

When you were born again, you were completely removed from the world's system and translated into the Kingdom realm where God has dominion. We received His health care plan, His life insurance plan, and His retirement plan. We have His employment benefits where He takes care of all of our needs. Holy Spirit dwells within us, helping us to advance God's Kingdom by preaching the Gospel and healing the sick. It's a pretty exciting life! There's an adventure waiting every place you go, and you never need to take a vacation or retire!

Jesus stated that the ruler of this world had nothing in Him. We never read about Jesus going to the doctor or getting in an accident. The life of the Holy Spirit flowed out from Him and nothing evil could touch Him. If He touched a disease, it died instantly. Jesus lived His later years on the earth as a man filled with the Holy Spirit, just like you and me. He came to show us how to do it.

We can't get a "double portion" of God's anointing. Since we have the same Holy Spirit Jesus had living inside of us, how could we get a double portion of Him? That term is a reference to Elijah & Elisha in the Old Testament when the Holy Spirit came upon them, but He never lived *inside* them. So when someone talks about a "double portion anointing," remember that it is impossible because you have been given the fullness of the Spirit.

Since we have the fullness of the Holy Spirit, the only thing that can limit how powerfully He flows out of us is ourselves. We cannot

MAY 3

receive any more than we already have, or else that would mean that the Father is holding out on us; and that would be impossible, because in Him there is no darkness at all. He is a never-ending source of life and power, and now that we are a part of His Kingdom, only His rules apply. We only need to learn what we have received by inheritance and how to utilize it. This simply requires putting feet to your faith!

MAY 4

Life By The Spirit

Read: John 7:37-39 (KJV)

*L*et's focus on this phrase in parentheses contained in verse 36, (*"But this spake He of the Spirit, which they that believe on Him should receive"*)

These words give us some important insight. It says that those who believe on Jesus *should* receive the Holy Spirit. In other words—it's not an option. If you are in Christ, you have received the Holy Spirit. So, what does that mean?

It means that we are required to live in response to the Holy Spirit living inside of us in everything we do and say. No, not like a robot. Nor like a marionette, where every move is controlled by heavenly strings from above. The Holy Spirit never forces Himself upon anyone. He usually nudges from within to guide us by an inner voice, but it's still our choice. It would be much easier if He would just do things for us so that we wouldn't have to do them, but He is there to assist, not to take over and control us.

The more we relax and don't fight or strive, the more natural it will be for us to flow with Him, no matter how big or insignificant the need is. This is not an overnight journey, but a lifetime of getting to know Him, learning to be able to pick up on His voice, and continuously and intentionally choosing to walk with Him every moment. It requires consciously and purposely turning away from other influences—no matter who or what they are.

Every human heart truly longs for God. This is why people find themselves in addictions, depression, or bad relationships. They are trying to fill the vacuum in their heart for Jesus with other things that never really satisfy. It's like the song my kids used to sing when they were little from the Doughnut Man:

MAY 4

"Life without Jesus is like a doughnut, like a doughnut, like a doughnut. Life without Jesus is like a doughnut, there's a hole in the middle of your heart!"

The Holy Spirit fills up the hole—that emptiness that nothing else can satiate. You can be certain that Holy Spirit wants to fill you to overflowing, like a geyser bursting out of you. He bubbles up from within, bringing life, joy, and peace with continual satisfaction!

MAY 5

A New Language

Read: Mark 16:17-20, 1 Corinthians 14:14-15

*W*hen we receive the Spirit's power, we also receive a new language. It's not any of man's known languages; it is a spiritual language we receive from the Holy Spirit. I admit that speaking in other tongues is awkward at first. I struggled with it myself. It's very unnatural; which is why it is so powerful!

I'll be honest. I only found out about becoming baptized in the Spirit after nearly five years of struggling in my relationship with the Lord. Up until that time all I knew was that the Holy Spirit was called the Third Person of the Trinity. Other than that, I figured He was just hanging out in heaven floating around looking holy.

Once I was filled with the Holy Spirit, I didn't struggle any longer trying to live a godly life. Holy Spirit gave me strength of character I never experienced before. But unfortunately, after I got baptized in the Holy Spirit and spoke in my new language, once again I was told; *"Now you're good to go."* I didn't understand the purpose for speaking in tongues, so I seldom prayed that way unless it was an emergency.

One day, when I was very ill and felt like I was close to death, I asked Holy Spirit to show me what to do. There were many voices screaming and taunting me in my head, sometimes it was deafening! I had nightmares while I slept at night. I tried to read and confess the Word, and it did help to a point, but I needed power. I needed strength of spirit, mind, and body. The Holy Spirit gave me the answer I needed! He told me to pray in the spirit for an hour every day. I didn't understand why, so I didn't do it right away. Then He told me to get a book by Bill Hamon called *Seventy Reasons for Speaking in Tongues*.

MAY 5

Once I got the book, I didn't start to read it right away and every time I'd see that book lying around, Holy Spirit would say, *"Read that book!"* So I finally obeyed. I wish I would have listened sooner. That book explained why we need to pray in the spirit. So, I set an alarm on my phone to go off at the same time every day. When that alarm went off, I'd set the timer to make sure I prayed for the full hour. I want you to know that praying for an hour is no magic time frame. This is just what the Lord told me to do because it was exactly what I needed to build up my spirit.

Soon, as I began to pray in the spirit every day for an hour all that junk: the fears, the nightmares, the turmoil inside of me was being flushed out. I grew stronger in my inner man. I began to receive greater understanding of the Word. I was able to hear from the Holy Spirit easier. It really became the game-changer for me. Yeah, it's weird at first—but it works!

Eventually, I didn't have to set an alarm to remember to pray. I began to pray all the time; washing the dishes, walking my dog, folding the laundry, or driving down the road. Its become a natural, normal way of life for me now. Holy Spirit has answered so many prayers since then, and even healings have taken place as a result of praying in tongues. I've seen relationships restored and just the ability to be more sensitive to the Holy Spirit has added adventure to my once "hit or miss" relationship with Him!

John G. Lake once said that praying in the spirit was the making of his ministry! If that was the key to the miraculous healings he did, we all should be encouraged to pray in the spirit every day, as often as we can. Holy Spirit knows precisely what you need. Even though you may not understand what the words you speak in the spirit mean, they just might be the catalyst to bring about a miracle in your life!

MAY 6

Effective Armor

Read: Ephesians 6:10-20

It's God's armor of protection. I believe it is more offensive than defensive. I'm sure most of us have seen pictures of a man wearing a Roman suit of armor with each of the parts labeled in accordance with the passages of Scripture in Ephesians.

Paul was making an analogy. He was giving us a visual image to identify each of the virtues we have in Christ and their benefits. We often stop short of the whole concept, and as a result we are unable to glean the important truths Paul intended for application. Let's take a closer look at verses 18-20:

> *"**Praying always** with all prayer and supplication **in the Spirit**, being watchful to this end with all perseverance and supplication for all the saints and for me, that utterance may be given to me, that I may open my mouth boldly to make known the mystery of the Gospel, for which I am an ambassador in chains; that in it I may speak boldly, as I ought to speak."* (Emphasis added)

We see from these verses that praying in the spirit is what makes the armor, i.e. the virtues of God, effective. If you've ever tried praying in your normal, native language for any length of time, you get tired pretty fast and run out of things to say. Praying in the spirit is the most effective way we can pray, especially for the most difficult situations.

We can also see that Paul asks the church at Ephesus to pray in the spirit for him because he was in jail for the sake of preaching the Gospel. He needed boldness to preach effectively under those circumstances. The people he witnessed to needed listening ears so they could receive. In order to take ground (souls) for the Kingdom, praying in the spirit can give us the right words to say

MAY 6

so that they can receive Christ. Holy Spirit gets stirred up on the inside giving us boldness to approach someone and lead them to salvation, a word of encouragement, or heal a disease—whatever is needed!

MAY 7

Revelation In The Spirit

Read: 1 Corinthians 14:18, Colossians 1:24-27

Paul had an exciting relationship with the Holy Spirit. It is interesting that even though he was not one of Jesus' original twelve disciples, he wrote about more revelation of Jesus than most of them; even though they spent over three years with Him every day. I believe that as a result of Paul praying in the spirit, he was the one God used to reveal the mystery that was hidden since the beginning of Creation. It was the greatest mystery of all time! God's plan from the very beginning, hidden until just the right time: **CHRIST IN YOU!**

No one knew this mystery. If they had, it says they never would have crucified the Lord of Glory. The Pharisees had had enough of one Jesus messing with their religion and control of the people. The demons had had enough of Jesus healing people and casting them out. Now there would be thousands and thousands of "Jesuses" with the same Holy Spirit, the same miraculous ability and authority, wreaking the same havoc on all their selfish, evil plans!

Paul had the revelation of Christ living in us! No longer is it a mystery hidden to be revealed at a later time. Christ has been revealed to all! Man, I don't know about you, but if praying in the spirit can reveal to us things we normally wouldn't be able to see, I'm going to be a prayin' fool! LOL!

MAY 8

Miracle In The Womb

Read: Psalm 139:1-18

*O*ver four years ago at the time of this writing, my daughter was due to give birth to her second son. During one of her last appointments, the doctor discovered that the baby was not in a head-down position for delivery. He informed her that either the baby would have to be turned or she would need a c-section.

Since it was a Friday late in the afternoon, the doctor told her that she would need to go to the hospital early Monday morning to have an ultra sound. If the baby wasn't head down, they would have to push hard on her stomach to try to turn him. It was going to hurt. If that didn't work, when she went into labor, they would have to do a c-section.

She called me on the phone in tears after her appointment while she sat in her car in the parking lot. I said, *"Oh no! You're not having a c-section! I had one of those and it was a horrible experience! And they will not hurt you by pushing on your stomach to turn the baby! The Lord's going to turn your baby!"* I told her that we should pray together in the spirit and listen for what Holy Spirit would tell us to do. It is absolutely wonderful to have a daughter who is born again and filled with the Holy Spirit! There's a special spiritual connection that goes deeper than a normal relationship between a mother and a daughter.

After we prayed in the spirit for a few minutes, I heard the verse of Scripture in Psalm 139:5, *"...You laid your hand upon me."* That was exactly what we needed! How appropriate, since Psalm 139 describes how God knows every intimate detail of our bodies as we are formed in our mother's womb! I shared this verse of Scripture with my daughter and I told her that we would decree together that

MAY 8

the Holy Spirit would lay His hand upon the baby, turn him in her womb, and he would stay in the proper position until birth.

As I spoke that verse and we prayed in the spirit, my daughter exclaimed, *"Mom! He's moving!"* At that moment, the baby turned in her womb! When we went to the hospital Monday morning to have the ultrasound to check his position, in five seconds the doctor said, *"Yep, he's head down!"* The baby remained in the right position until he was delivered! No c-section, no complications! Praise the Name of the Lord! And THAT is *all* the result of praying in the spirit!

MAY 9

Directed Prayer

Read: Proverbs 12:17-28

When we speak to someone, the words directed to them can have a healing effect or a hurting effect. It's always wise to choose our words with consideration and care to the person we're speaking to.

In the spirit realm, words are swords! They have the power of life and death. Isn't it remarkable that, when we first come to Christ, we immediately desire to change our vocabulary? Even better than this, is receiving your own special spiritual language to communicate with God. It's like a secret code just between you and Him!

Did you know that when you pray in tongues that you can direct your prayers toward a specific issue? You don't have to sit there babbling, hoping you're speaking the right words. If there is a situation in your body you need healing for, you can direct praying in the spirit toward that. All you have to do is think about that issue, start praying to Holy Spirit, being conscious that you are having a conversation with Him. Expect Him to answer back by keeping an ear out for His voice. He may show you a picture in your mind. He may give you a particular verse of Scripture. He may tell you to go do something. He may give you wisdom about the situation. Whatever it is, be sure to listen and obey. This way it will be easier for you to hear from Him again the next time.

Since our words are like swords, the ability to pray in the spirit is a fool-proof way to pray perfect prayers because it by-passes our natural mind. With accuracy and precision we have an effective way to dissolve problems in a much shorter time than praying other ways. Those long-standing issues can be quickly eliminated! You'll be amazed how the Holy Spirit steps in to help!

MAY 10

Knowing the Future

Read: Acts 27

*P*aul's life and the 276 men on the ship were certainly in big trouble! Yet, there Paul stood, as confident as he could be! He knew God told him that he was to stand trial before Caesar, so he was not afraid of dying in the storm. I can just see him shaking his head at all these experienced sailors and saying, *"I told you! You should have listened to me!"* God had spared the lives of all the men for Paul's sake!

Paul saw the angel when it came and stood beside him and spoke. I'm sure it was sent to encourage him, just like when the angels attended to Jesus. The angel told Paul what would happen to him in the near future. There have been a few times, after I've had several consistent days of praying in the spirit, that I know things before they happen. For example, in the morning while getting ready for church, sometimes I already know the message or things that are going to happen in the service before I ever get to church. It isn't anything earth shattering, but it is very cool! I experience the service before it happens and then relive it a few moments later, like déjà vu!

Since Paul prayed in the spirit a lot, and I've experienced many cool things by praying in the spirit, it's incredible how something so simple can do so much! Praying consistently in the spirit causes our spirit man to rise up and be in control. It makes us feel like nothing can stop us! It's like flowing with the Holy Spirit and thinking what He's thinking by knowing it in our heart! That's the language of the Spirit—knowing! The more we pray in the spirit, the more intimately we will know Him, and He will show us things to come!

MAY 11

When Strivings Cease

Read: John 2:13-17, Romans 12:9-13

In Christ Alone

In Christ alone my hope is found;
He is my light, my strength, my song;
This cornerstone, this solid ground,
Firm through the fiercest drought and storm.
What heights of love, what depths of peace,
*When fears are stilled , when **strivings cease!***
My comforter, my all in all—
Here in the love of Christ I stand.
    Words & Music by Keith & Kristyn Getty & Stuart Townend, 2002

*T*he musicians who composed this beautiful song testify that the lyrics "encapsulate the life, death, and resurrection of Christ." I only shared the first stanza of the song above. I want to focus on the line that says *"when strivings cease."*

Many Believers have a strong passion for Jesus. Jesus Himself was consumed with doing His Father's will and not His own. He said in John 4:34,

> *"My food is to do the will of Him who sent Me, and to finish His work."*

In our Scripture reading for today, it says in verse 17, *"Zeal for Your house consumes Me."* Have you ever asked yourself what the difference is between striving and having a zeal for the Lord? Striving has a connotation of human effort, trying to make something happen. Zeal is much the same as having an ardent pursuit for

MAY 11

something. How is striving and zeal different when it comes to the things of God?

I asked the Holy Spirit one day what the difference is and He said, *"Zeal has confidence."* Think about that for a minute. Striving has an element of doubt, almost like trying to convince God that He needs to do something He already promised He gave you. Zeal is confident that we already have it and He is working with us so we can see it and utilize His promise. Striving is usually partnered with fear and doubt, whereas zeal is bold and confident that it's already yours. Striving also zeros in on a particular problem, where zeal looks at the fullness of Christ's finished work made available.

I have experienced time and again, when I choose to embrace confidence and speak boldly—like stepping out on a limb—He is always there to back me up. The Lord helps me see the bigger picture more clearly. It cuts out the rabbit trail of emotions and thoughts that lead to nowhere but frustration and exhaustion. Striving takes quite a bit of effort to pull my mind out of a tangled mess and get my head on straight. It's not worth the wasted time and energy.

Approaching the Lord with zeal and confidence gives Him something to work with. Keeping yourself in faith and building yourself up through praying in the spirit is a huge help! So let's keep our spiritual fervor and throw off striving! It's a shortcut to keeping our relationship with the Lord red-hot and eliminating sheer exhaustion!

MAY 12

The Grass Is Greener

Read: John 14:27 (Mirror Bible)

*W*hen my children were young, I read them a book entitled *The Grass is Always Greener* by Jez Alborough. It is the story about a flock of sheep and a lamb named Thomas. Events developed as the entire flock kept looking at the other pastures surrounding them. They thought their shepherd was intentionally keeping them from enjoying the greener pastures. The entire flock escaped the pasture to explore another, seemingly greener, pasture nearby—except for Thomas. He stayed right where he was munching on grass while the rest of the sheep were like, *"So long, chump!"*

The rest of the flock pridefully trotted away, believing they knew better than their shepherd and Thomas. After they all scurried into the new pasture and began chomping on the grass, they scoured the landscape again. Another pasture looked greener than the one they had just moments earlier escaped to! Eventually, after scampering from one pasture to another, they ended up right back where they started! But Thomas never left! When the flock came barreling through the gate, Thomas looked at them like, *"What's wrong with you?"* while the rest of the sheep stopped in their tracks, their faces covered with blank stares.

Obviously, the moral of the story was that the grass isn't greener on the other side of the fence, and if someone is rebellious enough to leave where he is, hopefully, someday he'll find out that what he had was the best all along! One disgruntled sheep caused the whole flock to question their shepherd's provision for them—except for the little lamb, Thomas, which no one paid any attention to.

Comparison breeds mistrust in our relationship with God. Comparing ourselves to other people and what they have is dangerous because it feeds the insatiable flesh, if we give in to it. I

MAY 12

am emphasizing much needed caution when we compare our lives to others. Sometimes people try to live with one foot in the world and the other foot in the Kingdom. It just cannot work that way. They think that God is holding out on them. They become their own worst enemy, fighting against themselves. I've seen it way too many times where people refuse to give their lives fully to Christ and trust Him, and they are some of the most miserable people I've ever known. It's very sad to see. The wrestling inside of themselves and believing they are missing out on something in the world, or that God is withholding something, is nothing but a lie. Christ frees us from ourselves! That is true freedom! The grass is the greenest right where we are—in Him!

MAY 13

The New Man—Part 1

Read: Ephesians 4:20-24

One of the saddest things I've seen in the Body of Christ is a mixture of the world and God's Kingdom. We can see it everywhere. Many times there is little difference between the Church and the world. The Church has the same ills—sickness, lawsuits, promiscuity... you name it! None of us is infallible. We all need to "walk circumspectly, not as fools, but wise" as Paul says in Ephesians 5:15.

Paul tells us to cast off the old man and his former way of living. In other words, there should be an obvious change in the way we live now that we are in Christ. Paul tells us to *"be renewed in the spirit of your mind."* This means that our attitude should be different. If you were a depressed person before you came to Christ, depression was part of the old man who died. Now you are to see yourself in Christ! He was far from depressed! We take on His life and attitude and leave the old ways of the life we lived behind—forever! No revisiting! No more identifying with that old self! He is now our joy and our strength!

We have been re-created in the character and nature of our Father. Made in true righteousness and holiness; our lives should reflect these virtues! Each of us is responsible for our own attitude and conduct. We are commanded to come out and be separate from the word's system. When we come together as a whole, there will be greater impact and influence affecting those who do not know Christ. No longer will they see us as a bunch of hypocrites that don't practice what we preach.

Each of us has the responsibility to live as Christ, and continue to be renewed in our mind so we can live it—free of disease, division, judgmental attitudes, promiscuity, you name it! Whole in spirit, soul, and body!

MAY 14

The New Man—Part 2

Read: Colossians 3:8-17

*T*he Greek word *new* is referring to something having a different quality or nature than before. This is the new humanity created in Christ, which all Believers share individually and corporately. Paul is encouraging the Colossians to put on their new spiritual nature which is in union with Christ. It's a new kind of humanity! A different breed! Imagine if everyone put on Christ! What a wonderful world this would be! The corruption and decay we see now would all disappear!

We, as Believers, must hold ourselves to a higher standard than the rest of the world settles for. This standard has been set by Jesus. Remember Paul said that *"to live is Christ, and to die is gain."* In the context of the verses before and after, Paul is referring to his imprisonment because of preaching the Gospel. Let's read it the way Philippians 1:21 is expressed in *The Message Bible*:

> *"...everything happening to me in this jail only serves to make Christ more accurately known, regardless of whether I live or die. They didn't shut me up; they gave me a pulpit! Alive I'm Christ's Messenger; dead I'm his bounty. Life versus even more life! I can't lose."*

We know that Paul himself had to cast off everything he had gained as a Pharisee under the law so that he would find himself in the righteousness of Christ. The new nature we received through Christ has re-created us into people with an entirely new standard of living and a new nature that desires those things that are pure, just, and right—especially when it goes against the world's system. In the days ahead, I believe we are going to see the gap ever-widening between the true Church and the world. Will we value the character and fruit of the new man created in Christ to do good

MAY 14

works, or will we allow ourselves to be eroded little by little and compromise? If we stay in Christ, He will be magnified in our lives and in our death—if that is the cost we must pay to follow Him.

MAY 15

Protected & Provided

Read: Ezekiel 34:25-31

Did you ever think about the miracle it was for God to sustain the Israelites in the wilderness? Think about it! Fresh manna every day! They didn't have to plant gardens and grow their own food. Their clothes never wore out. How could that be? Did they give their hand-me-downs to others as they outgrew them, or did their clothes grow with them? Did their shoes grow with their feet?

We never read about any wild beasts attacking them and eating them for lunch—except when the snakes bit them because of their own stupidity. We never read about marauders going on a killing spree and plundering them. Nope! God protected them and provided for everything they needed for forty years! Talk about faithful!

What about us now? The Bible says we have a better covenant with better promises, right? It seemed so much easier when God just did it all. Would I have been among those who were fearful and complained all the time like the Israelites? Probably!

Right now we have it better than they did because we have the Holy Spirit living on the inside of us. God had to make up for a lot of the Israelites' foolishness back then, but we don't have any excuses now. He gave us His ability, character, and nature. Personally, I have never gone a day in my life without food or a roof over my head—no matter where I've been. I'm thankful for that!

The key for us now is learning how to cooperate with the Holy Spirit. We have a relationship with Father, Son, and Holy Spirit that people in the Old Testament only dreamed of having—God on the inside! If we don't have exactly what we need at the moment, He can show us how to receive it. It's a union and an exchange far beyond comparison. If we know that we have the benefits of protection and provision, we can trust Him to care for us. I encourage

MAY 15 ———

you to keep a journal of your own personal testimonies, like a book of remembrance. Whenever you get discouraged, open up your journal and recall His faithfulness!

MAY 16

It's Personal

Read: John 5:17-21

I think it is rather mind-boggling that Father God chooses each of us and makes it His own personal ambition to pursue a relationship with us. Sometimes I seem like the "Queen of Questions!" Not in the sense of questioning Him because I'm full of doubts, but more along the lines of inquiring help for something that needs to be done, or how to apply the truths in His Word to gain understanding. Quoting what Jesus described in the *Wuest Translation* of John 5:18:

> "He was saying that God was His privately owned, unique Father, a Father in a way in which no one else had Him for a Father, making Himself equal with the deity."

This is the reason the Pharisees were so hacked off at Jesus! To them, it was like He was comparing Himself to be equal with God. Truth is—He was! I wonder what it would look like if we, as His body, began to only say what the Father says and only did what we saw the Father do, like Jesus.

It's certainly taboo to discuss a personal, intimate relationship between a husband and his wife. That kind of *knowing* is hard to describe because no one else can know each other in the same way. It is also hard to describe the depths of our relationship with the Lord because it is unique and personal—Spirit to spirit. And this is the way it's supposed to be. I'm not saying that we should not share our relationship with the Lord with others, but there are some things that are personal and indescribable. He is jealous toward us!

Is it any wonder that, in the Old Testament, when the Israelites worshiped false gods, that God called it adultery? He was their own personal God in a way that no other god could ever be toward humanity. No other god could or ever would give a thought to

MAY 16

revealing himself personally and extending life, love, and healing to his children like our God has done for us. I wonder if any people who worship gods like Buddah, Baal, or Allah ever receive answers to their prayers. Do worshipping these gods ever fill their deepest longings like Christ does? I don't know anyone I can ask, but again—I'm the "Queen of Questions" and I'm just curious.

It's personal. I love that about Him! To know that He is inside of me right here feeling everything I feel, knowing and caring about my thoughts, and always being ready to help; wonder and awe fill my heart just thinking about Him! And if you long to know Him this way, just ask Him to reveal Himself to you and He will!

MAY 17

Bewitched?

Read: Galatians 3:1-5

Paul gives the church at Galatia some pretty harsh correction. With much passion, he wrote crucial instructions, which concerned the way they were going about their faith in Christ. False teachers (Judiazers) had infiltrated the church and began to pervert the true Gospel, which he had brought to them.

In the *Wuest Translation*, instead of using the word *foolish*, Galatians says *unreflecting*. It seems that he is saying, *"Didn't you stop and think for a minute that their teaching goes against everything I taught you?"* They were not able to discern the false teachings they heard from the Judiazers from the truth that Paul had laid for them as a foundation for their faith.

The word *bewitched* means *false representation* or *to malign someone by making false statements about them*. This is what the Judiazers had done regarding Christ. Why? Because they didn't know Him! But the Galatians did, and yet they allowed people they had no relationship with to tell them what their relationship with Jesus should be based upon (The law).

That leads me to question: *How many times have I taken someone else's word about God as the truth, instead of what I know in my sprit?* Or *How many times have I agreed with something based on a person's experience rather than Biblical truth?*

Look how culture has infiltrated the church and caused us to compromise truth. It's not always easy to zero in on religion and harmful false doctrines, especially since we may have heard man's interpretation of a particular Scripture and we skim over what the verses say in context. We need the Holy Spirit to give us "fresh eyes" when we read the Bible.

MAY 17

What about a doctor's report? Do I take a doctor's experience and knowledge over the many Scriptures that say I'm healed? Do I listen to church doctrines that say that healing, miracles, signs, and wonders all passed away with the early church?

It is important that we take responsibility for our own lives and doctrine (teaching/beliefs), as it says in 1 Timothy 4:16,

> *"Watch your life and doctrine closely. Persevere in them, because if you do, you will save both yourself and your hearers."* (NIV)

MAY 18

Oh The Body!

Read: John 6:53-58

"*Oh the Body of Jesus! Oh the Body of Jesus! Oh the Body of Jesus! He heals me from head to toe!*"

Have you ever thought of singing the song, *Oh the Blood of Jesus*, by replacing the word *Blood* with the word *Body*? It's been a habit in many churches to only focus on the Blood of Jesus washing away our sins and to forget about how He gave His Body to heal ours. No, I'm not minimizing the washing away of our sins at all. Of course where we spend eternity is important; but how fast would you like to get there?

Paul had a revelation of this when he addressed this problem in the 11th chapter of First Corinthians. Many of the Believers were dying prematurely because they were not recognizing Jesus' Body and giving it the same gravity and value as His Blood. Unfortunately, we're still doing the same thing today, and as a result, many Believers are dying before their time from sickness and disease or living with pain and suffering in their bodies.

It is interesting that the Pharisees condemned Jesus for claiming to have authority to freely forgive sins. They could have cared less that he exercised His ability to heal blind eyes or cleanse lepers— they were enraged only because of the day (the Sabbath) He chose to heal them! Today many Christians do the opposite— magnifying above everything else that He forgives our sins, and scoff at the idea of divine healing. That's why, for salvation, people are typically taught they must say "The Sinner's Prayer" to be saved. Again, we forget about the body—that Jesus sacrificed Himself for both parts—spirit and body. This is what makes us a living human being; a body with a spirit. He had to die for both parts or man would only be half-way redeemed!

MAY 18

Here we are in the church today magnifying His Blood and forgetting about the other half that is just as important. What good am I to anyone if I'm lying in bed consumed with health issues? Pay close attention to Jesus' words in John 6:57,

> *"As the living Father sent Me, and I live because of the Father, so He who feeds on Me will live because of Me."*

Jesus relied completely upon the life of the Father to keep His body alive and disease-free. As the Father lives inside Jesus, and Jesus lives in the Father; because Jesus lives inside us, we have His life and the life of the Father inside of us too! We also must rely on His power to give us health, life, and strength! *Oh the Body of Jesus!*

MAY 19

Far Reaching

Read: Psalm 103:3

*H*ave you ever wondered how the stripes Jesus took on His body for our healing could be as effective today as it was 2000 years ago? We know that 1 Peter 2:24 says, *"by whose stripes you **were** healed."* If we were healed 2000 years ago, how can this affect us now? Is this something we must receive and apply ourselves or do we already have healing?

I was thinking about these questions as I was reflecting on Psalm 103:2 which states: *"Who forgives all our iniquities, Who heals all our diseases."* We have been taught very well in the church that Jesus can forgive the worst of sinners—murderers, rapists, the worst of the worst; there is absolutely no sin that is too great that the Blood of Jesus could not pay for, forgive, and wash away, right? Yes! Say yes and you are correct.

Let's think about those of us who are born again. Has Jesus paid for and washed away *every* sin we have ever committed and has He already forgiven us for *every* sin that we will commit in the future? Yes! So, is it accurate to say that Jesus' Blood is so far reaching into our past, present, and future that His Blood has already been applied and paid for ***all*** of our sins? Yes!

Now let's think about the second part of verse two: *"Who heals **all** our diseases."* Jesus offered His Body in the place of ours for healing of disease 2000 years ago at the same time He shed His Blood for our sins. Is the power and authority of the stripes on His Body as affective as His Blood to forgive our sins? Yes! Is the sacrifice of His Body as far reaching into our future to have cured *every* disease before we ever suffer with it? Absolutely!

"Far as the curse is found..." as that old Christmas hymn *Joy to the World* proclaims. His Blood is far reaching into our future and has

MAY 19

already forgiven every sin, and His Body is far reaching into our future and has already healed every disease! Pretty cool, eh?

MAY 20

Works Witness

Read: John 5:30-36

Jesus said that he had a greater witness than that of John the Baptist. He also said, and I quote the *Wuest Translation* of verse 31,

> "As for Myself, I am not able to be doing even one thing by Myself...because I am not seeking the desire which is Mine but the desire of the One who sent Me."

Jesus emphatically stated that He could not do any works—the miracles of healing and multiplying food, etc.—without His Father's help. These works were very important because Jesus claimed that He came to show us the Father. In order to reveal the Father to us, He had to be able to think, talk, and act like the Father as a man full of the Holy Spirit.

Jesus pointed out that John was not the only witness that He was the Messiah. Jesus said He had a greater witness than that of a man—the Father's works. The miracles He did testified and pointed to the Father. He stated in verses 36-37 in the *Wuest*:

> "But, as for Myself, I have a witness greater than that of John, for the works which the Father has given Me in order that I might bring them to a final consummation, the works themselves which I am **constantly performing**, they are bearing witness concerning Me to the effect that the Father has sent Me on a mission." (Emphasis added)

I like the way the *Wuest* says **constantly performing**; which means He's still doing those works today. The only thing different is the location where He does the miracles from. Back then it was only from Him, today it is from us. Now the miracles point to Jesus and reveal Him, the Father, and the Holy Spirit. The works we do bear witness of Him and we should be constantly performing and testifying so we can display Jesus to others and set them free!

MAY 21

The Nod

Read: Matthew 4:1-11

*T*he devil's first temptation, I believe, was probably the most challenging. After fasting for forty days, His belly was growling from hunger. Of course, He could have turned stones into bread at any time during the fast if He wanted to, but He knew the importance of having power over His flesh.

Was the devil's second temptation a major deal for Jesus? Who would be like, *"Oh, hold me back! I just don't think I can keep myself from jumping off a building to see if I stub my toe or not!"* It reminds me of something my dad used to say to me when I was growing up, *"If someone tells you to jump off a bridge, are you going to do it?"*

If you look up the temptations in the book of Luke and compare them in the order they are listed in Matthew, the last two temptations are switched. Not that it matters, it's just a fun fact. The last temptation in Matthew is where it gets interesting.

I read somewhere that in the original Greek, Luke says something quite different than most translations. In Luke, where the devil tells Jesus that if He would bow down and worship Him, he would give Him all the kingdoms of the world. The original Greek says that the devil is not asking Jesus to bow down; just a nod of acknowledgement was all he wanted. Just a nod. Just a nod—that's it—and everything would have gone down the toilet from there!

In light of this perspective, we're challenged to give ourselves a heart check. What areas in your life have you simply given "the nod" in agreement with lies— especially where disease and pain are concerned? Symptoms that persist can wear us down and seem to become a part of us because of dealing with them every day. Sometimes it takes a lot of effort not to give in—to give the nod and just put up with pain. It can certainly be overwhelming when there

MAY 21 ———

are several serious issues going on at the same time. But don't do it! Don't give in! Don't give "the nod!" Keep a straight course and keep your head up! Be strong and courageous! Remember that the Holy Spirit is right there to help!

MAY 22

Teaching & Preaching

Read: Matthew 4:23-25

*T*hese verses give us a snapshot of Jesus' daily life. This was the way He revealed the Kingdom of God and demonstrated what it had to offer mankind. Jesus not only taught, but preached the Gospel of the Kingdom. He demonstrated the Kingdom's dominion over every disease by healing the multitudes.

What is the difference between teaching and preaching? In order to teach, we are bringing forth ideas and concepts, showing how to apply them to bring growth and maturity. It is giving specific instructions and the "how to's." Preaching is a proclamation of truths that demand a response.

The *Wuest Translation* defines preaching as, *"making a public proclamation as a herald with that formality, gravity, and authority as must be listened to and obeyed."* (Matthew 4:17) We have a tradition of *offering* salvation to people through alter calls and the sinner's prayer, however, Jesus wasn't making an offer; He was making a proclamation that demanded a response. Is there choice involved? Yes, but not as a suggestion. Christ's sacrifice brings every soul to the point of choosing or not choosing—there is no in-between.

What about where physical healing is concerned? Many ministers today are teaching how to heal the sick and how a Believer can receive healing for themselves. Yet, after all the teaching on the part of the minister and the learning on the part of the person in need, there comes a point where a decision must be made.

2 Timothy 3:7 states, *"always learning and never able to come to a knowledge of the truth."* (NKJV) There must come a point where a response must be made—where the rubber meets the road, so to speak. We all must come to this point, or we will end up circling around the same situation again and again. Truth has been

MAY 22

preached. Truth has been taught. It's time to settle it once and for all. No more back and forth. No more questioning.

It can be quite a challenge to get to this place. I believe the more we as the body of Christ stay immovable against sickness and disease together, the greater results we will experience for ourselves, our loved ones, and when we minister to others. The Bible has laid out the truths that are very clear. We must separate these truths from our experiences in the past and not view the truth through the lens of our experiences. Those that have split the Gospel in half and removed physical healing from the atonement will have a greater challenge receiving healing. If we enforce the full Gospel with formality, gravity, and authority that must be obeyed; healing will become normal for the Body of Christ. We will stand out from the rest of the world. This will create a curiosity that draws people to experience the whole Gospel—freedom in spirit, soul, and body.

MAY 23

Climate Control

Read: Titus 1:5-16, Proverbs 25:28

If you live in a temperate climate zone like I do, you experience extremes in weather. In winter, it can be blustery and cold with below freezing temperatures. In the summer, it can be smoldering hot with stifling humidity. I'm certainly thankful for heating and air conditioning to escape these extremes.

When I lived in Kenya, their weather was nearly perfect. They have a wet and dry season, but they do not experience the four seasons like we do here in the U.S.A. The temperatures are usually around the 70s or 80's year round, depending on what part of the country you live. They were able to open the windows and doors of their homes every day. The sun rose and set at almost the same time every day. They didn't need heating or air conditioning to control the climate of their homes. Not too hot, not too cold!

If it wasn't for the mosquitoes, it would have been perfect! If we didn't close the windows at the same time every day when the sun started to set, one of those buggers would get into our bedroom and sing a song in our ear all night or suck our blood for a midnight snack! Forget about turning on the lights to smash its guts with a vengeance, cuz the moment we'd turn on the lights, it would hide.

We have an "indoor climate" within each of ourselves that we must maintain; much like setting the thermostat in our homes to regulate the temperature. We don't open our windows and let the heating or air conditioning escape. Sadly, this is where many Believers struggle the most—conquering their own flesh/thought life. Our spirits need to be kept in the place of ruling over our minds and our bodies. Sometimes, there's a pesky mosquito that comes singing the same mantra in our ear in the form of a bad thought. I wish it was as easy as smashing it with a rolled up newspaper, but that's

MAY 23

usually not the case. That is where Holy Spirit as our Helper comes in, especially when it comes to physical healing.

Setting the "spiritual thermostat" of our environment means cooperating, developing trust, and obeying the leading of the Holy Spirit. We must also submit our emotions and feelings under the leadership and authority of the Holy Spirit. Our thought-life must be subject to Him consistently and habitually, much like sleeping with a mosquito net tucked around our mattress to protect us from pesky mosquitoes so we can sleep in peace. This usually only becomes effective with regular practice and persistence. We can become our own worst enemy if we don't control our thoughts.

Once our thought life is consistently submitted and our actions and words align with Holy Spirit, the body can then follow. In the same way we submit our thoughts to the Word and Holy Spirit, we can submit our physical bodies to the authority of the Holy Spirit and Christ's finished work.

The transition in our thinking must go from, *"I'm waiting for God to heal me,"* to, *"Body, you are healed! Thank you Jesus!"* and stick with this truth no matter what the lying symptoms say.

I used to get bad headaches in my forehead from sinus pressure. If it went on for days, my stomach would get upset and dizziness and pain would keep me bound to the sofa. I'd reach for my natural remedies for some relief, but sooner or later the sinus pain would come back. Finally, I'd had enough of this cycle and when a headache would start, I'd say, *"No, you can't have a headache or sinus pressure, because you are healed!"* I decided to enforce this truth instead of reaching for any remedies, which were temporary at best. A few times the headaches would start and the pressure tried to return, but I resisted them. Now, I can honestly say that I don't have build up, pressure, or headaches from sinuses anymore! Thank you Jesus!

MAY 23

Enforcing the truth that I am healed because of Christ in me, therefore, I cannot have pain, has helped me build upon this healing for other long-term annoyances that don't belong in my body! I'm healed! Therefore I CANNOT have_____. You fill in the blank. Stick with that, and watch it disappear!

MAY 24

Take This Cup

Read: Matthew 20:20-28, Luke 22:42-44

I had been taught in the past that these Scriptures in Matthew spoke specifically of the physical suffering that Christ paid for our lives; that He was saying in essence, *"Are you willing to undergo a baptism of suffering as I am going to suffer?"* Meaning that our lives from now on will be nothing but suffering in whatever form that means: sickness, death, accidents, tragedy...etc. and somehow this would bring glory to God. Fortunately, none of that teaching is true! But I'd like to take a look at these verses in a different way, applying the New Covenant.

When Jesus was in the garden praying that this cup would pass, He had previously enacted the New Covenant in the upper room with His disciples. He drank from the cup and ate the bread as He instructed His disciples to partake with Him. What were they joining themselves to? A Covenant that required denying themselves and their own lives and living every day as a result of the impact this New Covenant brought. It meant that all other Covenants were null and void. All other commitments were secondary to this New Covenant. The suffering is the persecution from other people—not sickness and tragedy. But anyway, enough about that!

When James and John's mother requested that her sons sit at Jesus' right hand, He wasn't offended like, *"Oh you selfish woman! Why should I choose your sons over anyone else?"* He basically said, *"Awesome! They want to be great in the Kingdom? Here's how: become a servant like Me."*

When He said, *"Can you drink the cup that I am about to drink."* He was referring to the New Covenant, which would require complete devotion. Jesus was fully committed to finishing the assignment for which the Father had sent Him. This covenant kept Him in His

MAY 24

greatest moment of trial, while He wrestled in the garden sweating His Blood in aguish of soul. He was asking the disciples to keep their commitment by sharing in the New Covenant with the same intensity in which He was committed.

When He said, *"Can you be baptized with the baptism that I am baptized with?"* What baptism did Jesus have? The baptism of the Holy Spirit! Basically, He was saying, *"Can you stick with Me till the end? I will send Holy Spirit to help you."*

If the disciples never followed through in their part of the New Covenant, you and I would not be able to share in it today. They had to be just as committed as Jesus was. Yes, every one of them was martyred or persecuted harshly. They stood strong to the end, committed to the Covenant they entered into on the night Jesus broke the bread and offered the cup—the Cup of the New Covenant.

When you and I take the cup and the bread of the New Covenant, the requirement is still the same: everything and everyone else in secondary. The exchange is this: His life for our life. We get what He has, He got what we have. Does persecution come along with this trade off? Yep. But that's nothing compared to sharing in freedom from disease, sin, and death. It's a cup of covenant and commitment; a cup for eternity.

MAY 25

Delivered From Authority By Authority

Read: Colossians 1:9-14

"*Who delivered us out of the tyrannical rule of the darkness and transferred us into the kingdom of the Son of His love, in whom we are having our liberation, procured by the payment of ransom, the putting away of our sins; who is a derived reproduction and manifestation of absolute deity...*" (Colossians 1:13-15, *Wuest Translation*)

A person's authority cannot be overruled unless someone else has a higher authority than theirs. That means that that person no longer has authority—it's been nullified. Jesus said that **all** authority, in heaven, on earth, and under the earth, was given to Him by His Father (Philippians 2:9-11).

We know that Jesus said that He gave us the keys to His Kingdom. Keys represent authority. He also told us to *"Go"* in His name. He gave us His authority to act in His place; to do what He would do if He were here on the earth. It's still His authority, but we get to use it as our own; it is included in our inheritance because we are in Him.

However, many people believe that they may give the enemy authority, or give the enemy an "open door" to wreak havoc in their lives. They believe that this "open door" is the result of some unknown sin they did somewhere along the way that let sickness in their body, or it is the consequences of some other bad decision. Scripture says that one can allow certain circumstances from bad choices that they made. This would be as a result of sowing and reaping the consequences, not as a result of God lifting His protection off of them or allowing the enemy to teach them a lesson. God just doesn't operate that way. The Bible says,

MAY 25

"In Him is no darkness at all..." (1 John 1:5)

We cannot give the enemy any authority because it isn't ours to give away. All authority belongs to Jesus. The enemy was completely stripped of whatever authority he had by Christ's sacrifice. Whatever disease, pain, or situation you are facing, you have authority over it. You can be confident of that, because the Bible says it's so.

That does not mean that you need to go around yelling at the devil, *"I rebuke you! I rebuke you!"* Just ask Holy Spirit what to do, or not to do. Pray in the spirit and the answer will come. Holy Spirit will give you the courage to move forward. You do have the authority over whatever situation is going on in your life; Jesus gave it to you to establish His Kingdom on the earth. If something in your life doesn't look like it would in heaven, then you have jurisdiction. Use it! You were delivered from the enemy's authority once and for all by Jesus' authority!

MAY 26

God, Are You Crazy?

Read: Matthew 10:16-40

I have a very old book, written in 1903, entitled *The Holy Spirit and the Human Mind*, written by Ashley S. Johnson. On page 167, the author refers to Acts 1:4-5, where Jesus says that the disciples would receive power from the Holy Spirit to be His witnesses. Johnson says:

> *"From one standpoint it appears that the whole thing was placed, without reserve or equivocation, in the hands of the apostles. From the other standpoint it appears that the whole thing was placed, without reserve, in the hands of the Holy Spirit. Where is the truth? In both..."*

In John chapter 6, when Jesus fed the 5000, that same multitude tried to follow Him. Jesus eventually gave them an ultimatum: *"Eat My flesh and drink My blood, or else you can have no part in Me."* Well, forget that! They thought His expectation was ludicrous; disgusted, they walked away. He turned to His disciples and questioned, *"Well, do you want to leave too?"* They realized that they had nowhere else to go because Jesus is everything they needed. When it came time for Jesus' death, burial, and resurrection, only 120 remained.

If you do the math, there were a minimum of 5000 people following Jesus from place to place as He set the oppressed free, and only 120 remaining devoted to Him at His ascension—that was a mere 2.4% commitment rate! Pretty bad odds for setting up His Kingdom on earth! I often wonder if God is crazy for putting His Kingdom in the hands of men. Think about it! The success of the Kingdom requires 100% commitment from you and me! Believers can be so fickle; they don't follow through with their promises. God must have a lot more confidence in us than we have in ourselves! He knows that Holy Spirit is our Helper to heal, deliver, and save. The truth is that

MAY 26 ———

it does take both the Holy Spirit and us together to bring God's Kingdom here on the earth. He needs us and we need Him! It's a perfect partnership!

MAY 27

Watershed Realities

Read: Colossians 1:21-23

A watershed is *a crucial dividing point, line, or factor.* It is a place that we come to where a decision must be made and there is no turning back. When we come into the Kingdom of God by choice, it brings us to a crossroad where there is no going back to our old way of living. Many people do not understand the gravity of what being "born again" means. We've been relegated to a "someday when we get to heaven" possibility, but until then, life just stinks. It's God's sovereign will for you to suffer so that you can see your need for Him and He can teach you a few things through your suffering along the way. That's the gospel most of us have heard. This is why when someone makes a commitment for Christ, and then when things go wrong, as they do many times in life, people fall away.

There is a reality in life we all have to face: Where we will spend eternity and what happens until we get there? How much of a choice do I have in the matter or is it all up to God's sovereignty and fate? The decision of whether or not to live for Christ is a decision we all must make, and it cannot be based on or influenced by anyone else. No excuses. This is a watershed reality. People don't like the fact that they play a part in what happens in their lives after salvation. They'd rather chalk it all up to everything being God's sovereign will—in other words, it's all His fault.

When it comes to physical healing, we are faced with another watershed reality: a choice must be made. We've been taught that sickness is God's way of teaching us something. False! The Holy Spirit is our teacher, not disease. We've been taught that sometimes God heals and sometimes He doesn't. False! The Bible says that we are already healed and that Jesus healed everyone who came to Him—no exceptions. But what about so and so? They believed

MAY 27

God would heal them and they died! So if it's God's will to heal every person, why don't we see them healed? Is it God's will for every person to be born again? Yes! Is everyone born again? No. No one knows why everyone isn't healed; but the more I get to know the Lord personally, I see a deeper reality of His heart than I ever understood before. He truly does want everyone born again *and healed*. Why else would He have paid for it with such a high price? I don't give someone a gift and expect them to shove it under their bed and forget about it. I consider what might be a blessing to them and then I expect them to use it!

For me, I know that I cannot afford to allow my experiences to alter the truth written in the Bible. If I'm going to be effective at praying for other people to be healed, I cannot allow the times that people didn't experience healing to stop me from praying for the next person. I choose to believe whole-heartedly that they will experience their healing. The Bible says that they shall recover.

And there it is—choice. Choice is that watershed reality; the crossroad we come to time and again when things don't look like they should. Every opportunity provides itself the choice to quit or to keep going with God. Sometimes life throws one punch after another until, by the time you stand up and gain your wits about you, another punch comes and knocks you down. We've all been there at one time or another, like the words on the Morton® salt container: *"When it rains, it pours."*

So, what do I do when healing evades me, or a loved one goes astray? What do I do when I've got bills up to my eye balls and no job in sight? I find myself like the disciples, after Jesus tells His multitude of followers that they have to eat His flesh and drink His Blood or they can have no part in Him. The multitudes left because they wanted a free meal ticket. What He asked of them was too much in return. Jesus then asks His disciples, *"What about you? Are*

MAY 27

you going to leave too?" And Peter responds, *"Where are we going to go? You have the Words of Life!"*

They had ample opportunity to leave at any time. Multitudes followed Jesus everywhere He went. But where were they during His crucifixion? Where were they during His resurrection? Where were they on the day of Pentecost? Jesus' true followers numbered only 120. They all had a choice, and they all chose. I'm choosing to stick with Jesus. I made my decision almost three decades ago, and I don't plan on turning back now. He *is* my watershed reality.

MAY 28

The Reward

Read: Isaiah 52:13-15

The Moravians were a group of Believers that lived together in Hernhutt, Germany, during the early 1600s-1700s. In the beginning, there was much division in their relationships with each other. They decided to set themselves in prayer. The quarreling began to dissipate, and out of their prayer developed a deep love and devotion for Christ and for one another. Out of their devotion for each other and the love they experienced in Christ, a zeal for the rest of the world burned in their souls. Many of them left their family and their country, sent as missionaries to unknown regions of the world.

Two men in their early 20s, David Nitcshmann and Johann Leonard Dober, learned of an island in the West Indies where about 3000 Africans were sold to an atheist slave owner to work in the sugar cane fields. These slaves would live and die, never having the opportunity to know Christ. These two men, deeply moved by the plight of the slaves, bravely pledged their lives to Christ. They sold themselves into slavery to the godless slave owner so they could preach the Gospel of salvation to the slaves on the island. As the men got on the ship, their families and friends waved good-bye weeping, knowing they may never see them again.

As the distance between the edge of the shore on which their families stood and the ship grew wider, the two men linked arms as one of them lifted up his fist to heaven and cried, *"May the Lamb that was slain receive the reward of His suffering!"* This statement became the rally cry of the Moravians and fueled their passion further to send missionaries around the world!

Is there any risk too great, or price too high to pay for the sake of preaching the Gospel? As long as we play it safe, the church will

MAY 28

continue to remain soft and barely effective. As the Moravians pledged their lives and reputation for the sake of following Christ, we too must value the privilege to preach the Gospel, pledging our lives, families, and fortunes. It is only with this attitude and fortitude that others can see the value of Christ's sacrifice for themselves and, in turn, model a true demonstration of the salvation, healing, and freedom that was freely given to them. Let the declaration of the Moravians be echoed throughout the church once again: *"May the Lamb who was slain receive the reward of His suffering!"*

MAY 29

Kingdom Seeds

Read: Mark 4:26-32

When my children were young I had homeschooled all of them. During science class we learned about how seeds germinate. I always found it fascinating how a tiny seed could grow into a huge tree. We learned that, when the dirt received the seed, it began to vibrate, although you couldn't see it happen. It's like the ground got excited it was receiving life!

It's bewildering that, with all of the technology and knowledge we have today, no one really understands how life transforms from a dormant seed into a mighty tree. Yes, we know that the right conditions must be met like, water, temperature, and air. Something wondrous happens when new life sprouts from the ground, and that we had a hand in it just by planting a seed.

The Bible says that the Kingdom of God is like a seed. Under the right conditions, the Kingdom was birthed and continues to grow. How? Just like the seed of a plant germinates with the help of the right elements, the Kingdom of God grows when it is preached, taught, and demonstrated.

Every time a person receives Christ, the Kingdom advances. Every time a person is healed, the Kingdom advances. Every time the Gospel is preached the Kingdom advances. It has something to do with the words we speak, or don't speak for that matter. Something wondrous takes place and new life is born! There is energy and excitement when a person is born again, much like when dirt receives a seed!

No one understands how this happens, this new life; this new birth. But all of heaven rejoices! So preach! Teach! Heal the sick! Deliver the captives! By the words you speak, you cause the Kingdom to grow!

MAY 30

Blood Speaks

Read: Genesis 4:3-12, Hebrews 11:4, 12:22-24

It astounds me how, immediately after Adam and Eve fell, the first sin committed by man was murder! You'd think that it would have taken quite a few generations for the effects of the Fall to be evident. But murder? That's pretty extreme! Cain murdered his own flesh and blood! It's still a hard fact to comprehend. We read how he wrestled in his heart and came to the place of extreme envy, which drove him to such anger that he had premeditated to kill his own brother. God even warned him and presented him with a choice:

> "So the Lord said to Cain, 'Why are you angry? And why has your countenance fallen? If you do well, will you not be accepted? And if you do not do well, sin lies at your door. And its desire is for you, **but you should rule over it**.'" (Genesis 4:6-7, Emphasis added)

Even though Cain did not have the help of the Holy Spirit inside of him like we do today, God still expected him to get a grip on his emotions. Cain chose not to, and he let his emotions fester out of control, blinding him with rage to commit the murder of his brother with his own two hands. The Bible says that Abel's blood cried out from the ground for vengeance! It's an eerie thought that Abel's blood had a voice—a voice that God heard crying out to Him. God was compelled to answer with justice. Why? Because Abel's sacrifices to God were righteous and Cain's were not. Could it be that Abel's blood was encoded with the heart of righteousness he possessed, that it shouted a message against injustice?

Abel's blood still speaks today, as recorded in the Bible, of both righteousness and judgment. Yet, we are told that Christ's blood speaks a better word than that of Abel's. Why? The voice of mankind's

MAY 30

blood cried out for justice against the tyrannical rule of slavery to sin and disease; Christ's blood answered with judgment on iniquity and all of its affects, ministering righteousness in its place.

The righteousness of Christ is the only kind powerful enough to satisfy the wrath man brought upon himself as a result of the Fall. Christ's blood is still moist on the mercy seat in heaven (Hebrews 9:11-15). It has never lost its effectiveness against sin's oppression. It will NEVER lose its power—as the old song says—it reaches to the highest mountains and flows to the lowest valleys! Oh the blood that gives me strength from day to day—it will NEVER lose its power!

MAY 31

The Incredibles

Read: 1 Peter 1:13-2:3

*H*ave you seen the movie *The Incredibles*? It is an animated film from 2004 about Mr. Incredible, Elastagirl, and their three children who possess superhero powers. Each member of the family is a thrill-seeker, showing off their unusual crime-fighting abilities. As the plot unfolds, they are perceived as more of a disaster than a helping-hand. Ungrateful government officials blame the family for wreaking havoc, even though they had the best of intentions to save mankind from evil dictators scheming to take over the world. They are ordered by law to suppress their supernatural capabilities, join civilian life, and just be "normal" like everyone else. The mother is reduced to the role of June Cleaver, while the father begrudgingly punches the 9 to 5 daily grind—but its killing him inside!

My favorite scene is when the father comes home from work so frustrated from the pressure of conforming to an average life, that he grabs his car, lifting it overhead, intending to smash it to pieces! He glances left and right to see if anyone is watching, catching a neighborhood boy staring with bulging eyes and a gaping mouth. He smirks with a chuckle and lowers the car down gently in the driveway. Even though he's got what the world considers "The American Dream"—the family, the house, the white picket fence, he is the most miserable man on the planet! He hates his job with a passion and he feels himself dying inside! Hopeless and disgusted; he is forced to suppress his true identity as a superhero and live a life of mediocrity.

Knowing he was born for more than the "average Joe" life, desperately seeking to save his sanity, he sneaks out with his best friend, Frozone, lying to their wives under the guise of a weekly night out at the local bowling alley. Together, they find crimes being

MAY 31

committed and swoop in to save the unsuspecting victims. These secret outings are the only way the father can keep from losing his mind and hold on to his true identity of a superhero.

Can you identify with Mr. Incredible in this movie? Did you ever look at yourself as a superhero with superpowers commissioned to deliver the world from corruption? As a son of God, this is exactly who you are! Do you know that you have been born again for more than an average life? There is a voice on the inside reminding you that you are here for a purpose! The little things you have accomplished this far may fail compared to what you dream of doing for the Kingdom in your future. Will you settle for less and look back on your life some day with regret?

May this devotion be the springboard to launch you in the right direction! No more excuses! Life is too precious and too short to live with remorse because of not living your dreams! Will you allow the "paralysis by analysis" or the discouragement of others to keep you "small" in your own eyes? What abilities do you possess that the Lord has placed inside you, but have been left dormant? God created you for an *incredible* life, equipped with His supernatural power to heal the sick, raise the dead, and set the oppressed free! Merely praying about your future can be an excuse for inactivity. Start putting feet to your dreams. Don't let life pass you by. Faith often means stepping out on nothing—and finding something there!

JUNE 1

DNA

Read: 2 Peter 1:2-4

Archaeologist Ron Wyatt discovered the Ark of the Covenant underneath Jesus' crucifixion site. He discovered that the blood of Jesus had spilled through the cracks in the ground unto the mercy seat below. The scientist, Richard Rives, performed the analysis on Jesus' 2000 year old dried blood—a procedure which can only be performed on *living* blood!

A genetic analysis revealed that Jesus' blood contained 23 chromosomes from His mother Mary, the same as all normal human blood—but only 1 chromosome from the Father! All normal humans receive 23 chromosomes from the mother and 23 chromosomes from the father, thus proving that Jesus' Father is God Himself!

We have been given Jesus' DNA through a spiritual blood transfusion when we are born again. We receive the Divine Nature of Christ! When He walked this earth He was never sick. We have His divine nature through the Holy Spirit living inside us, giving life to all of our flesh. Jesus knew that the Father was in Him and because of this relationship, He was able to live free of every evil in this world—it could not touch Him!

I remember what the Lord told me when I was very sick. He said, *"I am healing you from the inside out."* I eventually understood that He meant He was living inside me, and as a result, I was receiving a constant stream of life flowing into my flesh, making me whole.

Every generational curse was broken the moment you were born again. The earthly family you were physically born into has no effect on your genetics any longer! Now your lineage goes back one generation—to God the Father Himself! Most mainstream churches don't teach this. Maybe the topic of generational curses sells a lot of books and keeps members of the congregation dependent on

JUNE 1 ———

their pastors—I don't know. But Scripture clearly shows us that Jesus became the curse for us in Galatians 3:13. We've got the life and blood of Jesus Himself flowing in our veins! What started as a spiritual rebirth became a physical reality in our body, keeping us healthy. His Word becomes flesh! We originated from our Heavenly Father, born from above with His Divine Nature, character, and life—His DNA—the <u>D</u>ivine <u>N</u>ature of the <u>A</u>lmighty!

JUNE 2

Faith Killer

Read: Mark 5:21-24, 35-43

The most effective faith killer is living by emotions, while thoughts are the fuel that keep them running. Before we find ourselves in a situation where we are in over our head, it is of utmost importance to govern what we give our attention to. When bad news strikes, our first reaction can set the tone for how we allow the news to make or break us. This is why it is paramount that we develop habits for practicing self-control when we are not facing a crisis. God never intended for anyone to live in a state of anxiety or panic attacks.

Let's peer into the scene where Jairus pleads for Jesus to come and heal his daughter. Jairus runs out of his house to track Jesus down; time is not on his side, the situation—critical. In the midst of a tumultuous multitude, he desperately pushes himself through the mob to come face to face with Jesus. He finally stands eye to eye with the Master, only to be interrupted by the woman with the issue of blood. Meanwhile, his precious daughter dies.

The bearers of bad news frequently appear in the middle of chaotic moments, don't they? They tell him, *"Forget it, it's too late. Your daughter is already dead."* Jesus refocuses His attention from the woman back on Jairus and affirms him, *"Don't be afraid, only believe."*

This is a perfect set up! Right in the midst of confusion, doubt and fear, Jesus looks into Jairus' eyes and says, *"Don't be afraid! Only believe."* How do you do that when your worst fears have come upon you? By applying this right now—everyday! Don't wait for a life and death situation to take you off guard! Faith automatically comes when we read or hear God's Word. It's what we choose to do with what we hear that makes it effective. What value do I place on God's solutions? Do I look at the Word as a source of absolute truth

JUNE 2

regardless of my experiences? This was one hard lesson I had to learn for myself. If I hadn't made the decision to intentionally push thoughts and emotions aside and replace them with Scripture, I'm not sure that I would have recovered as soon as I did when I was fighting for my life.

Many times the help of man is useless. We can find ourselves with nowhere else to turn but to Jesus. No one else can relate to our pain. Like Jairus, Jesus is our only hope. We must reject all other voices, even our own. If we don't put value on Scripture and confidence in the Holy Spirit's help, we can find ourselves swimming upstream against a strong current.

When my dad was diagnosed with cancer, at one point, he had been healed; cancer-free in his entire body—I believe as a result of taking authority over it in Jesus' Name! A few months later he began having seizures and they found several tumors in his brain. By then, he had fought for two long years and he was ready to give in. His physician being the bearer of bad news, told him he only had a short time to live. My first thought was, *"Where's this doctor so I can give him a piece of my mind! Who does he think he is? He's not God! He doesn't have the right to tell someone how long he will live!"* When I told my dad this, he replied, *"Well, he's the doctor! He's the one who went to school."* I responded, *"He's not God, he's just a man, education or not! You don't have to listen to him and he has no right to tell you how long you can live. If God can make you cancer-free in your body, He can make you cancer-free in your head too!"* Unfortunately, my dad didn't understand what I was trying to say. He believed the words of the doctor and shortly afterward, passed into the arms of Jesus

I cannot emphasize enough how important it is to avoid living by the ups and downs of our emotions fueled by what other people say, no matter how educated they may be. Emotions aren't real, they are just feelings fed by thoughts and opinions. When we act on

JUNE 2

those emotions by the choices we make—that's where the trouble begins and fear can try to take over. Take a moment and separate yourself from your emotions. Refocus your attention on the Holy Spirit. Get a grip on yourself and take a deep breath. Recognize that Holy Spirit is right there inside of you and ready to help. Draw from His strength. Pray in the spirit and ask Him what to do, then listen and obey. As Jesus said to Jairus, *"Don't be afraid, only believe."*

JUNE 3

Pursue, Overtake, Recover ALL

Read: 1 Samuel 30

*I*n 2017, I was fighting for my life against Lyme disease. It was a time where I seemed to continually face death day after day. To make matters worse, I was alone much of the time. My husband worked in New York, four hours away, and only came home on the weekends. My sons worked the nightshift, so they had to sleep most of the day and work all night. The medicines that doctors had prescribed were making me worse, and I didn't know what was going on in my body. I couldn't eat, I couldn't sleep, and my mind was in constant torment. I couldn't walk without crutches because my knee was hot and swollen, I had to lay flat on my back with a pillow under my knee because I couldn't straighten my leg completely.

One week, my husband decided to take me with him to New York for the first time so he could keep a better eye on me. The drive there was nothing but agony and my body racked with pain over every bump in the road. Could anything get worse? Well, it did...

My son was home by himself getting ready for work. He had purchased and old gun from a coworker that didn't have a safety switch. He went out in the woods with his gun, checking on some suspicious critter activity. When he jumped over a ravine, the gun became unsnapped from the holster, flew out, hit a rock, and shot him. The bullet passed through one part of his body and lodged in his arm. Alone in the woods, several yards from the house, he had to keep himself from going into shock as blood spilled out from three different holes in his body. He somehow got himself back to the house and called 911. The ambulance and police came and took him to the hospital.

I received a call on my cell phone from the policeman, but thankfully, my husband was the one who answered it. I admit that upon hearing this news I completely lost it! Could anything else go

JUNE 3

wrong? Here we were four hours away, not knowing whether our son would live or die. Oh, he said he was fine when we talked to him on the phone, and the police said he would be fine, but were they just saying that to keep us from worrying? We didn't know the full extent of the damage from the bullet where he was shot. Four hours seemed like an eternity to get to the hospital back home in PA. I cried uncontrollably as we packed up and threw our belongings in the truck to bear the pain in my body once again on the drive back home to the hospital.

BUT GOD...

A week or so prior to going to New York, while I was alone in prayer, I asked the Lord for a verse of Scripture as His promise that He would help me get through this illness and assure me that I would live and not die. He gave me 1 Samuel 30, where David and his army returned to Ziklag to find their wives and children had been kidnapped by the fierce Amalekites. Their city was burned and there was nothing left. When David and his men saw the desolation of the city and that their wives and children had been kidnapped, they cried until they had no more tears to cry. They began to turn on David and blame him for their troubles. *"If we weren't out fighting with you, we could have been here to protect our families!"*

But David, wiping away his own tears of grief, *"strengthened himself in the Lord his God."* He inquired of the Lord what to do. *"Shall I pursue this fierce army, and if I do, will I overcome them?"* And the Lord answered and said, *"Pursue, for you shall surely overtake them and **without fail recover all**."* In verse 18-19 it says,

> *"So, David recovered **all** that the Amalekites had carried away, and David rescued his two wives. And nothing of theirs was lacking, either small or great, sons or daughters, spoil or anything which they had taken from them; **David recovered all**."* (Emphasis added)

JUNE 3 ———

I told no one about this promise of Scripture the Lord had given to me. I kept it in my heart. Right after my husband and I received the call from the police about our son being shot, we grabbed our belongings and my husband threw them into the truck. On my way limping from our apartment for the endless drive to the hospital, deliriously blinded by tears, at that exact moment I received a text on my phone on What's App. It was a message from a dear friend in Kenya, Africa who knew nothing of the situation about my son, stating:

"Dear Sister Michele,

From 1 Samuel 30 we see king David in a desperate situation and didn't know what to do. Ziklag was burnt down and his family taken. The people with him just wanted to stone him. He felt alone and confused. THEN HE DREW SOME STRENGTH FROM INSIDE OF HIM. He encouraged himself in the Lord. Later the idea of PURSUING, OVERTAKING and RECOVERING ALL came up. We pray for you that some strength may rise up from within you, even as we pray. Jesus is still Lord, Healer, and Deliverer."

Those words stung my soul with shock and amazement! That was GOD! He was letting me know He was right there with me; that I would overcome Lyme disease and my son would be alright! If that wasn't amazing enough, this event happened on a Wednesday afternoon and my son was back to work by Monday! Doctors could not remove the bullet from his upper arm because it would cause more damage to remove it then leave it in his arm. The other place the bullet had passed through had missed a vital organ by millimeters!

Although this was a horrifying event during one of the worst times in my life, God had been faithful—He had kept His promise: **"Pursue, for you shall surely overtake them and without fail recover all."**

JUNE 4

Never Tired

Read: Psalm 121

"I will lift up mine eyes unto the hills—from whence cometh my help. My help cometh from the Lord, which made heaven and earth...Behold He that keepeth Israel shall neither slumber nor sleep." (KJV)

This was my grandmother's favorite chapter in the Bible. She was a godly woman who faithfully took care of my grandfather while he suffered from MS most of his life. He was diagnosed with the disease when he was about thirty-six years old and she cared for him for over forty years until he went home to be with the Lord. She cooked the best meals and baked cookies of every kind you could imagine for all her neighbors at Christmastime. She never drove a car. When my family and I lived in Texas, she wrote letters to me about what she did during the day: walked to the post office, walked to the store, hung out the laundry, cooked dinner. She was a remarkable Proverbs 31 woman whose arms were strong for her tasks. Her letters made me tired just reading them, and I was in my 20s at the time with 3 small children!

Looking back, I remember fondly the things she did for my brother and me when we were young. When it was our birthday or Christmas, she bought us exactly what we asked for. She is an example to me how the Lord never tires of us. He doesn't roll His eyes and ignore us when we ask Him for something. He won't shrug us off when we repeat our problems for the hundredth time. He is constant, unwavering, steady, and never changing—always faithful.

He doesn't look at us the same way we look at ourselves. He sees the good. He sees something redeemable. He sees worth. He is our loudest cheerleader, reminding that we can overcome—even when all the odds are stacked against us. So, no matter how bad it looks, remember, He's awake and He's listening for your voice. He is an ever-present help in your time of need!

JUNE 5

Completely Blessed

Read: Exodus 23:25-26

*G*od thought of everything! He is a God of blessings, not a god of curses. He protected His people, Israel, from harm. Even when they didn't keep their part of the covenant, He kept His.

Imagine all of the food you eat and the water you drink as blessed. That's quite an exceptional promise, especially these days with GMO's, toxic pesticides, and harmful additives in our food. It could drive a person crazy, reading labels and avoiding contaminated water! Did God know what we would be up against with the 21st Century food supply?

He made a covenant with Israel that He would bless their food and protect their bodies. He promised that women would not have miscarriages and that everyone would live to a ripe old age. Since He did it for His people under the Old Covenant, wouldn't He do it now?

God made our bodies amazing. He thought ahead when He created us. He knew that mankind would need intelligent, strong immune systems to fight against disease after Adam & Eve no longer lived in the Garden of Eden. What about now? Did He know that we would be exposed to the many toxins and pollution in our world today? There is no way possible to avoid exposure to every toxin. Much of it is intentional, as we have experienced in the past few years.

So what do we, as Believers, do? If Jesus was walking this earth today, what would happen to His body? Would He become full of toxins and sick? No, He wouldn't. Why? Because the Holy Spirit living in Him would keep Him just as safe and healthy now as He was when He laid His hand on a leper or anyone else that was sick or had died from disease.

JUNE 5

How is this possible? Jesus lived by faith too. The Bible tells us that anything that is not done in faith is sin. Everything Jesus did had to be done as a man of faith, just like us, or there is no way it would be fair of God to expect us to do greater works than Jesus, or even do *any* of His works for that matter.

Some people believe the crazy lie that if a Believer lays hands on a sick person that disease can jump on them. My friend, this is not biblical. There is absolutely no where in the Bible that supports this belief. There is no record of Jesus or any of the disciples getting someone else's disease as a result of laying hands on them to be healed.

Furthermore, we have the same Holy Spirit as Jesus. He's not a "mini" Holy Spirit, or of less power or quality than the Holy Spirit in Jesus. He is the exact same Spirit. If the life of Holy Spirit was powerful enough to wipe out disease when Jesus was on the scene, that same Holy Spirit can protect us from the toxins and diseases of our day. How? By faith. Believe that same protection Jesus had with Holy Spirit is also inside of your body making you well, repelling toxins and disease, and keeping life in your body! Amen!

JUNE 6

Overflow

Read: John 7:37-39

*O*ur lives are not meant to be like a dammed up river with debris obstructing the flow of water. Jesus said,

> *"Whoever believes in Me, as Scripture has said, rivers of living water will flow from within them."* (NIV)

Where did Jesus describe the rivers flowing from? *Within us!* This world is designed to distract and pull us away from our relationship with Christ. There are so many things that compete for our attention in one day, that if we don't continually guard our minds and hearts, we will be dragged into the world's enticements. When we are preoccupied with problems and challenges, we stop up the life and flow of the Holy Spirit inside. We dam Him up and hinder Him from flowing out.

Jesus sent the Holy Spirit to fill us up to capacity, but how do we let Him overflow from us into other people's lives? The woman with the issue of blood in Mark chapter five is one of my favorite stories. She touches Jesus' robe and power flows out from His garment and into her body. It says her "fountain of blood" (can you imagine a fountain of blood seeping from her body every day?) was immediately stopped, after twelve years of misery! The power in His garments from touching His body flowed into her. No wonder the Roman soldiers cast lots for His clothes while He was on the cross! There was power in His clothes to heal and deliver!

The life inside of Jesus was the Holy Spirit, and He is the same Holy Spirit inside of you right now. He can flow out of us like rivers of living water by just being conscious of Him residing inside us and allowing Him to flow with power. So get out there! When you see a person who is walking with a cane or riding a scooter, take the time to minister healing. If you have permission to lay hands on

JUNE 6

someone, imagine the life of Holy Spirit flowing from your hands into their body and healing them! The more you share Christ with others; you will recognize the life of God overflowing like a river raging during a thunderstorm!

JUNE 7

Priests

Read: Leviticus 8

This account of the priesthood is extraordinary because of all the details. Everything God told Moses to do was carried out perfectly. The priesthood of Aaron and his sons in the Old Covenant is an example of Believers in the New Covenant.

The Old Testament priests were the entire tribe of Levi set apart for special service to God in His tabernacle. They were clothed with special garments so that they didn't sweat. They wore a turban on their heads with a gold sign engraved: HOLINESS TO THE LORD (Exodus 28:36). They were anointed with a combination of oils that were never supposed to touch their skin, only their garments. This oil was not to be used for any other purpose than anointing priests.

When Aaron and his sons prepared the animal sacrifices, it was a bloody mess. We've never had the experience of laying our hands on an animal's head to transfer our sins. We didn't have to watch its throat slit, blood spurting as it collapsed on the ground, tremoring while the sacrifice bled to death—all because of a sin we committed. We never stood by watching the Romans scourge Jesus until He was a mangled, shredded mass of flesh and blood that paid the ransom for all our sins and diseases. We get off easy.

To sum up our life in Christ, it is imperative we comprehend that *believing* is the *most* we must do and it is also the *least* we can do—and all that is required of a priest in the Kingdom. Yet there is something deeper that beckons us. It's that longing in our hearts that nothing else can satisfy. It is inexpressible with human words, yet drives us to the end of ourselves to find it. And when we do, we never want anything else; nothing else satisfies. It's that fellowship spirit to Spirit called the secret place. That secret place isn't a closet

JUNE 7

or a prayer room—it's internal. It's that place inside of us that no one else knows and is sacred to Him and Him alone—that is the priesthood. It's ministering to Him before we minister to others in His Name. This is where we find His heart, and it is where we find ours; complete in Him.

JUNE 8

Joy

Read: Psalm 30:2, 11

The Psalmist says that God had turned his mourning into dancing, removed his sackcloth, and clothed him with joy. Sackcloth was a sign of deep mourning and overwhelming distress.

The word for *joy* or *gladness* in this verse is much more than just happiness and relief that our troubles are over. These words are translated as *blithesomeness, exceeding gladness,* or *mirth*. *Mirth* is a strange word. It means to rejoice with hilarity and uncontrollable laughter! Imagine that! Transitioning in an instant from extreme sadness, depression, and confusion to blithesome, uncontrollable laughter!

I recently watched the video of a group of radical Believers baptizing people in several large animal troughs in a barn. This was no solemn assembly! They were enthusiastic lovers of God! I could feel the energy, excitement, and expectation drawing me in as though I was there! The worship music was blaring, as groups of people gathered around each of the troughs clapping and singing while each person was baptized. One particular young woman had been sick for quite a long time, experiencing excruciating pain throughout her entire body. As she was immersed in the water, she was instantly healed! She arose out of the water, drenched and wailing uncontrollably, *"He loves me! He loves me!"* They were tears of joy and awe! Imagine experiencing extreme pain one second and the next second totally free! Now that's *mirth*! Joy inexpressible! Laughter uncontainable! Praise the Name of the Lord!

JUNE 9

Confident Expectation

Read: Hebrews 4:1-11

*H*ebrews 4:1 in *The Passion Translation* says,

> "Now God has offered to us the same promise of entering into His realm of resting in confident faith. So we must be extremely careful to ensure that we all embrace the fullness of that promise and not fail to experience it."

We have the opportunity for situations to **not** take years to come to fruition, because it was meant for us to experience them now. The whole purpose for Christ accomplishing everything He did was for us to live it in the natural, not just the spiritual. Confident expectation is the key to experiencing things quickly. Getting a picture in your mind of how it ought to be, instead of how it is, is extremely beneficial.

I've been on both sides of the spectrum, as I'm sure you have too. There's nothing more frustrating than knowing something belongs to you, yet it seems to evade you. It requires a total shift in our mindset from: *"God, will You?"* To: *"God, I know You have!"*

It's an amazing experience to sit back with confidence knowing you've got your healing and then watch it happen right before your eyes! I believe that God wants us to have immediate healing every time, but many times we get in our own way. It's perplexing to me how we can experience the "high" when God comes through in a situation suddenly and miraculously. Then when a new situation arises that seems more challenging, in the same breath we may think, *"Ok, You did that, but can You do this too? Cuz this is much worse!"* Don't act like you're so holy and have never done that! LOL!

This is why entering His rest is so helpful. You must choose that, no matter what it looks like, God will come through once again,

JUNE 9

just like He did every time before. We cannot afford the luxury of dwelling on the circumstances or calling and texting all of our friends for their advice, complaining about our problems over and over. All that does is energize the hamster running on the wheel. You gotta jump off that rat race! It takes you nowhere and exhausts you physically and mentally.

I believe that the sooner you enter His rest and confidently expect results, it comes faster. The yo-yo back and forth pushes His help away. Not because He is unwilling to help us, but because we get so entangled in the circumstances that we cannot see or hear clearly. Then, confusion and fear set in like a cloud. I've seen it happen way too many times! It seems like we don't want to let go of control, but letting go of control is the exact thing we need to do! It's a catch-22, so to speak.

It's like a person grabbing the steering wheel of their car all white-knuckled and wide-eyed. There is something to be said about letting Jesus "take the wheel." Peace is ready to flood away the fear. Rest is ready to calm the pulsating heart. Confident expectation is not necessarily knowing HOW He will work it out, but knowing He WILL. A thousand pounds will slip off your shoulders as you rest in the realm of confident faith!

JUNE 10

Yeshua

Read: Matthew 1:18-24

Jesus is the English form of the Hebrew name *Yeshua*. Parents named their children, in Bible times, according to either of the following customs:

1. An observable characteristic
2. A prophetic role the child would fulfill

Consider the twins, Jacob and Esau, for example. Esau means *hairy*. It's kinda gross to imagine delivering a baby covered with so much hair over his entire body that his mother had to name him "Hairy!" Definitely an observable characteristic! He was a "man's man" who loved hunting and rugged living. No wonder he was his father's favorite.

Jacob meant "heel" because he grabbed a hold of his brother's heel and let Esau pull him out as they were birthed. Jacob was a bit of a wuss and a "mama's boy," hanging around home all the time. Both of these men are examples how they got their names.

Jesus was named by His Father *Yeshua*, meaning *salvation*, for both reasons. It was an observable characteristic and a prophetic roll He would fulfill. *Salvation* means *"to save, deliver, rescue."* Jesus was and performed all of these things for us in every area of our lives whether spiritually, physically, or emotionally. He is Savoir and He performed salvation for all! His Father said,

> *"...and you shall call His name Yeshua (Salvation), for He will save His people from their sins."*

JUNE 11

Garbage Can Religion

Read: Romans 6 (The Message Bible)

*Y*ears ago, in 1992, my husband and I had rededicated our lives to Christ. The night we both got baptized in the Holy Spirit at church, someone came up to us and said, *"I don't know what they were praying with you about at the altar, but God says you are supposed to go home and clean out your house."*

It took us three days to go through all of our stuff and throw out the junk from our old lives. We had received a new life in Christ and we didn't want the books, music, posters, movies, (you name it), with all kinds of witchcraft and evil things we didn't even know we had! We filled up an entire dumpster with garbage! We wanted a clean slate and we never wanted to go back to our old lives!

Life can be like that, sometimes. You make a clean break from something from your past, but a few years later, you're tempted to go dumpster-diving into all the old stuff that was cleaned out of your life! Little by little those old habits and old ways of thinking can creep back in until you find yourself swimming in garbage again. How did that happen? Revisiting the memories from your past, mixed with your new life in Christ and—Walla—garbage can religion!

Our relationship with Jesus requires active participation every day. It's easy to drift and get drawn away by responsibilities and demands of everyday life. Unless you live on an island alone, people will always have needs they may expect us to meet. We can't be like the man who said to his wife, *"I told you I loved you twenty years ago and I said I'd tell ya if it ever changed!"* in our relationship with Jesus. It will not maintain itself. It is extra challenging because we must live out of our spirit and not from our mind. In order to do that, we must guard our hearts and minds from taking a dive into the disappointments of our past. It is paramount that we continually

JUNE 11 ———

recognize ourselves dead to self and alive in Christ Jesus. That old life ain't worth thinking about or revisiting ever again! So keep yourself from eating out of the garbage can from your past. Whom the Son has set free is free *indeed*!

JUNE 12

Success In Failure

Read: Exodus 3

Thomas Edison, the famous inventor, had more failures in his lifetime in the beginning than successes. In addition to improving the incandescent lamp, he invented the x-ray machine, the motion picture business, and even the tattoo pen, among many other inventions we still use today. If he would have quit, think about all of the things we would be doing without right now!

He is famous for many quotes about success and failure:

> *"Many of life's failures are people who did not recognize how close they were to success when they gave up."*

> *"Never get discouraged if you fail. Learn from it. Keep trying."*

> *"Our greatest weakness lies in giving up. The most certain way to succeed is always to try just one more time."*

> *"I have not failed. I've just found 10,000 ways that won't work."*

> *"Restlessness is discontent and discontent is the first necessity of progress. Show me a thoroughly satisfied man and I will show you a failure."*

Moses is the perfect example of someone in the Bible who was a huge failure before he was a success. When he was born, Pharaoh ordered all baby boys to be killed. He escaped death, was adopted by Pharaoh's daughter, and raised in that same king's castle... think about it! His own mother was paid to nurse him until he was old enough to live in the enemy's palace. Amazing! Yet, when he realized the injustice against his people and tried to take matters into his own hands before he was fully qualified to be Israel's deliverer, he failed big time and had to flee for his life!

JUNE 12

He settled in the foreign land of Midian, on the backside of the desert. He became a shepherd—the lowliest form of occupation for an Egyptian. Moses probably just figured that this was his lot in life and he believed that he was a failure. His encounter with the burning bush came unexpectedly. Israel had been crying out for God to deliver them from slavery, yet after 350 years of hearing Israel's cries, God did not consider it a waste of time for Moses' full preparation to take *another* forty years. Imagine the heartache of forty years of failure!

God told Moses that He would prove Himself as the "I AM" by bringing him back to this same mountain with all of the people of Israel, fully delivered from Pharaoh. What looked like failure was really preparation. Moses knew that wilderness like the back of his hand. God had actually guided him to the region of Midian, although Moses thought he was just trying to save his own skin. It seemed like a random place to run, yet it prepared him to be the Deliverer that was God's answer to Israel's misery!

Maybe there have been a lot of failures in your life. You know, like I do, that you have the call of God on your life, but nothing seems to be working out the way you had expected. When I look back over the years of my own life, I too, see a lot of failure. I sure learned a lot along the way about what doesn't work! I think that was Thomas Edison's main point as well. What looks like failure in our eyes, is really a process of elimination—we find out what doesn't work so that we can do what does! It would be a lot easier if God would just drop a big movie screen in front of our eyes and show us what would happen with the choices we'd make. Yet, we aren't wired that way. There is something within our humanness that drives the need for us to experience life's lessons entirely by our own volition (or stubbornness).

God patiently and tirelessly walks with us through the maze of life's failures and builds a repertoire of what He considers

JUNE 12

accomplishments, where we have seen failure. Just know that you are never stuck in your current situation. Whatever roadblocks are seemingly in your way—they do not have to be your lot in life. Begin to see yourself on the other side. Like Thomas Edison and Moses, remember that there is always success in failure—we simply need the right perspective to see what God sees. So don't quit!

"A righteous man may fall seven times and rise again!" (Proverbs 24:16)

JUNE 13

Grit & Grace

Read: John 14:12-18

Intestinal fortitude. It was a term coined by Dr. John W. Wilce of Ohio State University in 1915. In other words It's a nice way of saying, *"Do you have the guts?"* or *"Show me what you're made of!"* In other words: *"No guts, no glory."*

Jesus said that we could ask the Father *whatever* we want in His Name and that, by doing so, He would be glorified. Many situations in life cannot be solved by human effort. That's where grace comes in. Grace is an easier word to define than to explain how it works. It's coupled with faith. Both are abstract nouns that are only described effectively thorough experiences.

The other day, my hubby and I had a financial need. I prayed one night that a check would come in the mail from somewhere that owed us money that we were unaware of. That next day, less than 24 hours later, there was a check in the mail from the IRS (of all places!) telling us we didn't get our full refund back for our taxes! Well, whatdoyaknow? Coincidence or grace? Grace to help in a time of need (Heb 4:16)!

When situations look hopeless and we've exhausted all of our own grit and stick-to-itiveness, grace is always there. Holy Spirit is like Hamburger Helper, when you need a helping hand! So, look for grace—that helps in a time of need. Expect it! God's throne is built upon it! Amen!

JUNE 14

Matthias

Read: Acts 1:15-26

*W*ho was Matthias? He was only mentioned once in the Bible, yet he filled an important position with the twelve apostles. It was prophesied that Judas would betray Jesus in Psalm 109:8 and he would need to be replaced,

> *"Let his days be few, and let another take his office."* (NKJV)

There were important specific characteristics that would qualify Judas' replacement. Many people teach that the disciples got it wrong and that Paul was supposed to be the disciple that replaced Judas. They say that Matthias was man's choice, but Paul was God's choice. I totally disagree. Who cares, you might ask?

Well, for one thing, an essential qualification was that Judas' replacement had to be a disciple who had been with the twelve from the beginning. That leaves Paul out for sure. Why didn't they just leave the number at eleven? Prophetically, Peter pointed out that according to Scripture, someone must take Judas' place. Second, in the book of Revelation, there are specifically twelve apostles to the Lamb (Revelation 21:14) signifying that they would hold a prominent place in God's Kingdom. (There are other apostles, obviously, like Paul, but specifically twelve apostles to the Lamb).

Historically, research describes Matthias as one tough character! It is recorded that he was among the seventy sent out by Jesus in Luke 10:1-24. Matthias preached the Gospel in Ethiopia and Macedonia. At one point he was imprisoned for preaching about Christ. He was arrested by cannibals. While imprisoned, they forced him and the other prisoners to drink poison to make them blind. But it didn't work! I bet He remembered Jesus' words before He was lifted up into heaven, *"...and if they drink anything deadly, it will by no means hurt them."* (Mark 16:18). He also prayed for the

JUNE 14

other prisoners' eyesight to be restored. Matthias also got released miraculously from prison, but was later stoned and beheaded as a traitor to Rome for preaching the Gospel.

So who cares about Matthias? He was one radical dude who confronted religion and bravely gave his life as a martyr for Christ! Knowing the history of these seemingly insignificant people in the Bible inspires us to realize that no one is unimportant to God. Each of us has an essential role in the Kingdom and we all have been given the same responsibility to preach the Gospel. Testimonies about heroes of faith give us fortitude and embolden us to stand strong in our present evil generation. Even if it means we must die for our faith; we know that we are not alone because we are surrounded by that great cloud of witnesses, including Matthias, who have courageously gone before us (Hebrews 12:1)!

JUNE 15

We're All Sons

Read: Galatians 3:26-4:7

*W*hat if Jesus told you that He wanted to give **you** the ability to do signs and wonders, like healing the sick? Have you ever thought about God using **you**? It is a popular belief that only certain "anointed" people have been given a special gift to do miracles and heal the sick because they are highly favored, but well, for the rest of us "peons"—forget it! That is, unless you are one of the few privileged people who received an impartation from one of these "anointed" individuals. Otherwise, well, sorry... you just don't qualify.

It is unfortunate that we have been taught to put our faith in a man's anointing. There isn't one Scripture to back up these beliefs. As a matter of fact, it's just the opposite. In today's Scripture, we can clearly see that no matter what race, gender, or occupation—we are all one in Christ. Jairus was the ruler of the local synagogue, which would be much like the town mayor for us today. He had a prominent social standing among the religious leaders, yet that held no bearing whether or not Jesus would raise his daughter from the dead. A few seconds earlier, Jesus healed the woman with the issue of blood. She was an outcast of society. Yet Jesus didn't qualify who would be healed and who wouldn't.

As a matter of fact, who did He select as his disciples to carry on the works of the Kingdom after He ascended into heaven? He chose a small group of uneducated, ordinary men. What about you? If you choose to apply what the Bible says you are as a son who has received an inheritance in God's Kingdom, then you can also walk in the miraculous! I will go so far as the say that it is *expected* of you to do signs and wonders. Anything less is not demonstrating the fullness of the Kingdom. It's actually abnormal for us **not** to be doing the same works as Jesus, with even greater results. He

JUNE 15 ———

told us to outdo Him! Any good Father wants their children to go farther and accomplish more than themselves, right? So go get 'em, tiger! Renew your mind continually to the truth, and then be bold and act on it! This is the way the Kingdom works and there are no selected favorite individuals. We choose, we apply, and we experience the results!

JUNE 16

Seized With Power

Matthew 8:16-17, Acts 1:8 (The Passion Translation)

*I*n Matthew 8:17, it says that Jesus *took* our infirmities. In Acts 1:8, it says that we will *receive* power when the Holy Spirit comes upon us. These two words are the exact same Greek word #2983— *lambano*.

The *Strong's Concordance* says *lambano* means *"to seize or remove."* Thayer's says *lambano* means *"to take up a thing to be carried; to take upon one's self, to remove or take away with the notion of violence, to seize, take away forcibly, to take to one's self, to make one's own."*

The dictionary says *seize* means *"to take something eagerly, aggressively or by force, for example: like when you jump at a chance, to grasp suddenly and forcibly, take or grab, to take by force, capture or conquer."*

When we compare these two different Scriptures, we can easily see that Jesus has violently, forcefully taken our diseases upon Himself and He replaced them with the power to overcome with the Holy Spirit. There was a great exchange that took place and most of us didn't even realize it! Many places in the Bible the translators used different English words for the same Greek word. By doing this, it is hard to understand the gravity of what had been accomplished for us through Christ. That's why we have to dig beyond the surface for ourselves and find out what really belongs to us! We've got to study the Word for ourselves!

No wonder it says that the Kingdom of heaven suffers violence and the violent take it by force (Matt. 11:12)! Christ was no wimp! Neither was John the Baptist, who was in prison when Jesus made this statement. Jesus emphasized that John wasn't a pansy in a king's palace wearing fancy clothes gorging on delicacies. He was a messenger of the Kingdom of God that was juxtaposed to the

JUNE 16

world—and for that he was beheaded! After this statement, Jesus rebuked the cities that had rejected His mighty works.

We were *seized* by the power of the Holy Ghost! Our diseases were *seized*! There was violence involved when Christ took our place in order to give us the power and authority He has. So—be as bold and confident in seizing the Kingdom as the Kingdom is in seizing you!!

JUNE 17

Birds Live!

Read: Matthew 6:25-34

When I was about twelve years old, an elderly couple was a friend of our family. They were going on vacation to Hawaii and they asked me to "bird-sit" their two pet parakeets. I had never taken care of birds before; all we ever had were dogs. I loved animals, so I was glad to care for them the two weeks they would be away. The man, in particular, enjoyed these birds. He talked kindly and whistled to them to say good-bye. I didn't want to let them down because he loved them so much.

As you know how things go sometimes, you can do everything to the best of your ability and disappointments still come, no matter how hard you try. About one week into caring for the birds, the male bird didn't look so good. What can you do for a bird, really? It's not like I could take it to a vet. I didn't know what to do. I knew the man would be so upset if his bird died while he was away, and I certainly didn't want to be responsible for killing it!

So you know what I did? I spoke to the bird and told it that it couldn't die. Then, I prayed and asked God to heal it. Within a short time, the bird looked much better and, by the time the couple had returned, the birds were both doing well. Whew! Thank you Jesus!

I didn't know that this was called "faith." Most times, we don't need to know all the details. We only need to trust like a child. A bird near death received new life? Why not? He's the God of the impossible, isn't He? Aren't we worth more than many parakeets?

JUNE 18

It's a Gut Feeling

Read: Colossians 3:12 (KJV)

The third chapter of Colossians says in verse twelve:

> *"Put on therefore, as the elect of God, holy and beloved, bowels of mercies, kindness, humbleness of mind, meekness, longsuffering..."*

Yes, oddly enough, it's referring to our intestines. And no, I don't have an obsession for potty humor! According to the Greek mindset, they were a very passionate people. They expressed a lot of emotion through theater and poetry. To them, the bowels were regarded as the seat of passion, such as anger and love.

To the Hebrew mindset, the bowels were the seat of tender affections, especially kindness, benevolence, and compassion—nicer guys to hang around with, I suppose.

It's important to keep these things in mind when we read the Bible. Understanding the culture and mindset of the writers helps us to more accurately grasp what we have been given to experience the fullness of the Kingdom. The English language is sometimes very flat and lifeless unless the translators took the time to explain in detail what was being expressed. That is why I like to compare many different translations/paraphrases such as the *Wuest*, *The Message Bible*, *The Passion*, and even the *Mirror Bible*.

Bowels in the *Strong's* is #4698 *splagchnon* which means *"strengthened from the spleen; an intestine, bowels, inward affection, tender mercies"*

The spleen is a part of our immune system, so there really is a transformation that strengthens us to the point where Jesus' life literally affects our health! The inward man is the seat of all our passions,

JUNE 18

affections, and desires. He completely transforms us from the inside out—emotionally and physically!

The above information is saying that the new man is transformed down to his guts—to what drives him. The very seat of his passions and desires are transformed into the image, likeness, and the same passions that drove Jesus to live life as He demonstrated it!

JUNE 19

Endued

Read: Colossians 3:12, Luke 24:49

"Put on" in Colossians 3:12 is the same Greek word as *"endued"* in Luke 24:49. Inspiring! Isn't it? They both mean *"sinking into a garment, array, clothe, endue, put on."* Both are # 1746 in the *Strong's Concordance*.

Colossians commands us to clothe ourselves with the godly virtues of the Holy Spirit. Luke also shares a directive from Jesus, telling the disciples that they must be endued with the Holy Spirit's power.

Spiritual fruit and spiritual power are working together, providing us with the right attributes to be the most effective in the Kingdom. Both are necessary elements, and we are commanded to be clothed with both. We do it. Holy Spirit helps.

It always amazes me how much responsibility the Father entrusts to us. Sometimes I wish He wouldn't have, honestly, because it would be so much easier if He would just do it all. But then we'd just become lazy and not be able to fully enjoy the power He has given to us. He desires for us to experience His life in a dynamic, close relationship with Him.

It's like a child. If you do everything for them, they never learn for themselves. They never grow. They stay totally dependent to the point of being unable to be a productive citizen in society—always a burden on everyone, acting like co-dependent adult children. The Father knew better. He wants us to fully rely on Him, yes, but we also have to do something. For example, we have to take the time to read the Word, pray in the spirit, lay hands on the sick, or give of our time and resources to help someone. God does it through us; and it takes character and the power of the Holy Spirit to help us be effective. It does take effort—a lot of effort to stay Kingdom-minded. It doesn't happen by unconscious osmosis and

JUNE 19

passivity. We must be willing participants—partners in Covenant, clothed with fruit; endued with power!

JUNE 20

Power Annihilates Weakness

Read: 2 Corinthians 13:1-7 (The Passion Translation)

As Christ was crucified a "weakling" and now lives robed in God's power, we also were weak until we crucified our old lives through faith in Christ. Now together, we live in God's triumphant power; the power He demonstrated when He raised Christ from the dead!

Think about it! We're no longer wimps, subjected to the corruption in this world! We are seated in Christ in heavenly places; far above all rule, authority, power and dominion and every title that can be given! In the weakness of the flesh, God's strength is made strong!

The flesh: our emotions, thoughts, feelings, etc. can very easily control us if we let them. That's probably the most challenging aspect of living for Christ. It's not the devil. It's our own self! But thanks be to God who always causes us to triumph in Christ Jesus! He has given us the power and the provision to overcome even our flesh!

His power is made perfect in our weakness, so that we are no longer weak, but strong in the Lord and the power of His might! The key is to begin looking at ourselves with a new perspective. Not the perspective of constantly *needing*, but of constantly already *having*! This is HUGE! And I cannot emphasize this strongly enough! If we have a habit of looking at our circumstances as lacking, then that is what we will get—more lack! Something changes when we shift over to the mindset of *having* and thanking Him for it. Stop the "what-if's" and the "how's"—the constant questioning and trying to figure things out. The Holy Spirit is there to show you His way of approaching that circumstance to enable you to overtake it! Listen to Him! Lean on Him!

JUNE 21

Mouth Guard

Read: Proverbs 21:23

The *Passion Translation* advises:

> "Watch your words and be careful what you say, and you'll be surprised by how few troubles you'll have."

The *Message Bible* warns:

> "Watch your words and hold your tongue; you'll save yourself a lot of grief."

The biggest way to blow it is by shooting our mouth off. We would save ourselves a lot of heartache by setting a guard over our mouths. Sometimes, we'd like to tell people to go "pound sand" even though they may deserve it. Remember this: Thomas Jefferson once said, "When angry count to ten before you speak. If very angry, count to one hundred."

When you look back on the situation, you'll be glad you didn't say something you cannot take back. James 3:2 in the NKJV says,

> "If anyone does not stumble in word, he is a perfect man, able also to bridle the whole body."

I like the part where it says a man is able to control his entire body by what he says or doesn't say. Let's apply this where physical healing is concerned. We all have a natural tendency to dwell on the negative, but what if the way you think about yourself and your own self-talk actually affects the "you" that you see? According to Scripture, this is true!

> "For as he thinks in his heart, so is he." (Proverbs 23:7, NKJV)

I wonder how much trouble we could avoid if we changed the way we spoke and the way we see ourselves. Could we create a strong,

JUNE 21

healthy body just by speaking and thinking the right things about ourselves and then acting on it? I believe we can! This old song by Bing Crosby makes a valid point:

> *You've got to accentuate the positive*
> *Eliminate the negative*
> *Latch on to the affirmative*
> *Don't mess with Mister In-Between*
> *You've got to spread joy up to the maximum*
> *Bring gloom down to the minimum*
> *Have faith or pandemonium*
> *Liable to walk up on the scene*

I made up my mind over a year ago to get strength back in my legs since the muscles had become weak when I was sick. I decided to make my body submit to the life of the Holy Spirit within me by walking my dog first thing every morning—no matter how much my knees hurt. And you know what? Slowly, but steadily, strength came back and pain left! Walking wasn't the only thing that affected me. I pray out loud in the spirit so that my spirit rules over my mind and body. I believe our prayer language has the ability to transform us from the inside out! So, forgo the complaining and act solely on truth—you will surely avoid a harvest of grief!

JUNE 22

The Life-Giving Spirit

Read: 1 Corinthians 15:42-45, John 6:63

*T*he *Wuest Translation* records Jesus' words in John 6:63:

> *"The Spirit is He who makes alive. The flesh is not of any use at all. The words which I have spoken to you, spirit are they and life."*

It makes no difference what help we can try to find in man, be it a doctor, medicine, or natural remedies—they all have limitations. Without having a spirit, we'd all cease to exist. But the Spirit gives *His life* to our flesh. How much more do we have *eternal, resurrection life* working on the inside and releasing life to our flesh, now that Jesus has taken up residence in our body? 1 Corinthians 15:45 states,

> *"The first man Adam became a living being; the last Adam became a life-giving spirit."* (NKJV)

Notice it doesn't say *"the second Adam."* If it had said the second Adam, there would be need for a third Adam, a fourth, a fifth, and so on. But Jesus was the *last* Adam; meaning there was no need for another. He finished it. There is no other way to receive life.

Jesus, being the last Adam, is a life-giving spirit. What does that matter when we live in a flesh body? We read in our verse for today that the Spirit is the only way to receive life—eternal, resurrection life. The flesh cannot give resurrection life to the flesh.

Have you ever had someone cuss you out? The words they said played in your head over and over again the next few days. The more you thought about what that person said, the more ticked off you became! Remember how those words seemed to stick to you like glue and nag at you?

JUNE 22

Now think about some kind words someone said to you. Those words really encouraged you and built you up to the point you started to think, *"Hey, I guess I really can make a difference! Wow!"* And you began to feel really good about yourself.

Look at the rest of the verse that declares Jesus' words are *spirit* and they are *life*. Everything Jesus has to say about you is Spirit and life. When we read His words, they strengthen our spirit man, which in turn strengthens our mind and our physical body. That's the way the Spirit works—from the inside out! They build you up and give you the confidence to overcome; Spirit to spirit we touch, receiving life! It's how His Word becomes flesh!

JUNE 23

Possessing Life

Read: John 10:10 (Wuest Translation)

Superabundance means *"an amount or supply more than sufficient to meet one's needs, the state or an instance of going beyond what is usual or needed"*

Jesus said in John 10:10 in the *Wuest*,

> *"I alone came in order that they might be possessing life, and that they might be possessing it in superabundance."*

Did you ever think about what this may look like? Jesus was our example of a superabundant life. Whenever He needed something, He made it appear. Whenever something was wrong, He fixed it. He was always willing to help other people; He didn't need it for Himself.

It is perplexing how many in the body of Christ still question God's willingness to heal, even though Scripture is very clear about physical healing. Our experiences with diseases and pain are quite the opposite. Jesus never taught His disciples *how* to heal the sick. They saw Him do it, then He commanded them to do likewise; it wasn't an enigma.

Jesus was aware of the Holy Spirit's ability within Him. He possessed life and life possessed Him!

Possession means *"to have or own it, have as property, belonging to, to have under one's power or control"*

That's the reason He came—so we could possess His *superabundant* life for ourselves and retain more than enough to give away!

JUNE 24

The Communion Experience

Read: 1 John 1:3-4 (The Message Bible)

John gave a report about what He and the early disciples experienced in their lives day to day with Jesus. He wrote about it so we could experience Him too. There is one sure fire way to keep us from experiencing a relationship of close communion with Jesus, and that is by constantly believing there are hindrances.

So, stop right there! That's the hindrance! There are no hindrances to receiving and walking in everything Christ gave to us, except one thing: You believe there is a hindrance. It's just another way of looking at the spiritual with natural eyes. We continue to see lack or the need for more of something; something to be fixed, filled, or replaced. But in the spiritual, with God, everything is already fixed and prepared to jump over and make the natural as whole as the spiritual. It is done! So,

1. Stop looking at yourself
2. Stop believing you are hindered
3. Look at Jesus as having fulfilled all and is in all—nothing lacking. He moved in and hell moved out—period!

He is constantly supplying your needs and never, ever runs out! No hindrances anywhere! He is our Completer—the One who made everything whole! What Jesus accomplished was done, finished, and complete. It was done and still continues to be done! It wasn't just done and stuck back in time, 2000 years ago. It's finished for all time: past, present, and future! No, my mind can no longer be a hindrance; I have the mind of Christ! My mind is renewed and continues to be renewed daily when I read the Word and communicate with Holy Spirit. So when I get somewhere in my future, He's already there; ready, able and willing to meet me there, fully supplied!

JUNE 25

Simple?

Read: Romans 4:13-25

I read a book some time ago which stated that physical healing was simple. To be honest, it really hacked me off! How could the author say that healing was *simple*? At the time, healing was anything but simple for me! *Simple?*

What I didn't understand was the difference between the circumstances and the solution. The circumstances were difficult. A physical illness has many factors involved: finances, relationships, symptoms, etc. It can be complicated. The solution is what is simple. That is what the author of the book was saying; that the *solution* is simple.

We know what the solution is: Jesus! Applying what Jesus accomplished is challenging when we are going against what our mind and body are saying. The symptoms try to speak louder than what we know in our spirit and according to the Word. We choose to believe that Jesus is our Healer! We choose to give Holy Spirit and God's Word first priority. So, in all actuality, it isn't the solution that is complicated. It's all the other stuff trying to avert our attention. Like Abraham, we must refuse to consider our own body and what it is saying through symptoms.

Healing *simple*? It's really just like anything else: the more you practice it the easier it becomes. I remember when I first started consistently praying for the sick at Wal-Mart and everywhere else I went. I even made house calls to terminally ill people and unfortunately, they all died. I thought, *"What is wrong with me!"* It was very discouraging, to say the least! But I just kept at it. Now, most of the people I pray for get healed and/or experience improvement immediately! And it happens easily! I believe it is supposed to be as easy for us as it was for Jesus. I don't think He would have told

JUNE 25

us to do anything that He didn't do Himself. We're supposed to get the same results! It *is* simple—Jesus did the hard part! I keep myself out of the way—what I think, what I see, and what I feel—just like old Abraham did and watched that baby come forth!

JUNE 26

What Did You Say?

Read: Proverbs 18:7, James 4:17

*T*he snare this Scripture is talking about in Proverbs is a trap that is carefully set to catch an animal. Think about this statement: What a person speaks can be like a trap that they set for themselves, much like a trap set for an animal. That person is bringing about his or her own destruction! Yikes!

It's a simple fix, right? Just stop saying all the negative things about yourself or the circumstances in your life and start declaring what the Scriptures say you are and what you have! But most Believers don't! Unfortunately, they'd rather call their friends and ask for advice, but then they don't even follow it! Some revel in sympathy, rather than to change the way they talk. It is unwise to seek advice from one friend, and then share the advice suggested with another friend, just to ask for an opinion about the advice received! Ugh!

Have you ever heard the definition for insanity? It's *"doing the same thing over and over again and expecting a different result."* This Scripture is very clear: we can set a trap for ourselves by the words we speak! We actually have a part in our own destruction!

When I minister to people, some of them say, *"But..."* When I hear that, I can tell almost everything that person is going say means they really didn't hear a thing I said. In all honesty, they don't want to change the way they have been doing things! They just want their circumstances to go away, but they really don't hate their circumstances enough to change their words or what they do. It's very hard to watch someone self-destruct by their own doing! It breaks my heart, honestly.

There is a saying that is very true: *"The pain of remaining the same must be greater than the pain of change."* In other words, which is more painful: to stay the way you are, or to change? To remain

JUNE 26

the same is more painful than change in the long run, even though there may be no quick fix. To break old habits and to change the way we think and the way we talk is a lot of hard work! But in the long run, life is so much more enjoyable! We will not be ensnared any longer by the words of our own mouth. When we discipline our thoughts and retrain them to think like the Scriptures, circumstances change! We let Holy Spirit on the scene!

JUNE 27

Just Do It!

Read: James 2:14-26, Matthew 5:42

The title of our Devotion for today sounds exactly like the slogan for a major athletic company. They have a point: put on the shoes, do the stuff! Otherwise, what would be the point? Fashion? What does that accomplish? This is the main point of chapter two in the book of James. He says that if we have faith and we don't *act* on it, then we really don't have faith. Basically, our faith is equal to that of demons because although they believe, they do not *act* on their belief in God either.

We've all done it at one time or another when someone has a need—we hear about it and we say, *"I'll pray for you."* But then we don't do anything to help them. *"Vaya con dios!"* (Spanish for *"Go with God"*) we may say, and promise to pray for them, but most times we don't even follow through. Think about all the opportunities that pass us by every day to bring the Kingdom of God on the scene!

Sometimes, it's clearly a financial need. Oh, see that bum at the street corner begging for money? *"Yeah, he's just going to buy alcohol or drugs anyway. I can't give God's money to a bum!"* They have a need, you have the goods! They will listen! It's a perfect opportunity to offer to pray with them. Maybe they really do have a legitimate problem. Maybe they need healing in their body! You will never know what you're capable of until you step outside your comfort zone and do it!

So, *"Just do it!"* Get out there and act on your faith! You say you believe in healing, but do you pray for the sick? James says, *"I show you my faith by what I do."* Faith isn't passive. Faith is aggressive *action*. It's bold and uncompromising!

JUNE 28

The Father's Business

Read: Luke 2:41-52

Jesus' focus always amazes me. He adhered to the mission that His Father sent Him to accomplish, and He knew He only had a few years to complete it. The religious leaders tried to throw Him off a cliff, but He just walked right through the crowd. He knew He was not destined to die by bashing His head at the bottom of a mountain. He wasn't terrified in the storm, like the disciples, when He calmed the wind and the waves because He knew He wasn't appointed to die by drowning in the sea. He wasn't afraid to go back to Bethany so He could raise Lazarus from the dead, even though the Jews had previously threatened to stone Him. He knew He had an appointment to die on a cross.

There are so many things that try to distract us from fulfilling God's call on our lives. There are many good deeds we can do to serve, but they may not have the greatest impact. Scripture is clear: we are all called to preach, teach the Kingdom, and to heal the sick. Each Believer may have a unique way of going about it, but nonetheless, the call is the same for all of us.

The question is, *"Where is your focus?"* Maybe there are some adjustments you could make to be more fruitful. Maybe there are some things you could eliminate. Take a quick evaluation of your life. Are you doing what you know God has called you to do? Are you being the most effective at what you're doing? Are you about your Father's business?

JUNE 29

The Runner's High

Read: 1 Corinthians 9:24-27

I remember when I was a teenager; I would spend many of my afternoons during the summer running. I grew up in the country, so it was easy to find a challenging back road. One of my favorite routes had two iron grate bridges to cross over. I'd run a mile to the first bridge, two miles to the second, and home again. It was a total loop of about five miles. I'd sprint as fast as I could without stopping, no matter how many hills there were to conquer!

When I would run those country roads in the summertime, I'd thrust myself through the heat beyond the verge of exhaustion. I pushed my body as far as it thought it could go. Homeward bound, my legs began to wobble like Jello® beneath me; then, suddenly, a second wind hit! Energy I didn't know I possessed surged from the inside! This is what it was all about—the stage where it was easier to keep running than it was to stop! I had reached the tipping point where my legs seemed to have a mind of their own and they could just keep running forever. Adrenaline set in and I could run like the wind! I had made it to "the zone." That was the prize I was running for! With the wind in my hair, my breathing in sync with the rhythm of my legs; there was nothing quite like it—the runner's high!

Did you ever take notice how a runner runs a race? He locks his eyes on that finish line and runs with all he's got; if he so much as glances to see who might be gaining on him, it slows him down and could cost him the prize. He thrusts out his chest and runs as fast as he can. Breathing is rhythmic and intentional: in through the nose and exhaling through the mouth helps him pace himself. If he only uses his mouth to breathe, he will tire faster. It also keeps his emotions under control.

JUNE 29

A runner pushes himself beyond any limits he has previously experienced. He gives it all he's got, mentally and physically, to get to that finish line—not looking back to see who might be catching up to pass him. He beats his body and makes it his slave to win the prize!

Paul says in our Scripture reading for today that he disciplines his body and brings it under subjection, so that he himself would not be disqualified. He says he runs with *certainty*, meaning he is being deliberate in his preaching to avoid being ineffective to others as well as to himself. He keeps his focus, not allowing persecution to side-swipe him from behind. He is purposeful, doing whatever is necessary to win the high prize of his heavenly calling.

Paul was intentional, bold, and focused about everything he did to preach the Gospel. He was the kind of guy who was either all in or all out—there was no in-between. He didn't mince words. And that's exactly the same kind of focus and attitude that will benefit us as well. Imagine where we'd be right now if Paul hadn't been totally committed to preaching the Gospel? We wouldn't have the Bible we hold in our hands today. He took the little bit of opportunity he had in prison to pray for the churches he'd planted and to write personal letters, encouraging them. He made the most out of his circumstances; and it is still benefitting us today, thousands of years later! He didn't let prison stop him, he didn't let lack of provisions stop him, he didn't let the threat of death in every city stop him, and he didn't let what people said about him stop him.

Go for it! Run in such a way as to win the prize of your high calling in Jesus Christ! You will never be satisfied with your life if you settle for mediocrity. With the Holy Spirit giving you His life and longevity, He's got a track already set for you to run. Don't look back! Just RUN! Gain momentum! Cross that finish line to VICTORY! There's nothing quite like it—the runner's high!

JUNE 30

Hit Me With Your Best Shot

Read: John 6:41-69

*R*emember the song from the 80s by Pat Benatar, *"Hit Me with Your Best Shot?"* That was exactly what I was facing when I was in Junior High. There was a gang of nine girls that wanted to kick my butt! I don't know why; I never did or said anything to them. One day, I was informed that I was on their "Beat up List." Was I scared? Yes, at first. The one girl was very tough; she was the leader of the pack. Their intimidation went on for most of the school year. They would come up behind me, mock me, and try to kick my shoes out from under my feet when I wore clogs. One of them was on my school bus, and she made it her aim to let me know how much she hated me, threatening with her fist! I couldn't get away from them!

I'm the kind of person who sits back and observes for a while before I do anything. I was hoping it would all end when their leader got expelled from school, but it didn't. One morning, I was at my locker and one of the gang came up from behind and started taunting me. At that point, I'd had enough! I turned around and punched her in the face! You back me into a corner and I'm comin' out swinging!

Unfortunately, I got detention for an entire week. She got nothing. Even one of the teachers on the school board came to my defense, emphasizing that I wouldn't have hit her if she hadn't been relentlessly antagonizing me.

Oh, that's not very "Christian" of you! Maybe you're a better Christian than me. I had had enough of trying to settle things peacefully. We sometimes try to do the "nice Christian thing" to our own detriment. That's where we must draw the line. You don't have to take anything that isn't in agreement with what God has already said about you. Jesus didn't put up with people's excuses in John

JUNE 30

chapter 6. He never ran after anyone and said, *"Oh wait! Is that too hard for you to eat My flesh and drink My blood? I'll change it! I'll make it easier for you! Just don't leave Me!"* He didn't compromise His message to accommodate people's whims. He said, *"You want bread? I'm the bread of life; eat of Me!"* Their response was, *"Ugh! No way!"*—It was their choice to make. They chose to be offended and walk away.

Now, I'm not suggesting that we go around punching people. Obviously, we're adults now—not children, and we shouldn't act like children. I'm sure you figured out, that back then I knew nothing concerning Biblical instructions about how to respond to bullying. However, as Believers, there are times when we must take a stand, especially when it comes to a doctor's report! We cannot afford the luxury of wallowing in self-pity because of a bad report. We cannot allow symptoms of pain to kick our butt! We do have a choice in the situation: roll over and die, or stand up and resist! Disease is just a big bully on the block threatening with words. But we have God's Word on disease which is sharper than any two-edged sword! Use it to defeat the bully!

So, come out swinging! Let the words of Pat Benatar's song put the punch back in your attitude toward disease:

Hit Me With Your Best Shot

Well you're a real tough cookie with a long history
Of breaking little hearts like the one in me
That's OK, let's see how you do it
Put up your dukes, let's get down to it

Hit me with your best shot,
Why don't you hit me with your best shot
Hit me with your best shot
Fire away!

JUNE 30 ———

You come on with a "come on"
You don't fight fair
But that's OK, see if I care
Knock me down, it's all in vain

I'll get right back on my feet again

JULY 1

Essence

Read: John 10:27-33

The NKJV in verse 30 states, *"I and My Father are one."* As compared to the *Wuest Translation* which says, *"I and the Father are one in essence."*

Essence is the core nature, or most important qualities, of a person or thing. That puts us in good company with Jesus! Jesus didn't depend on anything He could say or do by Himself. He totally depended upon the Father for absolutely *everything*! By living this way He was the full expression of His Father. Like I said, we're in good company. We aren't expected to muster up anything from within ourselves to live in the Kingdom. Everything we need is supplied through Christ.

Sometimes it seems like this is a scary place to exist, yet when we actually begin living this way, it is total freedom! It's a paradox, like most things are when we compare them with the way the world functions against the way the Kingdom functions. Oh, need some money to pay the temple tax? Go fishing and you'll find a coin in the first fish's mouth you catch. Need some food? Just thank the Father for the little you've got and He'll multiply the rest.

Think about all the days of Jesus' life here in earth. When He was thirty years old and began His ministry, all of His needs were provided for as He went. He never starved. He had the best clothes, not some cheap garment. He never got sick and needed a doctor. He was kept safe in the storms and from those who wanted to take His life before He was ready to lay it down.

Essence makes me think of a sweet-smelling perfume wafting through the air. Jesus had a certain "air" about Him that drew people to Him with awe and wonder. He was everything they were looking for and everything they needed. He was one in character

JULY 1

and quality with the Father. This quality caused men to desire their original created value and position. There was something within Jesus that stirred hope and joy; something that sparked life! It was the essence of their Creator, Deliverer, and Father drawing them back into union with Him!

JULY 2

Who You Gonna Call?

Read: Jeremiah 33:1-3

When the car breaks down, we call a mechanic. When the air conditioner breaks, we call the AC man. What about when the impossible breaks loose? We call on God! He's the only one who can answer that call!

Impossible is not in God's vocabulary. The fact is, it shouldn't be in ours either. So, who are you gonna call? Well, not the Ghost Busters (LOL!). God is the master at fixing impossible circumstances!

Sometimes, I think He loves to show off! Think about the Red Sea splitting in two! All those sharks were swimming around looking for an easy meal but they hit a wall trying to snack on some Israelites as they sauntered by! When the water rushed back, the Egyptians became the shark food! Talk about destroying your enemies! That one was a doozy!

One afternoon I was cutting some vegetables for supper with a sharp knife. Oops! The knife slipped! I felt pressure, but there was no cut! I thought that I had cut myself pretty bad. But there was no blood, only a red line where the knife had slipped! Whew! Thank you Jesus! He protected me from my own carelessness!

That incident wasn't a first for me. You mean we don't have to have accidents? Yup! Think about all the things God can protect us from: car accidents, storms, burns, you name it! He's the God of the impossible! So, who are you gonna call?

JULY 3

Three Ways To Renew Your Mind

Read: Proverbs 16:32, Hebrews 12:9

*O*ne of the most challenging, yet necessary, things we will ever need to do to live the Kingdom life effectively is to renew our minds.

1. Repetition

    This is how habits are made, whether for the good or for the bad. When it comes to applying Scripture to bring about transformation of the way we think, repetition is the key. The human mind retains information more effectively when it is repeated again and again over a period of time. Then, in the near future, repeat the information to reinforce it. Be a student of the Bible and dig into the meaning of specific words by using a Concordance. Ponder the Scriptures that you read throughout the day. Ask the Holy Spirit to give you insight. Personalize specific verses and speak them out loud, thanking Him for providing what you need.

2. Keep a journal

    It doesn't have to be anything fancy; just a notebook will suffice. When we write by hand instead of typing, our brain retains information better. Write the date and the Scripture you read for that day. Record what the Holy Spirit teaches you so you can refer to it later. Take notes on special instructions or wisdom Holy Spirit reveals to you. I cannot emphasize how vital it is to keep a handwritten record of the things Holy Spirit teaches you. I have several stacks of notebooks from the past that I can look back over the past thirty years of walking with the Lord and I can see my growth and His faithfulness! Sometimes I am reminded of some pretty powerful revelations I didn't know I knew way back then! I recall to memory situations I was going through at the time

JULY 3

and how the Lord brought me through. If I hadn't been diligent to write these revelations and experiences down, they would be forgotten.

3. Speaking in tongues

   Yeah, it's weird and awkward at first, but you gotta get past that. This gift is God's way of communicating with your spirit without having to go through your mind. You are praying spirit to Spirit; the deepest part of you communicating with the Father of your spirit. If you want to be strong in your spirit, praying regularly in your own personal prayer language is vital. Your understanding of the Bible will increase. You will hear the Holy Spirit more easily when He speaks to you. You will have wisdom before you need it. I cannot emphasize the benefits of this treasure enough!

Our mind can become "unrenewed" if we think about the wrong things too. We can undo the good if we read the Bible and then go about life like everyone else and speak whatever comes to our mind with no filter. We shouldn't read *"By His stripes we are healed"* in the morning, and then when we run into a friend at the grocery store start unloading our list of aliments just for conversation. We must be consistent with truth!

JULY 4

It's Working!

Read: Romans 10:8

You've been diligent. You have read and applied Scripture to the extent that it has become your first thought, instead of your last cry. You *know* that healing belongs to you—you're fully convinced! No matter what you feel, you know it's a done deal! No one can tell you otherwise! But...

The symptoms are still there. The pain is still there...

What do you do?

Don't look at it as long-term—consider it as already done. Reckon that pain, that disease, as already changed. It wasn't there before; it can leave just as easily.

It's working. You have received an anointing that *abides*. Holy Spirit is ministering health. He's touching all of your flesh right now. He's imparting resurrection life to every cell of your body. There *must* be change; there *is* change! It might be slight, it might seem gradual, but there is change. It may even feel like nothing is going on! But in truth, healing has come! It's working! He's working in you right now! Life is there! Rejuvenation is there! Energy and strength is there!

Cooperate with that fact; the fact that Holy Spirit is living inside you. The prayers are working, the Word is working, the anointing of Holy Spirit is working...and just thank Him for it! Take the load off yourself. It's done. Now rest. He's got this! He's got you! It's working!

JULY 5

Flesh Of His Flesh

Read: Ephesians 5:21-32

*P*aul uses the metaphor of the relationship between a husband and wife as an example of Christ and His church; which is an outstanding revelation from the Holy Spirit considering the fact that he had never been married!

The analogy when a man leaves his mother and father and becomes one flesh with his wife, is relating to a person leaving the world and joining himself to Christ. The man's life is not his own anymore. It says he becomes "one flesh" with Christ.

Now, please don't misunderstand me, I'm not trying to get weird here. The point I'm attempting to make is that this verse of Scripture is referring specifically to our flesh, not the spirit. Traditionally, we've limited everything as spiritual, and as a result, we have not benefitted from the blessings of wholeness as we should. Christ paid a physical price with His body so that we would be able to receive physical benefits, especially healing.

How does this work? What begins in our spirit by faith in Christ ignites life and makes us one in spirit with Him. All of who He is possesses our spirit by the Holy Spirit. In response, the Holy Spirit imparts life to our soul, which in turn, imparts health and life to our flesh. The life of Christ saturates our entire being, spirit, soul, and body and we become flesh of His flesh and bone of His bones!

JULY 6

The Will

Read: Hebrews 10:1-10

The will. We have all been given our own free will. God won't even force His will upon people because He allows everyone to make his own choices. He may send people to influence us and draw us to Himself, but He never forces anyone to comply with His will—it's totally 100% our choice. That can definitely be a positive thing, but can also lead to unnecessary tragedy.

It is common vernacular in the church to talk about the *will* of God. Believers use it casually for practically anything that is going on in our lives; then we tack on the Scripture: *"God works all things out for good to those who love Him!"* (Romans 8:28) It's as though we think we can deduce that He's the one orchestrating every event that happens in our lives, regardless of our own choices.

What is God's will? God's will is His CHOICE. What does He choose for us? To have every spiritual blessing in Christ! He chooses for us to be conformed to the image of His Son and to live as Jesus lived on the earth. God's will is His Word. Anything outside of that isn't His will, or what He has chosen for us.

One of the biggest debates is whether or not it is His will (or choice) to heal us *every* time we need healing. And the strange thing about that question is that God revealed Himself from the beginning as *"Jehovah Rapha—The Lord Who Heals You,"* (Exodus 15:26) and He finished His will by sending His Son to pay the price for our healing with His own body. From the beginning to the end, He proved and demonstrated healing for ALL people—even pagans in the Old Testament, like Abimelech and Naaman the leper—all the way through to the New Testament. He healed pagans like the Syro-Phoenecian woman's daughter, the Centurion's servant, or the Roman soldier Malchus, whose ear Peter had chopped off.

JULY 6

Whether they were society's worst of the worst or held in high esteem, it didn't matter. He healed them all just the same. Why? Because it is His will, His choice *all* the time! He proved it over and over again! We can rest assured that it is His will, His choice for us to be healed today. It is strange that we still question that today. He never demonstrated any other outcome in the Bible. Why believe anything less now?

JULY 7

Hypostatic Union

Read: Hebrews 1:1-4

Hypostatic is just as fancy word that means *personal*. It is defined as the personal union of Jesus' two natures—the human and the divine. The word *hypostatic* isn't as important to remember as is the concept. This does not infer that Jesus is two separate people; one human and the other divine. It is the union of the human and the divine in the one person of Jesus Christ—the God-man.

Hypostatic comes from the Greek word *hupostasis*, and only appears five times in the New Testament. Hebrews 1:3, in *The Passion Translation*, is the most descriptive of Jesus:

> *"The Son is the dazzling radiance of God's splendor, the exact expression of God's true nature—His mirror image!"*

In this verse of Scripture, it is evident that both the Father and the Son share the same nature. What makes this union of the human and the divine natures in Christ so magnificent is that we have someone to connect us with the Divine. Jesus fully represents us to God, at the same time He fully represents God to man.

What causes this union to be even more mind-blowing is the fact that this same union is offered to us! Does not Scripture say, *"As He is so are we in this world?"* (1 John 4:17) Since our lives are hidden in Christ, we are human in a physical body, but our spirit has been made alive by union with the Holy Spirit. It is His life and power that oozes from the inside out!

We are fully human and fully divine because of Christ! With this in mind, we no longer look at ourselves in our humanness and its limitations. The expression of the life of Christ bursts forth in light, life, and miraculous ability as we do the works Jesus demonstrated out of the Father's love for people!

JULY 8

Judas

Read: Matthew 26:46-56, 27:3-10, Acts 1:15-21

There is so much emotion in the events happening in this account of Jesus' arrest. His own disciple and friend, Judas, betrayed Him and set in motion Jesus' trial that led to His crucifixion. Judas had healed the sick and cast out demons with the other twelve. He had experienced life with the Master personally and in close fellowship for over three years. Were these events as cut and dry as we perceive?

Other writings suggest that Judas was tricked into betraying Jesus, others deduce that he was just a crook blinded by greed. Whatever the case may have been, he will always be remembered as a traitor and entitled as the "son of perdition" (John 17:12). Another interesting fact is that Judas was the only disciple that was not from Galilee.

We read in Acts that Judas ended his misery in anguish of soul. He repented by returning the money to the religious leaders for handing Jesus over. He ended his own life because he couldn't live with himself for what he had done. Whether he was forgiven or not, we'll never know for sure on this side of eternity.

Have you ever done something you swore to yourself you'd never do? Have you ever let yourself down by not living up to your own expectations? Little by little, you find yourself in a place you never thought you'd end up, surprised at your own human depravity. I remember being in that place before I came to Christ. It's a place where you're so low that the only direction you can go is up. Yet, somehow Jesus finds you. Psalm 40:2 says,

> *"He lifted me out of the slimy pit, out of the mud and mire; He set my feet on a rock and gave me a firm place to stand."* (NIV)

JULY 8

It isn't a bad place to be if you've come to the end of yourself; then you're ready to live your life God's way. When there's no other place to go but up, and when you're that low, it can only get better. Jesus stretches out His hand to pull you up out of that slimy pit. He gives you a firm place to stand, and that place is in Him. Now, you no longer have to rely only upon yourself, well, cuz you know where that got you! He restores your soul.

There are a lot bad of memories from the past that the Lord has helped me to forget. The first step was to stop thinking about them—things people said or did that fueled my injustices. When you can look back on certain people with compassion, instead of anger or revenge, you'll know you're on the right track. We cannot afford to give other people the responsibility to validate our identity. We must solely put our trust in Christ alone. Jesus paid for us to be whole in our soul just as much as in our physical body. It says in Isaiah 53:5 *"...the chastisement of our peace was upon Him..."*

So take His hand. It's there—outstretched to you in whatever situation you're in. Forgive yourself. Receive His forgiveness. Let Him pull you out of that slimy pit and set your feet upon a rock! He desires to make you whole!

JULY 9

Malchus

Read: Luke 22:44-51, John 18:1-11

*T*hese two accounts of Jesus in the garden praying and the events leading up to His death, stir us with much emotion. In the Gospel of John, Jesus strode boldly up to His accusers and met them eye to eye. *"Who are you looking for?"* When they answered, *"Jesus of Nazareth,"* He did **not** say *"I am He."* He said, *"I AM."* The word *He* was added by the translators, but it isn't there in the original language. Why is this important? Jesus was making a statement that implied much more than He said.

In Exodus 3:14, God referred to Himself as *"I AM"* when He revealed Himself to Moses. He told him, *"Tell them I AM sent ya!"* Jesus was indentifying Himself with the Father—the Great *"I AM"*! At the mention of THE NAME, Jesus' enemies fell on their backsides with such force; it was as though a great gust of wind had knocked them over!

Another interesting event was when Peter's passion to protect Jesus became full blown by chopping off a soldier's ear. Malchus was an enemy, a Roman soldier sent to arrest Jesus. Most of us would have said, *"Let him bleed to death, he deserves it!"* But...Jesus responded, and I love the way it is opened up to us readers in Luke 22:51 in the NKJV,

> *"But Jesus answered and said, 'Permit even this.' And He touched His ear and healed him."*

What a response! He healed his ear! Imagine the shock of having his ear chopped off, the pain he felt, and the blood squirting out everywhere! Then, Jesus touched his ear and it was instantly made whole! It doesn't say he picked up the ear that was chopped off and put it back on the side of Malchus' head. It says Jesus touched his ear and healed him, which leads me to think the old ear was still

JULY 9

lying there on the ground and the dude got a new ear! (Sorry if you're a bit queasy from my description, LOL!).

The events surrounding Jesus' arrest seem chaotic, but Jesus knew exactly what was going to happen to Him; He was in control the whole time. In the midst of His most trying hours, His compassion toward His enemy still ruled over the anguish He wrestled with in His soul just a few moments earlier when He sweat great drops of blood. Jesus is able to abruptly "switch gears" by saving this enemy soldier, who probably would have gone into shock and died. Talk about controlling your emotions!

In the midst of tragedy, Jesus remained calm and in control. His relationship with the Father and Holy Spirit, which He had developed over the course of His life, was the key factor in His ability to react with compassion to heal verses act in retaliation, even though He had every right to defend His innocence. It is a reminder for us to remember, that in tragic situations, with the help of the Holy Spirit, we too, can remain calm and in control. We will be able to hear clearly what He tells us to do and act swiftly, boldly, and with confidence!

JULY 10

Avoid The Noid

Read: Song of Solomon 2:15

Do you remember the creepy little character in the *Dominos Pizza* commercials back in the 1980s? He was always trying to destroy Dominos Pizzas, but he was never successful. For whatever reason, my brother-in-law likes the Noid so much that he got a tattoo of it on his arm. Because of the tattoo, he ended up starring in a commercial on TV for *Dominos* just a few years ago!

To me, the Noid was just a weird, ugly, annoying character. Imagine some menacing, ghoulish creature sneaking around stalking the delivery boy to sabotage your take-out dinner!

Sometimes, there can be little things lurking around in our lives that we are unaware of—things we have held on to for so long that we don't realize that they have become a part of us. You know—those character flaws or typically responding to situations with worry and anxiety. Do you flip out and vomit your emotions on friends and family members? Do you use something physical like alcohol or anti-depressants, in an attempt to manage your emotions?

I know life can be overwhelming sometimes, but the solution should not be worse than the problem. Emotions can be like that creepy little Noid on the lookout to destroy your lunch. And the strange thing about emotions is that they are so unreliable that they change from one moment to the next. People that are ruled by their emotions are down one minute and up the next. It's like a roller coaster ride that never ends—up and down, round and round—so exhausting!

One thing for sure is that emotions, when out of control, keep us from *abiding* in the vine. The grapes on the vine are like the fruit we are expected to bear to give glory to Christ living inside of us as His nature and character are revealed.

JULY 10

Jesus said He came to give us His peace and not what the world gives. I love the verse in the Psalms that says, *"What time I am afraid, I will trust in Thee."* (Psalm 56:3 KJV). That verse always calms my soul when I think about it. God's Word is so precious to me. It's the one thing I run to when I need help; and Holy Spirit is always there to help lead me into truth and get my emotions in check. When I ask Him for a verse of Scripture, He usually gives me something specific that pertains to my situation, or He tells me what I need to do. I hold on to His instruction because it becomes my life-line to the solution.

I remember many situations over the years of my life that were so overwhelming, I couldn't think straight. I'd ask Holy Spirit for a verse of Scripture, and then I'd meditate on it and speak it frequently. God came through every time! Sometimes it was a life-threatening situation, or a relationship on the verge of irreconcilable differences. As God honored His Word, I learned how dependable He is!

So the next time you find yourself in a terrifying situation, don't grab your phone. Don't grab a bottle or a pill; leave the Oreos® in the cabinet. Grab your Bible and talk to Holy Spirit. He knows exactly what you need!

JULY 11

Information Warfare

Read: Luke 12:22-34

*T*here is no doubt that we are living in a time of "information warfare." Whether the topic is food, exercise, finances, politics, or spiritual things we are constantly being bombarded with information. Most of it is pure rubbish. The real challenge comes when we are looking for the right answers and need a solution.

It is inconceivable how timeless the Scriptures are! Yet, we usually find that the answers we need are the exact opposite of the information the world dishes out. In fact, the information the world puts out is forever changing. For example: Many years ago a scientist named Galileo discovered that the sun was the center of the solar system, not the earth. For that, he was excommunicated from the church as a heretic. Today, we know this as a fact. Another example is food. A few years ago information poured out about how good it is to eat margarine, which is mostly man-made ingredients, verses butter, which is natural. Currently, they have retracted that "wisdom." It's ridiculous! Information is forever changing.

The world tells us to "stock up!" The Bible tells us to give and it shall be given back in abundance. The Bible instructs us to be kind to our enemies and do good to those who despitefully use us. The world tells us to take revenge. According to Scripture, we lose to gain and we die to live. The world is always the opposite.

Although the information surrounding us is confusing at best, Jesus' instructions, *"And do not seek what you should eat or what you should drink, nor have an anxious mind"* (Luke 12:29 NKJV) are still just as effective today as when He first spoke them. His point was, *"We've got a job to do. Don't get encumbered with your worldly needs—I'll take care of that; just go about My Father's business in the Kingdom."* So whatever your needs are, don't look to the world

JULY 11

with its ever-changing plethora of choices. You've got two sources of constant help any time you need it: Holy Spirit and the Word. You'll be sure to avoid confusion just by keeping your options pure and simple!

JULY 12

Arise

Read: Mark 2:8-12, Mark 5:40-42

Arise. Such a simple yet powerful word! Jesus spoke this word and the man who was paralyzed got up and walked. Jesus said, *"Arise"* and the little girl, Jairus' daughter, came back to life!

What power is contained in this little five letter word? Resurrection Life! It's the word Jesus spoke to make the man walk again. Usually when a person is paralyzed, other organs in the body are affected as well, not just the legs. There was more going on here than meets the eye. When Jesus healed someone, they were made whole. In the Hebrew understanding, that meant "Shalom"—peace, nothing missing, lacking, or broken.

Whatever sickness that little girl had that took her life was gone when Jesus said to her, *"Arise."* She was fully restored to her parents, healthy and strong! All of her organs were functioning perfectly in her body. So ***ARISE!*** Be healed and whole right now in Jesus' Name!

JULY 13

Living In Gratitude

Read: Romans 5:8-11

When I think about the New Covenant and all that is included in Christ through His sacrifice, it blows me away! Sometimes it challenges me to remember: *"Wait! I can't earn this!"* Whether it is physical healing or any other need I have, my *doing* doesn't earn me anything! The time I spend studying and reading the Bible, or in prayer, is really all for my own benefit. It will not give me "brownie points" with God or influence His desire to help me. He already desires to bless me—whether I give money to my church or not; whether I help the poor and needy or not. These things I do *as a result* of my relationship with Christ out of gratitude—not to gain it.

According to Scripture, we don't belong to ourselves any longer. We live in response to the willing sacrifice Jesus became when He took our place. First Corinthians 6:19-20 says, in the NIV, *"...you are not your own; you were bought at a price..."* The most inspiring part that brings me gratitude, in response to Christ, is that I am free from myself! I no longer have to be driven by my own human nature and desires. Jesus destroyed the sinful nature of man and gave us power over it. Romans 6:6 declares that our old man was crucified with Him and that we are no longer slaves of sin. That includes sickness as well!

Nope! We can't *earn* physical healing! It is received the exact same way salvation is received—by faith in Christ alone! Why? Because it is included in the New Covenant. His body was broken so our body could be made whole. His blood was shed to remit (wash away) all our sins.

If you've ever questioned whether there was something you did to deserve sickness, the answer is "NOPE!" Now, I'm not saying

JULY 13

that natural consequences don't happen sometimes to people who are intentionally harming themselves. But would God withhold healing from any person doing these things? Would He withhold salvation from them? The answer to both questions is a resounding *"NO!"* Would He withhold healing to them, even if He knew they'd go back to their old lifestyle? A resounding *"NO!"* is in order. Why? Because healing isn't based on how good or bad we are, and neither is salvation! Healing and Salvation are solely based on the Covenant our Father God made with His Son Jesus Christ, and we can't earn it or mess it up! It is given by believing in Jesus alone!

Yep! God is THAT GOOD!

JULY 14

A Habitation

Read: John 14:15-27

*O*f all the Saints in the past, the one person I have enjoyed reading about the most is John G. Lake. I came across an autobiography about his life and faith over twenty years ago. His intensity for God has always stirred me more than anyone else. One of his most inspiring quotes is:

> *"The Holy Spirit is not simply given that you may be a channel and always a channel. No sir! But instead of that, the most significant thing the Word of God portrays is that Christ indwelling in you by the Holy Ghost is to make you a son of God like Jesus Christ, God-anointed from heaven, with the recognized power of God in your spirit to command the will of God."*

He says so much contained in this one little paragraph that if you never understood the purpose of the Holy Spirit before, you would after reading Lake's description of our identity, and what we're supposed to do with it. Many Believers today would consider it heresy to think we could command the will of God! But this is exactly what Jesus demonstrated.

The Holy Spirit was sent by Jesus to *live* and *dwell* inside us, not come and go like He did in the Old Testament for prophets and kings. Some religious people talk about "hosting" the Holy Spirit, like He's a guest that floats into our lives under the right conditions or an atmosphere that has been set by hours of worship. Then, when it's all over, He leaves until next time the atmosphere is to His liking and He feels welcomed. But, my friends, Scripture does not support this belief.

Jesus said He and the Father would make Their home in us (John 14:23). He also said He would never leave us—even to the end of

JULY 14

the earth (Matthew 28:20). Hebrews 13:5 says *"I will never leave you nor forsake you."* In the Greek, this is one of the most emphatic statements in the New Testament. It contains two double negatives meaning in English, *"I will never, ever, ever forsake you."*

The Holy Spirit will never leave you! Sometimes we do sense Him stronger than others, but that is not because He left and came back. It is simply because we aren't as aware of Him because of distractions. The Holy Spirit has nothing better to do than to stay with you all the time! That is where He wants to be. He was sent to be your Helper. He wouldn't be a very good helper if He was fickle and didn't want to show up because the atmosphere wasn't to His liking or all of your ducks weren't in a row, so to speak.

So whatever situation you're in today or tomorrow, Holy Spirit is right there with you in the thick of it. In reality, He's waiting for us to involve Him rather than us waiting on Him! He never leaves—Nope! Never!

JULY 15

The Miraculous

Read: John 10:37-42

Have you ever seen a miracle? Have you ever experienced a miracle for yourself? If you are born again, you are a miracle! In fact, being born again is the greatest miracle! Why? Because a new person has been resurrected! Your old self was the walking dead, and now you have been born from above into a completely new person!

Have you ever heard testimonies of people that used to commit the most heinous crimes and how they were born again; how Grandma's prayers or their Mama's prayers brought them to Christ, after years of rebellion and wild living? I love this quote by T.L. Osborn: *"Everything about Christianity is miraculous. If we don't have the miraculous in Christianity, we have a philosophy."*

Since the very origin of our new birth is miraculous, we should expect a life of experiences in the miraculous! Most of the Church has been conditioned to sit and hear a message once a week and then go back to "normal" after a half hour of a motivational speech. Many have been relegated to a philosophy to live by, verses life-changing power in order to be equipped to give it to others. Look at the life Christ demonstrated and taught His disciples! He taught them by demonstrating the miraculous. He even said, *"If you don't believe My words, believe My works!"* (My paraphrase).

Everything about true Christianity is miraculous! Why settle for a philosophy? You were (re)born for more than that! Don't settle for less!

JULY 16

Life Without Limits

Read: John 15:1-17

*W*hat if every request you prayed was answered? (The ones according to Scripture, not the ones like: *"God give me a Mercedes cuz my Mazda isn't good enough."*) One of the most hindering beliefs is that God is only in Heaven or in the atmosphere around them. They relate to God being up there in heaven and that He has to hear them banging on the doors of heaven to the point of exhaustion just to get their prayers heard before He *might* decide to answer. Some talk about grabbing on the horns of the altar and not letting go till God answers! My question is, what altar are they praying at, cuz that sounds like the Old Testament to me! Jesus is our once and for all sacrifice.

I have personally experienced many more answers when I approach a situation like this: *"Holy Spirit, I know You are aware of my circumstances because You are right here in them with me. I know that You already have the solution cuz Jesus paid for it. Please show me what to do."* Next, with confidence, I start praying in the spirit, expecting to hear His instructions. I *know* He's here and that He already *has* the answer. When I approach the situation with confidence, I usually receive an immediate response.

My daughter had to go to the hospital because she was in premature labor with her third son. She was only 34 weeks into the pregnancy. She had planned to give birth at home with a midwife and not even involve doctors or hospitals. It was about ten o'clock at night when she called and told me that she and her husband were headed to the hospital. I told my husband that I had peace about the situation, but I was going to stay up, pray, and listen to what Holy Spirit had to say. I began to pray in the spirit. That always shifts my mind away from anxiousness and fearful thoughts of *"what if"* scenarios.

JULY 16

As I prayed in the spirit, this verse came to me: *"Tell the righteous it will be well with them."* (Isaiah 3:10) Those words leaped out at me! I knew it was confirmation of the peace I had already sensed from Holy Spirit, that everything was going to be fine with my daughter and the baby. I praised the Holy Spirit for His answer as I continued praying in the Spirit, thanking Him that all would be well as He had said. I received a phone call from my son-in-law that the contractions had stopped and the doctors found nothing wrong in any of the tests. I continued to pray with thanksgiving until she went home at 2am. Then I went to sleep.

I can't tell you how many times God has answered situations so specifically, right in the middle of what could be a mess! Things always work out so much more effectively when I come to Him with boldness and confidence, verses crying and questioning! He tells us to boldly come to His throne of grace to find help in our time of need! Holy Spirit, our Helper, is ALWAYS on the scene!

JULY 17

The Guarantee

Read: John 6:26-27, Ephesians 1:13-14

When we purchase a car or a house, it is typically required that we pay a percentage as a down payment, called earnest money, that proves our commitment to follow through with the purchase. Otherwise, the property or car will be sold to someone else who is able to pay the price in full.

The above Scriptures tell us that the Holy Spirit was sent to live inside us. He is the deposit, or the down payment securing our salvation. The word *guarantee*, in the original language, means that the Holy Spirit was given as a pledge for the "purchase payment" as security for the rest. In other words, He was given in earnest until our full redemption.

One day God is going to "make good" on His deposit and fully bring us into everything He promised, laid up for us in heaven. He sealed us as His own precious possession with the Holy Spirit. The Holy Spirit is the seal, or mark of ownership, in a Believer's life. The Holy Spirit is the guarantee of our inheritance.

The Holy Spirit is like an engagement ring given by Christ, the Bridegroom to the Church—His Bride. The Holy Spirit is the down payment, the earnest money, in the long-awaited marriage. We are the Father's purchased possession, bought by the blood of His Son.

If you've ever wondered whether God would make good on His promise to live in eternity where He is, here's how we can be sure He'll make good on His Word: We're signed, sealed, and delivered as a guarantee by the Holy Spirit!

JULY 18

Signs

Read: Luke 2:8-20

Signs

"Sign, sign, everywhere a sign
Blocking out the scenery breaking my mind
Do this don't do that, can't you read the sign!"
Song by 5 Electric Band, 1971

*T*his song has been running through my mind lately. Did you ever have that happen to you? Sometimes I wake up in the morning and the first thing that comes to my mind is an old song. My husband and I frequently joke around and relate circumstances to different songs we grew up hearing on the radio.

A few years ago I was in a major transition in my life. I was no longer a mom homeschooling her children, but had become a new grandmother with all her children grown into mature adults living on their own. I think they call it "Empty Nest Syndrome." What was I going to do with the rest of my life? I never imagined myself as a granny!

One day, I was in a store and I heard the song by Elton John, "Crocodile Rock." I didn't think much of it at the time. A few days later, I was in another store and the same song was playing on the intercom. *"Hmmm, that's a coincidence,"* I thought. Then I forgot about it. About a week later I was driving down a back road listening to a Christian radio station. When I drove over the crest of a hill, the station switched over to a secular radio station all by itself! It was playing the song "Crocodile Rock!"

"Okay, Lord, now You got my attention! Are You trying to tell me something?" I laughed because I knew at that point it was more than just a coincidence! When I returned home, I looked up the

JULY 18

lyrics of the song. What stood out to me was the line: *"I never knew me a better time and I guess I never will."*

Aw, man—that was *exactly* how I was feeling! Like my best days were over! God was showing me that my best days were ahead of me, not behind me! God can use any number of things to speak to us every day. Whatever situation you are facing, Holy Spirit is speaking. Pay attention to any signs He might be showing you. You don't have to get all weird about it. Our relationship with Holy Spirit is for real. He's never silent and He's never still; and He does have a sense of humor!

JULY 19

He's Got It!

Read: Matthew 8:5-13

*T*here are so many times when Holy Spirit gave me that *knowing* in my spirit—that inner witness that something was going to turn out a certain way. For example, my son had an issue with his tailbone. He started to have sharp pain for no apparent reason. No injury had occurred; just inflammation and pain to the point where he couldn't sit straight.

I've learned that Holy Spirit is involved in every healing. I prayed for my son and I didn't feel a release of the Holy Spirit flowing through me or anything; although I know I cannot afford to put my trust in what I do or don't feel. The next day, I was asking the Holy Spirit about my son's healing and He reminded me that I had prayed for a lady a few years ago who had fallen and injured her tailbone to where she could hardly sit. After prayer, she was healed and the pain never returned.

The confidence for my son's healing was complete when I heard Holy Spirit's instructions. I knew it was a done deal. When Holy Spirit gives me information to help, I know for sure He's got it! I texted my son the next day and asked him how he was doing. He said he was almost 100%! Yay God! Just like the Centurion who had taken Jesus at His word; when he returned home he found that his servant was healed at the exact time Jesus had spoken.

I'll admit that sometimes my confidence doesn't always flow naturally. Usually, that is because, somehow, I got my own thoughts too far into the situation and I don't hear from the Holy Spirit as easily as I should. He never ceases to amaze me with His patient, constant help. I don't always realize that the ideas He brings to my mind are His because they are so simple. The thought that came to my mind about the lady being healed from the same pain my son

JULY 19

had was not my own bright idea. I had totally forgotten about it, as it had happened over two years ago. Holy Spirit was pretty genius by bringing that back to my memory! A simple reminder was all it took to give me the confidence I needed.

I encourage you to make it a habit of paying attention to the thoughts that come to your mind. This is one way that the Holy Spirit is communicating with you. If a thought about a circumstance comes to your mind that is helpful, stirs your faith, and gives you confidence; you can be sure it isn't your own brilliant idea—it is His! From that point on, just consider it done!

JULY 20

Done!

Read: John 19:28-30

Several years ago, when I lived in Texas, I received a phone call from my aunt in Pennsylvania. She told me that her daughter, my newly married cousin, was desperate to have a baby. She had been to fertility doctors and had tried everything but nothing had worked. She wept and grieved daily; her heart ached to hold a baby in her arms. My aunt is the most compassionate person I've ever known and she was in anguish for her daughter. Being a Believer herself, she asked me to pray.

Shortly after our conversation, I began to pray for my cousin. It was almost like at the same time I opened my mouth to pray, I heard the Holy Spirit say very loudly, *"Done!"*

The next time I spoke with my aunt on the phone, she told me that my cousin was depressed and wept day after day, longing for a baby. I told my aunt what the Lord had told me: *"Done!"* My aunt responded, *"Oh, Michele! She is inconsolable and weeps every day! Her shoulders sink with despair and hopelessness. She just sobs, hanging her head!"*

"Well, I know what I heard and she's going to have a baby!" I assured her. Shortly after we had that conversation, my cousin got pregnant! Man that was simple! Today that precious baby is now a brave, beautiful young woman who works as a nurse; ministering compassion to every patient she meets!

"Done!"

JULY 21

The Resurrection

Read: I Corinthians 15

If there is one chapter in the Bible that consistently speaks about the resurrection throughout the entire chapter, it would be First Corinthians 15. Paul states that the message he preached was the message of Christ, raised from the dead. To remove the message of Christ's resurrection would be destroying the message of the Gospel. He goes so far as to say that our faith is useless if Christ was not resurrected. He lays his reputation on the line and states that he, as well as all the other Believers who preach the Gospel, would be false witnesses spreading lies if they didn't preach Christ's resurrection. Paul further says in verse 17, that if Christ isn't alive, then we are lost in our sins and our faith is just a fantasy. Jesus declared in John 5:24 in *The Passion Translation*,

> "I speak to you an eternal truth: If you embrace My message and believe in the One who sent Me, you will never face condemnation. In Me, you have already passed from the realm of death into eternal life!"

The Father is the source of life and He has given His Son the authority to impart life to us! This isn't a *someday maybe when you go to heaven* promise—it is for now! The moment you came to Christ, you entered heaven's eternity. Resurrection power is giving you life through Jesus' life inside you!

Jesus demonstrated authority over death when He raised Lazarus from the dead, the widow of Nain's son, Jairus' twelve year old daughter, and when He Himself was resurrected by the power of the Holy Spirit.

Paul had received resurrection power through the Holy Spirit. He demonstrated that power when he raised Eutychus from the dead; after he had fallen asleep and dropped to his death from a third

JULY 21

story window due to Paul's long-winded preaching! Scriptures testify, in Hebrews eleven, that women received their dead raised back to life!

We have evidence that raising dead people back to life is not a strange phenomenon, but a *normal* part of true Christianity. In fact, without the resurrection from the dead, our faith is futile and we are left without hope!

It's fascinating to hear the testimonies from groups of Believer's traveling around the globe as Dead Raising Teams; ministering salvation, healing, and resurrection from the dead. We are truly living in exciting times! I've experienced praying for someone and raising them from the dead from a drug overdose, as I had shared before. So, don't fear if an opportunity comes your way. As a Believer, you are fully equipped with the power of the Holy Spirit to do the same works as Jesus, Paul, or any of the other Believers in his day!

JULY 22

Who's Got Who?

Read: Acts 10

In the *Wuest Translation* of verse 45 it proclaims:

> "...because also upon the Gentiles the gift of the Holy Spirit had been bestowed with the result that now He was in their possession, for they were hearing them speaking by means of languages [other than their own and not naturally acquired], and extolling God."

What I find interesting about this Scripture is that this is a repeat of Acts chapter two, but specifically for the Gentiles. God intentionally made it a point to show all of us who were not born in the lineage of the Jews that we get to share in the inheritance of Christ, and now there's no distinction between the two.

It is further fascinating the language the *Wuest Translation* uses by describing the Holy Spirit as *"in their possession."* It goes on to say that the Gentiles were speaking in different languages and extolling God; which they did with the help of the Holy Spirit.

Let's consider how *possession* is defined in the dictionary: *to have as property; own, to have under one's power or control, to have as a quality, characteristic, or other attribute.*

So who had who? Did the Gentiles possess the Holy Spirit or did the Holy Spirit possess them? Both! Pretty cool, huh? They possessed/owned Holy Spirit and He possessed/owned them! They were under Holy Spirit's power and displayed His character from that moment on! There was an infusion of life that had taken place in their spirit and they were now included in the Kingdom!

JULY 23

Confidence Needed

Read: Acts 8:26-40

I recently read the story of John G. Lake and his dying sister. He had a very close relationship with her since childhood and received a message from his mother that, if he didn't come to see her right away, it would be too late. Lake had previously lost eight brothers and sisters. Their family had suffered a lifetime of illnesses and, as a result, sorrow had become their lot. This was one of the main reasons Lake pursued healing with everything in his being. He hated sickness with a passion and vowed to learn how to heal the sick through John Alexander Dowie.

When Lake arrived at the house, his sister was already gone. Her little baby was asleep in the crib nearby. Their parents wept uncontrollably at the side of her bed, but something inside of him would not let her go! His wife was healed just a few weeks prior of a heart condition, and his brother and another sister had recently been healed of terminal illnesses. He could not accept death for his precious sister!

He began to cry out to God, *"O God, this is not Your will, I cannot accept it! Dear Lord, she cannot go!"* Lake was in dire need of someone with faith in God that he could call for help. He sent Dowie, who was 600 miles away, a telegram, *"My sister has apparently died but my spirit will not let her go. I believe if you will pray God will heal her."* He received a message back, *"Hold on to God. She will live."*

Dowie's response created what Lake described as flashes of lightning to his soul. He prayed out loud, abolishing death and sickness, while speaking life. When he turned to look at his sister, he saw her eyes blink and her husband had seen it too! Five days later, the

JULY 23

family was gathered together to enjoy Christmas dinner and, for the first time in nine years, everyone in the family was well!

When I ponder the events in this story, I wonder if Lake really needed Dowie's help. After all, Dowie was 600 miles away. Lake believed he needed Dowie to agree with him for his sister and this gave him the confidence he needed to stir up the Holy Spirit inside him.

Consider Philip in our passage for today. He was all by himself in unfamiliar surroundings. Yet, an angel spoke to him and told him where to go. Later, the Holy Spirit picked him up and transported him to another place so he could continue preaching. If that's not enough to give somebody confidence when they need help, I don't know what is!

I wonder if that is all some of us need at times—just a little boost to get to the other side. Whether its help from a friend in the faith or Holy Spirit telling you what to do, that little boost is enough to give us the confidence we need at the time to see the miracle we need to come forth!

JULY 24

No Decapitation

Read: Colossians 1:15-23

*A*n accurate understanding of the New Covenant brings with it the knowledge that God, as our Father, does not look at us separate from Christ. He sees us "in Christ"—perfectly united with absolutely no distinction. This is why He (Jesus) is called the head and we are called the body—we are inseparable.

Anytime we put ourselves in a lower class than Christ, it is like decapitating a head from its body. I know this is an interesting way of describing it, but it's true! This gives us a clear picture of what it is like for a person to see themselves with any other identity than Christ.

Think of it this way: Look at your body with Jesus' head on it instead of yours. You are seeing yourself in Christ. He is your identity. Any time you compare yourself to another person other than Christ, it's like putting that person's head on your body.

The Bible tells us that we have been given the mind of Christ, the nature and the character of Christ, and that we are complete in Him. No other identity will cause us to live the victorious life we are called to live. Our Father even honors the words we speak the same as He does Jesus' words! There is no favoritism! He didn't spare His own Son, but surrendered Him for our sake! He has freely given us everything Jesus has—yes, even His glory!

Ouch! Did I step on somebody's religious toes? Well, it's true! He gave us His glory! Many well-meaning preachers will say that God won't share His glory with anyone. Wrong! It's proven right there in the Old Testament in Psalm 8:3-6, and the New Testament in John 17:20-23, that we were crowned with the same glory! Would we really have been made in His image without Him giving us His glory? No! So let's not separate ourselves from our identity in Christ. No decapitations here!

JULY 25

Eyes And Ears

Proverbs 20:12

*P*ersonally, I can't stand to wear glasses of any kind, even sunglasses. Everything just looks wonky. I had tried to wear contact lenses and my eyes got so dried out that no amount of eye drops helped. My eyes became bloodshot with bulging red blood vessels. The ophthalmologist tried several different types of lenses. He gave up on me! Nope! Just can't do it! So any problem with my eyes just had to be healed by Jesus cuz I couldn't stand any other way.

God made our eyes and our ears to perform functions that we need to get us through life. He created our eyes to be able to see and our ears to be able to hear perfectly. So if you need healing for your eyes or ears—this is for you!

It says here in Proverbs that God made *"the **hearing** ear and the **seeing** eye."* God did not make eyes and ears that do not function properly. Ears were created specifically to hear and eyes were created specifically to see. Got "floaters" in your eyes or loss of vision? Be healed now in Jesus' Name! Got ringing in your ears or hearing loss? Be healed now in Jesus' Name! Now expect to see and hear clearly!

JULY 26

Faith Over Fear

Read: Psalm 27

"*Faith over Fear*"

I have seen this statement a lot these days since the "plandemic" hit the world. An article from a popular Christian website I recently read mentioned that not wearing a mask was throwing common sense out the window as much as not wearing a seatbelt in your car. They called not wearing a mask *"flagrant disregard of the reason and rationality He's (God) employed us to use."* The author further stated that not wearing a mask was "testing" the Lord like Israel had done in Numbers 14:42-43 when they wanted to confront the Amalekites and Canaanites, even though God adamantly declared He would not go with them if this is what they chose.

The editorial also referenced the event when the devil tempted Jesus, taking Him to the high point of the temple, commanding Him to throw Himself down, and enticing Him by quoting Psalm 91. Since Jesus response was not to put God to the test, the author of the article believed this was equal to someone not wearing a mask, because this would be similar to testing God.

I don't agree with this person's use of these Scriptures to back up his belief, though, I must say that I was very grieved by the position the church worldwide had taken during the lockdowns. We, overall, exhibited anything but faith over fear by shutting down our buildings, wearing masks, practicing social distancing, and turning our facilities into vaccination sites. This trial displayed how deep the world has infiltrated the church—who is meant to be God's ruling, governing authority in the earth *over* sickness and disease.

There is nothing in Scripture that implores us to use common sense, in fact, it's quite the opposite. One third of Jesus' ministry was healing the sick and setting people free. Laying hands on a

JULY 26

leper to heal him is not using common sense—it's using God-sense. God's mandate to His church is to advance the Kingdom by healing the sick. Jesus told the twelve when He sent them out in Luke 10:9, *"Heal the sick there, and say to them, 'The Kingdom of God has come near you.'"*

My point is simply this, at some point you gotta trust God plain and simple. Man's common sense clearly has limitations. A mask can't keep you free from all germs, a seatbelt can't always save people from dying in car accidents, and jumping off a high place...well, that's entirely up to you! The Bible doesn't say that faith overcomes fear, it says that *love* defeats fear. Faith doesn't believe in some *thing*. Faith believes and trusts in God alone; and when you're in faith—His perfect love casts out all fear!

JULY 27

Under Or Over?

Read: Mark 4:35-41

From the days of old, "under the weather" was a nautical term coined by sailors as they traveled on tempestuous seas. Crewmen and passengers feeling sick were sent below deck to protect them from the weather. They would literally be "under the weather." Today, we use the term frequently as a polite way of saying someone isn't feeling well. Some make claims about how the weather affects their body, *"Oh, I can tell it's going to rain tomorrow! I can feel it in my bones!"*

A few weeks ago, my grandson was at my house. My daughter had taken him and his brothers for a walk up the hill and it suddenly became extremely windy. I went outside to help her with the boys and, before I could get to her, my four year old grandson came running down the driveway wide-eyed in stark terror yelling, *"Mimaw, a 'tormato' is coming!* (His way of saying *tornado* LOL!) *Hurry! We have to hide!"* A few days prior, there was a tornado warning near his house and they had to seek shelter in their basement until the storm passed.

I told him, *"No we don't have to hide. You just tell that tornado to go away in Jesus' Name!"* He said, *"You can do that to a tormato?"* Trying to hold a serious composure at his four-year-old terminology, I explained to him, *"Yes you can! Jesus spoke to the wind and the waves, remember? You don't have to be afraid of the wind."* We spoke to the wind and commanded it to go away. In a short time, the weather returned to normal.

It's common vernacular for people to accuse the weather for their sickness or pain. As children we grow up hearing all of the reasons why we can get sick: put your coat on before you go outside when it's cold, don't go out in the rain, don't get wet feet, etc.

JULY 27

Jesus chided the disciples after He spoke to the storm, *"Why are you so afraid? Haven't you learned to trust yet?"* (*The Passion Translation*) Most of these men were experienced fisherman, but I don't think that was in their favor. They had probably persevered through many storms and fear had gripped their hearts, remembering previous fishing expeditions when their lives were in danger.

It's a good idea to think about what we're saying and why we say it. Our beliefs are affected by the words we've heard while growing up, and sometimes, we just say things out of habit. Remember that life and death are in the power of the tongue!

Are we *under* the weather or *over* it?

JULY 28

Fill 'Er Up!

Read: Luke 4:1-15

I remember when I was a little girl, probably about four or five years old, after we went to church as a family, sometimes we'd try to go out to eat. Not much was opened on a Sunday in those days (I know I'm showing my age!). I remember one time in particular, we were almost out of gas and there were no gas stations open. We finally found one—you know, the days when you didn't have to pump your own gas and all you'd have to say is, *"Fill 'er up!"* to the attendant. You'd get your oil checked and your windows cleaned too, and you didn't have to get out of your car! It was called a "Full Service" gas station. Those days are long gone!

In our Scripture for today we read that Jesus, being *filled* with the Holy Spirit was led into the wilderness. After He defeated every temptation that the devil could come up with, it says He returned to Galilee in the *power* of the Spirit. He didn't get weaker from the temptation or the fasting. He remained steadfast. He was filled with the Spirit at His baptism and stayed filled with power.

I have had heard this statement many times: that we are just "leaky vessels" that need to constantly be filled up again, kinda like burning up the gas in your car and you have to pull up to the service station and say, *"Fill'er up!"* again and again.

The word *filled* in the Greek means: *replete, covered over, complete, full*. Jesus was full of the Holy Spirit and the Spirit never waned or left Him. God had told John the Baptist,

> *"The one you see the Spirit descending upon* **and remaining** *is He who baptizes with the Holy Spirit...this is the Son of God."* (John 1:32-34, NKJV, Emphasis added)

JULY 28

Whenever we feel like the Holy Spirit isn't near and God feels far away, it isn't because He left. It is because we became preoccupied with other things and our awareness of Him has diminished. The Holy Spirit never "leaks" out of us. Where would He go? In a puddle on the floor? Would He leak out like air from a tire? Kinda silly, isn't it? Especially when Jesus promised that He'd NEVER leave us or forsake us!

God is a Full-Service Attendant!

JULY 29

Slime

Read: Psalm 41:1-3

The past few days as I sit here writing this devotion, my husband and I have been severely annoyed with bad colds. I was hacked off at myself for letting it even take a hold on me. I know better! When I felt the first signs, I just dismissed it as nothing. I should have held that stance.

Anyway, today was the turn around. Why today? I don't know why I didn't have this epiphany sooner—day one would have been nice, but nevertheless, it came! I always look for that connection with the Holy Spirit. The one that says, *"Done!"* and this release in my spirit comes and a *knowing* in my spirit grips me to the point of realizing, *"AH, I've got this!"*

This is how it happened: I was doing all the things I'm supposed to do: read the Word, pray in the Spirit, etc. There I was, by myself in the kitchen, heating up leftovers for dinner and I got this sense in my spirit that I was healed! I felt something lift off of me, like a weight, and everything started to get better from that point on! The slime began to dry up from that moment on! Yay! Thank you Jesus! The cool thing is that I wasn't even thinking about being healed! I was thinking about the food I was making cuz I hadn't eaten all day. Then *Boom!* There it was!

I love that! It's hard for me to describe what that feeling is. I don't even like to call it a feeling. It's a *knowing* that suddenly hits my spirit on the inside and a weight lifts off and I am free! Whatever it was is gone and peace reigns!

Bye-bye slime! Hello freedom!

JULY 30

Entanglements

Read: Hebrews 12:1-3

*H*ebrews chapter twelve begins by referring to the martyrs in chapter eleven that surround us daily, observing what we're doing for the Kingdom so that we all receive the promises of God, becoming complete in Him together. There are some things we need to do along the way so that we can finish our race victoriously. The writer of Hebrews talks about *weights* and *sin*, both of which are waiting to ensnare us.

Weights are burdens we carry like cumbersome loads on our back, weighing us down. To merely lay them aside sounds so passive. The Greek meaning of *lay aside* means *to put away, cast off, put off*. In other words—*throw them off!* There, that sounds more fervent than just plopping a heavy backpack on the ground and walking away!

We cannot run with endurance if we've got heavy burdens and the distractions of sin taking our eyes off of Jesus. We've got to throw off those heavy loads (distractions) and start running. This is exactly what Jesus did with our iniquities and diseases. He took them upon Himself and became them; then He cast them off forever!

The Passion Translation speaks about these entanglements as wounds that have pierced us like an arrow sticking in our rib cage, which would keep us from running our race with freedom. We cannot run holding on to our wounds or they will always distract us. Imagine a person trying to run with an arrow stuck in his side! Ouch!

Forgiveness is not a feeling. It is a choice. I know people can do some horrible things. But it's over. Don't ruin your future by holding on to the wounds of your past. *Let it go...let it gooo.....* Ok, I'll stop singing...

JULY 30 ———

Remember Jesus. He took it all upon Himself and cast it off, every offense, every wound, and every entanglement. It's gone! Yank it out, cast it to the ground and get going! Run with Jesus toward your finish line!

JULY 31

Get Carried Away

Read: Matthew 8:16-17

The word *bore* in this verse is #941 in the *Strong's Concordance*. It is the word *bastazo* in the Greek and it means *"to lift, bear, or carry, take up."*

Thayer's says it means *"to take up with the hands, to take up in order to carry or bear; to put upon one's self, to bear what is burdensome, to bear away, carry off, to take away or remove by curing them."*

Did you read that? ***"To take away or remove by curing them"***

That's what Jesus did with our sicknesses and diseases. He took them upon Himself with force, grabbing them and taking all diseases upon Himself; then He carried them off far away, leaving us cured!

I don't know about you, but whenever I learn something unimaginable Jesus did for me before I ever knew I needed it, I get beside myself! I'm in awe and wonder of just how thorough He was! When He said, *"It is finished!"* He really meant it! But it's wonderful to discover again and again just how complete His death, burial, and resurrection truly is! It never gets old!

So get carried away with His life resonating inside of you! He carried away your diseases so you could get carried away with Him!

AUGUST 1

You Carry Him!

Read: Matthew 13:33

This thought recently came to mind that, if heaven was here with me right now, things would look a lot different, and I'd certainly feel a lot different. The second that thought came, Holy Spirit interjected, *"Heaven is here and it's inside you!"*

I consider that, since Heaven *is* heaven because God lives there; He is the One who makes it so wonderful. Without Him, it wouldn't be glorious, right? Imagine all the benefits Heaven has: no sorrow, no pain, and no disease; everything is perfect!

I realized in an instant, that what I was thinking was a human perspective based on perception and experience, and it was far from Biblical. It is bizarre how we can get lost in our own reasoning so easily! Thanks be to Holy Spirit who leads us into **ALL** truth!

Holy Spirit was right on top of this, reminding me of Jesus' words just like He said He would do! Jesus said that the Kingdom of God is within us! Meaning God's reign, the rule of Christ and His domain—inside us! What is on the inside should be experienced on the outside! The challenge is getting that truth through our thick noggin!

I like Jesus' example comparing the Kingdom of heaven to a woman mixing leaven into a batch of dough to make bread. She kneaded the dough until the yeast permeated and affected every part of the loaf. If she didn't mix it thoroughly, she'd end up with a lopsided loaf or a brick! Remember Jesus referred to Himself as the Bread of Life! Jesus was saying that heaven was meant to be incorporated into our lives and then expand; literally taking over, affecting our entire being—spirit, soul, and body, until its influence causes us to arise to our created purpose: displaying heaven on earth!

AUGUST 1

Think of it this way: Heaven came inside us when Christ moved in. As we recognize Christ's redemption in every area of our lives, He continues to expand beyond us to other people. Of His Kingdom, domain, rule, and authority there will be no end; it will only continue to expand!

Stop for a minute and think about Holy Spirit living inside you right now, taking over your body and every system: your circulatory system, reproductive system, and digestive system. Think about Him saturating your thoughts with peace and joy. Imagine Him expanding beyond yourself into the atmosphere around you to everyone you live with and people you walk past.

Some time ago I met a man at a prayer meeting and he said to me, *"You carry Him! I can see Christ in you and all around you! You carry Him well!"* I was stunned! I thought that was an interesting way of putting it: *"You carry Him."* But we do! And the more that we are aware of Him and heaven living inside us—His life, His rule, His domain, the more we will put Him on display to share Him with others!

So get out there and remember heaven is on the inside of you expanding and making you whole, working its way on the outside. *You carry Him!*

AUGUST 2

Food's Deception

Read: Acts 28:1-10

Many experts claim that the food we eat can either keep us healthy or make us sick; especially today with the modern ways of farming, GMO's, pesticides, chem-trails, etc. We are led to believe that paying a few dollars extra for organic foods will keep us healthy.

When I read the Gospels, I see that there were multitudes of sick, lame, diseased people everywhere Jesus went. They ate the "Kosher" diet, didn't they? The nation of Israel was forbidden to eat anything "unclean," right? Then why weren't "God's Chosen People" living in divine health because they ate the diet God commanded them to eat?

In our modern day, "experts" claim that the *Mediterranean Diet* is the best diet in the entire world! Yet, we read here in Acts chapter 28, that the ruler of the island of Malta, smack dab in the Mediterranean Sea, was sick with dysentery. Bad water, you might say. Really? This is the Mediterranean, the best foods and purest water on an island 2000 years ago before pesticides and GMO's. Why didn't his diet keep him well?

We read about every sick person from the island rushing to Paul for healing! But wait! They ate the *Mediterranean Diet* and they were sick? Coconuts, pomegranates, etc.—they still needed healing! Paul was eager to impart the life of Christ and heal them all! This is a perfect example that we cannot put all our trust in anything on earth or our own wisdom to live a healthy life! Food? Nope! Medicine? Nope! Supplements? Nope! Jesus' complete redemption for our spirit, soul, and body? Yep!

AUGUST 3

Just Be

Read: Psalm 119:89

*E*ven though Psalm 119 may be a lengthy chapter to read, I love how many times it references God's Word. The Psalmist comes to the conclusion that, regardless of the trial he experiences, one thing is sure: *God never changes His Word.* That's a difficult thing to fathom since we live in a culture where people seldom keep their word. That is the main reason many question whether or not God will keep His Word, because it is unheard of for someone to keep their word 100% of the time.

What is also amazing is that God is certain to follow through and back up what He said with His actions. I've seen His faithfulness to me and my children over and over again, just as He promises.

How can one be sure that He will do what He says He will do? That's where we have to settle it. We have to determine for ourselves that this is the way it will be and not back off our decision, especially when it comes to physical healing. To doubt means to be undecided in your heart. You've got to settle it! Once you settle it, you can be at peace and begin to hear from Holy Spirit more easily. When we're tossed back and forth with indecision, our thoughts are so loud we cannot hear Holy Spirit.

Once we determine in our mind that God will do what He said and that's that, we can *just be.* We don't have to try to figure anything out because the outcome will be what He said it will be. It may look like chaos on the outside, but you can still have peace on the inside where it counts.

You don't have to TRY to be healed. JUST BE.

AUGUST 4

Juggernaut

Read: Matthew 11:1-5

A juggernaut is an overwhelming or unstoppable force. It can also be an object that crushes everything in its path. This is the perfect metaphor for the Kingdom of God!

Previously, in Matthew chapter 10, Jesus sent out His disciples with some pretty specific instructions. He delegated His authority to them and directed them to preach that the Kingdom of God was at hand; then He commanded the disciples to cast out demons and heal the sick. He warned them that they would not win a popularity contest with the religious leaders or their family members; in spite of all of that, they were not to fear death.

The difference between us and the disciples in the Gospels is that Jesus gave them *delegated* authority. On this side of the cross, we have *inherited* authority. How? Christ is our inheritance. Everything He conquered He gave to us because we are sons and daughters—equal to Jesus as God's Son. Romans 8:32 says, *"He who did not spare His own Son, but delivered Him up for us all, how shall He not with Him also freely give us all things?"* (NKJV)

Jesus demonstrated the Kingdom by making the lame walk, cleansing lepers, opening deaf ears, and raising the dead. Everywhere the world's system had caused corruption, Jesus restored it. He commanded us to do the same works He did—even greater!

Since the Kingdom of God is inside us, Holy Spirit infuses with our spirit and unites us with Christ; we become complete from that moment. As we renew our mind to the Word, grow in our relationship, and comprehend our full redemption; we discover that Jesus' atonement was for our mind as well as our physical body. How much of the effects of the Kingdom we experience in our everyday lives is entirely up to us. As we cooperate with the Holy Spirit

AUGUST 4

and act on what we learn, making it a vital part of our lives, the Kingdom expands within us, taking over our mind with truth and our body with health. From there we learn to give it away to others and expand the Kingdom beyond ourselves.

Was any person or evil force able to stop Jesus from finishing His Father's mission? No! Has the Kingdom of God been altered or defeated today? No! Can it ever be conquered? No! As a matter of fact, it will eventually take over this world! How? Through you and me! That was God's plan from the beginning—to get His Spirit back into man so He could rule and reign through His children. I cannot fathom why the Father puts that much confidence in us! But He does! The Kingdom of God is a juggernaut—an overwhelming, unstoppable force forever advancing and taking over!

AUGUST 5

Play By The Rules

Read: Luke 10:25-37

My husband would deny this if you ask him, but every time we play a game together, he suddenly remembers a rule about the game. Funny thing is—he only remembers the rule when I break it! He's done that so many times I call them *"Rich's Rules of Order"* (pun intended), because he's changed the rules in the middle of a game so many times! LOL! I can be a very competitive person, so I don't back down easy. One way or another I'm in it to win it!

Whenever I play a game with my youngest son, he always wins, especially Monopoly. He rolls the dice with the perfect number almost every time, and he ends up with all the property and all the money before I can get around the board once! I'm sure he holds the *Guinness World Records* for the shortest time to win a game of Monopoly!

However, I'm the Checkers champ. My grandfather taught me how to play when I was little. You see, he had MS and was confined to a wheelchair, so playing Checkers was one of the few things he could do. His strategy was this: don't move your back row; that way the opponent cannot get "kinged." However, you've got to be pretty smart with the rest of your checkers to hold on to your back row. My family claims that's cheating—I call it strategy.

Jesus said that the only rules we are to live by are to love God with all our heart, with all our soul, and with all our strength, and to love our neighbor as ourselves. If everything we do is summed up in these two commandments, we have fulfilled the law. It's a tall order; easy to say, not so easy to live. However, this is God's strategy to overcoming the world. Treat evil with kindness, anger with a soft answer, and extend mercy instead of revenge.

AUGUST 6

The Label Nazi

Read: 1 Corinthians 6:12

*S*everal years ago, after my family and I had returned from living in Africa, there were so many challenges, that it was overwhelming. Because of the stress of it all and not knowing how to control my thoughts and emotions, I became very ill.

I was severely fatigued. Just vacuuming the floor left me exhausted for three days on the sofa. Other symptoms I had left me so debilitated that I couldn't leave my house. No doctor could find anything wrong with me, so I turned to self-diagnosis and Google. I know now what a big mistake that was, but back then I thought it was my only hope. I began the journey of self-medication with natural supplements based on the symptoms I experienced. I also drastically modified my diet. I deduced that we had eaten pure and healthy in Africa without all the pesticides, preservatives, and GMO's here in America, so food must have been the culprit.

I became a "Label Nazi" and anything containing high fructose corn syrup or partially hydrogenated oils was banned from entering my home! I remember standing in line to check out at the grocery store with my cart full of expensive "healthy" organic foods, while the person in front of me piled his cartload of junk foods and frozen foods on the checkout counter. I thought, smugly to myself, that he was a fool in bondage to junk food, while I was the educated one. The man didn't appear to have any physical issues, but I concluded that there was no way he could be healthy! I realize now that I was the one in bondage and he was the one who was free to eat whatever he wanted without fear.

I was so extreme with label reading that I could have written a novel entitled *Mein Kampf of Dietary Restrictions*! When my husband and I had the opportunity to travel to Puerto Rico with his job, I went

AUGUST 6

to a local store and bought baby food in jars so I could eat "healthy" and avoid what was served in the cafeteria for lunch. I went so far as to ask the hotel's kitchen to hard boil a dozen eggs for me! I missed out on birthday cakes with my family and eating our normal traditional Christmas cookies because I believed gluten and sugar were my enemies. When I say that I bought the lie hook, line, and sinker—that would be an understatement! The more I feared eating certain foods, the more control I gave it.

Over time, I noticed that all of my efforts never brought a cure for my symptoms—only more restrictions. I began to question why "experts" would say eggs are bad and cause cholesterol to rise, and then suddenly eggs were good for us. Fish oil was supposed to prevent heart attacks, but then it was eventually touted as bad for men. There's articles popping up constantly that are designed to convince us that you shouldn't eat a certain food or it will cause us to become overweight or cause inflammation, so you might as well go out in your yard and eat grass—but wait!—there could be pesticides out there! YIKES!

I had to change the way I thought about food and the control I gave it over my life. I began to realize the power I had given to man-made supplements and man-made advice about what was considered healthy and what was not. The wake-up call came when the Holy Spirit convinced me that I had trusted man's wisdom over God's. As I was reading the Bible one morning, this Scripture hit me right between the eyes, *"All things are lawful for me **but I will not be brought under the power of any.**"* (1 Corinthians 6:12 NKJV, Emphasis added).

I saw how, over time, I had allowed myself to be brought under the power of man's rationality about food. It had brought me little benefit and much frustration. So, how did I get out of it? I began to eat the opposite. No, I didn't begin to gorge myself on junk food, but if I wanted to eat something, I ate it. I began to eat bread

AUGUST 6

again and foods containing sugar, if I wanted it. I stopped limiting myself from only eating green apples and grapefruit to eating red apples and bananas ("experts" said green apples and grapefruit were lowest in sugar). Are red apples bad? No! It's just an apple, right? Ridiculous, isn't it? That's exactly what bondage does to us. It brings so much confusion, fear, and restriction that we condemn our own consciences by what we accept as truth. That's not the freedom Christ died to give us.

I began to change my thinking as I ate in freedom. Sometimes I had to tell myself, *"Body, this is just food. It has no power to do you harm, only good."* I refuse to read labels now. I prefer *not* to know the ingredients. I've certainly come a long way. I don't have the symptoms I used to be plagued with. No more "Label Nazi!" We don't have to live in fear of food or any symptoms it may cause. Nothing shall by any means harm us! (Luke 10:19) If I would have known this back then, I could have saved myself years of grief—and I could have enjoyed more chocolate chip cookies!

If you haven't read Tony Myers' book *"Knocking Food Off Its Pedestal—Eating Your Way to Divine Healing and Supernatural Health"* I highly recommend it! It was very helpful for me to put food in its proper place.

AUGUST 7

Truth & Wisdom

Read: Psalm 51:6 (KJV)

*T*his may not be the most obvious Scripture regarding physical healing, but Holy Spirit gave me this Scripture while praying for a close family member.

When you think about it, God created all of our organs to function according to His wisdom. No scientist can fully understand the complete workings of the human body. For example, he cannot explain how our organs were created to work in tandem. While declaring that our organs align with God's wisdom, we can trust that He will make each part function according to His design.

We discover that He *desires* truth in our innermost parts and He *makes* our bodies to know wisdom. He makes everything function perfectly from the inside out! I'll take that over man's wisdom any day! God doesn't *practice* medicine on us like a doctor, He *is* medicine! His words are spirit and they are life—the cure for whatever ails us!

Symptoms are nothing more than lies that our bodies speak. God's word is truth to combat those lies. As we establish truth in our hearts and minds, it will be experienced in our bodies.

Proverbs 2:20-22 is one of my favorite Scriptures because it describes, in detail, the steps a person can apply for healing: *"My son, pay attention to my words; Incline your ear to my sayings. Do not let them depart from your eyes; keep them in the midst of your heart; for they are life to all who find them and health (medicine, the cure) to all your flesh."* (Parenthesis added)

If you look up the Hebrew word for *health* in a concordance, you will see that it means: *health, cure, medicine, physician, wholeness, repair thoroughly, sound*. It is derived from the Hebrew word *rapha*,

AUGUST 7

used in Isaiah 53:5, that says, *"And by His stripes we are **healed**."* Every organ in your body must function with the truth and wisdom in which God created it to function! Amen!

AUGUST 8

Childhood Terror

Read: Isaiah 41:10-13

During the summertime, when I was a little girl about ten years old, one of my favorite things to do was picking berries. I knew where to find every type of berry growing wild when it was in season. At the end of May through the beginning of June, wild strawberries grew all over the field behind my house. I would pick large bowls of these tiny strawberries and fill the refrigerator with them. On Friday nights, when my parents went away for the evening, I'd sit in front of the TV and eat my strawberries while watching *The Love Boat* and *Fantasy Island*. I know—I'm showing my age...

In the middle of June, after the strawberries finished for the season, black raspberries grew in the sticker bushes behind our house. One evening, after my Dad had come home from work, I was in the field picking raspberries. My Dad, being a carpenter, was hot and sweaty from a hard day's work and headed straight to the shower. Suddenly, something was crawling towards me. I couldn't see what it was, but a lump of weeds was slowly inching its way closer and closer as the grass crinkled near my shoes. I assumed it was a snake! The problem was—there was only one way in and one way out!

I began to scream for my Dad to come and save me! *"Daaad! It's a snake! Help!"* Thoughts were running wild through my mind about a snake slowly, tormentingly; coiling its body around my ankles! The grass kept steadily moving as the lump approached my feet! I must have been screaming for at least a half hour before my Dad heard me. Finally, he ran up in the field where I was and lifted me out of the raspberry bush! Whew!

I never saw what was under the weeds—I just assumed it was a snake! My mind ran wild with terror, imagining what that snake

AUGUST 8

would do to me once it reached my legs! I had enough berry picking for that day!

That's exactly what fear does! We imagine something is out there coming for us, but we never actually see it. Our minds run wild with possibilities, yet they seldom ever happen and we get all worked up for nothing. I wished I'd have had the courage to jump over that lump. It might have been a turtle. If it was a snake, my screaming certainly would have scared it away. Taking a moment to think rationally, I would have remembered that harmless garter snakes, which were always around our house, do not kill their prey by constriction.

But that's what fear does. It tries to paralyze us and make us feel helpless when we are not, especially when it comes to physical healing. Fear is the bigger enemy, not the disease itself.

Our Scripture reading for today is one that the Lord had given to me when I was dealing with Lyme disease. Fear tried to overwhelm me many times, but when I was able to see it as just a force trying to affect my emotions like that "snake" in the grass, I refused to give into it. This verse always turned my focus back to the Lord, knowing that His right hand meant that He was there to save me, just like my Dad rescuing me out of that raspberry bush!

AUGUST 9

Kick The Can

Read: Ephesians 4:20-24

*D*id you ever play *Kick the Can* when you were a kid? My brothers and I often played that game during a hot summer night at twilight on weekends while our parents went away for the evening.

We'd use an old *Maxwell House* coffee can. To determine who was "it," each of us would put one of our feet into the center of a circle and say *"Eeny, meeny, miny, mo, catch a tiger by the toe. If he hollers let him go. Out goes Y-O-U!"* Of course, me being the youngest, I got stuck being "it" more often than my brothers, who were three and five years older than me.

To play the game, we all stood in the driveway. One of my brothers who was not "it" would kick the can as hard and as far as he could. The person who was "it" (which was usually me, crying and complaining) would have to run after the can while the others ran and hid. The person who was "it" had to retrieve the can, stand it upright in the driveway at the previous location, find the others, and tag them before they could get back to the can. If they touched the can before they were tagged, they were "safe." Needless to say, I usually spent the entire evening being "it."

Kick the Can was one of the more harmless things we used to do. Usually, mischief found us. We were merciless toward each other when our parents weren't around. We broke a lot of things from picking on each other and taking revenge.

One time my middle brother was so frustrated from being picked on, he threw his math book and the corner of it got stuck in the closet door. The boys spent the rest of the evening repairing the door and turning the part with the hole toward the inside so it would never be seen. Our parents never figured that one out!

AUGUST 9

I look back on those memories and laugh now; I sure got into a lot of mischief when I was growing up. One of the principals in high school said that I was like a magnet to trouble because I was always in detention for something stupid I did.

Though *Kick the Can* was definitely one of the more innocent things we did as kids, when I came to Christ as a teenager, I had to put my mischievous ways behind me (well, most of them!). That took a lot of undoing and learning what was acceptable for a Believer who is supposed to represent Christ.

That is one thing I realize that many Believers do not understand. Some never learn that they cannot bring their old thinking and old ways of living into their new life in Christ. We receive a new nature. We put off man's ways and put on Christ. These two worlds are in total opposition to each other. We cannot live with one foot in the world and one foot in Christ. It's not *"Eeny, meeny, miny, mo"* anymore. We choose how effective our lives will be for Christ. No more games.

That's not to say "no more fun!" I'm the biggest jokester. I love some competitive fun. I can dish it out as much as anyone else and I can take it too; yet where living for the Lord is concerned, everything we say and do should be to the honor and glory of the One we represent.

AUGUST 10

Mercy Triumphs Over Judgment

Read: Micah 7:18, James 2:13

When someone does something wrong, especially repeatedly, and we have been hurt by him or her, it is human nature to want to see that person get what's coming to them. We may think that God's wrath will cause that person to stop what he or she has been doing, repent, and turn toward God. Most times this isn't the case. It is because we DON'T get what we deserve that causes people to turn to Him.

I'm not saying that some of us don't go through the school of "hard knocks" by our own doing. But when we find God's mercy instead of His anger; His kindness instead of judgment—that's what draws us to Him.

In *The Passion Translation*, James 2:13 says, *"and remember that judgment is merciless for the one who judges others without mercy. So by showing mercy, you take dominion over judgment."*

I like that! By showing mercy we take dominion over judgment. God delights in showing mercy. Mercy was there when I needed it several years ago when I fully committed my life to Him. I deserved judgment. Instead, I got mercy.

I think that, most times, we are our own worst critic. We also project the same judgmental view that we have of ourselves upon God. But He never sees us with a critical eye. He sees Jesus. He sees us perfectly hidden in Christ. In this perfection, He provided mercy over judgment. Now we can give that same mercy to others.

AUGUST 11

Healing Is NOT A Reward

Read: Romans 8:1-2

Just as there is NOTHING one can do to earn their salvation; there is absolutely NOTHING anyone can do to earn their healing. Can't give an offering for it, can't tithe for it, and can't do good works for it—NOTHING. It is all by grace.

Just as none of us deserves salvation, we don't deserve healing either. We don't deserve mercy or forgiveness. What price could we pay for our own lives? That would depend on its value. God believes we are worth the price of His only Son. That really takes the pressure off, doesn't it? Any hindrance to receiving healing is only because of believing that there can be a hindrance—nothing more.

Knowing that I can never be good enough to receive healing gives me a sigh of relief. Go ahead, take a deep breath and let out a sigh of relief!

When we are in Christ, we live under the law of the spirit of life. The law of the spirit of life *MADE* us exempt from the law of sin and death. To be exempt means: *to be free or released from some liability or requirement to which others are subject.* Imagine that! Exempt from the law of sin and death! Sickness does NOT apply for us, thank you Jesus!

Our body is Christ's body. We don't own it anymore. He paid a ransom for our lives with His own life. We are Jesus with skin on—and it's all by grace!

AUGUST 12

Loaded

Read: Psalm 68:19-20

I like the sound of that—*daily loaded* with benefits! That reminds me of Psalm 103, which tells us to not forget *all* His benefits: He forgives *all* our iniquities and heals *all* our diseases. Our Scripture for today takes it even further. He provides *"escapes from death."* Notice that the word *escape* is plural. Can you remember any times where God saved you from death? I know I can!

Sometimes, when I'm driving and I take my eyes off the road to do something, I have the sudden urge to look up and quick swerve to get back on the road. Other times it's the slip of a knife, or my dog yanking me to the ground as I hit my hip on a rock, yet stand up with no pain! Whatever the need, Holy Spirit is on top of it before I need it.

One thing is for sure, time has no effect on whether or not healing is available. We can look back and reminisce about the days of our youth and remember when certain body parts worked properly without any assistance, right? Should time have the power to change all of that? If it worked perfectly then, it can work perfectly right now, especially if we are in Christ. Big Mo (Moses) was of aged glory until 120 years old. He climbed that mountain one last time to see the Promised Land without eyeglasses or a cane. I'm sure he wasn't huffing and puffing all the way up the mountain. And that was under the Old Covenant!

So remember that you're cocked and loaded! Loaded with His benefits of forgiveness, life, and deliverance because Jesus lives inside you! That's even better than what Big Mo ever experienced!

AUGUST 13

Dead Works

Read: James 2:14-26

Dead works are things that people think they can do to make themselves right with God. Living works are things we do as a *result* of our faith in Christ. Anyone who wants to work the works of God consistently does it as a result of believing in Him, not because they are trying to get His approval.

It is interesting that verse 25 says that we are justified by our faith *and* our works. Just sitting around while we agree that something is true, does not prove that we really believe it, because our actions will always display what we believe or don't believe. Sometimes I've got to take a big step back and examine myself. When I see a person on a scooter at Wal-Mart with no legs, do I believe that God can use me to heal that person just as easily as the man walking with a cane? In our human eyes, one is more difficult than the other, but not for Jesus.

I heard the story of a woman and her baby at one of John G. Lake's meetings. The baby was born without a foot and his leg was shorter than the other. Lake prayed for the baby and turned and walked away. The mother screamed! When Lake spun around to look, a foot had suddenly appeared on the end of her baby's leg! She set him down to take his first steps. Both legs and feet were perfect!

We can limit ourselves if we don't just step out and take the risk. We don't do these works because it makes us righteous, but because we *are* the righteousness of God in Christ. No one person is more righteous than any other. We don't need another person's anointing. We don't need a "double portion" of anything. We have the Anointed One living inside of us with good works prepared in advance for us to do!

AUGUST 14

What Do You Want Me To Do For You? (Part 1)

Read: Luke 18:35-43

Blind Bartimaeus cried out when he heard that Jesus was passing by. No doubt he had previously been told that Jesus was the Messiah. He had no problems believing, but the religious leaders did. Isn't it strange that Bartimaeus couldn't see Jesus, yet He believed He was the Messiah, but the Pharisees could see Jesus, and they didn't believe? It proves that a person's perception influences him more than what he can see with his physical eyes.

The man cried out for Jesus. *"Shut up!"* the crowds told Him. But He cried out all the more. Good job! Because Jesus heard his cry and it stopped Him in His tracks.

The question was simple, *"What do you want Me to do for you?"* Don't you think He could tell the man was blind? Wasn't it an obvious, no-brainer? Yet Jesus still asked him that question. Why? It was to encourage the man to be bold. Would he go so far as to believe the Messiah would heal **him**, a lowly outcast beggar of society?

"What do you want Me to do for you?" questioned Jesus standing, face to face with the man.

"Lord, that I may receive my sight." The man requested boldly.

"Receive your sight." Jesus simply responded.

The man immediately received his eyesight. No hands laid on him, just the simple words: *"What do you want? Here you go."*

That's all it took!

AUGUST 15

What Do You Want Me To Do For You? (Part 2)

Read: Psalm 33

*W*hile no one knows for sure who wrote it, Psalm 33 is beautifully descriptive. I'd like to focus on verse nine: *"For He spoke, and it was done; He commanded, and it stood fast."* (NKJV)

Much like the blind man receiving his eyesight in our devotion from yesterday, where Jesus simply spoke the words *"Receive your sight,"* and Bartimaeus was immediately able to see, this Psalm reminds us how God spoke the world into existence. It is another example where He spoke and it immediately appeared.

There was no delay when God spoke. There was no delay when Jesus spoke. They spoke and it was done! Healing is the same for us now. How? Because God announced Jesus arrival prophetically hundreds of years before He came, and Jesus fulfilled every one of those prophecies. There is nothing we can do that can add to it, reduce it, or delay it. Healing is always available now, just the same as salvation is always available. So the question stands for us today: *"What do you want Me to do for you?"*

Jesus' answer is a little different, on this side of the cross, than it was for the blind man. Jesus' reply today would not be *"Receive"*, because if you are in Him, you have already received! *"Well, then, where is it?"*, you might ask. Inside you! The Healer Himself is touching you from the inside out! The moment you realize that, you will discover peace. In that place of peace is rest. In that place of rest is freedom. In that freedom is health and life! Whatever has afflicted you lifts off right now! It's all connected because it's all Jesus! It's His nature transforming you from the inside out! What God spoke and what Jesus did still holds true for us today!

AUGUST 16

A Defeated Mentality

Read: Romans 8:5-6

One sure way to tell whether we are living in the spirit or the flesh is by doing a quick inventory on our thoughts. I'm not sure why, but some people seem to be addicted to drama. Their lives are like a roller coaster ride, up one minute and down the next. Questions and *"what if's"* plague their minds constantly.

Did you ever notice that there is nothing that suggests a wimpy or a defeated mentality in Scripture? Do things *always* turn out the way we want them to? Obviously, stuff happens in this life we cannot always control, especially when it comes to the choices other people make. Still we can choose *how* we react to it.

What about when it comes to healing? Fear is usually right there trying to overwhelm our thoughts. Recognize it as a lie that is trying to play on your emotions—and get rid of it! Dismiss any thoughts that aren't true, and kick fear out quickly!

One thing that helps me get my head on straight and push my emotions out of the way, is praying in the spirit. It stirs up the Holy Spirit inside me and I can hear Him much easier. That always brings me to a place of stability when I don't know what to do. I listen and expect to hear Holy Spirit tell me what to do.

Occasionally, He reminds me of a problem I overcame in the past to encourage me. Other times, I'm given a verse of Scripture to help me focus on truth, or He will show me something specific. For example, today I was praying about something, as I sat in the dark early this morning; I opened my eyes and happened to look at a box of tissues nearby that said, *"You Got This!"* on the box!

Is that a little corny? Maybe. But I received it as though I had the victory over what I was praying about, and within a few hours the

AUGUST 16

issue was resolved. Whatever way the Holy Spirit uses to speak to you is personal. It doesn't have to be anything earth-shattering, but rather something simple—even a box of tissues. He knows how to get what He wants to say across to you. He's personal like that!

AUGUST 17

The Man In The Mirror (Part 1)

Read: 2 Corinthians 3:18

Man In The Mirror

"I'm starting with the man in the mirror
I'm asking him to change his ways
And no message could have been any clearer
If you wanna make the world a better place
Take a look at yourself and then make a change"
Song by Michael Jackson, 1987

When I think about the man in the mirror, I see a person looking at himself but seeing a reflection of Jesus instead of his own. This is what the Bible reinforces from Genesis to Revelation, yet most of us don't fully see ourselves in His image.

The message in the song by Michael Jackson is about noticing other people's needs instead of being self-absorbed. The most effective way not to be self-absorbed is to do the works Jesus did. He was the perfect example of *selflessness* as He fed the hungry, healed the sick, and set the oppressed free!

I like the *Mirror Bible's* translation for 2 Corinthians 3:18. It paints a descriptive picture of how we are supposed to envision ourselves:

> *"The days of window-shopping are over! In Him every face is unveiled. In gazing with wonder at the blueprint likeness of God displayed in human form, we suddenly realize that we are looking at ourselves! Every feature of His image is mirrored in us! This is the most radical transformation engineered by the Spirit of the Lord; we are led from an inferior mind-set to the revealed endorsement of our authentic identity. You are His glory!"*

AUGUST 17

We have a natural tendency to overcomplicate things by trying to change ourselves. This approach is seldom effective. The easiest, most Biblically accurate approach is to read about what Jesus did in the Gospels and do it yourself. That's the Great Commission. Jesus saw the man in the mirror: His Father. If you want to see change; then be the change you want to see. See Jesus; the Man in the mirror, because that is who you truly are!

AUGUST 18

The Man In The Mirror (Part 2)

Read: 2 Corinthians 4:10

*O*ne of the most important truths we need to understand and put into action is the fact that Christ lives inside of us! Many of the most powerful men and women of God, who saw themselves as dead and alive to Christ, are the ones who have left us the greatest legacies.

Paul is one of the first people we read about who had a dramatic transformation from strict religion, to a man dead to self, but alive *in Christ*. A few of the most powerful people I know, who are effective in the Kingdom, have the image of Christ embedded deep within them. Signs and wonders follow them. We, too, must recognize ourselves *in Christ*.

Recently, I had faced a physical challenge. After three days of having enough of it, I went to pray in the spirit and listen to what Holy Spirit had to say. One thing He said to me is, *"Your body isn't your body anymore. You are Christ's body. He bought you. His life is your life."* YEAHHH! The lights came on! Jesus can't be sick! Ha! Got my head on straight and decided I'm healed. I got up and planned to catch up on the dirty dishes and laundry and get back to life. Later that day the fever left.

This is one thing I want to become stronger and stronger in me: that Christ's life is my life and that my body is His body. He paid for it with His own blood. It belongs to Him and Him alone—not to sickness. I like the *Mirror Bible's* translation of 2 Corinthians 4:10,

> *"Wherever we go, whatever we encounter in our bodies, we bear witness within us of the fact that Jesus died our death; in this same body, we now exhibit His life. The fact that we co-died in His death confirms that we now co-live in His resurrection!"*

AUGUST 19

Baked Beans & Applesauce

Read: Exodus 15:22-26

What I love about this account of Moses and the children of Israel is purely incredible! Over a million people just came out of Egypt, healed by eating the Passover Lamb; which we know represented Jesus. They were walking along and somebody decided he was thirsty, so the rest of the people realized they were thirsty too, and the entire multitude began to complain to Moses. There was a problem: the water was unfit for drinking.

These are healed people, remember? So what does God do? He heals the water so that nothing can hurt them! Moses threw a piece of wood in the water and the water's chemical composition immediately changed! This represented Christ's death on the cross. Hmmm... changed its chemical composition? Isn't that what happens to our bodies when the life of Christ comes to live inside of us?

I love the way God protected them by healing the water! These were a healed people and God promised to keep them that way. So what about us? Isn't that why we pray over our food?

When I had a lot of health issues, I blamed food as the culprit. I had heard the saying by Hippocrates—touted as "The Father of Modern Medicine:" *"Let food be thy medicine and medicine thy food."* And I bought into that lie and began the process of eliminating foods from my diet. The problem was that eliminating foods never cured the health issues I was having. It put off some of the symptoms, yes, but I became so fearful of eating that I didn't enjoy life anymore.

A friend told me the story of a woman he knew in his church. This woman had a lot of food allergies. She had eliminated so many foods from her diet that all she could eat were baked beans and applesauce! That was my wake-up call! I decided from that moment on

AUGUST 19

that was NOT going to happen to me! I realized that I was on the same path, and the more foods I cut out of my diet, the less I would be able to tolerate! Baked beans and applesauce? What a disgusting combination! Please don't allow yourself to ever fall into that kind of trap, because the more foods you eliminate, the less you may be able to enjoy.

You know, there is nowhere in the Bible, Old Testament or New Testament, that says that food kept a person healthy. In fact, Proverbs 4:20-22 says, *"My son, give attention to My words; Incline your ear to My sayings. Do not let them depart from your eyes; Keep them in the midst of your heart; For they are life to those who find them, and health (medicine, the cure) to all their flesh."* (Parenthesis added)

There is no place in these verses that say anything about food giving us health or curing disease. Hippocrates got it all wrong. I learned a very hard lesson—not to take the advice of some dude living hundreds of years ago, who never knew God or His Word. If I had turned to the Bible, I would have seen that there are many Scriptures that talk about life and health. I would have been reminded that Proverbs says it is the words of my own mouth that can bring life or death.

I've witnessed churches offering the option of gluten-free bread for Communion, to be considerate of those with gluten intolerances. I understand why, but isn't healing what the bread represents? To eat the bread is to receive our healing by Christ's body that was broken for us. Eating the bread will keep us from becoming weak, sickly, or dying prematurely (1 Corinthians 11:30)! Don't let the fear of symptoms keep you in bondage like I did. Look at your food the way Israel looked at the waters of Marah when they saw the floating piece of wood. The water was healed before they drank it. We've got an even better Covenant, built on better promises!

AUGUST 20

Transmutation

Read: Matthew 17:1-8, 2 Peter 1:1-4

*"When the life of Jesus comes in, the death of your soul ends. When the Spirit of God comes in, your **dead** nerves come alive. God, by the Spirit, takes possession of the blood and the brain and the bone. He dwells in the very cellular structure of your whole being. His quickening **life** regenerates you and generates **life** in you and by the Christ of God you come forth, not a dead senseless lobster, but a **living man**, a **living** Christian."*
Quote by John G. Lake

Transmutation means to change or alter in form, appearance, or nature— especially to a higher form. *Transmutation, Transformation, Transfiguration,* and *Metamorphosis* are all synonyms. This is what the three disciples saw here in Matthew 17 on the Mountain of Transfiguration. Their eyes were opened to Jesus clothed in His glory; what I believe was always there, but on this occasion, their eyes were opened to see it.

The word *transfigure* is where we get the word *metamorphosis*; like when a caterpillar is changed into a butterfly or a tadpole becomes a frog. This reminds me of a children's song, *"Bullfrogs and Butterflies—we've both been born again!"* If you think about it, both the caterpillar and the tadpole are transformed into something totally different than how they began life. Their abilities changed. A caterpillar crawls slowly on the ground, and eventually gets wings to fly high above the trees! A tadpole swimming in the water loses its tail and grows legs to hop on land; no longer captive to a pond, but a master of the land as well.

Even their diets change. The caterpillar is no longer reduced to gorging itself endlessly with roughage but, as a butterfly, begins flittering to every flower, slurping up sweet nectar with its straw-like

AUGUST 20

proboscis. The tadpole's appetite changes from algae and decaying sludge-like vegetation, to the life of a carnivore!

When we are in Christ, our appetites change, just like the caterpillar and the tadpole. No, I'm not talking about the food we eat. I'm referring to our desires. The music we used to enjoy, the TV programs and the friends we used to associate with no longer satisfy; even our language changes. How we spend our time changes. Our desires suddenly become His desires.

When Christ comes to live inside of us, we undergo a *metamorphosis* of spirit, soul, and body. Our spirit becomes infused with Holy Spirit. We receive the mind of Christ, and our body becomes ignited with life! We "morph" from a mere human into a supernatural being!

I know a brother in Christ who had received a blood test. The nurse called to question him about abnormal substances found in his blood—qualities that are not "typical" of most humans. He just laughed and said it was Jesus!

At the physical level, our DNA is changed. Just like the example of the brother in Christ, his blood had become full of the life of Jesus' blood. Our bodies become charged with supernatural energy and strength. We become partakers of His divine nature from the inside out. *Transmutation* has taken place—we have morphed into a higher life form.

What was once natural, earthly, and selfish has been touched by divine life! Our new heavenly nature brings us into the likeness of God's Son, with His life coursing through our veins! A chemical reaction has taken place in every cell, making us full of divine life—*transmuted into the Supernatural!*

AUGUST 21

Healing's Promise

Read: Jeremiah 30:17

*W*hether it's the *Old* or *New Testament*, we can find God's consistent promise of healing. Whatever type of healing is needed, be it emotional or physical, we can find at least 100 verses of Scripture in the Bible referring to our health.

Did you know that inflammation is not always a bad thing? It's actually a sign that the body is trying to heal itself. Inflammation has its role. There's a lot of hype about inflammation these days, and I'm not saying that there isn't *any* truth to it, but just like anything else, things can get blown out of proportion.

It's fascinating how God created our bodies to heal on their own when we get a simple paper cut. The body immediately sends help to the wound site to clean up and repair the damage. It proves that wholeness and restoration have always been a part of God's plan for us. Even a tree knows how to heal itself if it gets a cut in its bark. Sticky sap seeps out of the injured area to seal it up and keep it free from insect invaders until it heals completely.

Healing was God's idea from the beginning. He never sends sickness or disease to teach us a lesson. We have the Holy Spirit as our teacher. There is never any darkness in God, only light and goodness. Even old Abraham prayed for King Abimelech so he could have children, way before Abraham could have any children of his own. Like Abraham, you can pray for others to be healed even if you need healing in your own body! As a matter of fact, the more you pray for other people to be healed and you see them improve, it will encourage you for your own healing. You've got to have something in order to be able to give it away, right? You do! You have the life of Christ in you; more than enough for yourself and to give away to others!

AUGUST 22

No More Affliction

Read: Nahum 1:9

One of people's biggest fears, after they have been healed, is the return of the symptoms. We can see, in this Scripture that God already thought of this: *"He will make an utter end of it. Affliction shall not rise up a second time."* I like that!

During special healing services, the room is pumped with faith so strongly that you can feel it in the atmosphere! Someone goes up to the altar for prayer and he or she is immediately healed! Once that person goes home, the symptoms often return shortly afterward. Why does that happen?

I believe one of the reasons is that the physical body has programmed itself to send the signals of pain and symptoms to that area. Any change is foreign to it so it tries to revert back to what it was used to, like muscle memory when we exercise. We usually cannot go back to that person to be prayed for again, so what do we do?

This is when you have to tell your body what it is supposed to feel like. You have the same ability, the same Holy Spirit, and the same authority, that the person who prayed for you has—so use it! Have confidence that the pain, sickness, or disease is completely healed; then expect them to leave. **You did not lose your healing!** Don't believe that lie! If it left before, it can certainly leave again!

God's got you covered. Affliction shall not rise up a second time! Continue to see yourself healed and doing the things you could not do before. Don't give up and don't back down. Remember that the Holy Spirit is there to help you. In most cases, the best thing for you to do is enforce that you are healed, and then forget about it. Go do something that will get your mind off it completely. After a while, you will have forgotten about the pain and symptoms and recognize that you are healed!

AUGUST 23

Who's The Light?

Read: Matthew 5:14-16, John 8:12

In Matthew, we read that Jesus said that we are the light of the world. He says, in essence, no matter where you are, whether in a public place or in your own home, your light should not be hidden. It (you) should shine (show) the Christ that is within you to everyone by the good works you do. Jesus never called us anything other than what He called Himself, and He never told us to do anything that He Himself didn't do. In fact, we know that He challenged us to do greater works (John 14:12).

In John, Jesus says that He is the Light of the world. When Jesus said, *"He who follows Me shall **not** walk in darkness, but have the light of life."* The word *not* is a double negative in the Greek stating emphatically *"no, never!"* Meaning that, when we are in Christ, we will **never, no never** walk in darkness. Darkness can refer to such things as death, fear, depression, and disease. Do any of these things belong to God? NO! We can be certain that these things are never from Him!

It is stated in 1 John 1:5, *"This is the message which we have heard from Him and declare to you, that God is light and in Him is no darkness at all."* If there is only light in Him and never darkness that means that we never have darkness in us as well.

So who is the light? Jesus is! We are! Everything He is, He gave to us! As He is so are we in this world, right? There can be no darkness in us because we are in Him and He is in us!

AUGUST 24

I'll Trade Ya!

Read: Mark 8:34-38

When I was young, one of my least favorite foods of all time was mashed potatoes. My brother, who always sat next to me during dinner, loved them. Since the kids in the family ate at the counter while my parents ate at the table behind us, my brother and I would always trade food. I'd whisper to him, *"I'll trade ya my mashed potatoes for your vegetables."* He was always glad to trade.

I hated mashed potatoes so much that I didn't make them until I was married and my first son was about five years old. He exclaimed to one of our friends, *"My Mom made a new invention!"* She replied, *"What's that?"* He stated emphatically, *"Mashed potatoes!"* She got a chuckle from my son's answer! I'm still not thrilled with the idea of eating mashed potatoes today. I don't exactly know why, I just hate those piles of white, chalky mushiness!

Jesus made a great exchange: His life for ours. He simply gave us the offer: *"I'll trade ya!"* It says here in our Scripture reading for today, *"For whoever desires to save his life will lose it, but whoever loses his life for My sake **and the gospel's** will save it."* (NKJV) It's living by a totally different set of standards than the rest of the world.

My life before Christ was like that plate of mashed potatoes with liver and onions on the side—disgusting! Oh, liver and onions? That's another story for another time. I'm so glad Jesus said to me, *"I'll trade ya!"*

We get to scrape off our messy plate and start over with something much better: A brand new life with all the best He has to offer!

AUGUST 25

Let Me Introduce You To You

Read: 2 Corinthians 4:6

In the *Mirror Bible*, 2 Corinthians 4:6 says,

> "The light source is founded in the same God who said, 'Light, be!' And light shone out of darkness! He lit the lamp in our understanding so that we may clearly recognize the features of His likeness in the face of Jesus Christ reflected within us."

The farthest thing from God's mind was to create another religion and call it Christianity. His intention was to reveal the image of Himself in human form in the example of His Son, and then to reproduce that same likeness in all of redeemed humanity.

Jesus is our brother, the firstborn. Since He is our brother and we have the same DNA as our Father; we are bone of his bone, flesh of His flesh, blood of His blood (Ephesians 5:30).

God's purpose was not for us to merely find ourselves in His Word, but to become that Word—a living epistle. As we mature in Christ, we find that more of Him is revealed in us; much like the unveiling of a work of art on display.

So let me introduce you to you. Friend, this is Jesus. He is who you are: from your hair to your toenails; the inside to the outside. Just as He is complete, you are complete. If God were to paint a portrait of you, it would look exactly like Jesus, because when your Father looks at you—all He sees is Him!

AUGUST 26

Party Time!

Read: Psalm 104

I like verse twenty-five of Psalm 104 that says the sea is *teeming* with innumerable creatures. The word *teeming* means: *to become filled to overflowing, abound, to be present in a large quantity.* God never does anything on a small scale. He's always way beyond more than enough—He's *superabundant*.

I love the fact that I don't have to do anything to earn His desire to hang out with me all the time. That would be a real drag. He never says, *"Ugh, you're just too much right now; I need a break!"* As a matter of fact, it's the exact opposite. He enjoys hanging out with us! That's why He sent His Holy Spirit!

Jesus says in John 10:10, in the *Wuest Translation,* "*I alone came in order that they might be possessing life, and possessing it in superabundance.*" The most effective way to possess life in *superabundance* is to know Him experientially; which involves our active participation. When you think about it, that's what having a relationship with Him is about: experiencing life together continually moment by moment, holding a conversation with Him that never ends.

Every cell of your being echoes with the zoe life of God. It's like your body is so resonating with the life of God, there's a party going on inside! Each of your cells is doing "The Bump" with the other cells around it vibrating back and forth with life!

It is vital to envision your body receiving life from His Body. What we imagine with our minds has a greater potential to become a reality. The more we make a habit of thinking about His life and energy exuding life and energy into our cells—especially an area that isn't functioning properly, the more we will experience it!

AUGUST 27

Reconciled

Read: Hebrews 2:14-18

"*Being one with the children of God presupposes the fact that He lived and died in a body exactly like theirs; being as fully human as we are, He is qualified to remove the dominion of death that was introduced as a result of Adam's fall. He delivered man from the lifelong dread of death. Death presents no further threat to man. His mission was to rescue, not the angels, but the seed of Abraham from their peril. He was obliged to completely assimilate every detail of His brothers' humanity so that, in His position as Chief Priest, His compassion and integrity would prevail effectively over their sins, to reconcile them with God. He experienced humanity's temptation with the same intensity, and under the same scrutiny, and was therefore qualified to represent them with immediate effect.* (Mirror Bible)

To be *reconciled* means to be made identical. When we reconcile our checkbook with the bank statement, if it's even a penny off, it's not fully reconciled.

We can clearly see from these Scriptures, that so beautifully express the complete sacrifice Jesus made; it was so that He could make us identical to Himself. There was purposeful intention in everything He did to complete us. Not one detail of full reconciliation was left undone. It was effective immediately.

I've learned that the more I understand this completeness and acknowledge His finished work, the more it intensifies. Deity was assimilated with our humanity and our humanity assimilated with Deity. There is no separating the two. They are fused together into one—reconciled, identical; so much so that when God looks at us, He sees Jesus!

AUGUST 28

Street Ministry Miracles

Read: Matthew 10

Thirty years ago, when my husband and I recommitted our lives to the Lord, we had a fresh start in our marriage and in our family. We met a man, Thomas, and his wife Elizabeth, who became our mentors for the next seventeen years. He was a "rough around the edges trucker dude" and he wasn't afraid to tell anyone like it is.

We were in our early twenties with two young children when we met them. We started a street ministry together the first year we got to know them. Every week we picked up at least a hundred large bags of clothes donated to our ministry. We'd make about fifty bologna sandwiches and serve baked goods donated by a local grocery store and take them to the worst part of town. Drive-by shootings and robberies were almost a daily occurrence in the area.

Every Sunday we would load up Thomas' truck with the clothes and food and set up in a vacant parking lot. He had an eight foot cross with a wheel attached to the bottom that he or my husband would walk around the neighborhood, inviting people so they could receive free clothes, food, and prayer. We also blasted Christian music from Thomas' truck to let everyone know that we had arrived. When the people heard the music, they would flood the parking lot.

As I look back on those memories, those were some of the best days of my life. I learned that Jesus could use me to heal the sick. I learned that miracles could be common place and not an anomaly. One of the first healings that took place was in a woman who had breast cancer. The four of us and our two children gathered around her in a circle and laid hands on her. A few weeks later she came back with the doctor's report that she was free of all cancer! Another lady was on disability for a back injury that caused her

AUGUST 28

constant pain. She came back a month later with papers informing her that she was off disability because her back pain was gone!

One Sunday, it was going to storm and Thomas commanded the rain to stay off the parking lot so people weren't prevented from coming. All of the food and clothes would have been soaked because we didn't have any shelter. When the rain came, it surrounded the parking lot in a circle around us, but we never felt one drop!

The most life-changing miracle happened to two men who had gotten out of jail a few days prior. They were walking down the road and asked a stranger where they could get some food. The man directed them to our parking lot. When the men arrived, they were both high as a kite on crack. Thomas began to tell them about Jesus, but they were cocky and resisted, as they sat eating their sandwiches.

Eventually, Thomas began to get through to them and the one man agreed to let us pray for him. The moment Thomas put his hand on the man's chest, the man dropped like a dead weight backward on the asphalt—slain in the spirit! He began to squirm and cry out that he was on fire! Thomas said, *"That's the fire of God burning those drugs out of you!"*

When the man finally stood up, his face was glowing and we led him and his friend to the Lord. The man's blue eyes were sparkling as he smiled from ear to ear. I'll never forget the brilliance in his face after his encounter with God! He was definitely not the same man!

Healing and miracles were so simple. Thomas showed us what to do, and we did it. We just followed his example and it worked! We never questioned anything. I can't tell you how many times God multiplied the food we distributed to the poor. We lived in constant awe of God as the supernatural became a part of our everyday lives; it seemed like something miraculous was always happening! I learned that all we have to do for the supernatural to happen regularly is: *"Go!"* Just like Jesus told His disciples!

AUGUST 29

Fish Bowl Fear

Read: Psalm 23

*M*y three year old granddaughter was visiting at my house on a Saturday afternoon. She chose a fish bowl toy from the toy box to play with. There are several colored plastic fish that must be pushed into the opening a certain way to go through the hole in the top. As she drops each fish in, the toy tells what color it is, *"That was a blue fish..."* and so on.

Once all the fish are inside, they must be removed from the bottom to play again. She took the bottom piece off to remove the fish, but instead of shaking them out, she stuck her hand inside to remove them one by one. The problem was that the hole was too small to remove her hand while holding on to the fish. When she tried to pull her hand out of the opening clenched in a fist, it hurt and she couldn't get her hand out. She began to get anxious and cry.

I knelt down beside her and calmly told her to relax her hand and pull it out. I showed her to how shake the fish out of the bottom and return the cover so she could do it again by herself; which she happily returned to playing the game without further complications.

I thought a lot about this simple situation. My granddaughter could have cried and fought to remove her hand in a fist, insisting not to let go of the fish. But the simple, calm instruction I offered helped her to let go and learn a more effective way to enjoy the game. Life is a lot like that sometimes.

Someone wisely once said, *"Life may change, but don't let life change you."* The more we hang on to past disappointments, the more destruction they can bring to our mind, emotions, and health. I've met many adults, well up in years, who still hold on to the abuse they suffered from their parents. Many play the same circumstances over and over, instead of renewing their minds to the Truth

AUGUST 29

offered in God's Word. Like my granddaughter's hand in the fish bowl, they refuse to let go and learn a better way to deal with life. Why let the past ruin your future? It's as simple as my granddaughter trusting my instructions. All she had to do was let go of the fish, remove her hand, and she was free. Her fear vanished. She was able to enjoy playing with the toy in a safer way.

Biblical restoration is much more than returning something to its former condition. It means to restore something better than it was before. I like *The Passion Translation's* version of Psalm 23:

> *"Yahweh is my best friend and my shepherd. I always have more than enough. He offers a resting place for me in His luxurious love. His tracks take me to an oasis of peace near the quiet brook of bliss. That's where He restores and revives my life. He opens before me the right path and leads me along in His footsteps of righteousness so that I can bring honor to His name. Even when your path takes me through the valley of deepest darkness, fear will never conquer me, for You already have! Your authority is my strength and my peace. The comfort of Your love takes away my fear. I'll never be lonely, for You are near. You become my delicious feast even when my enemies dare to fight. You anoint me with the fragrance of Your Holy Spirit; you give me all I can drink of You until my cup overflows. So why would I fear the future? Only goodness and tender love pursue me all the days of my life. Then afterward, when my life is through, I'll return to your glorious presence to be forever with You!"*

AUGUST 30

Think Healed

Read: Proverbs 23:7

One morning when I got up, for no specific reason, both my knees were swollen and painful. I got ready to take my dog for a walk like I do every morning. There was no question in my mind whether I should go or not, even though I walk nothing but up and down hills. Healed means healed, right?

Normally, at the first start of pain I'd lay my hands on whatever part bothered me and command it to leave, and on most occasions, it leaves immediately. This time, as I was about to do that, Holy Spirit said, *"Just think in your mind what you want."* So I did! I thought to myself, *"I want my knees to be normal."*

Immediately, my right knee became normal and all the pain and swelling left. The left knee stayed the same, but I decided to walk my dog anyway. By the time I got home, I had forgotten about the pain. Later in the day, I realized that it was healed! This was a whole new experience for me!

Think healed? Why not? If we think of ourselves as healed, healed is what we shall be! *"As a man thinks in his heart, so is he."*

AUGUST 31

No Prerequisites

Read: James 5:13-15

When a person needs salvation, most Christians would tell him that Jesus will receive him just as he is. He doesn't need to try to clean up his life before coming to Jesus. Jesus loves and accepts him no matter what he's done.

Later, when that same person needs healing in his body, he is told that he must forgive someone that has offended him or repent of whatever sin he committed, and only after he repents, God will heal him.

This type of teaching is totally disproved right here in our Scripture reading for today. Verses 14-15 clearly say:

> *"Is anyone among you sick? Let him call for the elders of the church, and let them pray over him, anointing him with oil in the name of the Lord. And the prayer of faith will save (sozo-heal) the sick, and the Lord will raise him up. And if he has committed sins he will be forgiven."* (Parenthesis added)

Notice the order in which the healing and forgiveness occurs. It says the man will be healed first when he is prayed for. Then it says **if** he has committed sins, he will be forgiven. Notice that the man did not need to repent first in order to be healed.

If sin cannot keep a person from being born again, it cannot keep a person from being healed. There are no prerequisites to either salvation or healing. No hoops to jump through. It's all by grace and faith, not self-effort.

SEPTEMBER 1

Iron Sharpens Iron

Read: Proverbs 27:17

*M*ost people never knew that Martin Luther, the great Reformer, had a right-hand man, Philip Melanchthon. Without him, Luther never would have had the influence to cause the Protestant Reformation of 1517. Philip was a brilliant Greek scholar of only twenty-one years old when he entered the University of Wittenberg in Germany. Luther's attempt to translate the New Testament into the common language was only a success because of Philip.

Although they were best buds, their personalities were quite different. Martin was outspoken and enjoyed socializing with others, while Philip was quiet and introverted. Philip said of Luther, *"If there is any one whom I love strongly, and whom my whole soul embraces, it is Martin Luther."* Together they made each other stronger—a bond that united them by the hand of God for the sake of the Reformation. Their mutual love sharpened one another. Alone, neither would have turned the world upside-down.

Luther taught Philip his theology of the Scriptures, while Philip taught Luther an extended knowledge of the Greek language. Martin's attempts to translate the New Testament were unsuccessful until he met Melanchthon. Martin and Philip were far from perfect, but together they made the perfect team for God to use to give the common people a Bible in their own language.

Philip Melanchthon was just a nobody to most of us, yet without his knowledge, friendship, and influence on Martin Luther's life, we might not understand the freedom we have been given in Christ today. The Protestant Reformation had an undeniable impact upon how we understand God's Word for ourselves. It's easy to take it for granted that we can drive to the Dollar store today and purchase a

SEPTEMBER 1 ———

New Testament for a buck, but this privilege came at a high price for a Martin and Philip.

Did Melanchthon and Luther understand the influence they would have on the world in the future? No, they didn't. They grabbed a hold of truth in the Scriptures and didn't let it go—no matter what anyone said and no matter what it cost them. They have certainly left a legacy for us to emulate!

SEPTEMBER 2

The Just Shall Live By Faith

Read: Romans 1:17, Galatians 3:11, Hebrews 10:38

Martin Luther was a Roman Catholic monk during the 16th Century. He wrestled with his own humanness and sin. Regularly whipping himself as punishment, he fasted and slept under wet blankets, believing he deserved the wrath of God. He had been taught that the righteousness of God meant judgment for sin, of which he thought himself to be the worst. After studying the Scriptures for himself, he received the revelation that righteousness is a gift—something he could never earn!

Most of us never heard the story of how Luther prayed for the healing of his friends. I assume that once he learned about grace through faith as a gift from God, he was able to apply it in other areas in life, especially physical healing.

Martin's friend, Fredrick Myconius, was on his deathbed in the last stages of tuberculosis. Luther wrote a letter to him demanding,

> *"I command you in the Name of God to live because I still have need of you in the work of reforming the church. The Lord will never let me hear that you are dead but will permit you to survive me. For this I am praying, this is my will, and may my will be done because I seek only to glorify the Name of God."*

When Fredrick received the letter, to him it was as though Christ was speaking to him: *"Lazarus, come forth!"* At that moment, Fredrick was healed! He fulfilled Luther's words by outliving him by two months!

Remember Philip Melanchthon, Luther's best friend? At one point, Philip was knocking on death's door. Luther prayed every verse of Scripture he knew about God's promises for healing. As faith rose up in his heart, he took his beloved friend by the hand and said, *"Be*

SEPTEMBER 2

of good courage, Philip, you shall not die." Philip later recounted that he had immediately regained his health. He said that he would have been a dead man if it had not been for Luther.

Martin had learned that salvation and healing were gifts from God—something that could never be earned. He grew in his understanding of God's grace. Through this revelation, he received the courage to stand strong and not recant the position he took against the Roman Catholic Church.

Luther lived by the words: *"The just shall live by faith."* It is one of the Scriptures quoted the most in the New Testament from Habakkuk 2:4 in the Old Testament. Since it was quoted three different times in three separate books in the Bible, I think it's obvious that God wanted us to get the point: *The just shall live by faith!*

SEPTEMBER 3

Entombed

Read: Colossians 2

One of my favorite t-shirts that my husband wears says **FREEDOM** on the front. On the back it says, *"There's nothing better than a dead Christian."* –Colossians 2:12. One day he wore it to church and an elderly man said, *"Oh, your shirt is telling me I'm better off dead!"* But he didn't understand the message. It's not talking about physical death, it's referring to the old man and his sinful nature and how we were resurrected in Christ. The *Wuest Translation* says,

> *"...in the putting off and away from yourselves the body of the flesh in the circumcision of Christ, having been **entombed** with Him in the placing into [Christ by the Holy Spirit], in which act of placing into [Christ] you were also raised with Him through your faith in the effectual working energy of the God who raised Him out from among the dead."* (Colossians 2:11-12, Emphasis added)

I like that—***entombed***! It sure creates a detailed picture in our minds of us literally being wrapped up in burial cloths and placed into the tomb with Jesus after He died! That old Adamic nature we were born into, without a choice, is now dead! When Christ was raised from the dead, we were resurrected with Him—raised to life! Hallelujah!

Colossians goes on to say that He gave us life together with Him by the same Holy Spirit. He forgave all our sins and obliterated every ordinance that was against us! Now our body belongs to Him! We are free from ourselves, free from our past, free from guilt, free from sickness and disease, free from every principality and power! That shirt got it right: **FREEDOM!!**

SEPTEMBER 4

Heirs

Read: Romans 4:13-17, Galatians 3:26-29

Abraham was described in Genesis 14:19 as *"Possessor of heaven and earth."* The above Scripture in Romans reaffirms this promise given to Abraham, that he would be heir of the world! How? Christ came through his lineage. Since we are in Christ through faith, we are included in this promise because Abraham is our father in the faith.

The Father said of His Son after His Resurrection, that He was seated at His right hand in the heavenly places *"far above all principality and power and might and dominion, and every name that is named, not only in this age but also in that which is to come. And He put all things under His feet..."* (Ephesians 1:21-22)

It's common sense, that if someone is an heir, the person who is deceased has to own whatever they are leaving as an inheritance. Christ gained the world back for us and also gave us His authority to use. We cannot give His authority away to anyone else—including the devil. I know that many leaders teach that we can give the devil authority to attack us if we open the door, but there is no Scripture anywhere in the Bible that supports this teaching. Christ gave us dominion because we are hidden in Him. It's His authority, period. Everything is under His feet, and because we are hidden in Him, everything is under our feet too.

We have been equipped with the Holy Spirit to put things back into order as the sons of God, just like Jesus did when He was here. If a person was sick, He made them well. If someone needed deliverance, He set them free. Scripture says He went about doing good everywhere He went (Acts 10:38). Man was created to have dominion over the earth. God created the earth for us, so in our modern day vernacular we would say, *"The world is your oyster!"*

SEPTEMBER 5

Blameless

Read: Psalm 84:11 (NIV)

*B*lameless. How's that even possible? The Psalmist is saying that God won't withhold anything from a person who is without fault. It's a works-based mentality. Since this is an Old Testament Scripture written to people under the Old Covenant, we must always read it in light of Christ's finished work on this side of the cross. Colossians 1:21-22 tells us,

> *"And you, who were once alienated and enemies in your mind by wicked works, yet now He has reconciled in the body of His flesh through death, to present you holy, and blameless, and above reproach in His sight."* (NKJV)

It's quite amazing that He sees us this way. Most Believers still blame themselves for mistakes they've made a long time ago, even before they were born again. But if you read further down in Colossians 1 to verse 23, it tells us that this is the message of the Gospel—to be found in Him holy, blameless, and above reproach!

Sometimes we are our own worst enemy. We pick ourselves apart, trying to make ourselves better people. We cannot do it! Why? Because it's already been done! He made you a totally new person. Now the Holy Spirit is inside of you, guiding you into all Truth (John 16:13)!

When you understand that Jesus made you holy, blameless and above reproach, you can see yourself as God sees you! The Holy Spirit shows you how to exhibit these attributes as you go about each day, talking with Him, living life through His Spirit empowering you, and showing you what is of the spirit and what is of the world.

For example, the Holy Spirit will always give you an inner witness on the inside that you are healed. It's a done deal, and your spirit

SEPTEMBER 5

knows this because your spirit is one with the Holy Spirit. Your body may be telling you something quite the opposite, and your mind is where what you experience wins out: health or sickness. It's a choice that doesn't make any sense to your mind, but it makes perfect sense to your spirit. You get to decide who wins, your body or your spirit!

Your spirit already knows the truth, but your mind must be renewed to agree with what is inside of you. When you are conscious of Holy Spirit inside of you, living in your identity as a son becomes easier as you practice it. You are holy, which means you are set apart for God—exclusively His. Whether you feel like it or not doesn't change this fact. Your entire being: spirit, soul, and body belong to Him! The first place to start experiencing this is to agree with God; then with the help of the Holy Spirit, act like it. Before long, you will like what you see!

SEPTEMBER 6

The Normal Believer

Read: Ephesians 1:3

What is considered *normal* for a Believer? The above verse tells us that every spiritual blessing is what is normal. I love it in *The Passion Translation*,

> "Every spiritual blessing in the heavenly realm has already been lavished upon us as a love gift from our wonderful heavenly Father, the Father of our Lord Jesus—all because He sees us wrapped into Christ. This is why we celebrate Him with all our hearts!"

I need these blessings in the physical realm, right? What is normal for a Believer in the spiritual realm is also normal for a Believer in the natural realm—the two co-exist. The physical realm receives its origin from the spiritual. Without the spiritual realm, the physical realm could not exist; but the spiritual realm doesn't rely on the physical realm to exist. The spiritual realm is greater than the physical realm.

What about physical healing? Sin is spiritual with the physical effect of disease. Disease began at the Fall, as part of the curse when sin entered the world. Disease, having a spiritual origin, is obliterated by spiritual means. The curse of sin and disease were forever broken (Galatians 3:13)!

It isn't normal for Believers to be sick. Sickness doesn't belong to us! We are told that healing is a sign of the Gospel to *Unbelievers* (Mark 16:16-20). There is an entire list of things Believers are able to do as a sign for Unbelievers. This is what is normal. Anything other than this is *abnormal* for God's children!

I realize that many of us are still learning what is normal for a Believer and what isn't. We shouldn't water down the standard

SEPTEMBER 6

set in God's Word just because we aren't experiencing it. We must raise our standard to match His, and then get out there and let the Holy Spirit confirm His Word through signs and wonders. If you never step out and minister healing, no one is going to get healed. It is normal and expected for Believers to be healthy and to minister health to others and set them free!

SEPTEMBER 7

Perfection

Read: Colossians 1:28

Most of us would think that perfection means that everything is just hunky-dory! According to the Greek, the word *perfect* is *teleios*—*without shortcoming and fully efficient, complete in growth, mental and moral character, mature, stable.* It has *nothing* to do with our circumstances. It concerns our *position* in Christ.

I like what it says in the *Mirror Bible's* translation,

> *"This is the essence and focus of our message; we awaken everyone's mind, instructing every individual by bringing them into full understanding (flawless clarity) in order that we may prove (present) everyone perfect in Christ."*

Paul is basically saying, *"I'm trying to open your eyes and help you to see who you really are—perfect in Christ!"*

Circumstances may never be perfect. Yeah, I wish they would be too! But part of being on the *more than conquerors'* side is knowing that we don't lack anything that we need to overcome. We've been given the fullness of a son to know how to handle whatever comes our way and put things back into their proper place.

The above definition for *perfect* says we have moral integrity and stability to be a mature son. I may not know what to do in every situation at first, but when I involve Holy Spirit, He always tells me what to do. That gives me the confidence that He's in it with me, so it's a done deal! Do I always see things instantly? No, I don't. But there is no time or distance in the spirit. If He says it's done, then it's done, and I don't waver—even if I don't see it right away. When I keep His perspective instead of what I see, the outcome is guaranteed!

SEPTEMBER 8

Nothing Can Compete

Read: Matthew 7:28-29

The religious leaders of the day could not compete with Jesus' wisdom. Why? He spoke with *authority*. He was not just a scribe copying the words of some important person. Jesus had taken His Father's words as His own because that is who He is—God's Word in the *flesh*!

In 2 Corinthians 3:1-3, Paul states that he doesn't need to write a letter to prove himself to anyone. He is inferring that *"the proof is in the pudding,"* meaning that the effect of the Gospel upon their lives was proof of his ministry. They had become living Epistles, with the Spirit engraved upon their hearts by how they lived their lives—pagans forever changed by the Gospel! Nothing anyone said could compete with the effect, whether it was spoken by Jesus Himself or by Paul. The Holy Spirit's wisdom and power are undefeated, even for us today.

Whenever we need wisdom, the advice the Holy Spirit gives is usually something we would never think of doing on our own. I love that about Him! That's what makes life with Him fun and exciting! I delight in the fact that I'm never limited to my own advice, especially when it comes to physical healing!

Holy Spirit is personally involved in every healing. He was with Jesus performing every miracle, and He is right here with us. Remember that no one can compete with Holy Spirit's wisdom. He is ready and able to help at all times—that is why He was sent by the Father! He will tell you the steps to take for your own healing, or for someone else's. It may be as simple as calling a friend to pray with you, or going for a walk to get your mind off of your symptoms. Whatever He tells you to do, you can be sure He will assist you!

SEPTEMBER 9

Kept By Power

Read: 1 Peter 1:3-5

As I was reading this chapter in 1 Peter, verse five stood out to me: *"who are kept by the power of God through faith for salvation..."* (NKJV)

It has been my experience, while studying Scripture using the *King James* or the *New King James* Bibles, the translators should have chosen more precise words. I had a hunch that the word *kept* meant more than just holding on to something; so I looked it up in the concordance, and found that my suspicion was correct.

Kept means *a permanently established military post, to hem in, protect, to be a watcher in advance, to mount guard as a sentinel.*

Power means *miraculous power*

Salvation means *rescue or safety, deliver, health, save*

With these words defined, we have a deeper understanding of what it means to be *kept* by the power of God! Holy Spirit is protecting us with military-type force! We can apply this to our lives as a promise that He will protect us from harm and sickness!

I'm thankful for the times, when I'm driving home alone at night on a winding back road, that God protects me from hitting a deer. I cannot tell you how many times just a few seconds made the difference of whether or not my car was totaled. One evening, I was driving a friend home from church. She saw a doe barreling out of the bushes lining the edge of the highway, heading straight for my SUV! Wide-eyed, the deer saw my car, flung forth her front legs—stiff-legged and skidded toward us! The doe came to a halt, turned around, and sprang back into the bushes! My friend exclaimed, *"I have never seen a deer do that in my entire life! When it saw your car, it skidded to a stop and turned around and jumped back into the*

SEPTEMBER 9

bushes!" Unfortunately, I didn't get to see what happened because I was keeping my eyes on the road. I am so thankful that I can trust God to protect me from demolishing my vehicle!

The confidence we gain when Holy Spirit highlights a Scripture pertaining to a specific need is very precious. We can be assured that when He shows the answer, He's also on the scene. Trusting in His protection from all harm and disease are a few of the most valuable promises we could ever commit to Him!

SEPTEMBER 10

The Governor

Read: Romans 8:6-8 (NIV)

"The mind governed by the flesh is death, but the mind governed by the Spirit is life and peace. The mind governed by the flesh is hostile to God; it does not submit to God's law, nor can it do so. Those who are in the realm of the flesh cannot please God." (NIV)

To be *governed* means *controlled, ruled, preside over, command, lead, and dominate.*

In the above Scripture, we see that there are two forces competing against each other to rule over the mind—the human nature and the Holy Spirit. Both forces are in complete opposition to each other and the mind is the battle ground. Where the mind goes, the man follows. A person cannot commit a sinful act unless he ponders it first. The opposite is also true; a person cannot live by the Spirit unless his mind is focused on spiritual realities.

We often don't realize that we do have a choice regarding what dominates our lives. The sinful nature drives us like a taskmaster, but the Holy Spirit gently leads or nudges us in the right direction. Take a quick inventory on your life right now. Do you have life and peace, or are you in turmoil? Who's your governor? The best news is that you don't have to settle for where you're at right now. You get to choose!

Paul fills us with hope by providing the solution! *The Passion Translation* says, *"So then, beloved ones, the flesh has no claims on us at all, and we have no further obligation to live in obedience to it. For when you live controlled by the flesh, you are about to die. But if the life of the Spirit puts to death the corrupt ways of the flesh, we then taste abundant life."* (Romans 8:12-13)

SEPTEMBER 10

Paul explains that our human nature has been depleted of its power to drive us—we are no longer under compulsion to give into what it desires. Living spiritually-minded exhausts human nature of its mastery! Let the governor, the Holy Spirit; give you a taste of abundant life!

SEPTEMBER 11

God's Timing

Read: Galatians 4:3-4

There have been instances where I have approached a Wal-Mart shopper who has an obvious physical problem. When I ask if I may pray with him or her for healing, those who profess to be Christians often respond *"It will happen in God's timing."* There is no convincing these "Believers" that God's timing for their healing was 2000 years ago at the whipping post!

While I realize there are certain situations that cannot be fixed immediately, these are usually related to circumstances where a person's will is involved—not because it is God's timing. If everything that happened depended upon God's timing, then He'd be the one to blame for the tragedies occurring in the world. He put man in charge from the beginning at the Garden (Genesis 1:26-28). If God had a choice, every person would be born again. We would never need to pray that God would work all things out for our good (Romans 8:28).

At best, the term "God's Timing" is just religious jargon. Events that happen or don't happen are not because there is a special timing—God is not holding out until just the right time. In most cases, the reason situations are delayed is on our part. Our emotions can get in the way, or we may not understand how to handle matters. The Holy Spirit is always patient, ready, and willing to help us overcome.

Does waiting for our healing change anything? No, the only result is suffering longer than we should. What is the difference between being healed today or tomorrow? Time and pain. That's about it. Why not be healed today? If we can believe healing is available in time, why not now? Time doesn't make it more available. The stripes of Jesus are as effective today as they were 2000 years ago, and will be just as effective tomorrow. Time doesn't change the fact that healing and salvation are always accessible! So, go ahead! Thank Jesus for making your healing available right now!

SEPTEMBER 12

Trust

Read: Psalm 138

How do you know whether or not you truly put your trust in God? How do you know whether or not you trust God to heal you, provide for you, or protect you? When you are being challenged and a thousand questions take laps around your mind, does that mean that you are *not* trusting God? Does it mean that you *doubt* Him?

The answer to all of these questions is a resounding NO! We can certainly be our own worst critic! The fact that you are born again proves that you trust God. Most times, all we need is a tweak in our perception.

It is more profitable to stop wondering whether or not we are trusting God. When we self-reflect all the time, we are not able to see the answer. It is best to look away from ourselves and our circumstances and look to Holy Spirit and the Word. Those who continually ask the question, *"Why?"* will seldom find an answer. It is best to put all of our human reasoning aside and pick up our Bible. Need an answer? I'm sure you will find it there.

Remember that you are in covenant with God through Christ. All that Jesus is and all that He possesses is equally yours. Simply acknowledge that you do trust Him, instead of questioning yourself. He's been faithful to you all of these years and He's not going to change now.

SEPTEMBER 13

Seize Or Receive?

Read: Mark 11:12-24

*I*n our Devotion for June 16th we discussed the meaning of the Greek word *lambano-"to take up a thing to be carried; to take upon one's self, to remove or take away with the notion of violence, to seize, take away forcibly, to take to one's self, to make one's own."* We compared Jesus seizing our sicknesses as part of our salvation so that we could be seized with the power of the Holy Spirit.

Today, we are taking a look at the word *lambano* again in the context of Mark 11—that famous teaching many of us have heard preached by popular ministers in the past about speaking to our mountains and commanding them to be removed.

The NKJV and the KJV use the word *receive* in verse 24. In our modern day understanding of the word *receive* it means *to take or acquire something given or offered.* That sounds a bit wimpy and passive to me!

If we read verse 24 like this: *"Therefore I say to you, whatever things you ask when you pray, seize them with force, and you will have them."* According to *Thayer's Concordance*, this would be a proper translation. Now it's got some "oomph" to it!

When we apply the idea of taking that mountain, we can think of it like the scene in the movie *Avengers* where Loki stands face to face with the Incredible Hulk. Hulk begins to lunge at Loki and Loki shouts, *"Enough! I am a god you dull creature!"* Hulk grunts and lunges at Loki, picks him up by his feet and smashes him into the floor several times, whipping him around like a rag doll! From a hole in the floor caused by the indentation of his body, Loki can respond with nothing but a faint whimper. Hulk struts away boldly, tossing his head over his shoulder, *"Puny god!"*

Imagine seizing your healing with force; knowing Jesus smashed it to pieces! Now that's more like it! *"Puny disease!"* No wimps here!

SEPTEMBER 14

High Things

Read: 2 Corinthians 10:3-5

Our actions usually reveal our thoughts and what we believe in our heart. Paul says that, even though we live in a body made of flesh, we do not use it to wage war spiritually. He says that our weapons are mighty in God. *Might* is the God-given ability to accomplish anything possible or impossible. Sounds like we can't lose, doesn't it?

Paul further goes on to explain that because our weapons are mighty in God, we have the authority to pull down strongholds, demolish arguments, and every *high thing* that tries to exalt itself against the knowledge of God. All of these strongholds, arguments, and high things are thoughts replaying in our minds that are contrary to what God says. Isn't that what the serpent did to Eve in the beginning? He challenged her with what she knew about God. That's exactly what man's wisdom does—it challenges God's wisdom. If we don't know who we are in Christ as sons and daughters, and if we don't understand the authority we have in His Name, we will continue to be brought down to a level that is not what is expected of a child of God.

When it comes to physical healing, the challenges confronting us are our imaginations and the physical symptoms screaming in our body. It can be very overwhelming. Yet, whether it is a thought in our mind or a physical symptom, they are both trying to exalt themselves above Christ and our knowledge of His finished work of the cross.

Bringing every thought captive does not mean it has to be a constant war. The easiest way to "cast down our imaginations" is to train our minds to think the opposite, according to what God says in His Word.

SEPTEMBER 14

For example, if you have a pain in your body, tell it that it is healed and do something to get your mind off it. With your mind focused on something else, you will realize the pain is gone and will gain confidence that it can be gone forever!

SEPTEMBER 15

The Faith Train

Read: 2 Corinthians 4:13

It doesn't make any difference the *quantity*, but the *quality* of faith with which we live by. We can prove this from Scripture because Jesus said we only need faith the size of a mustard seed to move a mountain. One particular characteristic of faith is that it is the most effective when we understand our *authority*. The quality of our faith is that it never draws back. We have been given the same faith and authority that Jesus has.

Faith speaks. It doesn't know whether what we say is true or not—we are the prophet of our own life. Jesus said we will have whatever we say, whether it is positive or negative. This is one of the most important keys to living in victory: Faith operates through *authority*, not *begging*. In fact, faith and begging are complete opposites! Faith says *"I have!"* and begging says, *"Please give me!"* Faith expects and speaks the promise. Faith speaks *to* the problem—not to God *about* the problem.

Faith is like a train on the railroad tracks. Once you set the train in motion, it doesn't stop until it arrives with the goods. Faith doesn't stop working until you experience what has been promised. It is helpful to keep the Faith Train on the tracks by believing that it is working, even if you don't see any evidence yet in the natural world.

In many situations, we must dig in our heels and be stubborn about God's promises. True faith says, *"This will be what I say it will be, and nothing else!"* True faith is not about the duration of time it takes. It is working, staying on track as long as you apply it, and it will accomplish what you sent it to do. It might be tempting to say, *"This is ridiculous; this isn't working!"* especially when you don't see any evidence of change. But don't do it! Don't derail your Faith Train!

SEPTEMBER 15 ———

Keep your faith on the tracks! Continue to persevere and speak life. Remember the authority you have been given in Christ, even over the most stubborn predicament. Your Faith Train is bound to arrive with the goods!

SEPTEMBER 16

Perfect Soundness

Acts 3:1-16

The account of the lame man receiving the strength to walk is the first miracle the disciples performed after being baptized in the Holy Spirit on the day of Pentecost. Peter stated to all those praying in the temple that it was the Name of Jesus and faith in His Name which caused the man to leap onto his feet for the first time in his life!

I love Peter's attitude! He didn't act astonished about the miracle. He acted like he wasn't even surprised; as though this was a natural thing and the people shouldn't be amazed! Well, technically it wasn't his first time around the block at performing miracles. He had been sent out with the twelve and he had seen Jesus heal multitudes every day.

I love the term *perfect soundness*. When the man was healed, he received what is called *integrity* in his body, according the definition in the Greek. It says in the Thayer's: *of an unimpaired condition of body, in which all its members are healthy and fit for use.* I like the sound of that, don't you?

The best thing about God's Word is that, if it is written, it's accessible for you and me! God doesn't give special privileges to some of His children and treat the rest like step-children. He's a generous Father! If you need perfect soundness in your body, you can be absolutely sure that it is available to you, just as it was for the man born lame. You have been given the same spirit of faith Jesus has; or else you wouldn't be born again. So, in the Name of Jesus, rise up and walk! Expect *perfect soundness* in every part of your body!

SEPTEMBER 17

Mr. Nobody

Read: Mark 9:38-40

*W*hat is remarkable about this man casting out demons in Jesus' Name is that he wasn't one of the twelve; neither was he among the seventy. Jesus never personally met the man. He never gave him instructions or His authority to do His works. The man had faith in Jesus' Name and acted without being told. This made the disciples look inferior, in my opinion.

The disciples took the responsibility upon themselves to inform the man that he wasn't one of them, so how dare he do what they were commanded to do! They didn't realize that there are no "elites" in God's Kingdom. All it took was faith and obedience in His Name. We don't even know the man's name! He's simply Mr. Nobody, doing Jesus' works. He didn't need someone standing over his shoulder telling him what to do, he just did it; and for that he is remembered in the Gospels.

It is a popular belief that we must wait for God's leading before we minister to someone. I've heard Believers testify that they've asked Holy Spirit to highlight certain people so they can pray for them. Ten other people could pass right by, hobbling with canes or riding scooters, and they will only minister to the ones they were given "special" information about.

We see the perfect example right here in Scripture that we don't have to wait for special instructions! Jesus already gave us the command to *"Go"* into all the world (Mark 16:15-20)! The greatest act of obedience is reading truth in the Bible and then acting on that truth by sharing it with others. We don't have to be super-anointed elite preachers. God uses a "Mr. Nobody" simply because he is available.

SEPTEMBER 18

Spiritual Gifts

Read: 1 Corinthians 12:1-11

Several years ago when I was a new Believer, my mentor said to me, *"Michele, if you see someone sick and there's no one else around, you go heal them. If you see a need, you go meet that need. You have all the gifts because you have the Holy Spirit."* Every time I read these verses, I always remember his counsel.

It wasn't until much later I heard ministers teach that the Holy Spirit doles out certain gifts to those whom He chooses. Honestly, that never resonated with me. I always believed that if there was a need, Holy Spirit would see to it that that need was met.

The "gifts" listed here in 1 Corinthians aren't really gifts, like receiving a special present from God. They are actually a list of the types of manifestations of the Holy Spirit. These are part of who He is—His character and nature, not just things He does.

Remember that this list of spiritual gifts was written to the most messed up church in the New Testament. The message Paul was attempting to explain is that, if there is a need, Holy Spirit's there to help give them a boost. It's not about qualifying anyone to be a super-duper, highly anointed person. No shirt with a capital *"S"* necessary!

As a matter of fact, we never read of Jesus using any spiritual gifts to meet the needs of the people because He walked in the fullness of the Spirit. He never needed the Holy Spirit to step in and give him a boost. He walked in the fullness of a Son.

Remember that Holy Spirit is always on the scene, prepared to help. You've got *all* the gifts because you have the Holy Spirit! No Super-Saints needed! Just step out and meet the need and you'll find the power to help whomever, wherever you go! Eventually you'll find yourself walking in the fullness of a son!

SEPTEMBER 19

Diseases Depart

Read: Acts 19:11-12 (KJV)

Paul was filled with the Holy Spirit—there is no doubt about it. The revelation he received about Christ coming to live inside of a Believer was the most valuable truth ever revealed in the history of mankind. He calls it the *mystery* that was hidden in past generations: *Christ in you,* the hope of glory (Colossians 1:26-27)!

This revelation of *Christ in you* is life changing! Embracing this truth is the difference between living victoriously or defeated. It requires a total mind-shift! I know a minister of the Gospel who, when he looks in the mirror says, *"I see you in there!"* to the Holy Spirit. He has such a revelation that Jesus is inside him, he bursts with joy and laughter everywhere he goes.

I believe Paul spent the rest of his life having personal experiences with Jesus. He was so sure of his identity in Christ and the new man he had become; he was able to do *unusual* miracles. I don't think he was deliberately showing off his miraculous ability. It was a natural result of knowing that the Spirit of God took up residence inside him. Even more amazing, is that demons and diseases departed because of the power in his clothes! They got one whiff of power and decided, *"Hey, this guy's holy! We're outta here!"*

If more Believers had the revelation that Christ has taken up residence inside of them like Paul, the body of Christ worldwide would explode with power once again—but we are gaining momentum! Hardly a day goes by that I don't hear of someone in a store, or on the streets, ministering healing to people. We are taking more ground together for the Kingdom!

SEPTEMBER 20

God's Prescription

Read: 3 John 2

To prescribe means *to lay down a rule or a course of action to be followed.* God's prescription for us to follow is for our bodies to be as healthy as our minds. In this book of devotions, I've written extensively regarding how a healthy thought life is directly related to our physical health.

Here in 3 John 2, we see the proof that it is God's will for us to prosper in all things; whether financially, in our bodies, or our soul. He desires for us to be whole in every area of our lives. It isn't possible to effectively follow Jesus' command to *"Go into all the world and preach the Gospel"* if we can't pay our own bills, if we're laid up in bed sick, or if we're depressed. John says,

> *"Beloved, I pray (wish, crave, desire) that in every way you may succeed and prosper and be in good health (physically), just as (I know) your soul prospers (spiritually)."* (Amplified Bible)

Below is God's Prescription for your life:

1. Renew your mind to the truth found in God's Word
2. Dismiss every thought that doesn't line up with God's Word and replace that thought with truth
3. Fellowship with like-minded Believers who can encourage you
4. Pray in the spirit often to keep yourself built up in faith
5. Act on the Word, praying for others or meeting their needs everywhere you go

By following these simple suggestions, we can stay healthy in our bodies, clear-minded, and focused. Jesus said we should concern ourselves with God's Kingdom, and in turn, never need to worry about meeting our own needs (Matthew 6:33).

SEPTEMBER 21

The Children's Bread

Read: Matthew 15:21-28

It was no surprise that Jesus would have an encounter with a non-Jewish person as He travelled through the region of Tyre and Sidon. I am amused at His first response to the Canaanite—He ignores her. I don't think it's because she is annoying Him. If that were the case, He would have given up on His disciples a long time ago!

The disciples were aggravated by her—no surprise there. There was hardly a time where they had a compassionate response to anyone not in their close circle of companions. They told her, *"Shut up and leave us alone!"* When she wouldn't stop crying out, like a bunch of tattletales, they complained to Jesus. In grade school, we used the term "nark" for anyone who acted like the teacher's pet.

Jesus told her, *"No!"* but she persisted all the more. I don't think He was holding out on her. I think He was challenging her to see whether she would give up or not. She wasn't leaving until her daughter was set free. What mother wouldn't try everything she could to help her daughter? Who could blame her for that?

Jesus informed her that it wouldn't be proper to cast the children's bread to dogs. What was the children's bread? Healing and deliverance! She didn't care that He had just insulted her by calling her a dog! She said, *"I don't care, just give me the crumbs from what is left over. That'll be enough!"*

Jesus changed His insult into a compliment. He commended her faith—she didn't take offence and just kept insisting that He must set her daughter free! He was the Bread of Life! She knew that He had the power to cure her daughter.

SEPTEMBER 21

Healing and deliverance belong to all of God's children. Healing is the children's bread because Jesus is the Bread of Life! He said in John 6 that anyone who eats (believes) in Him would have His life living inside of them! Healing is your daily bread because the "Bread of Life" lives inside of you supplying life to your body!

SEPTEMBER 22

Health & Cure

Read: Jeremiah 33:6

Whether it is written in the Old or New Testament, no matter who the people are, God makes no distinction; it is always His desire to heal. Whether it is a broken heart or a broken leg, the remedy is the same—Jesus.

Our Scripture verse says that God would bring health and the cure; then He would add to it the abundance of peace and truth. The word *cure* here is derived from the word *rapha* (healed) used in Isaiah 53:5 *"By His stripes we are healed."*

If a doctor gave you a prescription, you would follow the instructions on the label. Most medicines do not cure. Many just alleviate the symptoms so that the body can heal itself. If we want a complete cure, there is only one place we can go—the One who created our bodies. He knows how they are designed to function.

God's Word becomes new flesh when we apply it to our bodies! I've seen it over and over again. I've heard countless testimonies and I have experienced it for myself: God's Word *works*! His Words are spirit and they are life (John 6:63)!

Sometimes healing is slow because we must unlearn the teachings that religion enforced, and we have to replace them with what God's Word actually says. As our mind is renewed, the symptoms disappear! Our organs begin to function properly again because they are restored to health!

The reason I wrote this devotional is so that every day you can renew your mind to God's Word. As you renew your mind, expect those symptoms to leave. No, it doesn't have to take an entire year! But help is right here when you need it!

SEPTEMBER 23

Wise Guy

Proverbs 3:7-8

In the *Amplified Bible* God commands:

> "Do not be wise in your own eyes; fear the Lord (with reverent awe and obedience) and turn (entirely) away from evil. It will be health to your body (your marrow, your nerves, your sinews, your muscles—all your inner parts) and refreshment (physical well-being) to your bones."

In paraphrasing the first part of verse seven, we could say, "Don't be a wise-guy!" Sometimes we may think we know better than what God has to say, or that the doctor has the final word. But that is always far from the truth. I read the story of an elderly woman who had a disease that left her confined to bed. Her bones were so brittle that just moving her limbs could make them break. She was in agony, and her family members kept telling her it was okay to quit fighting and die because they couldn't bear watching her suffer.

When her family wasn't in the room, the lady would turn her face to the wall and pray. She knew some Scriptures about healing, so she would pray them over herself. One day, a family member came into her bedroom—in wide-eyed astonishment exclaimed, *"How did you get over there!"* She was sitting across the room in a chair—completely healed!

The woman had to push out of her mind everything her family said. She had to dismiss what her body was saying. She had to discount everything the doctor said. She couldn't afford to be wise in her own eyes. She honored God's wisdom above everyone's advice. As a result, the impossible became possible!

SEPTEMBER 24

Spiritual Reaction

Read: Luke 5:17-26

When I homeschooled my children, our favorite science experiment was watching the reaction between baking soda and vinegar. We never tired of the fizz and the foam erupting the moment those two compounds touched!

In our Scripture reading for today, there were two spiritual elements present for the paralyzed man to receive strength in his legs—faith and power. The man's four crazy friends brought the faith; Jesus brought the power. When those two elements mixed together in the atmosphere, a miracle was the result!

You know what? The same power is alive and active in your body right now! Did you know that you already have the faith you need for your own healing? If you are a saved, you already have faith because you used it to become born again!

The two elements needed for a miracle are already inside you! You've got *faith* and you've got *power*! Now that you know you already have what you need for your miracle, right now go do something you couldn't do. Expect there to be improvement in your body; then watch all the symptoms and limitations leave forever!

SEPTEMBER 25

No Weapons

Read: Isaiah 54:17

When a person is facing a stressful situation, this is one of the most popular verses of Scriptures. It's like the "go-to" verse for almost every problem. We cannot afford to forget when we read Scripture; it is a rule of thumb to consider who the instructions were originally spoken to. We find this verse in the Old Testament which means that we must filter it though the understanding of the New Covenant we have in Christ.

When reading this verse, we need to acknowledge that we are now on this side of the cross, where everything is finished. It says that no weapon formed against us shall prosper. Let's go to the New Testament for a more accurate account. Colossians 2:13-15 says that Christ has *disarmed* every principality and power! To *disarm* simply means that all weapons have been stripped away.

Since Christ disarmed the enemy, he has no weapons to form! All that is left now are words—suggestions and imaginations that influence our thinking. We can dismiss every thought, even if it comes in the form of a symptom in our body.

When our body tries to tell us, *"I have a headache,"* at the first sign of pain, we can command it to leave and thank Jesus for giving us authority over it. That's all. As Christ's body, we should be immune from disease and pain! The more we know the truth, that sickness and disease *cannot* belong in His body, the more we can hold our expectation to live free of all symptoms. Weapons? Ha! They've been obliterated!

SEPTEMBER 26

Never Dry

Read: Isaiah 58:11

I love the way *The Message Bible* expresses Isaiah 58:11,

> "I will always show you where to go. I'll give you a full life in the emptiest of places—firm muscles, strong bones. You'll be like a well-watered garden, a gurgling spring that never runs dry."

This verse of Scripture sums up everything we need, doesn't it? Direction for our lives, a long life, strength in our bodies, and continual refreshment! The first few times I read this verse, where it says "well-watered," I thought of it in terms of being *thoroughly* watered and refreshed. But after contemplating this idea, I realized "well-watered" means a literal well that is fed from and underground spring!

My home is a cabin in the woods. We have a well that is fed from an underground spring. Wells can be dug anywhere from 100 to 500 feet deep; some even 1000 feet deep! Very seldom do the springs that feed a well ever dry up because they come from deep underground. What is also an added plus is that our water is free! No monthly water bill!

The Garden of Eden was watered by a mist that came up from under the earth and watered the whole face of the ground (Genesis 2:6). The Garden was where every provision Adam needed was met. It was where he fellowshipped with his Creator.

Today, the Garden is inside us, where every need is met. The Holy Spirit is like rivers of living water flowing in our bodies. He never dries up because He is eternal. Imagine that! An eternal fountain of life inside your body—gurgling over!

SEPTEMBER 27

Words Like Swords

Read: Proverbs 12:18

"*Reckless words pierce like a sword, but the tongue of the wise brings healing.*" (NIV)

To be *reckless* means that one doesn't care about the consequences of his actions or words. If we measure this type of living against God's Word, we'll find that this is not the way we are expected to behave. For example, Psalm 138:2 says that God honors His Word above His own name. How is that possible when His name is above every name? A person's reputation is based upon what he says and how he acts. Years ago, a contract could be made by a verbal agreement and a hand shake. In our culture today, many do not follow through with their promises, but God isn't like that. He means what He says—His reputation is as good as His word.

I cannot emphasize how important it is to watch our words! If Jesus only spoke what He heard His Father speak, we can see that Jesus knew the value of His words. Imagine the damage Jesus could have done if He talked like most people do! Everything would have been destroyed!

What about our self-talk—our thoughts about ourselves? If we are careful to watch what we speak, but we find ourselves thinking the opposite, this is being double-minded. We won't be able to receive what God has promised because we're not able to divide the truth from the lies. Amos 3:3 says, *"Can two walk together, unless they are agreed?"* If our thinking, words, and actions are not in harmony with each other, we will experience confusion and lack of direction.

The second part of the verse from above says that wise words bring healing. We can read many examples in the Gospels how Jesus' words brought healing. He told the paralytic to *"Arise."* He told the nobleman, *"Go your way, your son lives."* Jesus never spoke one

SEPTEMBER 27

thing and then did another. Jesus' very words were the cure each person needed. Imagine if our words were like salve upon each other's wounds!

What if our words really were swords and we could see them cutting into ourselves or wounding someone else? Just because we may not see the immediate effects of our words—positive or negative, we should not be reckless with what we speak. The Word of God is just as powerful in our mouths as it was when Jesus spoke. He gave us His authority and ability to do the same works.

If we want to have the same effect as Jesus, our words and our thoughts must agree. When we say one thing and do another, or if we speak one thing and think another, it brings confusion to our hearts. We were meant to live in wholeness— not division. If we want to experience harmony in our spirit, soul, and body, it all starts with our words and our thoughts. Let's choose words that are like ointment pouring out!

SEPTEMBER 28

No Feeble Paupers

Read: Psalm 105:37

"*At last, God freed all the Hebrews from their slavery and sent them away laden with the silver and gold of Egypt. And not even one was feeble on their way out!*" (*The Passion Translation*)

A note in *The Passion Translation* says *"Not one of His tribes was a pauper"* or *"Not one stumbled."*

The Hebrew people were no longer slaves! The Passover Lamb had healed them. The beatings they endured from the Egyptians were healed. Their weaknesses gone! No matter how old or young, they all came out of Egypt whole and able to walk without stumbling!

God had given them favor with their enemies, so that the clothes they would need and the materials for building the tabernacle in the wilderness were provided. God was thinking ahead for what they would require before they had need of it. Gold, silver, jewels, and riches abounded! It didn't seem that way to the Israelites. They became thirsty and hungry and cried out for provision. Did God have in mind what He would feed them? Didn't He know that they would need food and water?

We know that the example of the children of Israel coming out of slavery and into the Promised Land is a metaphor for new Believers coming out of the world and into the Kingdom of God. God took the Hebrews out of slavery, but they wouldn't let go of their slavery mind-set. They received new clothes that would never wear out and they were made rich with the plunder of their enemies.

I wonder how many people still see themselves in bondage to the sin of their past when Romans 8:3-4 says,

SEPTEMBER 28

> *"For what the law could not do in that it was weak through the flesh, God did by sending His own Son in the likeness of sinful flesh, on account of sin: He condemned sin in the flesh, that the righteous requirement of the law might be fulfilled in us who do not walk according to the flesh, but according to the Spirit."*

In these two verses, it is telling us that sin was already judged—this is what it means to be *condemned*. Sin no longer has power over us. We don't have to identify with that old nature now that we are in Christ. For some Believers, they need to be reminded that Jesus not only took them out of the world, but He took the world out of them! They no longer belong to the world and its system any more than Jesus does! Talk about freedom and blessings! He came to give us a superabundant life! We received a new spirit, a new mind, a new heart, and a new body—with power and authority to boot! No feeble paupers here!

SEPTEMBER 29

Compassion

Read: Matthew 15:29-32

Compassion is more than having sympathy or pity for someone's plight. It is a deep yearning in your gut that moves you to do something to change the situation. It's more than empathy—like bringing a sick person a bowl of chicken soup to warm their belly—but delivering them out of their distress.

We read in Matthew that Jesus had compassion on this great multitude of people. Among them were the lame, blind, mute, and the maimed. It took Him *three days* to minister health to all of them! That's a lot of people!

On top of all this, at the end of the three days, Jesus was concerned about their provisions. None of them had eaten during this time and He didn't want them to pass out from hunger after He spent all that time healing them! Talk about thinking ahead! He didn't just care about them for the moment, but for their future lives after they would return home.

In verse thirty-two Jesus pronounced, *"I have compassion on the multitude, because they have now continued with Me three days and have nothing to eat. And I do not want to send them away hungry, lest they faint on the way."* Jesus' compassion motivated Him to heal and feed the people so they had more than enough!

There are about twelve different times the Gospels say that Jesus was stirred with compassion and healed, fed multitudes, or raised people from the dead. It is a good reminder to remember when we are moved with compassion for people that are suffering, we are also equipped with the same power to do something about it and deliver them from their plight!

SEPTEMBER 30

Just A Touch

Read: Matthew 14:34-36

*C*an you envision this multitude of people begging, pawing, and grabbing at Jesus' clothes so they could be healed! Was He offended? Did He try to push them away because He felt overwhelmed? No!

I'm assuming this multitude got the idea to touch His clothes to be healed because they had heard about the woman with the issue of blood. She had secretly touched His clothes and was immediately made whole! Here these people were, a few chapters later, receiving that same wholeness. It worked for them exactly the same as it had worked for her!

I believe the same thing would happen today if Jesus was physically here on the earth right now, but He isn't. However, we as His body are! If you need physical healing or deliverance from depression, you've got something better than Jesus' garment—you have the same Holy Spirit that permeated Jesus' body and flowed into His clothes! That very same Holy Spirit that raised Jesus from the dead is touching you on your insides—in every cell, every system, and every organ of your body, healing you from the inside out!

"Well, I don't feel healed!" You might be thinking. Did you acknowledge Him inside you before and then *expect* healing to be the result? Now that you are aware of Him touching you 24/7—not just one little touch like the woman with the issue of blood or this multitude—*but every day, all day and all night while you sleep*, you can expect there to be change! That's what faith is: knowing what is available and then expecting a result! Go ahead! Expect His life to penetrate your body, just like resurrection power permeated His clothes!

OCTOBER 1

Ride The Wave

Read: Isaiah 40:28-31

*T*hese verses say that God never grows tired or weary. That's astounding cuz you'd think we humans would have worn Him out by now LOL! But NO! He never tires of us! In fact, it says here that instead of growing weary of us, He gives us *His* strength and endurance!

The word *wait* in this verse does not mean to sit around and look for God to do something. It means to *expect* Him to renew us with His power and strength. Whether He will empower us is not limited to our age, because it says that even youths grow tired, become weak, and stumble. The difference is not in our age, but who we're connected to. Those who put their hope and expectation in the Lord will receive renewed strength to run, walk, and even soar like an eagle!

Did you ever see a flock of hawks soaring in the sky? They glide with ease in a circle without the need to expend a lot of energy from flapping their wings. These birds are riding a thermal wave. A thermal is a pocket of rising warm air that has been heated by the earth's surface from the sun. As the birds migrate, they glide from one thermal to another expending less energy as the wind carries them.

As we rely and trust in our God, we can soar upon the waves of His strength and energy, mounting up with dignity and majesty in Him, with renewed vigor and health—no matter how old we are!

OCTOBER 2

Renewed

Read: Psalm 103:5

*D*id you know that an eagle can reach the age of 20 to 30 years? Under normal conditions, an eagle will molt once or twice every year. This process of renewal preserves the bird's ability to replace old or injured feathers and happens over a period of several weeks. Restoration occurs symmetrically for their flight feathers, keeping their wings balanced in order to fly straight.

The word *Renewed* in Hebrew means *to rebuild or repair.* Much like the eagle's method of renewal, the Lord renews our youth. Are you determined to live a long, healthy life? I don't want to waste my life sitting in a rocking chair when I'm old, watching the world pass me by. I'd hate to look over my life with regret and lament, *"I wished I would have..."* Do you?

Psalm 103 in verse five of *The Passion Translation* says, *"You satisfy my every desire with good things. You've* **supercharged** *my life so that I soar again like a flying eagle in the sky!"* (Emphasis added)

SUPERCHARGED! Do you like the sound of that? God gives increased power that renews, rebuilds, repairs, and restores our bodies! Romans 6:4 reminds us, *"Therefore we were buried with Him through baptism into death, that just as Christ was raised from the dead by the glory of the Father, even so we also should walk in* **newness** *of life."*

Newness means *freshness, new with respect to age, renewal, youthful, regenerate.* In other words: live like you've been resurrected—because you have!

OCTOBER 3

Precious Communion

Read: Acts 2:42-47

*T*he early church held the sacrament of Communion as precious. They honored the elements and celebrated it together daily. One young man, Tarcisius, in the 3rd Century, was attacked and beaten to death by an enraged mob as he carried the elements of Communion. Rather than let the bread fall to the ground, he protected it with his life, earning the name "The Eucharist Martyr."

The elements of the bread and juice represent Jesus' body and blood that instituted and sealed the New Covenant. It's a covenant which promises that we will not be weak, sickly or die prematurely, and reminds us that sin—including all curses—no longer hold any authority over our lives.

Sadly, many contemporary Bible-believing churches have no idea what the bread represents. It's the first half of Communion! That's pretty disheartening, since Jesus walked around healing every sick person He met, isn't it? Paul warned the Corinthian church about forgetting the bread representing health for their physical bodies. The tenacity of the "Eucharist Martyr" shows us a glimpse how serious the early church was about the sanctity of Communion—they were willing to die for it!

Jesus instructed us to partake of Communion as often as we want. He told us to take it in remembrance of Him. In other words: DON'T FORGET WHAT I'VE DONE FOR YOU! DON'T FORGET WHAT MY BODY AND MY BLOOD REPRESENT! Yet many, like the Corinthian church, haven't listened!!

I encourage you to remember; when you eat the bread, you are sharing in Christ's body, broken for you, so that you can enjoy a long, healthy life! Keep in mind that since every curse of sin was destroyed—you are completely delivered! Cherish in your heart that the effects of the New Covenant can never be broken!

OCTOBER 4

POOF!

Read: Luke 2:41-52

*T*he Gospels indicate that, unexpectedly, after John the Baptist announced that Jesus was the long-awaited Messiah—POOF! Suddenly, Jesus began acting like He was God's Son. We get a tiny glimpse of Jesus' mindset as a young boy of twelve: He was consumed with His Father.

It cannot be possible that Jesus woke up on the morning of His baptism and decided to acknowledge His identity and His Father's mission. He had a relationship with His Father God throughout His entire life, and we only see a hint of it here in Luke's Gospel. He didn't impulsively develop His relationship with the Father. Growing up, He drew away to pray during the nighttime as a lifestyle, like the incidences we read about in the Gospels. Philippians 2:6-7 reminds us,

> *"Though He was God, He did not think of equality with God as something to cling to. Instead, He gave up His divine privileges; He took the humble position of a slave and was born as a human being."* (New Living Translation)

Jesus didn't automatically know the Scriptures. He had to learn them as any other Jewish boy in His culture would. Yet, He had to somehow realize that these Scriptures pointed to Him, like after His resurrection when He was walking with the two men on the road to Emmaus. He expounded the Scriptures to them about the things concerning Himself. He had to be fully convinced about the Scriptures that prophetically revealed Him.

I often ponder Jesus' confidence knowing He was as the Son of God. Imagine Jesus reading about Himself in the Old Testament a realizing, *"Hey! That's talking about Me!"* If Jesus Himself had to develop His relationship with His Father over the course of His life,

OCTOBER 4

before He was revealed as the Christ, I'm encouraged to search the Scriptures in the New Testament that are referring to me! For example, where it says I am a new creation in Christ and my old life has passed away, I too, can shout, *"Hey! That's talking about me!"*

OCTOBER 5

Strength To Strength

Read: Psalm 84:5-7

What do you think it means to go from strength to strength? This describes our strength increasing as we live in close connection with Holy Spirit. We may have been at one place in our relationship with God; yet as we continue to walk with Him, our strength increases beyond what we can fathom. In other words, we could say that we just don't know what we're made of! And here, it tells us that we are made of His strength!

The Valley of Baca was called the "Valley of Weeping" and refers to the difficult times we may pass through in our lifetime. But remember: we pass *through*. We don't remain there! Psalm 30:5 tells us that weeping may endure for a night, but we can be sure that joy will come in the morning!

No one is exempt from the hard reality that life isn't always a bed of roses. In spite of this, we can encourage ourselves by remembering that the joy of the Lord is our strength. Those pools of weeping that were filled with tears will once again be overflowing with showers of joy!

OCTOBER 6

Says Who?

Read: Psalm 103:1-5

A benefit is something that promotes or enhances well-being. The beginning of Psalm 103 uses the word *who* five times when referring to the Lord's benefits:

> WHO forgives all your iniquities.
>
> WHO heals all your diseases.
>
> WHO redeems your life from destruction.
>
> WHO crowns you with loving-kindness and tender mercies.
>
> WHO satisfies your mouth with good things so that your youth is renewed like the eagle's.

We could easily add to this list more benefits by placing the word "WHO" at the beginning of every line and adjust the words accordingly—I encourage you to do this! Meditating on God's virtues locks an in-depth description in our mind of the many benefits He has so graciously bestowed upon us! This affirms hope and trust, especially when we're facing a strenuous situation; these nuggets of truth dispel the temptation to question His goodness. This Psalm is the perfect reminder prophesying the many ways Jesus took care of what we'd need before we needed it!

OCTOBER 7

The Carrier

Read: Isaiah 46:4

*A*re you aware of the many references in the Bible pertaining to God's provision for us to live a long, healthy life? We've got these promises signed and sealed in His blood through the New Covenant, and a continual reminder of them every time we take Communion. He said we would not be weak, sickly, or die prematurely by eating the bread—representing His body which was broken for us.

Twice in this verse, God pledges to carry us to the end of our lives—until we're old and gray! Note that the words *bear* and *carry* are the same words used in Isaiah 53:4, where it prophesies of Christ *bearing* our sicknesses and *carrying* our diseases. These two words are synonyms and they both mean *to carry as a punishment so that the other person doesn't have to carry it themselves.*

He reveals Himself again as the "I AM," the One who is our protector, provider, deliverer. It is downright comforting to know that our Father will be intimately involved in our lives and carry us through until we decide we want to go home to be with Him!

OCTOBER 8

A Spiritual Nation (Part 1)

Read: Exodus 19:3-6, Revelation 5:8-10

From the beginning, God always desired to fellowship with and live among His people. We read about Adam conversing with Him in the Garden, to the glory cloud hovering over the tabernacle as God dwelt in the midst of His people. He knows every person by name and He is acquainted with all of their ways (Psalm 139).

It was also God's plan from the outset that His people would be a kingdom of priests and a holy nation set apart unto Him. This isn't limited to an Old or New Testament concept—the invitation is for everyone, for all time! He loves each one as His own special treasure! God announced His appeal to Israel and for all nations to reign as kings on the earth.

Do you consider yourself as royalty? Do you see yourself as a king or a queen, executing authority on behalf of God's Kingdom? You're not being prideful for seeing yourself in this position; after all, it was His idea! Being humble doesn't mean that you look at yourself like a worm squished in the mud. Humility means that you replace your own limiting human beliefs about yourself, believe who God says you are, and apply it with Holy Spirit's help. Remember Romans 5:17 affirms,

> *"For if by the one man's offense death reigned (as king) through the one, much more those who receive abundance of grace and of the gift of righteousness will reign (as kings) in life through the One, Jesus Christ."* (Parentheses added)

OCTOBER 9

A Spiritual Nation (Part 2)

Read: 1 Peter 2:9-10

Adding to yesterday's devotion, we maintain that God calls us a kingdom of priests, a holy nation, and His own special treasure again! We are a nation of people who trace their genealogy back one generation—our Heavenly Father! He delivered us from this dark, tyrannical world and re-birthed us into His Kingdom of freedom by grace.

It's like a pauper—the lowest outcast of society, begging in the streets. The rags to riches story: Without a clue, the beggar found out that he had royal lineage and was next in line to be king! A messenger searched for him in the slum and brought him into the castle. He is bathed, enrobed, crowned king, and handed the royal scepter. He is guided to his throne. From that day forward, he reigns as king over his people with justice and mercy, remembering what it was like to be one of them.

A king is set in place to rule with authority and responsibility. He determines what type of Kingdom he creates—oppression and injustice or compassion and integrity. A king, who is also a priest, is sent to *serve* others. Our commission, as Believers, involves delivering humanity from oppression and disease. We have authority and miraculous ability to rule over iniquity by setting every captive free because of our family lineage—Jesus, the King of kings!

OCTOBER 10

Spiritual Garments

Read: Romans 8:9

*I*n both the KJV and the NKJV, this verse is almost identical. I encourage you to look it up for yourself and compare them. The second sentence is what I'd like us to focus on for now: *"Now if any man have not the Spirit of Christ, he is none of His."*

The verb *have* is the Greek word *echo* and it does not merely mean *to hold on for use*. More accurately, it is defined: *to have in hand, to hold, wearing of a garment, to own, possess in mind, to be closely joined to a person*. Expounding on the true definition gives us a deeper understanding of what it means to "have" the Spirit of Christ!

It is advantageous for us to picture this information in our minds. Words create images and help us to grasp more fully what is being described. In the *Mirror Bible*, I love the way the translator expressed this verse with such accuracy, that it paints a clearer understanding of what righteousness looks like:

> *"But you are not ruled by a flesh-consciousness, (law of works), but by spirit-consciousness, (faith); since God's Spirit is at home in you. Anyone who does not see himself fully clothed and identified in the Spirit of Christ, cannot be himself."*

The words *clothed* and *identified* help us to see what we actually look like and who we are, verses merely just *having* Christ. We can recognize that when we do not see ourselves in Christ, we are not being true to ourselves! We are living a lie!

If we see ourselves labeled by a doctor, trapped in depression, or lacking in faith, we are not seeing ourselves clothed and identified with Christ. Remember, Christ is your life (Colossians 3:4)! We find out what we look like, who we truly are, and how the Father sees us in Christ—no variables. Any mutation of His perspective is missing reality!

OCTOBER 11

Milquetoast

Read: Acts 4:13

*C*asper Milquetoast was a cartoon character created by H.T. Webster in 1924, for his comic strip series entitled *The Timid Soul*, published in the *New York Tribune*. Due to the popularity of the cartoon, the word *milquetoast* (pronounced milk-toast), became common vernacular. The term is used to describe someone of a weak, unassertive, or timid disposition—in other words: a coward or a wuss. The word is derived from the foods milk and toast that are easily digested when eaten.

Paul desired to give the Corinthian church solid food, but they weren't mature, so he was forced to serve them milk (1 Corinthians 3:2). He referred to them as carnal babies, unable to handle true spiritual food because they were behaving like mere men, full of division and strife. They hadn't yet learned how to live in the spirit, even though Paul bottle-fed them every morsel of spiritual truth!

God's Kingdom is not a Kingdom of nervous, passive wimps, weak in character, slurping down toast soaked in milk (the fleshly appetites), constantly hungry and never fully satisfied. It is a Kingdom of meat-eating (spiritually fit) sons and daughters identified as Christ-men who are completely satisfied by the Spirit. In Acts 4:13 in the NIV it says,

> "When they saw the courage of Peter and John and realized that they were unschooled, ordinary men, they were astonished and took note that these men had been with Jesus."

Remember that this story took place immediately after they were filled with the Holy Spirit on the day of Pentecost. Peter and John had healed a man who was crippled from the time of his birth.

OCTOBER 11 ———

Notice it says, *"They saw the courage of Peter and John..."* How did they *see* their courage? After Peter and John had been arrested, they didn't hang their heads shuffling their feet in the dirt, stuttering with excuses! Peter, full of the Holy Spirit, boldly preached Christ crucified to the Sanhedrin with proof they could not deny! The lame man was standing right in front of them all, completely healed by the Name of Jesus! They had evidence to back up their words that could not be refuted! No milquetoast men here!

OCTOBER 12

Rich In Grace, Glory, And Mercy

Read: Ephesians 2:4-10

At first I thought it would be kinda silly to look up the word *rich* in the dictionary. Everyone knows that it means to have a lot of money, right? I was surprised by this definition: *made of or containing valuable materials.*

In light of these particular verses: (Emphasis added)

> Ephesians 1:7-8 *"In Him we have redemption through His blood, the forgiveness of sins, according to the **riches of His grace** which He made abound toward us..."*

> Ephesians 1:18 *" the eyes of your understanding being enlightened; that you may know what is the hope of His calling, what are the **riches of the glory** of His inheritance in the saints"*

> Ephesians 2:4 *"But God who is **rich in mercy**, because of His great love with which He loved us"*

Our Father is rich in these qualities because this is who He *is*! Because He consists of these attributes, we contain them as well. They are not merely qualities we possess; they have become part of who we are because we are part of Him! Take note that Ephesians 1:7-8 says, **IN HIM** we have all of these blessings! We are made of valuable materials!

OCTOBER 13

Cry Babies

Read: Numbers 11:1-15, 31-33

*V*erse four says that the children of Israel *"yielded to intense craving."* Ah! Their mouths were watering as they remembered the tastes of Egypt: the meat, cucumbers, melons, leeks, onions and garlic—savory foods in abundance! The manna had become boring and they were dissatisfied; they felt dried up from the inside. In other words, they loathed it! There were only so many ways manna could be prepared. They could fry it, bake it, or boil it, but at the end of it all, it was still just manna. It's like a cheap cup of coffee from a convenience store, no matter what flavor is added, like vanilla or hazelnut, it still tastes like burnt coffee!

The people were so upset, their entire families stood in the opening of their tents wailing! Imagine hearing over a million people crying at the same time! No wonder Moses was like, *"God! What did I do to deserve this? I'm not their Father! I cannot handle these people on my own; help me!"*

As a result, they got meat, meat, and more meat! As the quail landed on the ground, Israel immediately snatched up every little birdie they could, even staying awake through the night in desperation—as though they couldn't grab enough! They probably formed an assembly line: some captured the quail; others defeathered and gutted them, while the rest cooked. They may have even taken orders: *"How would you like yours? Well, medium, or some pink? Boiled, baked or fried?"*

Temptations are just that: intense cravings that urge people to forget the good things God has done for them in the past. We decide whether or not to yield to them. Unlike the children of Israel, we have the help of the Holy Spirit forming godly desires in our heart; yet we still must take responsibility for our choices.

OCTOBER 14

Tattletale

Read: Numbers 11:16-29

I laugh every time I read this account of Moses and the children of Israel! As a result of their bellyaching, Moses couldn't handle their issues by himself any longer. God said He would take of the Spirit of leadership on Moses and place it upon seventy of the elders. They would share in the burden of leading the people and Moses could then focus on more important matters.

These two men, Eldad and Medad, were supposed to join Moses at the tent of meeting, but instead they decided to stay home. When God sent the Spirit upon the elders, He also sent His Spirit upon Eldad and Medad. They began to prophesy in their tents just like the other elders who were gathered with Moses at the tabernacle!

This is where the story gets amusing: one man takes it upon himself to tattletale to Moses—as though the guy didn't have enough burdens! I love Moses' response! It clearly portrays the heart of God: *"Oh, that **all** the Lord's people were prophets and that the Lord would put His Spirit on them!"* Think of it! Over a million people prophesying by the Spirit of God instead of whining about their problems!

Fast forward to the New Testament in 1 Corinthians 12, where the gift of prophecy is available to **all** God's children! This was God's heart from the beginning. We know that our words have power! Using our ability to prophesy by the Spirit of God could change our own personal situations, other people's circumstances, and change the course of nations! Instead of wearing out our family and friends with all of our problems, we can tell our problems about God!

OCTOBER 15

Mary Jones And Her Bible

Read: Joshua 1:8-9

*M*ary Jones was a young girl who lived from 1784-1864. She was born into a poor Christian family in North Wales. Mary walked to and from church three miles both ways every week to attend Sunday school, where she learned to read. She desperately desired a Bible of her own. Her mother, being a widow by the time Mary had turned five, was too poor to afford a Bible of their own. The only Bible close to her was at a neighbor's house two miles away, and Mary walked there as often as she could to read it. At the age of nine, Mary decided she would work and save up money to purchase a Bible of her own.

Mary worked tirelessly for six long years to save up the 17 shillings needed to acquire her very own Bible. That was about a year and a half's wages in her day! In the summer of 1800, she was, at last, prepared to undertake the twenty-five mile trek to purchase her Bible. Loaded with a knapsack filled with bread, cheese, and her precious earnings, her mother sent her off to Reverend Charles Thomas' home to buy the Bible she dreamed of owning for herself!

When she arrived at Reverend Thomas' home, the Bibles had not yet arrived due to delays by the printers in London. Mary stayed in the house of the minister's maid for three days until the Bibles arrived. The preacher was so moved by Mary's tenacity to earn her own Bible that he gave her three Bibles for the price of one! That was quite a heavy load for a fifteen year old girl to carry twenty-five miles home, considering Bibles were much bigger and bulkier back then!

As Mary grew older, she read through the Bible four times in a year. She also memorized large portions that she was able to recite from memory as she grew old and was no longer able to read due to

OCTOBER 15 ———

blindness. Of the three Bibles Mary received, only two exist today and one of them is on display at the University of Cambridge. Mary died at the age of eighty, not far from where she was born. She was loved by many, and known by her generosity and love for the Word of God.

Today, the many things we desire are immediately available. We can order a Bible online and have it delivered to our house within a day or download it on our computer at the touch of a button! I wonder if having things so easily accessible may cause us to take for granted the things that are the most precious. If we all had to work six years and walk twenty-five miles to purchase a Bible for ourselves, maybe more Believers would honor God's Word with the same gravity as Mary Jones!

(Source: elnasmith.com)

OCTOBER 16

No Vengeance

Read: Luke 4:18-19

Jesus quoted Isaiah 61:1-2, here in the Gospel of Luke. It is interesting that He stopped smack dab in the middle of verse two, which continues with *"and the day of vengeance of our God."* This refers to the time of Jesus' second coming, when all things will be brought to completion at the end. Jesus first coming was to reveal His Father—not for vengeance. He had not come to condemn the world, but to save it by becoming our ransom for sin (John 3:17).

In the first part of verse two of Isaiah, Jesus was referring to what was called *Jubilee*, where any land or belongings Israel had sold, rented, or given away was restored to their family every fifty years and all debts were cancelled! Imagine what it would be like to receive this blessing today!

BUT...we do have a greater blessing than our material possessions returned! Through Christ, our right-standing with our Father was restored! We don't have to live in fear of any present or future judgment because Jesus became judgment for us (Galatians 3:13)! No vengeance! No punishment for screwing up! No retaliation! No fearful expectation of judgment! You didn't miss it, you didn't fall short! Rest in that!

OCTOBER 17

The Cloth

Read: Acts 19:11-12

We are men and women of "the cloth!" No, not the liturgical, religious kind, but cloths that are full of power, that when people touch them; all of their ailments are cured!

You know that the power of God is transmissible, right? That's why we can lay hands on the sick and they recover—not just from body to body, but inanimate objects we touch can transfer the power of God to heal or bring deliverance to others. I think that's pretty cool, don't you?

Paul didn't have an epiphany from God to use "prayer cloths" to heal the sick. It was something that happened organically. People had discovered a way to take healing and deliverance to loved ones who were unable to travel. They didn't have telephones back then to call and ask for someone to pray for them; or the ability to text someone to receive healing!

Today the prayer cloth can be the "modus operandi" as an effective means of bringing life to an individual. I've heard testimonies of people healed of cancers and various illnesses by this simple act of faith. And that's all it is—whatever the means of delivery; faith is the force accompanying the power!

OCTOBER 18

The Armor

Read: Ephesians 6:10-17

I love how *The Passion Translation* describes God's armor. One thing we need to remember, that this is **God's armor**. Many times our attention gets averted to the parts of the armor instead the attributes each part is meant to represent. Let's take a look beginning with verse fourteen:

> *"Put on truth as a belt to strengthen you to stand in triumph. Put on holiness as the protective armor that covers your heart. Stand on your feet alert, then you'll always be ready to share the blessings of peace. In every battle, take faith as your wrap-around shield, for it is able to extinguish the blazing arrows coming at you from the evil one! Embrace the power of salvation's full deliverance, like a helmet to protect your thoughts from lies. And take the mighty razor-sharp Spirit-sword of the spoken word of God."*

We are covered from head to toe with God's attributes! They are not pieces of a knight's armor we must put on and take off every day. We don't have to "pray" them on. We are already clothed with these characteristics because we are clothed in Christ! Just by being aware of them and acknowledging they belong to us is the same as putting them on and keeping them on. We can't take righteousness off if we're in Christ, can we? No! Because He *made* us the righteousness of God in Christ.

We have faith that protects like a shield and salvation covering our minds from evil thoughts. Truth girds our waist and keeps us fortified and standing strong! The Gospel brings peace, directing like a compass as we walk in the power of Christ. The Word in our mouth is like a sword that chops, slices, and dices lies into mince meat! The armor is comfy and fits perfectly like a glove shoring up our identity in Christ! We never have to take it off!

OCTOBER 19

Cursed Or Blessed?

Read: Exodus 20:4-6

There are a couple of important facts we should keep in mind when we read the Old Testament. First, we recognize who is being spoken to. The second important point to remember is that most of the Old Testament refers to the Old Covenant God had with Israel. Keeping these two important truths in mind, we know that God was not revealing Himself in a covenant relationship with any Gentiles at this time.

The Scripture I referenced for today's reading is relaying a conversation that God had with Moses on behalf of the children of Israel when He gave the Ten Commandments. This was a part of the Old Covenant between God and Israel. Now we can see that this "generational curse" does not apply to us on this side of the cross.

Furthermore, if this wasn't enough proof, it says, *"visiting the iniquity of the fathers upon the fourth generation to them that* **hate** *Me."* (Emphasis added) I don't hate God, do you? Again, more evidence that generational curses do not apply to us today.

Let's fast forward to the New Testament and the New Covenant every member of the human race has been offered—Jew and Gentile alike (Galatians 3:28-29). If we need any more proof, here it is in Galatians 3:13,

> *"Christ has redeemed us from the curse of the law, having become a curse for us (for it is written, "Cursed is everyone who hangs on a tree"), that the blessing of Abraham might come upon the Gentiles in Christ Jesus, that we might receive the promise of the Spirit through faith."*

So there we have it—*every* curse was completely removed through Christ and the blessing left in its place! No more generational

OCTOBER 19

curses! Any person stuck in a repeating pattern passed from a family member was something they had observed and made the decision to act on it by their own choice. As a result, it became a learned behavior pattern, not from a curse. If you (or anyone you know) is stuck in any type of addiction or bondage and you want to be free, I encourage you to read my first book available on Amazon:

Exposing the Enemy—Leaving the Rut of Bondage to Pursue Breakthrough and Destiny

OCTOBER 20

The Antidote

Read: Hebrews 7:22-28

I like verse twenty-five where it proclaims, *"He is also able to save to the uttermost..."* We learned that save is *sozo* in the Greek which means *to save, deliver, protect, heal, preserve, do well, make whole.*

The word *uttermost* means *all-complete, perfect, completeness, completely, perfectly, utterly.* In other words, it is the greatest, fullest, highest degree possible! This means we cannot be any more saved, healed, delivered, protected, or made whole than what we are right now in Christ!

An *antidote* is a remedy used to neutralize or counteract the effects of a poison. A chemical antidote is one that interacts with a poison and changes its chemical composition into a harmless substance. Oh, doesn't that sound like the change we undergo when Jesus steps inside of us and we obtain resurrection life? We receive a brand-spankin' new spirit and a blood transfusion! Our bloodline is now of the same lineage and composition as Jesus'!

Sin was the agent that poisoned humanity. Jesus' body and blood are the antidotes that neutralized sin's effect, making iniquity a harmless substance. Now we are saved and healed *to the uttermost*! That means there ain't no room for anything else!!

OCTOBER 21

You've Got Life!

Read: 1 John 5:10-13

Zoe is life like God has it! Do you have the Son? Then you've got life the way God has life! You don't merely have biological life; you've got supernatural life!

God's zoe life has set you free from death and has broken the *fear* of death (Romans 8:2). His life is eternal, which means it is in effect right now. It's not reserved up there in heaven only to experience once you get there. You stepped into life eternal when Jesus stepped into you! The more you are aware of His life, the more you will participate with its benefits.

This life of God is a creative force! It constantly generates energy in you; strengthening, renewing, and empowering your body on the inside—emanating to the outside—permeating the atmosphere surrounding you. Rivers of *living* water are bursting like a geyser from the inside out!

Have you ever been to Niagara Falls? People visit Canada from all over the world to experience its ambiance! The sound is constant; its power—mesmerizing! The roar of the water gushing over the edge is deafening! You cannot hear a friend next to you unless he yells! The mist sprays everyone standing hundreds of feet above. It is estimated that forty-four million gallons of water flow over the Horseshoe Falls every minute! Can you fathom anything capable of stopping the velocity of that river?

Close your eyes right now. Imagine the unstoppable force of the Spirit of God as a river of living water, like Niagara Falls, purging your body of all disease, sickness, and pain! Life is gushing, washing, and regenerating the cells of your body with unstoppable force! You are clean and fresh! Go ahead! Do something you couldn't do before! The more you are aware of His life-force, the more you will experience it!

OCTOBER 22

To Break Bread

Read: Acts 20:7

*I*magine the body of Believers sole purpose for meeting was for the sake of partaking communion together! They honored the Lord's Supper so much that it was a regular part of worship, not an afterthought or an addition for a special holiday.

There is more to taking the elements of Communion than limiting it for our healing and forgiveness of sins. This is a Covenant which meant the exchange of a life for a life. It means that every limitation has been completely removed.

In Acts 2:46 reports the new Believers gathering daily in houses to "break bread" together. This became an identifying mark of the early church. Why? They knew that the bread represented Christ's life that was exchanged for theirs!

When the two men were walking on the road to Emmaus after Jesus' resurrection, they compelled Jesus to come and stay with them for the night. When they sat down to dinner, Jesus broke the bread and then disappeared! The moment He broke the bread, their eyes were opened! Why? Jesus identified Himself as the Bread of Life—disclosing Himself by sharing His life with the world!

OCTOBER 23

Monopoly

Read: Titus 2:11-15

A monopoly is the absence of competition, where a specific company is the only supplier. The biggest problem with a monopoly is that the company can charge whatever price they want to the consumer. They hold control of an entire industry over a particular item or service. Basically, you're stuck! Pay the piper or do without!

My family has several different editions of the game *Monopoly: Ebay, Star Wars, Build Your Own Board, Army,* and *Baseball.* No matter which edition we played together, my youngest son monopolizes the entire board within the first few rolls of the dice; it's no fun because fair competition is out the window—he monopolizes everything! I don't know how he does it, but he always ends up with most of the properties while I'm flat broke! Do I sound like a sore loser? That's cuz I am! But that's the name of the game and he's certainly got a knack for it! A note in *The Passion Translation* for verse fourteen says,

> *"Uniquely His, we are monopolized by God, taken into Himself by grace through faith and surrounded by His love."*

Verse fourteen of Titus chapter two; recalls to memory that Jesus gave Himself so that He could purify us as His own special people. The word *special* means to be surrounded, like God has encircled you so that you can only belong to Him. In other words, He's got a monopoly over you! There is no other place you can go to receive what Christ has to offer. He set the price! It's like He wrapped His arms around you and declared, *"You're mine!"*

OCTOBER 24

Ekklesia

Read: Matthew 16:18

The *ekklesia* is a legislative body or ruling council summoned together for governing the affairs of a territory. In ancient Greece, it was understood as a select civil body convened for an official purpose. When Jesus referred to the church, the ekklesia was understood to be a politically independent body of Believers under no king but Jesus.

The word *ekklesia* is comprised of the words *ek*—"out from", and *kaleo*—"to call," meaning *"to call out."* The purpose of Christ's ekklesia is to be a people called out from the ungodly, worldly system, for the purpose of bringing His Kingdom on the earth as it is in heaven.

The Greek word for *church* is *kyraikos* which means *"pertaining or belongs to the Lord."* This definition has nothing to do with governing at all, and many times *church* is mistranslated in the Bible as *kyraikos* instead of *ekklesia*. A more exact translation of Matthew 16:18 is,

> *"I will build My legislative assembly and the power of death will not be able to overpower it."*

Jesus was declaring that He was the foundation of an assembly of called-out followers to reign over death and the affairs of the world. The Bible states that we are seated in heavenly places in Christ Jesus. If we weren't meant to rule over anything, we certainly would not have been placed on His throne with Him, where all things are under His feet! Psalm 82:3-6 commands,

> *"Defend the defenseless, the fatherless and the forgotten, the disenfranchised and the destitute. Your duty is to deliver the poor and the powerless; liberate them from the grasp of the*

OCTOBER 24

> *wicked. But you continue in your darkness and ignorance while the foundations of society are shaken to the core! Didn't I commission you as judges, saying, 'You are like gods, since you judge on my behalf. You are all like sons of the Most High, My representatives.'" (The Passion Translation)*

Jesus' intention was never to build His church like we understand it today—as merely a gathering of people to sit and listen to an encouraging message once a week and go home. Wherever Jesus went, the Gospels state that Jesus taught, preached, and demonstrated the Kingdom, as He healed the sick and set the oppressed free. We were commissioned to bring God's government on the earth—His EKKLESIA!

OCTOBER 25

I've Got A Name

Read: Revelation 19:11-16

I've Got A Name

Like the pine trees lining the winding road
I've got a name
I've got a name
Like the singing bird and the croaking toad
I've got a name
I've got a name
And I carry it with me like my daddy did
But I'm living the dream that he kept hid
Moving me down the highway
Rolling me down the highway
Moving ahead so life won't pass me by...

"*I've Got A Name*" is a single recorded by Jim Croce in 1973. The song reached the top ten on the Billboard Hot 100 after seventeen weeks on the chart. Sadly, Jim died in a plane crash on September 20, the day after the album's release. He never got to experience the thrill of his success!

What would it be like for us if we never got to experience Jesus and His life inside us? Do you remember what your life was like BC (Before Christ)? The New Covenant was ratified in Hebrews 9:11-12, when Christ came as High Priest, offering His own body and blood. He entered the Most Holy Place and obtained eternal redemption for all! He made us equal sons with Himself (Romans 8:17) and gave us His Name (John 16:23-24) to operate under His authority.

Philippians 2:9-11 tells us that God gave Jesus a Name above every name, and that at the mere mention of His Name, everything has to

OCTOBER 25

bow! Because He is King of kings and Lord of lords, we get to share in everything He is! We won't miss the thrill of success! Now we can sing like Jim Croce, *"I've got a Name, I've got a Name!"*

OCTOBER 26

My Redeemer Lives

Read: Job 19:25-27

Job was looking for a Redeemer—someone who would vindicate him or plead his case. The poor guy had no one to stand by his side during the worst trials of his life. His four so-called friends became his accusers. Even his wife abandoned him!

When someone is going through a tough trial, well-meaning people's advice can discourage, rather than encourage! I was told by several "trusted" Believers, on separate occasions, that God wanted me to go through sickness alone so that I would learn to trust Him. Another person told me that I must have done something wrong; that the devil got his hook in me and made me sick—so I should seek God and find out where I messed up—only then could He heal me! Sounds like Job's friends, doesn't it?

Please don't do that to anyone! It only makes them feel judged and abandoned! None of those words contained Scripturally-sound advice! It's difficult enough to be facing a life or death situation and to hear; *"Yeah, I know someone who died from that,"* is very cruel!

In the New Testament, the word *redeemer* means *to pay a ransom*. Our Father believed we were worth the price of His only Son so that He could make many sons (Hebrews 2:10). He paid our price so that we would not have to be sick and die prematurely, live in bondage to addictions, or be depressed! Our Redeemer was resurrected from the grave! We live because our Redeemer lives! Hallelujah!

So, go and set people free. Jesus didn't make people qualify themselves, and neither should we.

OCTOBER 27

Keep Mercy In Sight

Read: Romans 12:1-2

The NIV begins,

> "Therefore, I urge you, brothers and sisters, in view of God's mercy, to offer your bodies as a living sacrifice, holy and pleasing to God..."

I like the phrase: *"in view of God's mercy"*, which is only used in the NIV. *Mercy* is God's kindness joined with His desire to bring transformation. We are more apt to surrender when we are assured it is for our good. Renewing our mind brings these truths to the forefront. *The Passion Translation* in Romans 12:2 says,

> *"Stop imitating the ideals and opinions of the culture around you, but be inwardly transformed by the Holy Spirit through a total reformation of how you think..."*

The note for verse two says: *"Don't be squeezed into the mold of this present age."*

As we gather the above information together, we can see that God's mercy is the catalyst for transformation because trust is the foundation. As a result, Holy Spirit creates a metamorphosis of our minds and our hearts as He imparts truth, life, and understanding. Our response is the desire to fling ourselves upon His mercy and forsake every confining grip of this world's oppressive mold! On display, a limitless, powerful life is poured out from our being!

OCTOBER 28

Ambiguous & Capricious?

Read: Numbers 23:19

Does God constantly change His mind? Is He fickle and wishy-washy? Does He say something one minute and change His mind the next? Is He a mysterious being that is so impossible to get an answer from that we must beg, plead, and cry aloud just to get His attention? Is He ambiguous and capricious (impulsive, unpredictable)?

Part of you is probably saying, *"NO!"* right now, but the other part may be saying, *"...BUT sometimes it sure seems that way!"* I'm sure we've all heard ministers say that the problem is with us and not with God, but yet our situations still persist. We can get frustrated trying to figure out what the problem is asking, *"Why doesn't He just do this, when I know He is able?"*

I have discovered that, when I come to the Lord in *agreement* that He has already provided my needs; I avoid the emotional rollercoaster. Instead, I just thank Him! That removes a lot of pressure! I learned the hard way that He really hates begging, because begging is the total opposite of faith!

Listen! If you can receive what I'm saying here, it will revolutionize your prayers and your relationship with God. Most of us are not of Jewish descent. We were never under the Law of Moses. Almost everything Jesus said in the Gospels applied to the Jews under the Law of Moses. Jesus came as the last Adam born under the law to redeem everyone from the law, whether it is the Law of Moses or becoming a law unto ourselves by our own self-effort (Romans 2:14).

You cannot have a generational curse. You cannot be pilfered by the devil at any moment because of a target on your back. What you are is a son of God, made a co-heir with Jesus, and as a result of this relationship in the New Covenant, you have freedom, health,

OCTOBER 28

protection and provision. You have already received all of these things! They are applied by faith—believing you have already received them and thanking Him for them—not begging. We cannot be kings and beggars at the same time. We cannot rule with His authority if we don't believe He has given us everything we need for a victorious life.

So when you have a need, thank Him that it has already been supplied—it's already yours! That's why God gave His Son! If you need healing in your body, thank Him for it. Even if you are not experiencing complete healing, have confidence that you will, no matter what goofy symptoms your body expresses! You will experience complete relief by agreeing with Christ's full payment for disease, rather than begging Him for something He said He has already provided!

OCTOBER 29

God's Blueprint

Read: Romans 3:22-23

The *Mirror Bible's* version of our Scripture for today states,

> "Jesus is what God believes about you. In Him the righteousness of God is on display in such a way that everyone may be equally persuaded about what God believes about them, regardless of who they are; there is no distinction. Mankind is in the same boat; their distorted behavior is proof of a lost blueprint."

Jesus is God's blueprint for mankind! I love that! Like an architect designing a building, our Father drew Jesus as our blueprint. He replicated Himself in His Son as the pattern for our lives, and in turn He replicated Himself in us!

That blueprint becomes distorted when we conform or compare ourselves with the world's ways of living—called "keeping up with the Jones'". We can buy all the houses, furniture, clothes and beautiful things we desire, but in the end the houses need repair, the furniture breaks, and the clothes get stained or wear out.

We can fill our bellies with all the food we want: the wine and beer, drugs, and sex and end up down a deep, dark hole, hopeless and depressed. We can pursue relationships with people to find love and acceptance; only to experience disappointment and hurt when they let us down. Sadly, this is all the world has to offer and some of us don't realize it until we've wasted our lives for nothing in return.

But there's something about a Believer that's different than the rest of the world! Their lives are an expression of everything the human heart longs for—God's love and unconditional acceptance. Jesus is the redeemed glory of God in human life; the blueprint for mankind!

OCTOBER 30

No Cowards

Read: 2 Timothy 1:7

*M*ost people quote this Scripture believing that it arms them with power to make a demonic spirit of fear flee. A proper look at this Scripture, in context, by simply looking up the meaning of the word *fear* in a concordance, dispels an improper application of this verse.

Paul wrote this letter to Timothy, his son in the faith, to encourage him. Even though he was one of Paul's first converts in Lystra and had traveled with him to many of the churches he planted, Timothy was merely a young man. At the writing of his message, Paul was imprisoned in Rome and he had sent Timothy as a liaison to set things in order in the churches of Corinth, Thessalonica, and Ephesus.

Paul was encouraging Timothy not to forget his roots in the faith. He was reminding Timothy of the truth that was instilled in him from childhood by his mother and grandmother. He brought to Timothy's memory of the Holy Spirit, whom he had received when Paul laid his hands on him. Verse seven is referring to the type of spirit that the Holy Spirit is *not*. The Holy Spirit is *not* a spirit of cowardice leading to apostasy, but of miraculous ability, mutual love for others, and a mind that is stable and full of temperance.

Many were abandoning their faith because of the extreme persecution under the Roman emperor Nero. Paul had faith in Timothy's ability to lead the churches with sound doctrine. He expected him to persevere, even under intense suffering. Although Paul himself was under duress in a Roman prison for preaching Christ, He didn't want that to deter Timothy's position of leadership. Paul was warning him not to become apostate by abandoning the faith and responsibility which he was entrusted. Many were being martyred, imprisoned, tortured, and losing their families. Their belongings

OCTOBER 30 ———

were confiscated by the government of Rome. It is no surprise that Paul was writing instruction and encouragement to Timothy. The advancement of the Gospel depended upon him! No matter what, he had to press on and establish the churches on the firm foundation he had learned first-hand from Paul.

Whatever the circumstances we may be experiencing today, we can rest assured that a spooky, evil spirit is not the culprit. A mind that is renewed to truth can overtake any unbiblical thought pattern. Acting on the finished work of the cross is the key to experiencing a life of victory in every area! No apostate cowards here!

OCTOBER 31

Fear

Read: 1 John 4:17-19, 5:4

*F*ear is a substandard way of living, especially in the Kingdom. Fear is misdirected faith acted upon because of questioning and human reasoning. I personally don't believe that fear is always an evil spirit floating around waiting to pounce on unsuspecting victims. When a person is overcome by fear, it is because they are thinking "what if" about the many possible outcomes of their problems, or remembering a past experience that didn't turn out in their favor. Human logic created a stronghold in their mind by a rehearsal of continuing thoughts.

Our verse for today says that there is boldness in love, not fear. There is perfection (maturity) in God's love, not judgment. Summed up, this means that we are secure because of our position in Christ. I love the *Amplified Bible's* expression of 1 John 5:4,

> *"For everyone born of God is victorious and overcomes the world; and this is the victory that has conquered and overcome the world—our (continuing, persistent) faith (in Jesus, the Son of God)."*

What is there about you that isn't to love, since you have been made one with Christ? If you were to answer that question with a, *"Well, yeah, but..."* then the image you believe about yourself is not the same image your Father believes about you! I dare you to back up a few verses in 1 John and read 4:12-16. Backing up even further, we can read about the term *abide* all the way back to chapter 3. My Bible uses the subtitle *The Outworking of Love*. I like that because when there is something on the inside, it's gonna work its way on to the outside.

Fear works the same way. If your thoughts, emotions, and words are full of fear, then that's what will come out of you. Not because

OCTOBER 31 ———

an evil spirit made you do it, but because you saw yourself different than your Father does. It all comes back to choice. So choose to recognize Christ in you. He's still there whether you realize it or not. But as you begin to give Him more attention than all the other things, love will work its way up into your heart till it overflows!

NOVEMBER 1

Forever Branded

Read: Isaiah 49:16

When I think about belonging to Jesus, I feel a sense of security and peace, knowing that I'm His. This causes me to live in response to His influence on my life. He is the author of the desires that are written on my heart.

What is this draw, this connection, this sense of ownership? It is the branding of the Holy Spirit! We're forever marked by Him into the core of our being! The rest of our lives are lived in response to this "mark" seared on our hearts! This branding causes us to cast off every hint of a lower life!

We now recognize that we don't have to settle for a former way of thinking or existing! Whew! Effortless being! Effortless living! Effective living with no more striving!

So how does this apply to physical healing? Do we *get* healed or are we *already* healed? Tricky question, isn't it? Really, the answer to the latter question is the answer to the first question: Because we are already healed, we can experience the healing Christ paid for—right now. The finished work of the cross is the origin of our existence as Believers. Healing has been made available anytime, anywhere, to anyone who needs it. That truth has already been branded upon our heart by the Holy Spirit and our spirit already knows this as the truth.

Forever branded—this is what we are on the inside by Holy Spirit—the seal and mark of our belongingness to Him—forever saved in our spirit and forever healed in our body!

NOVEMBER 2

The Weight Of The Wait Is Over!

Read: Matthew 11:28-30

*W*aiting for God's promises to come to fruition can be a real drag! How much time is enough to wait for our healing, to wait for a loved one to come to Christ, or whatever else we may need? Is there something we are supposed to learn along the way? Is God waiting for us to "get it right" before He'll give it?

The answer is a big fat NOPE! The *weight of the wait* is over!

Several years ago, when I was facing my own life-threatening health challenge, a friend told me I was already healed! What? He blew my mind when he said that! My response to him was literally, *"Then I'm screwed!"* My instant thought was: *"If Christ already healed me then I missed out on it somehow!"* I had a flashback to third grade, when my classmates used to tease, *"When you were born they said, 'Get in line for a brain!—and you thought they said "train," so you didn't get one! Ha! Ha!'"* I'm serious! That's exactly how I felt when my friend told me my healing was already done!

So, you mean to tell me while I was in excruciating and debilitating pain, I *was* already healed? He hacked me off—to put it nicely! There I was begging, pleading, and crying for Jesus to heal me! Telling me that I was already healed did NOT make any sense! So, I continued on in my suffering, waiting and hoping for Jesus to someday make good on His Word.

Eventually, I began to understand! I didn't have to *wait* for my healing because Jesus bore the **WEIGHT** of my suffering! Since that time, I have seen many things healed in my body by just thanking Him that I'm already healed!

NOVEMBER 3

Silence Isn't Golden

Read: John 16:13-15

When a person is a "talker" we use the term, "Silence is Golden" in a nice way to express that they are rambling just to hear themselves talk. When referring to the Holy Spirit, silence isn't golden! Hearing Him speak is!

I've stated before that the Holy Spirit is never silent or still. As a matter of fact, He's quite a chatter-box! Why does it seem difficult to hear Him? Who's doing most of the talking, and who's doing most of the listening? When I've needed help with a situation, praying in the spirit helped shut out my thoughts and focus on Him. I can hear what He has to say more easily. Holy Spirit knows exactly what to do so that the situation is quickly resolved. Sometimes, His voice is loud and clear. Other times, He whispers, or shows me a picture. Whatever way He speaks, I grab it and act on His instructions immediately.

Jesus said that the Holy Spirit will guide us into all truth. He's really not the silent, passive type that we perceive Him to be. Jesus also said that the Holy Spirit will tell us of things to come. He will glorify Christ; He will take what belongs to Christ and declare it to us! That declaration is the answer we need! No mysteries or hide-and-go-seek! In Christ, everything that was hidden is now revealed!

NOVEMBER 4

Never Overcome

Read: Psalm 98 (The Passion Translation)

Defeated isn't in God's vocabulary—unless it refers to His enemies! I know what it's like to feel like I've been whipped, but when I take a step back and look again through Jesus' eyes, I see a totally different story with a completely different outcome. If I don't choose to run with His victory already won for me, then I will experience less than what He intended.

Our human nature compartmentalizes things into the tenses of time: past, present, and future. The idea of something completed in the past and continuing forever into the future is awkward and hard to wrap our minds around. It's called "Finished."

No matter how many times we've experienced victory, we'll say, *"Yeah, but will You do it **this** time, God?"* Yes! He will! Because *defeat* isn't in His vocabulary and, therefore, it shouldn't be in ours! At least three separate times, Jesus declared that nothing is impossible for those who believe. Believe what? That *nothing* is impossible!

Look at a box of complete pancake mix. Is it really complete? No! You must still add water! This is the way our natural mind thinks, *"It's complete, but I still have to add something!"* It is the "works" mentality that trips us up!

So take the "Im" (the I'm) out of impossible. When we look to ourselves the "I'm" gets in the way. Look at "possible" alone. There you will find His ability working all things out for His glory!

NOVEMBER 5

Who's In Charge?

Read: Psalm 115:16

*R*eligion teaches that God's Sovereignty means He's the grand Puppet-Master, orchestrating every event that happens in our lives. All troubles are metered to each person by the hand of a loving Father who gave satan permission to mess with us—just to teach us a lesson. If we don't tithe, we've opened the door to be cursed with poverty. If we don't break every generational curse, the sins of our forefathers will continue to wreak havoc in our lineage. If we don't plead the blood of Jesus on our family, they are victims of the devil's cunning traps...sadly; the list goes tirelessly on and on....

The strange thing about the cross is that we don't fully experience it—unless we apply Christ's *finished* work. Oh, it's always there, but we don't reap all the benefits for several reasons. One reason may be that a person is not born again; another may be that he is waiting on God to do something about his situation (hyper-Sovereignty of God belief), or that he is trying to work for what Christ has already done. We may fast and pray for forty days to no avail! *"But God, I did this and I do this and I do that...what the heck!!!"*

If we are doing anything with the mindset "to get" or "to convince God" that He needs to do something for us in response to all we're doing for Him, then we might as well walk the rest of our "Christian" days on a treadmill, going nowhere. I didn't say this to offend you, but to help you. Believe me, I was the proud owner of my very own shiny treadmill—wore the thing out!

Faith is ineffective when we're trying to make God see He needs to do something for us because we did X Y and Z to get His attention. Faith is effective when it is applied *in response to* Christ's finished work—His stripes for our healing, His blood for our sins, His

NOVEMBER 5 ———

resurrection over death, His defeat over every enemy...*ALL* of it! So just thank Him for it! As the result of His finished work, He put us back in charge here! The earth belongs to the sons of God. So, throw away the treadmill! Toss religion in the trash! Live like a son who's in charge! Cuz that's who He made you to be!

NOVEMBER 6

The Dash

Read: Luke 12:32

The *DASH*. Everyone has one. You are experiencing yours right now. It's that little symbol on a tombstone between your birth date and the date you meet Jesus. It's more important than the day you were born or the day you die. Why? Because opportunity awaits you in God's Kingdom!

When Jesus told us to *"Go!"*, He didn't specify China or Africa for specific people. He gave a general statement that included everyone, everywhere. He said, *"As you go..."* That means everywhere, all the time, wherever you are! And as we go we are to preach the Gospel, announcing that the Kingdom of heaven is here. We are to demonstrate His Kingdom by healing the sick, raising the dead, and casting out demons. We received the Kingdom for free; we freely give it away.

Did you ever hear the term "mad dash?" It is defined in the dictionary *as a wild and uncontrolled rush*, like a crowd of people causing a stampede for the door because the building is on fire! What if we lived our lives that way in the Kingdom, jumping at every opportunity as though it may be our last? Reaching that one person the moment you pass him by probably will be the only opportunity you will have to minister to him. Think of all the people you walk past at Wal-Mart, or everywhere you go. That's a lot of people!

We've all been given a dash. Whether it's a dull dash or a mad dash, the choice is entirely up to us! What are you doing with your dash?

NOVEMBER 7

Absolutely!

Read: Mark 10:17-22

The world doesn't like absolutes. Religion doesn't like absolutes. It means that we have to make some changes in our belief and our actions. Some people just aren't willing to adjust anything they believe. It's their way or the highway, and everyone else is forced to deal with their choices—like it or lump it.

They have a phrase in Kenya we heard quite a bit when we lived there: "Ji panga!" In Swahili, it means that you need to "sort yourself out." To us Americans, it meant that you better get it together or you'll find yourself in a bigger mess. We would joke about it and use this saying casually, but there was always an underlying truth to that phrase.

It is sad when we know people that are brimming with potential, but they won't make the effort to change. They continually make the same choices and expect a different result. It's heartbreaking to watch, but no amount of advice or help changes them. They refuse to "ji panga"—to sort themselves out.

Jesus didn't water down His message to make it more palatable for people. He made some pretty emphatic statements about Himself and, if a person disagreed, well, they were free to take Him or leave Him. Take, for example, the rich young ruler in our Scripture reading for today. Jesus didn't make accommodations to fit the man's lifestyle, even though He loved him. The guy came running up to Jesus, out of breath, storming past everyone to get to Him, yet he left hanging his head because he wasn't willing to meet Jesus' conditions. He thought his own efforts should be good enough.

Jesus put some stipulations about coming into His Kingdom: Believe He is the *only* Way, forsake your old life, love Him with all your heart, soul, mind and strength and love your neighbor as yourself.

NOVEMBER 7 ———

The Father also set up His Kingdom to work in "past tense." The Kingdom is openly available to all through faith that Christ accomplished everything—nothing more is needed. It's another absolute we cannot afford to live without!

NOVEMBER 8

Rain, Rain, Go Away!

Read: Romans 8:19-22

Rain, rain, go away! Come again some other day! Did you ever hear that rhyme as a child? I thought of that this morning as I prepared to take my dog for our walk. It's not easy to walk my dog on a leash while holding an umbrella. My dog, being part horse—has yanked me to the ground several times chasing a squirrel or a leaf falling from a tree! Where I live in the country there are hills, holes, rocks, sticks, and leaves that make walking like an obstacle course!

This is the third day in a row it has been raining and it's getting old. The moment I opened the door to step outside, it began to pour! I thought to myself, *"I'm not walking in this and I'm not taking an umbrella!"* I shouted at the rain, *"Rain, STOP!"* and within seconds it slowed to a light drizzle! Now that's what I'm talkin' about! I could care less about a slight drizzle. The entire walk was enjoyable from start to finish.

We don't always think about the authority we have been given over the elements. Most of us just deal with it, even though we don't really have to. Ponder Jesus' example of speaking to the wind and the waves. He was astonished that the disciples didn't do it first. Even when He spoke to the fig tree, it responded.

Whenever I'm on my walk and I see a tree or a plant not looking healthy, I believe it recognizes me as a son and it is looking to me to set it free from disease. I have a little evergreen tree that I speak to every day on the way back from my walk. Its needles were turning light green and brown. Since I started speaking to it, it is coming back to life and most of the needles are turning green again!

All of creation is groaning for the sons of God to quit putting up with degeneration and free it from bondage. One version of the Bible says that all of Creation is *"standing on tiptoe"* to see the

NOVEMBER 8 ———

wonderful sight of the sons of God coming into their own. Can you imagine what the world would look like if every Believer took their place of authority and commanded health and life everywhere they went?

NOVEMBER 9

I'm Out Of My Mind—Yeah! (Part 1)

Read: Luke 9:51-55

Out of My Mind

I doubt you've failed to see I'm out of my mind
Yeah it's for the sake of Christ that I'm this way
Ever since I gave Jesus all I have yeah I just
Can't keep this fire I've got inside, well you may think
It's a bad thing you say chill out you're just a little high strung
But the way I see it if I'm only seeking God's approval
Your disapproval won't bother me at all

Cause I'm out of my mind yeah
And I'm into the mind of Christ
I refuse to conform any longer
To the pattern of this world I'm living in
I'm not a good little church mouse boy any longer
From now on man I'm a man of God
Well you may think it's a bad thing you say chill out your just a little high strung
But the way I see it if I'm only seeking God's approval
Your disapproval won't bother me at all

Laugh at me, put me down
God told me such things would come
Disown me, you can ridicule me
I don't live my life for you
Cause you never died for me

Song by GS Megaphone

NOVEMBER 9

I encourage you to listen to this song on YouTube cuz you can really jam to it! It's one of my hubby's favorite Christian rock songs. There's a lot of truth in the lyrics. People will always have something to say about you, no matter what you do. I learned in life that some people are going to like me and some of them won't, but at the end of the day, I'm the one who has to lay my head down on my pillow at night and live with myself. My conscience has to be clean before God.

The account taking place in our Scripture reading for today happened after Jesus, and three of His disciples: Peter, James, and John, were on the Mountain of Transfiguration. Jesus had set His face to go to Jerusalem to celebrate the Passover for the last time with His disciples and then to be crucified. On their way, they traveled through Samaria for one last jaunt. Some of the disciples had been sent ahead to prepare for His coming, but the Samaritans rejected Him because they worshipped on Mount Gerizim. They believed that was where Abraham had gone to sacrifice his son Isaac. Samaritans were hostile to Jews who worshipped in Jerusalem.

James and John, having recently seen Elijah on the mountain with Jesus, had suggested that the Samaritans deserved to be struck by lightning, just as Elijah had done to his enemies in the Old Testament. (Funny how they believed they had power to call lightning down from heaven, but not to calm storms or multiply bread!) Their human reasoning, influenced by the cultural, religious, and ethnic hostility of their day, caused James and John to believe these people should be zapped and turned into crispy critters! Jesus declared, *"You do not know what kind of Spirit you belong to; for the Son of Man did not come to destroy people's lives, but to save them."*

Think about Jesus' response. He said they didn't *know* the Holy Spirit! Oh, they had seen miracles! They had done quite a few themselves, yet they still didn't *know* Him! They weren't seeing

NOVEMBER 9

these people worthy of the Gospel. This revelation that God was not a God of judgment, but of mercy, was foreign to them. Had they forgotten their previous visit to Samaria and Jesus' encounter with the woman at the well? Had they forgotten those who believed in Him as a result of her testimony? Knowing the Holy Spirit causes us to be out of our mind and into the mind of Christ!

NOVEMBER 10

I'm Out Of My Mind—Yeah! (Part 2)

Read: Acts 8:1-2

*R*emember Jesus' words to the disciples before He went back to heaven? He informed them that they would be seized with the power of the Holy Spirit to be His witnesses in Jerusalem, Judea, Samaria, and the ends of the earth (Acts 1:8). Jesus specifically mentioned the Samaritans. If you read further on in Acts, after the Believers were scattered because of Stephen's martyrdom, this was the exact progression the Gospel was preached. In Acts chapter 8, Philip traveled to Samaria and preached the Gospel to multitudes with signs and wonders! I don't think the Samaritans would have received the Gospel from Philip if half the region was burnt to a crisp by James and John previously calling down the fire of judgment upon them.

Have you ever heard a man testify how horrible his childhood was from abuse that he became addicted to drugs, stole from his mother, joined a gang, and did time in prison? As a result, the judgment of God came upon him; he repented and gave his life to Christ, right? NO!! Usually, it is with tears from the mercy of God he repents, not judgment. Oh, he knows he deserved it, but he receives kindness and mercy instead!

God doesn't look at people the way we see them. He had to give us a new mind and a new heart, or else we wouldn't care about anyone but ourselves. I like the lyrics to the song *"I'm Out of My Mind"* because it is the perfect expression how we cannot tailor our lives to fit the approval of others. We cannot afford to be a *"good little church mouse boy"* by conforming to religion. We cannot bow down to the world's standard of living— all for the sake of Christ!

There are plenty of "Samaritans" in our world today. We were all once a "Samaritan" in one way or another. Yet God's judgment did not consume us; instead His love and mercy embraced us and we became His. Now we're all out of our minds for the sake of Christ!

NOVEMBER 11

Help My Unbelief

Read: Mark 9:14-29

Of the three Gospels, Matthew, Mark and Luke, the account of the deliverance of the demon possessed son in the book of Mark is the most detailed. It is famous for the father's desperate plea for his son, *"Lord, I believe. Help my unbelief!"*

Unfortunately, many Believers repeat the father's words concerning their own circumstances. There are a few things we must consider before we accept this as the mantra of the body of Christ.

First, the most important fact to recognize is that this story happened before Jesus went to the cross. Neither the father nor the disciples were born again; they did not have the Holy Spirit, which is the Spirit of faith, living inside of them. The best type of belief they could offer was more like mental agreement.

The second point I'd like to make is that the disciples had previously been given the authority to cast out demons. The reason they couldn't cast the demon out is because they let the demonic effects of the boy foaming at the mouth and convulsing frighten them. They let their human reasoning get in the way of the power Jesus had given them. Jesus was displeased at their inability because He knew He was soon going to be crucified. The disciples were supposed to fill His shoes and they had failed. Once again, He had to take the reins and show them how it was done.

The disciple's problem in this story was no different than the father's. They were all confronted with the unbelief in their own hearts. Jesus told them that all things were possible to him who believes. We apply this faith by looking at Christ and His accomplishments, while ignoring our human inadequacies.

NOVEMBER 11

The last point I'd like to make is that those of us who are born again have been given the Spirit of faith. For us, we must choose between agreeing with the Spirit and the truth we know in our heart, or with what we are experiencing in the natural. No matter what is going on in our lives, we have already been given the victory. All the promises of God are *"Yes."* and *"Amen."* We can choose to waste our time fighting ourselves and trying to convince ourselves that we believe, or push all that garbage aside and recognize that we have the same faith Christ possesses.

The bottom line is: we are Believers! There is no such thing as an unbelieving Believer! Trust the Holy Spirit inside of you!

NOVEMBER 12

Have Your Healing Now

Read: Isaiah 53:10

When we are experiencing physical symptoms of pain and discomfort in our bodies, it does not mean that we are not healed. Symptoms are not a gauge to judge whether we are healed or not.

One of the few things the Old Covenant and the New Covenant had in common was healing. The only difference is how healing is received. In the Old Covenant, healing was based on obedience to God's commands. In the New Covenant, healing is based on Jesus' Atonement. Our belief in Christ's gift of life lets us in on the benefits. Isaiah 53:10 in *The Message Bible* states,

> "Still, it's what God had in mind all along, to crush Him with pain. The plan was that He gave Himself as an offering for sin so that He'd see life come from it—life, life, and more life. And God's plan will deeply prosper through Him."

It is ineffective to try to make symptoms leave, constantly rebuke disease, or fight the devil. You might as well beat the air. I've never experienced results from that approach. All it got me was totally frustrated and angry. I could not just "tough it out" no matter how hard I tried. And that was exactly the problem. I was trying to get symptoms to leave instead of having my healing!

I know what it is like to be overwhelmed with symptoms, but they are no match for the suffering Jesus took for our healing. The times I watched as my body did some really weird stuff I didn't know was possible, it took a bit of courage to confront it as a lie. I'd enforce the truth that I was healed, and because I had received healing way back when I received Christ, my body needed to respond to His life on the inside.

NOVEMBER 12

I'd speak to whatever part was bothering me and tell it that it was healed. Then I'd say, *"Thank you, Jesus!"* This is what I did every time the symptom tried to distract me, *"No, you're healed! Thank you, Jesus!"* Then I'd just go about my life as though I was healed, not dwelling on it.

I've had many things disappear by this simple approach. When they leave I don't always realize it because I refuse to let symptoms control me. They just leave cuz they have to! I'm having my healing now! You can too!

NOVEMBER 13

Waiting Or Persevering?

Read: Hebrews 10:35-36 (Amplified Bible)

*W*hat is the difference between waiting and persevering? They are so closely related that sometimes it's hard to tell.

Perseverance means *to persist or remain constant to a purpose, idea, or task in the face of obstacles or discouragement.* It has the idea of having strength of mind, courage, and endurance.

Waiting is *the act of remaining inactive or stationary.* It is a period of time spent basically doing nothing.

When we apply either of these approaches to physical healing, we can see these are two entirely different approaches. *Waiting* is more like hoping God is going to touch down some day and drop healing in your lap, so you're just going to wait until He feels like it is the right time. *Persevering* is taking what already belongs to you with courage and fortitude, enforcing it till you experience what is rightfully yours.

Waiting believes that someday you're gonna get it. Perseverance believes you already have it and nothing is gonna stop you from experiencing it. Sometimes it does take perseverance to experience our healing, but we're not sitting idle waiting for it, so don't fling away your fearless confidence! Live like you've already got it!

NOVEMBER 14

Trust Your Own Words

Read: James 3:5-12

"*God's word is preprogrammed. The seed is in itself. The ability to produce exactly what was promised is programmed into that word to produce after its kind...If you speak God's words the way God intended, you'll create the right image in the days to come, you will live it out in reality.*" – Charles Capps

Did you know that your own words have the authority to produce after its kind? Oh, yes, what we experience is usually because that's what we spoke over time. Many conversations take the natural course of complaining about symptoms. This only reinforces them!

I have heard well-meaning friends say the right things one minute, and the next time I talk to them, they regurgitate all of their problems. They are led by their emotions and don't make much progress overcoming their trials.

In our Bible verses for today, the examples James gives about the outcome of our words is very applicable. If we mix salt water with fresh water, the fresh water becomes salty. If we store rotten fruit with fresh fruit, the fresh fruit becomes rotten. The same result happens with our words. When we speak blessings one minute and curses the next, the blessings become corroded. Or if we speak Bible verses about healing, but then tell everyone about our symptoms, we confuse our own heart!

It may be easier to trust the words of another person instead of our own, but when the rubber meets the road, it's what we speak with our own mouths and what we believe in our own hearts that impacts our lives the deepest.

Trust your own words. You hold the power for what you experience right there in that little pink organ in your mouth! It turns the

NOVEMBER 14 ———

course of your entire life! Your own words brought salvation into your life, and your own words can certainly be a catalyst for your own healing!

NOVEMBER 15

God's Compass

Read: Isaiah 30:21

*H*oly Spirit; He's the calming whisper when chaos surrounds, the echo resounding confidence in uncertainty, and the voice over our shoulder clearing the way—He's God's compass.

At times when things spin out of control, Holy Spirit is like a spiritual machete chopping through the tangled mass of confusion. He's got you and He's holding you tight. You can sense Him if you quiet yourself for a few minutes. Lean in and expect to hear His instructions. With confidence, expect to hear and He will speak. He responds to our confidence and boldness.

A lot of Believers I know would love to hear God's voice more frequently and clearly. What they don't realize is that He is speaking to them more than they perceive. The easiest way to find direction and guidance from the Holy Spirit is to start going in the direction you have on your heart. Sitting around waiting to hear usually leads to inactivity and confusion. The Gospel is an *"as you go"* Gospel—not an *"as you sit and wait for a leading"* Gospel. It is as simple as acting on what you know.

Paul knew that he was an apostle to the Gentiles (Galatians 1:15-16). What did he do? He went to the Gentiles, where no one ever heard about Jesus. Did he sit and pray, *"Lord, where should I go?"* No, he just went. As he went, we only read of two experiences where the Holy Spirit said, *"Don't go to Asia."* And, *"Don't go to Bithynia."* Then Paul had a vision of a Macedonian man pleading for him to come and preach the Gospel to them (Acts 16:6-10). On all other occasions, Paul just went. Holy Spirit was his compass telling him where to go; all he had to do was to get going! God had already sent him!

NOVEMBER 15 ———

We have been commissioned to *"GO!"* (Mark 16:15). We don't need a special commissioning service for hands to be laid upon us to go. The same faith is required to act on it—so just cut to the chase; heal the sick and preach the Gospel. Holy Spirit will be with you everywhere you go; not only as a compass, but the power residing within you to do miracles!

NOVEMBER 16

Gummy Worms

Read: 1 Corinthians 1:27

It was late in the evening on a week night. Suffering in misery from a litany of symptoms, I was also experiencing incredible pain in my knee from infection and swelling. A friend gave me Tony Myers phone number and said he could help. He explained how Tony was miraculously healed of Lou Gehrig's disease. I needed someone who understood where I was at to help me out! At that point, I was desperate and would have done practically anything to get relief!

As I explained my situation, Tony offered to pray for me. Ah, at last the help I longed for! So, instead of the typical, *"Lord Jesus, we ask that You would..."* Tony states emphatically in his quirky southern accent: *"Gummy Worms!"*

My brain went _____ ... Yeah, he blew my mind! Then like a locomotive without breaks, a thousand thoughts barreled through my mind, one after the other: *"Why do I always get stuck with the "kooks?" "What kind of help is this, Lord?" "Now what am I gonna do?" "Is this some kinda joke?"*

"Hello, are you there?" Tony's question broke the silence. *"Yeah, I'm still here,"* I said with an annoyed tone of voice. I felt like hanging up the phone, but I didn't want to be rude. *"Now, check yourself out. Did you receive any improvement?" "Huh?"* I questioned like I had been suddenly zombified. *"Your knee; is there any improvement?"* Tony persisted. I'm thinking, *"What? You didn't even pray!"*

"What do you mean? All you said was 'Gummy worms.'" I shot back at him, extremely annoyed. *"I know what I said. I can say anything I want to and it doesn't matter what I say cuz it's not my words that matters. Now check out your knee; is there improvement?"* He shot back at me.

NOVEMBER 16

I thought about my knee...there was less pain! What the heck??? Tony explained why he didn't pray. I was so religious that I thought he had to pray a certain way to get healed. Well, honestly, none of that religious nonsense had worked up to this point; now he had my attention!

Tony explained that he had to distract me to get my mind off of the pain so I could receive. You see, when we've been in such a horrible state for any duration of time, our mind becomes so fixed on the problem, we can't think about anything else. He had to interrupt my normal mode of thinking and basically side swipe my mind. It was like a whack in the brain! Purely idiotic or pure genius—I don't know, but it worked!

I learned quite a few things about myself from that conversation! I didn't realize how religious I was! Throughout the following weeks, months and years, I decided to dump religion and let the Lord teach me His truth about healing. It wasn't easy. Really, the most important quality to possess is fortitude. I was willing to dump everything I thought I knew about Jesus and His ways. It took courage to persevere and replace false teachings with the Truth. It was worth every ounce of effort so that I could learn how healing had already belonged to me!

You can connect with Tony on Facebook and check out his YouTube channel; *Tony Myers Healing*, as well as my YouTube Channel and Facebook page: *East Coast Healing Center*. Tony and I are good friends and both of us are always available to pray with people. However, beware! He just might say, *"Gummy Worms!"*

NOVEMBER 17

Gluten-Freedom

Read: John 8:34-36

My hubby and I were at the beach shopping on the boardwalk in one of our favorite stores. It's a spice and tea shop. They carry many different blends of teas and spices we enjoy.

This particular visit, one of the ladies on staff was exuberantly ranting about articles she had read how coffee and certain foods cause inflammation and she was going to cut them out of her diet. Ugh! My mind quickly reverted back to the bondage I put myself through trying to cure symptoms with food. I had read many articles like that in the past and I wasn't about to fall for that trap ever again!

I honestly didn't interrupt her conversation. She flittered from one customer to the next repeating the same story. Sometimes you can't fix stupid—and I don't mean her, I'm referring to the source of information she was trusting in.

God gave us authority over our own bodies. If we don't exercise that authority and we hand it over to erroneous information by submitting to man's solution for health, we end up like a dog chasing its tail.

Today, when my hubby and I were at a restaurant, I heard the customer in the booth across from us ordering everything "gluten-free." I was just finishing up my BLT omelet loaded with Monterey Jack cheese—a food that previously would have caused me pain and inflammation in my joints. I had silently in my head just thanked Jesus for the freedom to eat whatever I wanted to eat. Freedom sure tastes good!

It wasn't exactly a walk in the park to push through the symptoms from eating bread, cheese, fruit, pasta and the whole list of foods

NOVEMBER 17

that caused pain in my body. But healed is healed, right? Healed people can eat whatever they want because Jesus gave every food for us to enjoy, not cause us harm. If He told His disciples that *"nothing shall by any means hurt us"* and *"if we drink deadly poison it will not harm us,"* shouldn't food be included in those lists?

I had to push past the fear of a food causing a certain symptom. Other people all around me ate whatever they wanted without symptoms, why should I be any different? So I intentionally eat stuff, even if my mind starts to say *"Uh-O!"*, I have found that I am free! I hope that you will be open to what I'm saying here. Jesus set you free. John 8:36 in the *Wuest Translation* says,

> *"If therefore the Son makes you free, you shall be free individuals in reality."*

NOVEMBER 18

Two Gardens, Two Lives

Read: Ephesians 1:3-12

What began in a garden ended in a garden; what began on a tree ended on a tree. Jesus was the sum total of everything; it truly was finished! In God's mind, we were in Christ before He created the world. In the Father's mind, Christ's sacrifice was already complete and He considered our lives hidden in Him before it all began! It's over! It's been over since the beginning! You were on His mind!

The two gardens represent two lives, or standards of living. The Garden of Eden provided everything, yet even in that, man still believed he was missing out on something; that's why the tree enticed him. When Jesus went to the garden to pray before His crucifixion, He wrestled with the *"Do-it-yourself"* mindset and conquered it once for all by submitting the *"Adam"* way of thinking to His Father's will. Romans 6:6-7 in the NKJV declares,

> *"Knowing this, that our old man was crucified with Him, that the body of sin might be done away with; that we should no longer be slaves of sin. For he who has died has been freed from sin."*

He orchestrated every event of His sacrifice and tailored it fill every void with exact precision! The fact that we do not have to crucify our own flesh sends a sharp, right hook in the face of religion! Blows your mind, doesn't it?

Our lives are now His garden. He is the "grounds keeper." Since we have given Him preeminence over our lives, the idea of fighting to gain healing, peace, joy, or freedom is futile! The more we learn about His goodness and generosity, rest from striving becomes our natural way of living. As a result, we, as well as others around us, experience the overflow of His Spirit unhindered!

NOVEMBER 19

Second Nature

Read: Hebrews 2:17

The term *second nature* refers to something a person has practiced frequently over time that comes naturally or instinctively. When an ability or trait becomes deeply engrained in your life, it is an expression of your capacity and character—for the good or the bad. As a result we become identified by that ability or trait.

Your first nature is what you were born with as a human, and we all know how that turned out! Your second nature is a habit that has become so engraved it naturally becomes a part of your character. So, can your second nature become your first nature? I believe that is exactly what God had planned all along!

As we get to know Holy Spirit, His impressions upon our heart become more pronounced and evident; so much so that we become just like Him! We are always told that we become like the people we hang around. People "rub off" on us, so we should choose our friends wisely.

Meditating on specific Scriptures embeds God's thoughts in the place of our natural thoughts. Over time, our thoughts become His thoughts. In response, we begin to live it out.

For example, most of us are familiar with Galatians 2:20, which states, *"I have been crucified with Christ; it is no longer I who live, but Christ lives in me."* Further reflection upon this Scripture denotes a life that has been replaced by Christ's life. Since we are dead; His life, His character, His thoughts, and His ability will be lived out through us. The application of this verse means that miracles are a part of our first nature! The supernatural becomes natural. The supernatural isn't supernatural to Jesus, its natural; therefore it should be natural for us!

NOVEMBER 20

God Sense

Read: 1 Corinthians 1:25-31

Common sense is sound judgment based on simple perception of the situation or facts. It's the basic level of practical knowledge and judgment that we all need to help us live in a reasonable way. While common sense is helpful for people in the normal course of life, it can really lead us into an inferior way of living in the Kingdom.

I remember several years ago at the church we attended, the pastor handed out a clothespin to every person in the congregation. We were told to write the word "REALITY" on the clothespin to remind us to stay *balanced* and take a reality check every so often. In all practicality, it sounds like a reasonable thing to do—as some people can be "out there" somewhere; but when we take this approach to the Kingdom, God's ways do not make sense to the natural mind. We need God sense, not common sense.

I recently saw a video of an African woman healed of a deformed arm. People were gathered around her in a circle to watch the miracle after she was prayed for. Within seconds, her arm began to shake. Her upper arm began to lengthen where it had previously been short and twisted. As I watched, her arm changed, and within a few minutes it was completely normal. It happened so fast that she almost passed out!

There is no reasonable human explanation for that miracle! It makes absolutely no sense! No doctor could have perfected her arm through surgery the way God fixed her arm! Common sense doesn't fit into God's sense. Our human perception and reasoning will always interfere with Kingdom principles! And they should because we are no longer of this world!

NOVEMBER 21

Truth

Read: John 17:17

*T*he exact definition for *truth* in a Biblical sense is *reality*. It is a state of being that is independent of human awareness. Jesus believed that the power of God's word had the ability to set His people apart, or sanctify them from the world. He trusted that what He had taught His disciples was enough to keep them from reverting back to their former ways of living. They had been radically changed by His message and they cherished the relationship they developed with Him. There was just something about Him that set Him apart from everyone else.

Truth will always have a certain "tang" to it. The disciples knew they were forever changed by knowing this Man. After Jesus asked them if they would like to leave when others had turned away, Peter stated,

> *"Lord, to whom shall we go? You have the words of eternal life. Also we have come to believe and know that You are the Christ, the Son of the living God."* (John 6:68-69, NKJV)

Pilate, when he stood face-to face with Truth and was unable to recognize it, stated, *"What is truth?"* (John 18:38) so he washed his hands of Him. The religious leaders had to lie about Jesus to arrest Him and have Him tried, but Pilate didn't want anything to do with Him. It was back and forth: *"You judge Him and sentence Him."* Then the Jews responded, *"No! Our laws don't allow us to kill anyone! You do it!"* It was like the old commercial for LIFE cereal, *"Did you try it?" "I'm not gonna try it! You try it!"* as the brothers pass the bowl of cereal back and forth, *"Let's get Mikey!"*

The religious leaders knew full well Jesus was the Messiah. They *chose* to reject Him because they didn't want to lose their status among

NOVEMBER 21

the people. Truth offends. If it didn't, it wouldn't be the truth! I often tell the Lord I want to live by the truth. I give Him permission to offend me anytime I need an adjustment in my thinking!

NOVEMBER 22

Copy Cat

Read: Hebrews 6:11-20

A copy cat is someone who copies the words or behavior of another; one who imitates other's work without adding any variation. For children, the old adage, *"Do as I say and not as I do,"* never works because children pick up on the bad habits of an adult quicker than the words they speak. The term *copy cat* is usually used as a negative connotation; but Paul, employing the wisdom of the Holy Spirit, uses imitating someone with a positive implication.

The sixth chapter of Hebrews has been largely misunderstood by not understanding it in its proper context. It is NOT referring to anyone who believed in Christ but walked away from their faith, implying that they could never be restored again! Here, we see the prime example of those turning back to live under the law of the Old Covenant verses choosing to live by faith under the New Covenant—it is as though Christ would have to be crucified all over again in their understanding.

The writer of Hebrews commands the body of Believers to mimic the faith of those who, through patience, possessed the promises of their portion of Christ's inheritance. He uses Abraham as the chief illustration for securing God's promise by faith. He encourages the Believers not to behave like illegitimate children, but to act like children of their true inheritance. God put His stamp of approval upon the promise by swearing on oath to fulfill it—it was forever unchangeable!

The author of Hebrews included Abraham and Sarah in chapter 11, along with many other examples of people whose faith we should imitate. These "heroes of faith" they all disregarded their earthly origin with its limitations, and by faith they *"subdued kingdoms, worked righteousness, obtained promises, stopped the mouths of lions,*

NOVEMBER 22

quenched the violence of fire, escaped the edge of the sword, out of weakness were made strong, became valiant in battle, turned to flight the armies of aliens, and received their dead raised to life again." (Hebrews 11:33-35 NKJV) And these were all people under the Old Covenant! Imagine what we can do under the New Covenant we have in Christ!!

They weren't sitting around waiting to possess their inheritance—they grabbed it by the jugular! So go ahead! Be a copy cat! You have an advantage those heroes of the faith didn't have—the Holy Spirit *living inside you!*

NOVEMBER 23

Hair Count

Read: Luke 12:6-7

"*Hair! Flow it, show it! Long as God can grow it, my hair!*" This is a line from the song *"Hair"* in 1968, by the Cowsills. Yeah, I know I'm showing my age—but this song always cracks me up!

We are led to believe that, as we grow older, our hair will thin, our hormones will give us ladies hot flashes, and our skin will get thin and wrinkly. When I turned forty, I began to have a series of health problems, including my hair falling out. Now, if you're a woman like me, your hair is your glory! I mean, who wants to look at a bald lady? *Ugh!*

I'm writing this devotion to all you ladies out there struggling with hair loss. That seems to be one of the most frequent things that women call me to pray with them about. Little is more horrifying than watching your beautiful locks wash down the drain every time you wash your hair, or finding strand after strand dropping on your clothes as you go about your day. Since I didn't know much about the healing Christ had already provided, I tried everything to keep my beautiful hair: supplements, shampoos, hormones...you name it. After all the frustration and tears, nothing solved the problem. Fear had gripped me with thoughts, *"What if I go bald? I don't want to wear a wig!"*

One of the verses of Scripture that the Lord showed me was Luke 12:7,

> *"Do not five sparrows sell for two copper coins? Not one is overlooked before God. Indeed, the very hairs of your head are all numbered. Stop fearing—you are more valuable than many sparrows."* (A note in *The Passion Translation*)

What is Jesus saying through this Scripture? A copper coin was the smallest, least valuable coin, equal to a tenth of a drachma. One

NOVEMBER 23

copper coin could purchase five sparrows. The earth is plentiful with so many sparrows that they are the least valued of all birds. Jesus was saying that even though sparrows are of such little value, our Father has not forgotten them. To Him, we are of much more value to Him than *many* sparrows—even to the finest detail of knowing everything about us, down to the very number of the hairs on our head! In other words, He knows what's going on with our hair!

After reading this Scripture, I came to the conclusion that because Holy Spirit is living in my body, He was giving life to my hair; so it should be shiny, thick, healthy, and beautiful. I found the following quote in one of John G. Lake's sermons. What he said gave me an encouraging perspective:

> *"Jesus went to heaven in order that the very treasury of the heart of the eternal God might be unlocked for your benefit and that out of the very soul of the eternal God, the streams of His life and nature would possess you from the crown of your head to the sole of your feet and that there would be just as much of the eternal God in your toenails and in your brain as each are capable of containing. In other words, from the very soles of your feet to the last hair on the top of your head, every cell of your being would be a residence of the Spirit of the living God. Man is made alive by God and with God by the Spirit. And in the truest sense, man is the dwelling place of God, the house of God, the tabernacle of the Most High."*

My approach changed from a desperate plea to boldness: *"Holy Spirit, You are giving Your life to my hair!"* I looked at myself square in the mirror and I told my hair, *"Hair, from now on you will be healthy, thick, and beautiful just like God created you! Thank You, Jesus!"* Even if I'd see a lot of hair in the drain or when I combed it, I began to care less. The sensitivity I used to feel in my scalp disappeared. New hair began to grow. I often looked at a picture of when I was younger

NOVEMBER 23

to remember what my hair was like. I used that picture to recreate the image I used to be in my mind. Whenever discouraging thoughts would come, I'd remind myself of that picture and say: *"That's who you are!"*

You don't have to settle for anything that is going on in your body that shouldn't be there. Dump the fear; remember God loves you! Know that He has kept a count of every hair on your head, down to the finest detail of your body—inside and out. He gave Jesus as payment for your freedom and life. Trust the finished work of Christ working in your flesh. Square your shoulders and confidently look at yourself in the mirror imagining the hair you used to have. Before long, you'll see those beautiful locks shining once again!

NOVEMBER 24

Cornucopia

Read: 2 Corinthians 9:8

A cornucopia, or horn of plenty, is a basket shaped like a horn overflowing with fruit, vegetables, flowers and grain symbolizing the abundance of a harvest. We typically see them in the fall around Thanksgiving. *The Passion Translation* for this verse says,

> *"Yes, God is more than ready to overwhelm you with every form of grace, so that you will have more than enough of everything—every moment and in every way. He will make you overflow with abundance in every good thing you do."*

In the notes referring to this verse, it states that Paul used a word found in classical Greek meaning *"independently wealthy, needing nothing."* That sounds like a cornucopia of God's goodness, doesn't it?

These days, when the world is shouting: *"Inflation! Supply shortages!"*, we have God's promise of provision that isn't limited to the earth's resources. We're connected to heaven's resources, even when it comes to healing. The systems we once trusted are miserably failing. It's imperative we learn how to function from the resources of heaven.

God brought Elijah bread every day from a bird and water from a creek. When those resources ended, he told him where to go for provision from a widow. God fed him, the widow, and her son, with an endless supply of flour and oil to make bread, sustaining them till the famine was over. Jesus also multiplied bread to feed thousands.

Whenever you have a need, just thank our Father for being an independently wealthy provider! Then, watch the creative ways He delivers it right to you!

NOVEMBER 25

Asking Or Having?

Read: Colossians 1:15-17

A muddy mixture of confusion is the result of combining an Old Covenant mindset with a New Covenant mindset. It's the main reason that Believers do not experience the blessings of health, freedom, and prosperity made available to them through Christ. Many sit waiting for God to do something He's already done. They question whether what they are asking for is His will for them or not, because it is taking so long.

I want to emphasize that what I'm saying here is of the utmost importance. If you will posture your heart to listen, it will transform your relationship with Jesus forever. I see this all the time! I am becoming more and more aware of it myself! So forgive me if I seem aggressive about this—I am, because I want to you experience the best God has given to you! It's the game-changer for a life lived in victory verses a life lived in defeat!

I will use the example of physical healing here, but you can apply this to every situation. When Jesus said, *"Ede panta tetelestai!"* meaning, *"Now all things have been finished,"* it's an oxymoron to ask Him for anything! It's a contradiction of the New Covenant's provision to be in need. There is no need for healing when healing was already a completed work by Christ's scourging—it is *FINISHED*! No do-over necessary! Done is done!

Stop asking Him to heal you! Our Father sees you as already healed because He sees you in Christ with everything Christ has. Agree with what God said about you—that you were healed by His stripes (1 Peter 2:24). When you begin to proclaim that out loud, your mind might act a little wonky and think, *"Huh? How can I already be healed if I've got pain?"* The more you affirm the truth to yourself, the more settled it will become in your heart. Your mind will begin

NOVEMBER 25

to agree with your spirit. Once that transition takes place, it's two against one and your body will have to submit. Health is the result! Thank Him for it and keep thanking Him! It's already guaranteed—He signed the New Covenant with His blood.

You see, our Father relates to us through Jesus' finished work. He sees it as over and done with, and so must we. Asking and asking is contrary to having. Asking and trying to make things happen by being a "good boy" or a "good girl" holds no bearing; that's the way the Old Covenant functioned. You cannot qualify yourself to deserve to be healed any more than you can qualify yourself to be saved—so get over it and have your health, cuz it's already yours! Thanks be to Jesus!

NOVEMBER 26

Blank Check

Read: Hebrews 4:9-10

*I*f I had an endless amount of money in my bank account and then I signed every check in my checkbook and gave you the whole thing, what would you do with all the money? Pay off your debts, buy a new car, or go on a cruise?—Probably all that and more, right? Or would you forget about the checkbook and call me on the phone, crying that you are so poor you cannot pay your bills, begging me for money? Your audacity would really tick me off!

Have you ever heard the saying that Christians are just a bunch of beggars telling other beggars where to get the bread? I used to hear that preached from the pulpit a lot! Sounds so humble, right? Even the Old Testament declares, *"I have never seen the righteous forsaken, or their children begging for bread."* (Psalm 37:25) Where anyone came up with that belief is beyond me!

Several years ago when my hubby and I had rededicated our lives to Christ, we helped serve in street ministry. We spent almost every waking moment gathering clothes and food to minister to the homeless. We had three boys at the time all under the age of six. Our youngest son was nine months old at the time and had just been released from the hospital after a month due to an infection in the joint of his elbow. To top it off, our car was on its last leg. A co-worker kept insisting that my husband and I visit his church because his pastor had received a special touch from an "anointed" man of God. When we arrived, no one greeted us. A few ladies sat in the front row during the entire service laughing because they were "under the anointing" from this certain popular preacher.

When it came time to receive the offering, the pastor said these exact words: *"If your kid is sick and your car is on its last leg then you aren't giving enough!"* My husband and I looked at each other and

NOVEMBER 26

began to cry! What? We tithed, we were in street ministry, feeding and clothing the homeless. Yet, our car was on its last leg, and our baby just got out of the hospital! What more could we give?

We left totally discouraged! We decided to turn our concerns over to the Lord and told him that if we were doing something wrong, we were open for correction. If the pastor was teaching in error, then God would show him as well. A few months later, the pastor had repented to his congregation for exalting a man and not exalting Christ. The person who had invited us to his church called and apologized. We were able to purchase a van for our growing family, and our baby continued to improve. We were relieved that God took care of it all!

Religion always makes us feel like we can never measure up; that we can never do enough, give enough, or sacrifice enough—as though it will earn us something in return; and if you don't, well, then you're cursed! The riches of His glory have been lavished upon us, supplying everything we need. Asking a hundred people to pray does not make it more accessible. Paying your tithes and giving offerings does not mean you deserve God to bless you. God does not think like man: *"You did this, so I'll give you this in return."*

God relates to man through the New Covenant—period! He took the "get" out of "getting" and the "work" out of "working!" So take a chill pill and relax! If you have been "church hurt", choose to forgive and move on! Don't let it hold you back any longer from what God has in store for you! You've got a blank check, so to speak, and the works we now do are HIS works: healing the sick, preaching the Gospel, etc. We have ceased from our own works and entered into His rest!

NOVEMBER 27

Yours For The Taking

Read: John 20:22

In two of the pervious devotions, June 16th and September 13th, we talked about the Greek word *lambano*, our English word *receive*, meaning *"to seize something with force and take it as your own."* That's what Jesus did with our diseases (Matthew 8:17). And our response is choosing to live in the freedom provided by the New Covenant. It's not the mamby-pamby way of opening up our arms as it's gently laid in our lap for us to gently hug. We grab a hold of what we have with force and don't let it go for nothin'!

In John 20:22, Jesus blew on the disciples and said, *"Receive the Holy Spirit."* There it is again—*lambano*—grab it with force! In this verse, we can take a further look at the definition of this word. Jesus was referring to the Holy Spirit. Up until this point, the Holy Spirit had rested upon certain people (except for Jesus), but not *in* them.

Here, when relating to the Holy Spirit, *lambano* also means *"to associate with Him as a Companion!"* Jesus was telling them to grab the Holy Spirit as their Companion from that moment on. Holy Spirit is the endorsement of their inheritance in Christ!

Hebrews 1:3 in the *Wuest Translation*, says that Jesus is the *"out-raying effulgence of His glory"*—the bright radiance of God's glory. That's what Holy Spirit looks like—dazzling radiance, pure blinding glory! And He, my friend, is living inside you right now as your forever Companion!

NOVEMBER 28

Implanted

Read: James 1:21-25

To implant something means *to fix or set it securely, deeply, and permanently in one's consciousness or habits.* This is the only place this word is used in the Bible. It is interesting that it is specifically referring to the Word, which we know is Jesus. Another word for implanted is *engrafted*.

I have an apple tree in my yard that will produce four different kinds of apples in one tree! How is that possible? Branches from three other types of apple trees were cut and grafted into the trunk to create one tree. Eventually, the engrafted branches grew and fused into the original tree. All the branches draw nourishment from the same trunk. When the tree blooms, each branch will produce its own type of apple! Now, I don't have to turn my yard into an orchard to grow a variety of apples! Pretty ingenious, isn't it?

James is unveiling the profound ability of the life of Christ becoming embedded into our nature. Our personality, emotions, and thoughts become a divine out-living expression of Jesus. We are doers of the words, instructions and habits of the Holy Spirit—not a mere listener who has no power to influence change. We have been implanted and engrafted into Christ. He is a living extension of who we are.

We are so one with Him that there is no longer any distinction. It's like my apple tree with four different types of apples. I cannot find any marks or scars where the branches were cut and grew together. If it wasn't for the tags left on the branches, I would not be able to tell which branch would produce the Granny Smith or the McIntosh. Is it far-fetched to expect to experience the health and energy exuding from Holy Spirit into our bodies? Absolutely not! We're implanted and engrafted into Him! His life is your life too!

NOVEMBER 29

I Think I Can!

Read: Psalm 18:28-33

The Little Engine That Could, published in 1930, is the story of a train loaded with toys that broke down at the bottom of a mountain. Larger engines were asked to help pull the train over the mountain but for various reasons, they refused. One little engine agreed to help. He's so small, he doesn't have much confidence in himself, but he decides to try anyway.

The little engine strained with all his might to pull the train up the steep hill repeating, *"I think I can, I think I can!"* Encouraging himself by repeating those words, inching his way little by little; he finds himself at the top of the mountain! He did it! All he had to do was think it was possible and he succeeded!

That was my favorite story when I was a little girl. I used to read it over and over again. My favorite part was when the little engine repeated, *"I think I can, I think I can!"* in cadence with his *"choo-choo"* rhythm of chugging up the mountain. The words he spoke had become the strength he needed to do what looked to be impossible.

That simple story still encourages me to this day. Throughout my life, I have found the courage I needed through God's strength within me. He's just like that—an incognito force available whenever a mountain is staring us down, giving us the courage to say: *"MOVE!"*

Whatever situation is trying to intimidate you, remember the words of the Little Engine That Could: *"I think I can!"* Because of Jesus, you can *choo-choo* chug right over that mountain!

NOVEMBER 30

The Crucified Flesh

Read: Ephesians 4:22-23

Religion has taught us that we must crucify our flesh and die to ourselves. I spent many years trying to kill myself over and over again. Die, die, die, you horrible flesh monster! The funny thing is, the more I focused on my failures, the more I failed! I used to set a goal every morning to try to go through one full day without saying or doing anything wrong—in the midst of trying to keep my cool while homeschooling my five children! Within the first fifteen minutes upon their waking up, the chaos would start and I'd flip out on them. The older two boys would antagonize the younger ones and then leave the room. Disappointed in myself, I'd try again tomorrow...Silly, isn't it?

I had read many books about being holy. Maybe I was misinterpreting what they said, but all it ever did for me was made me try harder only to become more frustrated. The real answers I needed were already inside me, but I didn't realize it until one day the Holy Spirit said, *"Michele, give yourself a break! Give yourself some grace!"* Confused, I responded, *"What? You know I'm doing this for You, Lord!"* It was almost as if He was saying, *"I know, but please stop!"* I realized that my self-effort was doing the complete opposite!

When nothing seemed to be going right, I'd think, *"What am I doing wrong?"* or *"What am I doing to hinder God from healing me?"* My constant self-analyzing and introspection was the problem! I was getting in my own way! When I asked Holy Spirit what I was doing wrong since my prayers were unanswered, He said, *"The only thing in your way is your believing that something is in your way!"*

"I can do all things through Christ who strengthens me" (Philippians 4:13) is more than just beautiful calligraphy for a coffee mug! The moment I think, *"I can't..."* it's a telltale sign of what

NOVEMBER 30

I'm thinking in my head and not in agreement with the *"I AM"* living inside me shouting, *"OH, YES YOU CAN BECAUSE YOU ALREADY HAVE IT!"*

Paul stated *"I have been co-crucified with Christ..."* (Galatians 2:20). Since we were crucified when Christ was crucified, dead is dead. If you walked up to a dead person in a coffin and insulted him, he doesn't care! He won't sit up and insult you back and lay down again! Most of us live like the flesh is still alive by believing we gotta do something to kill it. Once we realize we already died with Jesus and we arose in glory with Him, we can enjoy the life of freedom from ourselves that Jesus paid for us to live!

DECEMBER 1

Zachariah's Unbelief

Read: Luke 1:5-25

*V*erse six says that both Zachariah and his wife were blameless as far as the law was concerned. In other words, no one could have been more perfect under the law than they were. Both had come from the lineage of the Levitical priests—Elizabeth was a descendant of Aaron! Yet, in all of their outward perfection, they were still a disgrace in their culture because they couldn't have children. Add to it the fact that both of them were old and past the age of childbearing.

It was not by chance that the lot fell on Zachariah to serve as priest in the temple to offer incense, which only happens once in a priest's lifetime. God had heard Zachariah's heart cry for a child! Imagine! God heard his prayer and sent the angel Gabriel to speak to him! He told him he would have a son!

I don't know about you, but if I was praying about something for the hundredth time and an angel stood in front of me and told me the solution, I'd be pretty pumped! But Zachariah seemed to check out into la-la land because he had been overwhelmed with grief at the state of his childless condition for so many years. You would think that Zachariah would have snapped out of it, but he didn't. He came right back at Gabriel stating the obvious, *"How shall I know this? For I am an old man and my wife is well advanced in years."*

Gabriel was offended that Zachariah didn't believe his words! He said, *"I am Gabriel, who stands in the presence of God, and was sent to speak to you and bring you these glad tidings..."*

Because Zachariah didn't believe Gabriel, he was struck mute until the day his son was born. It sounds pretty extreme, but the situation would have been detrimental if Zachariah didn't keep his mouth shut! Gabriel knew he needed some extra help with that. If Zachariah would have kept speaking out his unbelief, He would have undone the promise with his own words!

DECEMBER 1

We can all become so overwhelmed with circumstances that have persisted for years that the solution, when presented, seems impossible. When focusing on the problem, it can look like a huge, unconquerable mountain! Zachariah was trying to rationalize with his puny human mind how he and his wife could bear a child. When Gabriel, who received the message straight from God, was ordered to appear to him, he mentally checked out. He couldn't fathom that he would have a child and that his shame would forever be a thing of the past!

Only speaking what the Scriptures tell us about our situation is a great place to start. Second, imagining ourselves whole and able to do what we couldn't do before is a huge part! Acting like Zachariah and thinking, *"I'll believe it when I hold that baby in my arms!"* isn't faith. Faith sees the impossible, acts on it, and then it becomes a reality.

A long time ago, one of my closest friends was unable to conceive. After many years without answers, a doctor diagnosed her with a certain disease that kept her from getting pregnant. She crocheted baby blankets for all of her expectant friends and donated her hand-made blankets to crises pregnancy centers. One day a friend told her, *"Why don't you make your own baby blanket in faith?"* So she did! I remember she also read Charles Capps' book, *"God's Creative Power for Healing"* and prayed the Scriptures in there over herself regularly. Within a short time, she was pregnant! That baby girl is now fourteen years old (at the time of this writing) with long, beautiful red hair, and a Believer in Christ! If my friend would have never acted on her faith, I don't believe she would have conceived.

Yeah, I get it. Sometimes it does take a lot of fortitude and persistence. Much of it is unlearning old habits and retraining our mind to think according to the truth. I understand, because I've had to do it for myself. As I renewed my mind to God's truth and began to act on it, my body began to change as well.

A transformed mind = a transformed body.

DECEMBER 2

Mary Wasn't Quite Contrary

Read: Luke 1:26-38

*U*nlike Zachariah, Mary wasn't contrary to the angel Gabriel. She wasn't caught up in a lifetime of agony in her soul longing for a child like he was. Gabriel appeared to her out of the blue (literally LOL!) and he told her that she would give birth to the King of all kings! She had the opportunity to respond with, *"Oh little old me?"* but she didn't. Instead, she offered herself without reservation, *"Behold the maidservant of the Lord! Let it be to me according to your word."*

The angel declared, *"The Holy Spirit will come upon you, and the power of the Highest will overshadow you; therefore, also, that Holy One who is to be born will be called the Son of God."* The Holy Spirit created a Holy Seed! The Holy Spirit brought forth that HOLY ONE called the Son of God!

Gabriel was wise. He encouraged Mary with the testimony of her relative Elizabeth's miracle pregnancy because she was previously barren. His point was: *"God did it for her; He can do it for you. For with God nothing will be impossible."* –Meaning that no word from God is void of power.

Mary went to see Elizabeth right away after her encounter with the angel. She found everything exactly as Gabriel had told her: Elizabeth was six months pregnant! Elizabeth also confirmed, through words of knowledge from the Holy Spirit, what Gabriel had spoken to Mary. She would be the mother of the Savior of the world!

When Mary entered Elizabeth's house, the baby leaped in her womb when he heard Mary's greeting! John the Baptist, the Messiah's forerunner, gave testimony to the Messiah before He was ever born! He had been filled with the Holy Spirit from his mother's womb, just like Gabriel had informed Zachariah!

DECEMBER 2

Isn't that what happens to us when we get born again? We are born into royal lineage by holy Seed! The Holy Spirit comes upon us and fills us with new life! From the moment of new birth, we are sanctified and made holy because of the Holy Spirit living in us. His life expands inside of us, and we grow in knowledge and understanding of who we are in Christ.

DECEMBER 3

Manual Or Emmanuel

Read: Matthew 1:23

I guess it would depend who you ask, but when we compare an automatic transmission with a manual transmission, the automatic is the better choice! Why? It's easier! It is a more stress-free driving experience! For me, driving stick is annoying because you have to be mindful of shifting with your hand and pushing too many different pedals with your feet—multi-task driving!

I was never good at driving stick. When my children were little, I borrowed my friend's manual car. My children sat in the back seat crying, "Mommy, please, stoooop!"—their heads jerking, and the car bucking, as I was grinding the clutch like fingernails on a chalkboard. I remember sitting on a hill at a traffic light as the car behind me approached—only it was me drifting backwards! Ah! This was NOT enjoyable in any sense of the word! It takes more coordination than I am willing to force myself to master.

We all know that *Emmanuel* means *God with us*. If we really believed God was with us; that He was living inside us, would we be experiencing life differently than we are right now?

God has told us that He is for us and not against us (Rom. 8:31). He promised that He would always be with us and will never leave us (Heb. 13:5). He said that He lives inside us (2 Cor. 13:5). Yet with all of this proof right here in the Bible, many people still find it challenging to trust Him completely with their lives. We tend to take matters into our own hands and try to work out our problems with our own human wisdom, much like taking control of every gear in a car.

Like an automatic transmission, Jesus has already prepared the ride ahead to be an enjoyable experience overall. How? Because *God is for us! God is with us! God is inside us!* We get to decide: Manual or Emmanual!

DECEMBER 4

The Incarnation

Read: Isaiah 7:14

Incarnation means *in flesh; a living being embodying a deity or spirit.*

John 1:14 states that *"the Word became flesh and dwelt among us..."*

I'd like to share the *Mirror Bible's* translation of this verse for a clearer understanding:

> *"Suddenly the invisible, eternal Word takes on visible form—the Incarnation, on display in a flesh and blood Person, as in a mirror. In Him, and now confirmed in us. The most accurate tangible exhibit of God's eternal thought finds expression in human life. The Word became a human being, we are His address; He resides in us..."*

This is a mind-blowing concept, that God would become a man; taking on the human flesh He Himself created! That flesh was His firstborn Son, Jesus—the visible human form of all of God's thoughts, desires, and words expressed in humanity! Even in all of this, it would not be complete without us!

Jesus was God incarnate, think of it—there has never been a second since Christ came that the world has been without Him in it! He sent His Holy Spirit to reside inside every person. We are the sole purpose of His intentions—Christ in us!

John G. Lake stated accurately: *"Christ is at once the spotless descent of God into men and the sinless ascent of man into God; and the Holy Spirit is the Agent by whom this is accomplished."* The incarnation: God with us; God *in* us!

DECEMBER 5

Three Gifts

Read: Matthew 2:1-12

The three gifts the wise men brought to Jesus were not exactly your typical baby shower gifts, where they? I researched the significance of these gifts the wise men gave to Jesus after His birth. From what I could find, the three gifts represented three of Christ's attributes: the gold referred to His kingship, frankincense represented His priesthood because it was burned as incense in the tabernacle, and myrrh represented His suffering and death.

In modern day usage, frankincense and myrrh are still among the most costly essential oils. Both are only found in certain parts of the world (the Arabian Peninsula and the horn of Africa). They are rare and could possibly become extinct.

It is interesting that Jesus received the gift of myrrh at the time of His birth. I mean, who wants to receive a gift the moment he is born reminding him of the horrible death he would die? It is heart-wrenching to think about! But there are two Biblical references to the use of myrrh regarding His suffering and death:

The first reference is in Mark 15:23, fulfilling the prophecy of Psalm 69:21 *"...and for my thirst they gave me vinegar to drink."* While Jesus was on the cross it says, *"They gave Him wine mingled with myrrh to drink, but He did not take it."* When myrrh was dissolved in wine, it became bitter. It was used as a mild anesthetic for pain—but notice that Jesus refused to drink it! He didn't take the easy way out, but chose to feel the full brunt of suffering for us!

The second reference is in John 19:39-40 after His death. *"And Nicodemus, who at first came to Jesus by night, also came bringing a mixture of myrrh and aloes, about a hundred pounds. Then they took the body of Jesus and bound it in strips of linen with the spices, as the*

DECEMBER 5

custom of the Jews is to bury." Myrrh was used as an embalming fluid for the dead because it protected the flesh from worms and bugs.

How awe-inspiring, that God had a divine purpose for something as seemingly insignificant as the gifts given to Jesus at His birth! If the Father was this detailed from beginning to end about His Son, Jesus, when He made Him an offering for us; it isn't far-fetched to believe that every detail we would need accomplished was equally fulfilled, down to the very last ingredient! That would include healing for every disease, deliverance from every mind-controlling thought, and divine life united with our spirit! That should make us want to shout and praise Him with all of our heart!

DECEMBER 6

Coming To A Tomb Near You!

Read: John 20:1-9

When Lazarus was resurrected from the dead and came out of his tomb, he was still wrapped in the grave clothes. Jesus ordered him to be set free. In John 11:43-44 we read,

> "Now when He had said these things, He cried with a loud voice, 'Lazarus, come forth!' And he who had died came out bound hand and foot with graveclothes, and his face was wrapped with a cloth. Jesus said to them, 'Loose him, and let him go.'"

When Peter and John heard the news that Jesus had been resurrected, they ran to the tomb! Peter entered and saw the linen cloths, which had been carefully wrapped around Jesus' body, just lying there. What is remarkable about Jesus' resurrection is that He was able to come out of His grave clothes without assistance, unlike Lazarus.

When Jesus arose, His body more than likely came through the cloths, proving that He was resurrected and not merely resuscitated. Jesus was able to escape the grave clothes without disturbing their form! He was able to return to life without any assistance! His body arose out of the cloths with them sinking where His body had been! A remarkable resurrection! If death couldn't hold Him down, certainly a few cloths couldn't!

Scripture tells us that when Jesus returns, those who have gone to sleep will arise from their graves! The same resurrection power will restore those bodies and bring them through their clothes, through their coffins, and through the ground to raise them up and meet their Savior with a brand new body—coming to a tomb near you!

DECEMBER 7

Will The Real YOU Please Stand Up!

Read: 2 Peter 1:5-12

*D*o you remember watching *To Tell the Truth* when you were a child? It was a popular game show on TV that was first aired in 1956. It consisted of a panel of four contestants, who fired a series of questions at three different people who all claimed to be the same person. The questions asked to each person were targeted to determine which one was telling the truth and who were the two imposters. At the end of the round of questioning, each of the four contestants voted whether person number 1, 2, or 3 was telling the truth about their identity. After the votes were in, the announcer said, *"Will the real (whatever their name was) please stand up!"* Each of the three people pushed their chairs back and acted like they were going to stand up, but the real person finally stood up straight and tall to prove he was telling the truth.

When we don't understand our true identity in Christ, we live our lives as impostors in a false identity. Our Father sees us the exact same way He sees His Son Jesus. That truth was very difficult for me to grasp at a time when I was very ill. What interfered most with receiving healing was my constant questioning, *"God, if You love me how could You have allowed this to happen to me?"* I had to face the unbelief in my own heart and realize that He didn't allow it. I did not fully know who I was in Christ. I had to stop my human questioning and set my heart to find the truth.

One morning, shrouded in misery and pain, I had this bright idea that I would throw myself on the floor before Jesus and sob until my tears covered His feet. I had the picture all played out in my mind how Jesus would be moved with sympathy and reach down His hand, tenderly wipe away my tears, touch me, and His power would surge through His hand into my body, heal me and raise me to my feet! Sounds like the perfect plan, doesn't it?

DECEMBER 7

Well, while sobbing uncontrollably, just as I was about to do my glory slide onto the floor at His feet, He sternly spoke very loudly to my spirit, *"Stop! Don't ever throw yourself at My feet again like a beggar! Stand on your feet and look Me in the eye as My equal!"*

"WHAT???!!! YOUR EQUAL??" My sobbing from self-pity immediately turned to awe! His words shook me to the core! From that moment on, my thinking regarding who I was in Christ was rearranged! I began to see myself as whole and healthy exactly as Jesus is! As I began to renew my mind with the Word, my body began to change. For me, it was a journey of both a radical mind-shift (like a lobotomy was taking place!), as new life in was emerging in my body! I realized I no longer had to bear the image of a low-life beggar trying to convince God to heal me! I could stand on His truth and look eyeball to eyeball into Jesus' beautiful face and stand toe to toe with Him! That's who I was all along—I just didn't know it!

In essence, Jesus was saying, *"Stop living like an imposter! Will the real you please stand up!"* When I allowed Him to change the image I had of myself to the image He made me, that is when I began to see results on my own, without anyone praying for me. And Peter reminds us in verse twelve in our Scripture reading for today, that we have been *established* in truth.

When we see ourselves as equal with Christ, we will understand that we don't have to accept a false lower identity. We can rejoice in the understanding of the cost He paid to recreate us in His image! WILL THE REAL YOU PLEASE STAND UP!

DECEMBER 8

Divine Infusion

Read: Mark 12:29-34

An infusion is simply the act of adding one thing to another to make it stronger or better. The qualities and properties of one substance now become one with the other. Once an infusion has taken place, usually it is impossible to completely separate them again. Tea and coffee are good examples of an infusion.

Today's Scripture gives the account of a dialogue that took place between Jesus and a scribe. The scribe dared to question Jesus after the Sadducees had their round of questions answered accurately. He was impressed with Jesus' wisdom, so he figured he'd take his shot at Him. The religious leaders were always looking for ways to find fault with Jesus' teachings so they could discredit Him as the Messiah, but it never worked.

The scribe, trying to trip Jesus up by questioning about matters pertaining to the Law of Moses, asked, *"Which commandment is greatest of all?"* Jesus replied correctly by quoting Deuteronomy 6:4, which was part of the prayers the Jews recited every morning and evening called the *Shema*.

What is interesting is that, when the scribe reiterated what Jesus said, in agreement he further expands on this truth. He did not use the exact same words Jesus used. He declared,

> "Right! Well! Teacher, truthfully you said, He is One, and there is not another except Him. And to be loving Him with your whole heart, and with your whole understanding, and with your whole strength, and to be loving your neighbor as yourself, is much more than all the whole burnt-offerings and sacrifices." (Wuest Translation)

DECEMBER 8

The scribe described loving God with your whole understanding. The word *understanding* actually means *a flowing together like two streams*. It implies a seamless merging or a fusion of thoughts as a result of combining two things together. Imagine God's thoughts infused into your thoughts so that the two become one! I love that!

This is what it means to have the mind of Christ! The origin of this merging is love! It all stems out of love! This is one facet of our "oneness" with Him! Infusion—Christ added to us to make us stronger and better; inseparable!

DECEMBER 9

Communion

Read: I Corinthians 11:23-26

Remember that the word *lambano* means *to seize with force, to grab and lay hold of, to be carried away, remove.* This word describes perfectly what Jesus did with our diseases and sins. Yet a further look at this word reveals even more! Communion is a time when we reflect on Jesus' total sacrifice for us. We have taken a thorough look at the Greek word *lambano* throughout this devotional, but there is more to grab! (Pun intended!)

The *Mirror Bible* expounds on the partaking of Communion as taking into yourself Christ's identity and victory as your own: *"Realize your association with My death, every time you eat, remember My body that was broken for you"* (1 Corinthians 11:24)

The NKJV uses the word *take* when Jesus instructed the disciples to break off a piece of the bread for themselves, as it represented His body broken for each one of them. *Take* is translated as *lambano* meaning *to associate with one's self.*

Here we see the completeness He intended for us in the association with Christ's body and His blood—it's personal for each one of us. Communion is a celebration of the incarnation—the divine deposit of deity into humanity.

When we eat of the bread representing His body, it symbolizes Christ coming inside our body and becoming one with us—deity forever joined with humanity—the incarnation complete! Oh, this is what it was about all along! God in us! To Him be all the glory!

DECEMBER 10

Mirage

Read: 1 Corinthians 6:19-20

A mirage is a French word meaning *"to look at, to wonder at."* It is an optical illusion caused by the refraction of light from the sky by heated air, which causes our eyes to see the appearance of a layer of water on a hot road. Our eyes can see many things that we think are authentic, but in reality they are nothing more than optical illusions.

The biggest hindrances to our relationship with Holy Spirit are the things in this natural world that appear to be more real than what is in the spiritual world. What trips us up the most is the belief of our inability to *see* with our spirit. We forget that the real person we are is a spirit with flesh draped around it. We are God with skin on!

I love the *Mirror Bible's* translation of 1 Corinthians 6:20,

> *"You are bought and paid for. All of you are His. Live your life conscious of how irreplaceably priceless you are. You host God in your skin."*

With this in light, we don't have to be a host for a virus, bacteria, or any type of disease! Our Father is not a guest; He is a permanent resident in our flesh! The mortgage was paid in full! God owns the property and holds the title deed! It was signed in the blood of His Son! We are a *living* house for the *living* God!

DECEMBER 11

The Master

Read: Hebrews 4:14-16

"For we do not have a High Priest who is not able to enter experientially into a fellow feeling with our infirmities, but one who has been tempted and tested in all points like as we are, without sin. Let us be coming therefore with boldness to the throne of grace, in order that we may procure mercy and find grace for seasonable help." (Wuest Translation)

Procure means to obtain something, especially with care or effort. If you procure something that is difficult to get, you obtain it. Jesus, as our High Priest, procured every ounce of our weaknesses with purposeful intention. When a person has had experience conquering something, they become a master at it. Jesus was not lacking the human experience. He became The Master, *"representing mankind in the highest place of spiritual authority."* (Hebrews 4:14, Mirror Bible)

Jesus experienced what we experience so we can experience what He experiences! How's that for simple theology? He was touched with humanity's plight in every way because He felt the pain we feel when we are sick, our loneliness and betrayal when others desert us, and the weight of temptation from the enticements of the world. Yet, He became The Master of them all!

DECEMBER 12

Tang

Read: Colossians 2

*T*ang was formulated in 1957, by food scientist William A. Mitchell, who also invented Pop Rocks and Cool Whip. It is a sweet, tangy, orange-flavored, powdered drink mix named after the tangerine fruit. Tang became a popular drink when NASA's astronauts drank it on John Glenn's Mercury flight in 1962 and in later Gemini space missions. Its fame grew from the misconception that it was invented for the space program because it was easy to mix in water. I remember drinking it as a kid every morning as a substitute for orange juice. Upon trying it again as an adult, I found it to be rather disgusting, maybe due to the fact that I have a strong aversion to fake tasting orange foods!

Truth always has a certain "tang" or "ring" to it. Yet, many times people mix in a little false with the truth to make it more palatable. Paul was constantly refuting the religious leaders who would come in after him promoting the law, and taint everything he had taught them about Christ. Here, in the book of Colossians, Paul sent a letter of encouragement, since he had not personally witnessed to this new group of Believers. The people in the city of Colosse had come to faith in Christ through Epaphras, one of Paul's converts from Ephesus.

In Colossians chapter two, Paul begins to instruct these Believers in Christ so they do not allow human reasoning to contaminate their new-found faith. In the *Wuest Translation* of verse four he informs them,

> "*This I am saying in order that no one may be leading you astray by false reasoning in the sphere of* **specious** *discourse.*" (Emphasis added)

DECEMBER 12

Specious is defined as *having the ring of truth but actually being false.* How can a Believer become firmly established in spiritual truth if there is a little of man's wisdom mixed in with it? Jesus told His disciples that the Holy Spirit is the Spirit of Truth; that when He would come He would guide them into ***all*** truth, and speak to them about the future. Everything Holy Spirit would do would always glorify Christ and take what belongs to Jesus and declare it to them. Jesus instructed them not to go *anywhere* or do *anything* until they received the Spirit of Truth! If the Holy Spirit was that important to the first disciples, would He be any less important to us?

Jesus sent the Holy Spirit to live inside us to be our Friend, Guide, Counselor, and to fill us with His life and boldness. Truth will always prevail, even when mixed with human error. The most important quality is that we should remain teachable. When we question something that is clear in Scripture, we must set aside our human rationalization and grab on to the Truth until it is a firm conviction within our being; especially when the situations deal with physical healing. There are many "opinions" out there, but what God says about healing is the *only* truth. If we want to experience the truth about physical healing, then we must settle it with the Word and choose to believe that above our experiences. Our spirit, which is joined completely with the Holy Spirit, will always resonate with the truth!

DECEMBER 13

The Empty Tomb

Read: Matthew 28:1-10

The women, along with the Roman soldiers guarding the tomb, were caught by surprise as the earth shook beneath them. They were awestruck at the sight of the angels perched on the stone, like CEO's overseeing the events of the Kingdom. Their demeanor, relaxed yet authoritative, displayed *"Aw, this is nothing!—Christ's resurrection is the real phenomenon!"*

We are stirred by the angels' words,

> *"Do not be afraid, for I know that you seek Jesus who was crucified. He is not here; for He is risen, as He said. Come, see the place where the Lord lay..."*

No longer a man bound in grave clothes, He was the promised risen Savior of the world! He had overcome even death! He had raised Lazarus from the dead after four days; being raised from the dead in three days was piece of cake!

Jesus left His tomb so we could leave ours!

DECEMBER 14

Gimme

Read: Psalm 19:12-14

Our prayer time does not have to consist of, *"God, gimme this."* Or *"God gimme that."* When I was a new Believer, I used to set time aside every night to hang out with Jesus after I put my kids to sleep for the night. For the first three months, I sat there complaining about the same problems I had over and over again! Whew! I had to realize for myself what a drag my relationship with the Lord had become when it was merely based on my asking and begging for things. I finally decided to shut up and listen!

Once I decided to spend time worshipping Him and sit in silence to listen, my relationship with Him began to grow. I learned to hear His voice and He began to show me visions about my future, preaching to crowds of people! I'd spend my entire day longing to spend that time with Him every night alone! I learned to lean on Him as my trust grew.

At one point, my son had dislocated my shoulder by throwing himself on the floor while I was trying to hold him. The pain was excruciating and I could not use my arm. My church was having a tent revival meeting with a special speaker and I really wanted to attend. I told the Lord, *"I want to be able to lift my hands to praise You!"*

That night, I was walking down the hallway in our house in the dark because I didn't want to turn on the light and wake up my children. I "accidently" rammed into the corner of the wall with my injured shoulder and it popped back into place! It hurt so bad it brought me to my knees in tears! But suddenly, I could lift my arm above my head without pain! I was healed! Whether it was clumsiness on my part, or the Lord making the most of an opportunity, I don't know! The important thing is that my arm was healed and I could use it to worship with all of my heart!

DECEMBER 14

Did you know that we don't need to use faith to get what the Bible says we already have? We don't even have to ask God for these things like health, provisions, joy or peace because He has already provided them! Where are they? Inside you and me! When we thank Him for the healing, the joy, the provisions—BAM! They come in the ways we least expect!

DECEMBER 15

Open Heavens

Read: Matthew 3:13-17

On the day that Jesus was baptized, the Bible says that the heavens were opened and the Holy Spirit descended upon Jesus and remained. Fast forward to the day of Pentecost, the Holy Spirit was poured out upon all flesh and *remained*! The sound of the mighty rushing wind was the Holy Spirit breaking through the earth's atmosphere like a sonic boom!

Bible-believing Christians are taught to pray for the heavens to open. There have even been books written about the heavens being brass (closed) over regions or certain people because of sin, but this just isn't accurate according to Scripture in the New Testament. Jesus took care of the problem of sin for all of humanity. There aren't little openings of heaven above certain people just because they are specially anointed Believers, or because God favors them above other people.

Giving of tithes and offerings does not make the heavens open over us and then make them suddenly close when we don't give. The heavens don't open when we avoid sin and close when we sin. It simply isn't about what we do or don't do! It's all about what Jesus already did!

Stephen saw the majesty of the heavens open while being stoned to death (Acts 7:54-60). He was in a state between earth and entering into heaven, as his spirit was transitioning into glory. His eyes were opened to see what was always there! Jesus next to the Father!

The heavens are open and will remain open! We don't have to pray them open; we don't have to try to get God's presence to come down! These events took place 2000 years ago! Holy Spirit *came* and *remained*! Hallelujah!

DECEMBER 16

Trouble

Read: 1 Thessalonians 5:4-11

As a teenager, I was a member of my church's volleyball team. Although it was my favorite sport, I wasn't very good at it—except for serving. I had a knack for delivering the ball in such a way that routinely caused the opposing team to mess up! Since we lived a little over a mile from our church, I used to ride my bike there for practice.

One evening, I had walked instead of riding my bike. My brother rode his bike to pick me up so I wouldn't have to walk home alone. On the way to the church, he found a family of baby raccoons whose mother had been killed by a car. He took off his shirt and wrapped one of the babies inside. When he picked me up, I had to ride home on the back of his bike holding the baby raccoon in his shirt like a sack as it squirmed for freedom!

When we brought the raccoon home, we decided to keep it as a pet to save its life. We brought it in the house and it would climb the curtains, swing from plant hangers, and make a mess of everything! Once it climbed up my leg to the top of my head and I couldn't get it off! Ouch! No matter what we did, we could not tame this raccoon! We named him "Trouble" because all he did was get into trouble—a complete menace! My brothers built him a pen outside, but he became even wilder. He grew pretty large and fluffy. Eventually, he escaped from the cage and we never saw him again.

There are some things we try to hold onto in life, like cherished habits, attitudes, or sins. We don't realize that they have become so engrained in our character and personality, that it's hard to imagine our lives without them—though they bring nothing but trouble. Whether we bring it into our house or try to keep it penned up outside when we're around other people, human instinct, left to

DECEMBER 16

itself, will always run wild. While it is sometimes hard to face these foibles, making excuses for them is like welcoming a wild animal into your home, causing nothing but destruction for everyone living there.

It can be something as simple as harboring a certain attitude and claiming that that's just the way we are wired, or as damaging as an addiction that has become like an illusioned friend. It brings a false sense of comfort because we don't remember what it was like to live without it. People learn to process their emotions through addictions and don't realize that they are trying to fill a God-shaped vacuum with a destructive shaped solution.

It can also be a circumstance a person is facing, where the thoughts and fears wreak havoc on one's health and destroy their ability to enjoy life. It is because the trouble has become more magnified, rather than the victory we have in Christ. A shift in our mindset can set us on the right track. Once a person is willing to admit that they have a problem, they can be able to envision themselves living life without "trouble" penned up inside them. Jesus came to set every captive free, and whom the Son sets free, is free indeed!

DECEMBER 17

Silent Night

Read: Isaiah 55:6-7

It is of the utmost importance to hear the voice of the Holy Spirit for yourself. It always seems easier to hear from God for the solution to somebody else's problem, but when it comes to our own needs, our questioning, fears and emotions can get in the way.

I have personally found that it is much easier and more effective for me to pray in the middle of the night. It's quiet and there's none of the day's looming demands distracting me. It's dark, so I don't get side-tracked with things in the room.

I value this time as a special treasure. It's not the time to request answers to any needs. It's not the time to voice all my problems. It's the time to be quiet and listen. Most times there is no need for words. We're communicating Spirit to spirit. There's an understanding that goes beyond words—an exchange where I "just know" what He's saying. The next morning when I wake up, the day is more like a continuation of our meeting together. I can hear His voice easier when I do pray for other people's needs.

The night Jesus was born, after the angels announced the arrival of the Messiah, *"Glory to God in the highest, and on earth peace, goodwill toward men!"* (Luke 2:14) There was a holy hush of awe over the entire world that night—a silent night! These moments are the most profound. No words are necessary, just an ear to hear! The Savior of the world speaks in the silence—all we have to do is set our heart to listen!

December 18

Conundrum

Read: Matthew 10:32-39

A conundrum is *a puzzling question or problem, a paradox or difficult problem* or *dilemma.*

The other day I made a comment to my youngest son that I did not like wearing a cross around my neck. He was surprised and asked why. I told him it is a symbol of Christ's horrible execution. He said, *"No, Mom, it's a symbol of freedom!"*

People put crosses on everything these days: shirts, bumper stickers, coffee mugs...you name it. The cross is *both* a symbol of execution and a symbol of freedom, which is why it is a conundrum—we can't have one without the other!

Jesus told His disciples before He went to the cross, *"You will weep and mourn while the world rejoices"* (John 16:20). Speaking about His death, but also about His resurrection He said, *"...but I will see you again and your heart will rejoice, and your joy no one will be able to take from you"* (John 16:22). But they had forgotten the part where He said He would see them again because they were so overcome with sorrow.

When we think of Christ's birth, the reason He came was to die! We cannot separate the reality of these two facts. Divinity became humanity so that humanity could share His divinity!

DECEMBER 19

Messianic Miracles (Part 1)

Read: Luke 17:11-19, Mark 9:14-27

According to Jewish tradition, there were four miracles the Jews believed only the Messiah could perform. The religious leaders themselves were able to heal certain diseases and cast out demons, but they were limited in their ability to set everyone free. They believed the distinguishing marks of the Messiah, that would prove His identity as the Son of David, would be to perform four specific miracles. I encourage you to research this information for yourself. I will discuss two of the Messianic miracles today and two miracles in tomorrow's devotion.

The first miracle we will address is the cleansing of leprosy. The Jews believed that God gave leprosy and only God could remove it. They base their beliefs on a few instances in the Old Testament: Moses' hand while he was at the burning bush, Miriam who was struck with leprosy for complaining against her brother's leadership, and King Uzziah who died for unlawfully burning incense in God's temple.

Jesus healed a man *full* of leprosy (Luke 5:12-14) and the ten lepers (Luke 17:11-19). Each account records Jesus' command to show themselves to the priests, according to the Law of Moses. Only the priests and the religious leaders were allowed to determine whether or not a person could return to society after they were healed of leprosy. Until the time when Jesus healed these lepers, there is no account of anyone being healed of leprosy under the Law. This is why the Jews believed only the Messiah could heal leprosy.

The second miracle we will discuss today is casting out a deaf and dumb spirit. The Pharisees were able to cast out demons. They did so by asking the person the name of the demon. The demon would speak through the person and tell them his name; then the

DECEMBER 19

Pharisee would call the demon by name and cast it out. Since deaf and dumb spirits couldn't talk, they believed that only the Messiah had the power to command it to leave. Jesus proved that He was the Messiah by casting out the deaf and dumb spirit in Mark 9:14-27, after the father had pleaded with Jesus to deliver his epileptic son.

When the religious leaders heard rumors about the miracles Jesus manifested, they could not have cared less—until they heard about Him performing the four Messianic miracles! As Jesus gained more popularity, their jealousy was aroused. They feared they would be knocked off their high positions of authority if all the people clamored around Jesus, so they refused to believe He was the Messiah. Until Jesus came on the scene, the sects of religious leaders were divided in their beliefs about certain doctrines. In spite of this, they united together and plotted to kill Him.

First, they sent a delegation of Pharisees to observe what Jesus was doing and teaching in order to bring back a report. The second step in determining whether or not He was the Messiah was to question Him—which they did constantly, trying to trip Him up. Lastly, they pronounced a judgment so that all the people would discredit Him as the Messiah. They claimed His power to cast our demons was given to Him by Beelzebub to discourage the people from listening to Him. If anyone continued to follow Jesus, they were kicked out of the synagogue.

DECEMBER 20

Messianic Miracles (Part 2)

Read: John 9, John 11

The four Messianic Miracles come from what is known as *"The Oral Law"*, which is commonly known as "the tradition of the elders." These beliefs are based upon specific passages of Scripture such as Isaiah chapters 35, 51, and 53. The traditions were passed down through generations and weren't documented until the second century A.D.

The healing of a birth defect is the third miracle that would prove Jesus was the Messiah. The Jews believed in generational curses, passed down from the person's ancestors as a result of sin. Jesus gave the blind man a new pair of eyes! He refuted the disciples' belief that the man was born blind as a result of his parent's sins. The reason Jesus healed him was simply to show His Father's works. We can see how much this ruffled the religious leader's feathers! They questioned the man over and over again, and further questioned his parents. They hoped they could trip the man up with their questions to discredit Jesus, but the man got snarky with them and teased, *"Oh, do you want to become His disciples too?"* They got angry and kicked him out of the synagogue, then schemed together to kill Jesus.

The fourth Miracle only the Messiah could perform was raising a person from the dead after four days. The Jews believed that a person's spirit hovered around the body for three days. After that, their spirit would leave their body and decay would set in. This is why Mary and Martha gave Jesus such a hard time when he came four days after Lazarus had died, *"Lord, if you would have been here...Lord, it has been four days and now he stinks!"* Hey, if Jesus could raise Lazarus after four days, then Jesus rising from the dead in three days was nothing, right?

DECEMBER 20 ———

Jesus performed every one of these miracles that had never been done before! It proved He was the Messiah, the Son of David!

But guess what? Even though Jesus performed these miracles, He said we would do greater thing than He did! So, let's go and show proof that Jesus is still alive!

DECEMBER 21

A Star Is Born

Read: Numbers 24:17, Matthew 2:1-12

Was the star the Magi followed an anomaly sent by God to lure them to the Christ Child? Some speculate that the star was a rare alignment of planets such as Jupiter and Saturn, which only happens once a millennium. Another theory suggests that the star was a super nova, particularly one recorded in history in 5 B.C., that lasted seventy days. This would have taken place around the same time as Jesus' birth.

The wonder of this star appearing and the prophecies concerning the arrival of the King of the Jews beckoned the wise men from the East to travel thousands of miles to worship Him, yet His own people were unaware of His appearing!

It was not to kings, priests, or prominent people in society that the announcement of the Messiah's arrival was proclaimed, but to lowly shepherds in a field and pagan astrologers from a foreign country.

The star is a reminder of His birth, His Kingship, and His Divine Nature. All of creation is still responding to this momentous occurrence! On that night over 2000 years ago a Star was born. No, not a phenomenon in the sky, but the Savior of the world—The Christ, the Son of the Living God!

DECEMBER 22

Faith's Response

Read: Romans 10:8-13

Faith is believing that what Christ finished in the past, is available NOW. Faith is not a future manifestation, waiting for God to act some day. Faith is Christ's finished work 2000 years ago made accessible to me NOW. If faith is not NOW, it isn't faith!

Yes! All the promises of God are "Yes" and "Amen." Yet, promises are always in the future. Physical healing is not future tense—it is past tense! If you can grasp what I'm saying here and take it to heart, it will really help you! Our faith is the response of a holy generation of blood-bought people, who have been made new creations in Christ living under a New Covenant that was ratified 2000 years ago. We are looking back as we live advancing the Kingdom.

If we find ourselves questioning, "When, God, when?", it is a telltale sign that we are looking for God to perform a future event that He has already accomplished in the past through Jesus' sacrifice. Is it finished or isn't it? Does Jesus need to add one more thing to what He accomplished? Absolutely not!

I encourage you to meditate on Christ's finished work for the rest of today. What does applying this mean for you? Since it was FINISHED, what should your response be? What should you be experiencing and enjoying that you have not been able to enjoy? See your healing totally resolved—yes, even that one you have been waiting for, for so long. Begin to see it as a past event that ended—this is faith's response!

DECEMBER 23

I Can't Believe It's—Butter!

Read: Deuteronomy 26:8-11

"Michele, would you like to go to Africa?"

"I'd love to go to Africa! You know it's always been my dream… When?"

"May."

"Of this year? You know its March…that's only two months to get my Passport and Visa…"

"Yes, I know."

"Ok, let me talk to my husband and I'll get back to you right away!"

It was 2006. I had recently told my new prophetic friend my dream to go to Africa and about a month later he asked me to go! There was so much to prepare! I was homeschooling my five children at the time. Taking this once-in-a-lifetime opportunity to travel by myself with a pastor I hardly knew to the other side of the world by myself seemed ludicrous! Was it brave or stupid to take such a risk? Either way, it was my dream and my husband said he'd do everything he could to help me go—including teach our children while I was gone for fourteen days!

I received a lot of tips from my friend about the culture for dressing and etiquette. It was a life-changing trip, and I wanted to do my best to honor the people we would be connecting with. One of the first things I needed to do was fix my hair! It was dyed blonde at the time. I went to the salon to dye it back to brown; the chemicals had over-processed my hair and burned my scalp! I didn't know what to do! It burned day and night making it hard to sleep with a burning sensation in my scalp!

DECEMBER 23 ———

My friend had suggested that we ask the Lord to show us things about our trip; the people we'd meet, the places we'd go, etc. One night, I had a dream about being driven on a dirt road by an African man. The orange-brown dirt road was very bumpy, full of cracks and crevices. I saw two women standing next to each other. I noticed white piles that looked like snow along the road, but in my dream it was butter! Everywhere it had "snowed" butter, which I believed to be a sign of blessing.

When I shared my dream with my friend, he said, *"Hey, why don't you put butter in your hair! Maybe that would stop the burning!"* I was desperate, so I did! I put butter on my scalp. And you know what? It stopped the burning! What a weird way to get healed, right?

As for the rest of the dream, it was like déjà vu! My host drove on the exact road I had seen in my dream to stay with him and his family! The two women were his wife and their house girl! It was like I had already been there and had met them! It was surreal to be in a place I never was before, yet—I felt like I belonged!

We attended a conference the following week. I had to pinch myself as I listened to them worship in Swahili. If God would go to such great lengths to give me dreams detailing what I would experience, why wouldn't He care about meeting my need for healing so I could take that trip without pain or suffering? Remember that God can use any means to bring healing to our bodies—even something as silly as putting butter in your hair!

DECEMBER 24

Alpha & Omega

Read: Revelation 22:12-17

Several years ago I had hung up a flag outside my house at the time of the year when we celebrate Jesus' resurrection. The flag said, *"He is risen."* My neighbor commented that she never thought of Jesus' resurrection at any other time except on "Easter Sunday." She thought it was odd and admitted that she was even offended that I put the flag up a few weeks before the official day. Later, she realized that His resurrection is for *every* day, not just for one day out of the year!

Whenever I set up my Christmas tree, the ornaments are manger scenes, crowns, and crosses. All of Jesus' life was summed up in these three symbols: His birth, His Kingdom, and His death—a life born of total sacrifice and total victory! There is nothing left unfinished! He is the prescription for all mankind's ailments—the Divine Antidote!

God finished what He started. He had Christ's sacrifice on his mind from the very beginning. Sometimes it's a hard fact to swallow that His life represents death and that His death represents life! We are reminded that He is the Alpha and the Omega—the First and the Last, the Beginning and the End. All of life and humanity was consummated in Christ!

DECEMBER 25

How Many Kings?

Read: Philippians 2:5-11

How Many Kings

Follow the star to a place unexpected
Would you believe after all we've projected
A child in a manger?
Lowly and small, the weakest of all
Unlikeliest hero, wrapped in His mother's shawl
Just a child, is this who we've waited for?

'Cause how many kings stepped down from their thrones?
How many lords have abandoned their homes?
And how many greats have become the least for me?
And how many gods have poured out their hearts
To romance a world that is torn all apart?
How many Fathers gave up their Sons for me?

Bringing our gifts for the newborn Savior
All that we have, whether costly or meek
Because we believe
Gold for His honor, and frankincense for His pleasure
And myrrh for the cross He will suffer
Do you believe?
Is this who we've waited for?
Only one did that for me
All for me, all for you...

Song by Downhere

I am sitting at my dining room table, listening to this song on YouTube while typing out the lyrics. A robin perched on the fence

DECEMBER 25

post and stared intently at me through the window. He cocked his head, as though he was listening to the words. After he flew away, immediately a blue bird came and did the exact same thing! Did you ever wonder if creation would recognize Jesus? I believe all of creation knows their Creator!

I encourage you to listen to this song for yourself. The words always bring me to tears during Christmastime. Whenever I think of Jesus' birth, I also reflect on His death. These events are inseparable. Humanity and time have been forever marked by His birth and His execution.

The *Amplified Bible* shows Jesus' commitment to our plight in verses 7 and 8,

> *"but emptied Himself (without renouncing or diminishing His deity, but only temporarily giving up the outward expression of divine equality and His rightful dignity) by assuming the form of a bond-servant, and being made in the likeness of men (He became completely human but was without sin, being fully God and fully man)...He humbled Himself (still further) by becoming obedient (to the Father) to the point of death, even death on a cross."*

How many kings? Only ONE did that for me!

DECEMBER 26

The Promised Messiah

Read: Hosea 6:1-3, Micah 5:1-5

*T*here are many Old Testament Scriptures that prophesy of the coming Messiah, the healings, His miracles, and His sufferings. Why did God make healing a part of both the Old Covenant and the New Covenant? Why was physical healing in the Atonement *included* with the remission of our sins?

The answer to these questions is: *Complete Redemption.* We can see, beginning in Genesis 3:15 and throughout the entire Bible, that there are references foreshadowing Christ with extraordinary detail in every book! This proves that God went to considerable lengths to unveil Christ as the atoning sacrifice for our sicknesses as equally as our sins.

Here, in the book of Hosea, we read of a prophecy in reference to Jesus' resurrection and how He had been torn to pieces, yet He was also gloriously raised from the dead on the third day!

Micah chapter five begins with the prophecy of the birthplace of the Messiah, written hundreds of years before Christ was born! In Matthew 2:3-6, the wise men inquired of King Herod where was He who had been born King of the Jews. He was disturbed that another King would try to overthrow his power; he called for the Jewish chief priests and scribes to tell him the prophecy which recorded where the Christ would be born. They referenced Micah 5:2:

> "But you, Bethlehem, in the land of Judah, Are not the least among the rulers of Judah; for out of you shall come a Ruler Who will shepherd My people Israel."

God pointed us to Christ throughout every book of the Bible and outlined with extensive detail regarding the purpose of His Covenant with Abraham, His Kingly lineage through David, His

DECEMBER 26

priesthood through Melchizedek, prophecies of the virgin birth, a description of His suffering and crucifixion...all fulfilled down to every last detail. Would He prophesy our healing in the Old Testament, demonstrate it in the New Testament, send Christ to be brutally beaten to secure our healing in the New Covenant and then choose to leave people sick and suffering now?

No, my friend! Healing wasn't left out for you or for me! We didn't miss the boat! God was deliberate down to the minutest detail, providing equally for both body and spirit! How do we receive this precious, priceless gift? Simply believe it is yours; continuing to thank Him for all that He has freely lavished upon you! See yourself healthy as you praise Him for depositing His life inside of you, and then my dear friend, you will experience what has been His desire for you from the very beginning: *Complete Redemption!*

DECEMBER 27

Simeon & Anna

Read: Luke 2:25-38

Luke's account of Jesus' arrival is the most detailed of all the Gospels. He shares events that we don't find in any of the other three books. We are given a detailed description of John the Baptist's miraculous birth as the forerunner to Christ's appearing. Luke's discourse of Jesus' dedication according to Jewish law is impeccable: the sacrifices given for the first-born son, the eighth day of a male's circumcision (which prove He was born under the Law), and named according to the angel's instructions at conception.

The lives of Simeon and Anna are inspiring. God had told them both about the coming Messiah and the mark He would make on their own personal lives. Simeon, whose name means *"he who hears"*, was promised that He would not die until he saw the prophesied Messiah. He was led by the Holy Spirit into the temple, and when he laid his eyes upon Jesus—his heart skipped a beat! The old prophet had the honor of holding God's promise in his arms! He prophesied by the Spirit of the salvation of the Lord—even to the Gentiles!

Anna was a prophetess who lived in the temple all of her life after her husband had died, fasting and praying! Obviously, the Holy Spirit was just as powerfully upon her. She came into the Temple at the exact moment Simeon was prophesying and she praised the Lord that the redemption of Israel had arrived at last!

I imagine the excitement for both Simeon and Anna, whose lives were so completely consecrated to God that they didn't do anything else. No distractions, no worries for provisions—just hang out with God until He fulfilled His promise to Israel—a promise they would both live to see! Now that Jesus was on the scene, their role was no

DECEMBER 27

longer necessary; the law was fulfilled and they could go home. A monumental shift had occurred in the course of human history!

In light of God's promise fulfilled in Christ as our own personal promise, can you imagine the impact we should all be experiencing? After all, we are *His body*! What would your current status be, if *every* area of your life was *completely* consecrated to Him? Where you see yourself in your imaginations—you are already called to live there!

DECEMBER 28

No Schism

Read: Psalm 103:10-12

Notice how the Psalmist expounds in detail how great God's mercy has been poured upon us, before he mentions the removal of our sins. His mercy and His forgiveness go hand-in-hand. It is interesting what he *didn't* say. He didn't say that our sins were removed as far as the north is from the south! Why? Because if you begin traveling north, you will eventually end up traveling south, but if you begin travelling east, you will never end up traveling west! East and west never catch up with each other! That's how far He removed our sins from us!

Imagine applying this view with physical healing! Since sins and sickness are equal, because they both originated from the Fall, it is safe to say that our sicknesses were removed as far as the east is from the west as well! A few verses earlier, in Psalm 103, the Psalmist documents that He has forgiven ALL our iniquities and He has healed ALL of our diseases—if you needed a reminder.

Think about this great chasm that existed between God and mankind. This schism, division, and disunion kept us separated because of the Fall. Adam's thinking became like the Absent Minded Professor; the old Disney movie from 1961. The professor was so absorbed in his experiments that he forgot his own wedding! Adam's mind became so sin-conscious; he forgot what it was like to live free! I think we can all relate to that on one level or another.

But now, we who were once far off were brought near by the blood of Christ (Ephesians 2:13)! There is no separation, no chasm, no schism! He cast our sins and sicknesses as far as the east is from the west! What He has, we have! Nope—No schism!

DECEMBER 29

No Class

Read: 1 Corinthians 2:12-14

*P*hysical healing is not in a class all its own. It's received the same way as salvation, but we have made it very difficult. We believed for our salvation with no external evidence. Why not the same for healing? The price was just as great— the sacrifice just as effective! A.B. Simpson, in his book *"The Gospel of Healing"* said,

> *"Matthew 8:17, He healed all that were sick, that it might be fulfilled which was spoken by Esaias the prophet saying, Himself took our infirmities and bare our sicknesses." This is quoted as the reason why He healed all that were sick. It was not that He might give His enemies a vindication of His Divinity, but that He might fulfill the character presented of Him in ancient prophecy. Had He not done so, He would not have been true to His own character, and if He did not still do so, He would not be—"Jesus Christ, the same yesterday, today, and forever." These healings were not occasional, but continual; not exceptional, but universal. He never turned any away. He healed all that were sick. As many as touched Him were made perfectly whole. He is still the same."*

Healing is not an ethereal, mystical object hovering in the spirit realm and we are left clueless to somehow make it magically manifest in the natural. The exchange was equal—His body for our body. The whipping was a physical act upon Christ's physical body. His crucifixion was a physical act upon His physical body. Yes, they both have spiritual effects, but to ignore the physical effects is inaccurate. If we believe we must say all the right words and do all the right things to win the jackpot; if we are waiting for God to make a spiritual truth a physical reality, we might as well have a boxing match with the air! It is already a reality! We live in *response* to this reality—not to gain it!

DECEMBER 29

Healing is not in a class all its own! I believed, therefore I have received. Isn't that how we all receive salvation? It doesn't come by waiting around for it. We must stop frustrating ourselves with constant questions and venting—that doesn't help at all. It actually does the opposite and pushes the simplicity of it away. If we know that we cannot earn salvation and forgiveness of sin by "works," then why would we think this approach would be effective to gain our healing?

Remember that our God is a good God and in Him is NO darkness at all. He is not up there withholding your healing for any reason. The more we refuse the lies and cooperate with truth, the easier experiencing healing will be. He heals because that's who He is and always will be: Jehovah-Rapha—*The Lord who heals you.*

DECEMBER 30

The Remedy

Read: Exodus 15:26

I hear many stories where people's lives are ruined due to "medical wreckage." Doctors prescribed a treatment and the person was left worse off than he was to begin with. Oops, a nerve was cut that shouldn't have been, or a problem improperly treated... sadly, the list goes on and on.

The Hebrew word for *doctor* is *rapha's* participial form *rophe'*. "I AM the LORD, thy physician"—Jehovah Rapha. His name is *"I AM."* God's names declare His character and His nature. He does not act contrary to His own name. We remember that *rapha* means *to mend, to cure, heal, physician, become fresh, repair thoroughly, make whole.*

LORD means *Self-Existent, Eternal One*. If we think about this description of God, He does not have to use any other source to exist. He doesn't need food, air, or water. He exists with all His needs met within Himself. If we compare that to life on earth, we see the exact opposite. People, plants, and animals all need to take in energy from some source to exist or they would die. We live in a world of consuming things; a world of limitations.

Picture this same eternal, self-existent God living on the inside of you! What other source for life do we need? There are no limitations for God, not in heaven and not on earth. So if your life is the result of medical wreckage, Jehovah Rapha is the remedy you can trust! He said, *"I AM the Self-Existent, Eternal One, and your Physician who cures you and makes you whole."*

DECEMBER 31

Personified

Read: 1 John 5:20

The *Mirror Bible* translates 1 John 5:20 as:

> "This is what has become distinctly clear to us: the coming of the Son of God is God's mission accomplished. He is the incarnate Christ. The moment all of Scripture pointed to has arrived. The Son is present. In Him God has given us the greatest gift, a mind whereby we may know Him who is true; and in the same knowing, to find ourselves there in Him who is true. Mankind is fully included and located in Him, in His Son Jesus Christ; this means that whatever Jesus is as Son, we are. This is the true God; this is the life of the ages."

He has not left us void of power, for all that He possesses, even down to His own Name, He freely gave to us! My dear friend, you are free! You are free to experience God in your flesh. Oh no, this doesn't make His power any less! It is the same miraculous power and authority it has always been from the beginning of time!

There you have it: CHRIST PERSONIFIED; God eternally in man! God took upon Himself the same human flesh He created, died as man, and resurrected as man; to live together as one in eternity. I don't know of anything more beautiful than this!

His Word became *flesh*...that's you and me!

Michele's Information

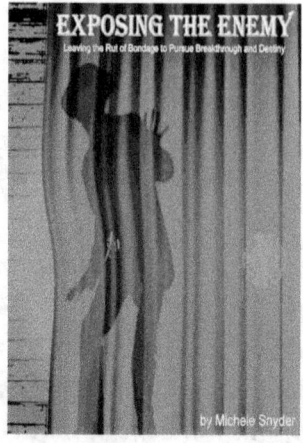

Amazon.com : Exposing the Enemy By Michele Snyder

https://youtube.com/c/EastcoastHealingCenterPA

Eastcoast Healing Center – PA | Facebook

Contact Information:

eastcoasthealingcenter.pa@gmail.com

Call for prayer 610-781-6332

I'm available for preaching engagements

Please go to Amazon and share your testimony how this book has impacted your life!

Tony Myers' Books

After living a life of atheism, Tony Myers was fighting for his life. He was completely paralyzed, and his body was shutting down. Diagnosed with Lou Gehrig's disease, a debilitating neurological disease with no cure or treatment options, all hope was lost. Then suddenly one day, Tony, determined to end his own life, found a miracle healing instead! During this journey you will cry, laugh, feel his wife's heartache, and then finally have a tremendous burst of joy as you celebrate his miracle with him and his wife Deb. Tony's honest, folksy telling of his story will make you believe he's sitting right in front of you drinking coffee! This story will encourage, motivate, and inspire you to believe in a miracle for yourself. If you are need of hope and encouragement, then this book is for you.

This book is the field manual as far as receiving healing for yourself is concerned. It is meant to awaken in the readers the mind of Christ and help them tap into the God-realm (i.e., "kingdom of heaven"). That's where we can receive the riches of Christ provided to us by grace, specifically, divine health and healing.

In this book, Tony Myers tackles tough issues related to food, our perceptions of food, and how to attain a healthy, supernatural life through simple practices and a fresh perspective of the things that go in our mouths. You'll learn how to avoid the pitfalls that keep you from healthy living from God's point of view and be able to correct the misinformation we've received along the way.

From where does human knowledge originate? What are the keys to living a supernatural life? *Pushing the Boundaries in Christ*, pushes the boundaries of what we think is possible. As children of a supernatural heavenly Father, the seemingly impossible is possible: physical healings, financial miracles, and operating in the gifts of the Holy Spirit. A workbook is included to push the boundaries of your mind.

Divine healing from the comfort of your home? Is that truly possible? The problem isn't getting new information. The problem is getting what's already available to work for you. Over many centuries, the simple message of the cross has been obscured and diluted by many religious and secular traditions. And that's exactly why and where this book comes in. Its purpose is to get you to see the simple truth of the Gospel as it's related to divine healing and health, without any unnecessary additives. This book is written in a simple, conversational style. It takes you from the Garden of Eden all the way to the present day. It shows you how the revelation about divine healing and health was offered by God, and how and why it kept on getting ignored and put aside. Most importantly, this book shows you what you can do to recover God's blueprint for your own health and how you can get the Gospel truth about divine healing to work for you from the comfort of your home.

www.ingramcontent.com/pod-product-compliance
Lightning Source LLC
Chambersburg PA
CBHW071947070526
44583CB00015B/1092